DATE DUE

3/14/03 BS			

Encyclopedia of American Public Policy

Encyclopedia of American Public Policy

Byron M. Jackson

ABC-CLIO

Santa Barbara, California
Denver, Colorado
Oxford, England

Library of Congress Cataloging-in-Publication Data
Jackson, Byron M.
Encyclopedia of American public policy / Byron Jackson.
p. cm.
Includes bibliographical references and index.
ISBN 1-57607-023-9 (alk. paper)
1. Political planning—United States—Encyclopedias. 2. United States—Politics and government—Encyclopedias. I. Title.
JK468.P64J33 1999
320'.6'097303—dc21 99-11371
CIP

05 04 03 02 01 00 99 10 9 8 7 6 5 4 3 2 1

ABC-CLIO, Inc.
130 Cremona Drive, P.O. Box 1911
Santa Barbara, California 93116–1911

This book is printed on acid-free paper ♾.

Manufactured in the United States of America

Contents

Encyclopedia of American Public Policy

Foreword

The *Encyclopedia of American Public Policy* is a valuable reference book for both college and high school libraries. It serves as a highly competent and authoritative resource that will answer a wide variety of questions regularly asked by students studying history, government, economics, and other topics in the social sciences.

Mark Twain, as astute an observer as there ever was of the American political stage, once said "the trouble with the world is not that people know too little, but that they know so many things that ain't so." As most librarians know, this fact is revealed, and then fortunately addressed, each and every day in the reference sections of America's libraries. Good reference books are therefore one of the bulwarks against misinformation and ignorance. A good reference book is an asset to the library collection, and one written for school and college libraries is especially appreciated. This is because it serves at least three purposes by:

- Providing quick and sufficient answers to its user's questions
- Serving as a resource for teachers to use in planning and implementing their curriculum and classes
- Saving librarians precious time while they assist their users to find answers and information.

The *Encyclopedia of American Public Policy* is more than just a good reference book—it fills a current gap in the reference section. There are several reasons why the work is invaluable: the depth and high quality of the information; the excellent, easily accessible organization and readability of the material; and the very helpful author's introduction, which provides a quick, easily understood overview of both the book and the field of American public policy. Dr. Jackson's extensive background in both research and teaching have surely contributed to the success of the encyclopedia.

Dr. Jackson did his doctoral research at the University of California at Berkeley during a time (1969–1974) when important public policy shifts occurred. He focused his research on police services in the major metropolitan city of Oakland, California. This provided him with a valuable, first-hand view of the relationship of a necessary and highly visible government service to its citizens. This perspective on the relationship of the government to its citizens is a vital, beneficial component of this book. Each topic and area of focus is explained in a manner that helps the user not only grasp the answer to the question at hand but also gain an understanding of the various functions of public policy.

Dr. Jackson's extensive teaching experience, spread over several decades at California State University at Chico, has given him understanding of the information needs and intellectual development of both the recent high school graduate as well as the college student. Having taught undergraduates for much of his career has allowed him to plan the *Encyclopedia of American Public Policy* for a wide variety of research and informational needs and render it readable by students.

The design of the *Encyclopedia of American Public Policy* accommodates the need for easy access and quick understanding of complex issues. This is achieved by its sensible, practical organization of this very broad, complex and changing field of study. The book breaks that knowledge and information into manageable, understandable chapters and brief articles, each focusing on important events and legislation in the area of public policy. There is extensive cross referencing and documentation, which serves both to spark the imagination and lead the reader into related areas of interest within and beyond the book.

The table of contents serves as a natural, convenient entry point into the book, listing the sections and the complete array of key concepts and terms that are included. Next, the very useful introduction helps orient the librarian and reader to the field of American public policy as well as to the layout of the book. The introduction is well worth reading, as it answers basic questions such as: What is public policy? What is the relevant historical background? How is government structured? What are the policy eras and how do they relate to each other and to current policy?

The first section of the *Encyclopedia of American Public Policy* is devoted to succinct articles explaining the important key concepts related to public policy. These are clear and direct, and include cross references to related concepts, people, events and terms. Key concepts range from technical, Latin terms such as *amicus curiae* or *cloture* to commonly heard but poorly understood phrases or terms such as due process or gerrymandering.

The rest of the body of the *Encyclopedia of American Public Policy* is organized into sections according to thirteen major areas of activity in the field of American public policy: agriculture, civil rights, commerce and transportation, communications, crime, economics, education, energy, entitlement programs, environment, health, housing, and labor. Each section begins with a chronological overview of how policy has developed over the course of American history. This allows the user to gain a sense of historical progression, a necessary step in grasping a full understanding of the facts, people, and events covered in the work. The chronology is followed by informational entries, provided in alphabetical order. These are arranged in the same manner as the key concepts, with extensive, relevant, and thorough cross referencing.

Both the librarian and the reader have much to gain from using the *Encyclopedia of American Public Policy*. It can be used to answer a particular question about public policy, or browsed to help one become acquainted with narrow or broad issues or interest areas of this important field of study. It may also serve as a supplemental text of readings for classes in the social sciences. The *Encyclopedia of American Public Policy* is a welcome addition to the library's reference collection, filling a gap that has existed far too long.

Peter Milbury, Librarian
Chico High School, Chico, CA

Preface

As a political scientist, I have a passion for the political history and development of American public policy. I have always been interested in the reasons that public policy was created and how the policy was designed to solve the social and economic problems of generations of Americans since the ratification of the U.S. Constitution in 1789. My favorite public policy eras were those of the decades that led to the Reform Era of American politics (1880s), the New Deal era from which emerged the major public policies that cemented a national government responsibility to improve the lives and conditions of Americans, and the three decades in the post–World War II era when social policy became the focus of American policymakers. These decades and the policy that came out of the Reform Era, the New Deal, postwar social and civil rights policy, and the later environmental policy era denoted times when the American government was actively engaged in change. These eras of change and public policymaking are exciting and fascinating to me.

I selected the policy areas covered in this encyclopedia on the basis of what I consider the major areas of government domestic political activity since 1789. The policy areas discussed here are: agriculture, civil rights, commerce and transportation, communications, crime, economics, education, energy, entitlement programs, environment, health, housing, and labor. These policy areas represent the bulk of government activity through the policymaking process in the twentieth century.

I have attempted to place the discussion of each entry in the context of the history of the policy era in which the entry fits. I have also tried to state the importance of the entry as it relates to the larger policy spectrum in American politics. For example, an entry in agricultural policy is discussed in the context of how the policy expands or changes the role of the federal government in the policy area. I also try to show how the policy or entry benefits or affects the targets of government action. What we discover in the process of American public policy is that policy has a purpose, and I am interested in how that purpose was met or satisfied by the development of specific public policies.

This encyclopedia was written for use by high school, college, and university students. My task was to discuss the topics and legislation in a manner that would be clear, understandable, and readable so that students would want to learn more about the various terms and legislation contained in the encyclopedia. Since political science and its subdiscipline of public policy are such broad subjects, my purpose was to link the historical elements of the development of public policy through the chronologies so that the reader could appreciate the lineage of public values expressed primarily through the growth and development of policy. One of the difficulties of studying and learning about politics and political science is delineating the boundaries of the subject. As a result of studying and teaching political science for twenty-four years, I feel confident in knowing the dimensions of the discipline of political science. The active part of the discipline—the creation and implementation of public policy—is the most fleeting and elusive aspect for students to clearly understand. When I was a college student I struggled with forming a clear sense of the range of public policy in American politics; the entries in this book were written with the goal of explaining the legislative process and how policy is actually made. I have attempted to describe and illustrate with examples the unique character of the legislative and policymaking processes.

Learning about public policy works best if the student of politics and public policy becomes involved in the political system or the policy process. Working with legislators at any level of politics—in a city council, board of supervisors, state legislature, or in the U.S. Congress—can be enriching and rewarding. I also encourage students to seek opportunities to work with interest groups because they learn the benefits of advocacy and networking that are essential to moving ideas onto the public agenda. The *Encyclopedia of American Public Policy* represents and documents the work, the advocacy, and the activism of many individuals and groups in the American political process. I encourage the reader of this encyclopedia to appreciate the political history that is the foundation of the legislative acts in the thirteen policy areas discussed herein, and I encourage the reader to use the material and ideas in these entries as a basis for political involvement to positively affect the public policy process. This is what the ancient Greeks called *praxis,* the practice of putting things that one learns into action. One of the enduring and rich aspects of the American political system is that there is a place for anyone who seeks opportunities in politics, and the explanations that I have offered of policy terms, concepts, and legislation illustrate the broad array of players in the drama of American public policy.

I must thank my wife Joan for tolerating my single-mindedness while I have worked on this very rewarding project. She has been an unwavering source of support for me, and her technical skills in helping me transform this work into something that I could store and modify on a computer will not go unappreciated. I also thank Alicia Merritt at ABC-CLIO who encouraged me and was always a source of kindness and assistance.

Byron M. Jackson

Introduction

What Is Public Policy?

Public policy affects all Americans in many ways. All of our laws result from public policy actions. Laws regarding speed limits on our roads and highways, possession and use of legal and illegal drugs, the licensing of family dogs, the advertising of alcohol and tobacco products on billboards and television: All aspects of life in America are regulated and therefore subject to controls resulting from public policy. The Food and Drug Administration determines the levels of food coloring allowed in basic food products. The Federal Communications Commission (FCC) monitors television advertising, and FCC requirements prohibit the sale of cigarettes over the airwaves. A local city planning commission sets rules and regulations for fence heights to ensure consistency in neighborhood designs. A community might restrict the cutting and removal of trees to promote aesthetics in an area.

Given all these regulations, many Americans feel there are too many, that rights are being restricted. Yet a main function of democratic government is to respond to needs as expressed by citizens. In this introduction I explain the dimensions of public policy as it evolved in the United States. I also outline the most important characteristics of the American political system, its structures, and its processes. Finally, I discuss the policy eras in American politics and how national needs and competing values dominated the policy arenas during the last 200 years. Accordingly, we now turn to what public policy actually is and how government engages in the policy process.

Public policy is generated in response to a problem or need, whether it be at the local, state, or national level. Elected officials are authorized to make laws and policies to solve problems and to satisfy needs. Quite simply, *public policy,* as defined by Thomas Dye, is what governments choose to do or not to do (Dye, 1995). Public policy is made up of the actions of government and the intentions that determine those actions. The process begins with a perceived problem or need that must then be solved or satisfied. Charles O. Jones calls this the *perception stage* (Jones, 1984). The citizens of northern California, South Dakota, southern Ohio, and Illinois experienced serious winter floods during 1997. In response to the problems caused by the extensive flooding, citizens in the affected areas soon had an interest in improving flood control measures to prevent future disasters. These citizens appealed to their government representatives for assistance. They sought government action in the form of public policy to directly affect the current and future problems that their states and communities faced. Once a problem is *perceived* as needing public action, then it needs to be clearly defined in terms of the nature and form of government action to be taken.

Government public policy decisionmaking comes as a result of how problems are presented to the government for action, something otherwise known as *getting on the public agenda.* Not every problem, no matter how deserving, receives government attention or action, and so all problems do not necessarily get placed on the public agenda. The *public agenda* is the category of issues and items discussed by government representatives and that, once reviewed, deserve public action. If a problem is perceived as serious enough, and if the problem has a real or potential impact on enough people, then government action will likely occur. Most public policies thus require evidence of support for action on the problem. Support adds legitimacy to the problem, enabling governments—at whatever level—to commit the resources required to solve the problem.

Some authors call this early process the *prepolicy stage;* others see it simply as getting on the government's agenda. For public policy to actually happen and for solutions to problems to truly occur, government representatives have to be convinced that problems are deserving of government attention, action, and the commitment of resources. Public policy, then, becomes a course of action, implemented by a government institution or official, for resolving an issue of public concern. The course of action is accompanied by laws, public statements, official regulations, sometimes visible patterns of behavior. Law is the basis for government action, providing the authority—and the coercion, if necessary—to bring about the change in behavior or the solution that is being sought.

Historical Background

In studying American public policy it is important to understand the historical context. For example, when the U.S. Constitution was ratified in 1789, the U.S. government was a new entity, and it was not in the business of making national policies and laws. It had just emerged from the difficult challenge of convincing enough elected representatives in the 13 new states of the merits of the new constitutional system. After the Constitution was ratified, the national government had to convince the states and their representatives that the national government had authority to *act* and to *govern.* The competing values and interests that emerged thereafter created several public policy eras that have dominated American politics since 1789.

The philosophy and structure of the American political system provides the setting for the emergence of public policy. The Founders believed in a form of government based on the concept of *democracy,* which was first implemented by ancient Greek city-states. In Greek, it means "authority of the people." American democracy is rooted in the Judeo-Christian tradition and in British history. Democracies emphasize the value of the *individual,* and early American colonists emphasized *liberty* over other goals of government. This belief in liberty is reflected in the Declaration of Independence, the U.S. Constitution, and the Bill of Rights (which comprises the first ten amendments to the original Constitution). *Political equality* is also an ideal of democracy, expressed in the Declaration of Independence in the phrase "all men are created equal." This did not mean that all people are born with equal virtues or abilities. It meant that all people (excluding male slaves and all women) were born with equal standing before government and entitled to equal rights. This belief in political equality lead to *popular sovereignty,* or rule by the people. This is best exemplified in Abraham Lincoln's Gettysburg Address, in which he spoke of "government of the people, by the people, and for the people." A second ideal of democracy is *majority rule,* which means that majorities rather than minorities determine policy decisions. If individuals are equal, then policies should be determined according to the desires of the greater number. The third ideal in the American form of democracy comprises *direct democracy* and *indirect democracy.* In a direct democracy, citizens vote on most issues. A town meeting in which local residents vote on issues before the town council is one example; this has been a common form of local government in New England towns for more than 350 years. Our national government is an *indirect democracy* or a *republic.* In an indirect democracy, citizens elect representatives (i.e., policymakers) to make decisions on their behalf. Therefore, at the federal level, members of Congress—and not citizens—vote to place bills into law.

The Structure of Government

The American system of government is referred to as a *federal* system. The term *federalism* describes a system in which power is constitutionally divided between a central government and subnational or local governments. In the United States, the states serve as subnational governments. We sometimes use the words *federal* and *federalism* interchangeably, that is, we say we have a "federal system," meaning two levels of constitutionally based authority. But we sometimes speak of the "federal government" in referring to the *national* government. The federal government in actuality consists of authorities in Washington, D.C., and the states. Therefore, state governors and state legislators are officials of America's federal system of government.

The principle of federalism was adopted in the Constitution in 1789. The Framers intended to establish a government that recognized two distinct levels or units of official authority: a national government and several state governments; both types derive their authority from the U.S. Constitution. Neither type can be destroyed by the other and neither is beholden to the other for its existence. The system of government that preceded the ratification of the U.S. Constitution was a *confederacy* created under the Articles of Confederation and Perpetual Union. Under a federal system, governmental units are coequal; under a confederacy, states hold more power than does the national government. The national government in a confederacy is largely a creature of the states, deriving its very power from the states. Thus, national government within a confederacy is weak, much more so than within a federal system. The Framers wanted to avoid the hazards associated with a weak national government, yet they wanted to preserve the coequal status of the states vis-à-vis the national government.

The predominant vehicle arguing for the adoption of a federal system that encouraged coequality between the national and state governments was a series of published articles known today as *The Federalist Papers,* or simply *The Federalist.* John Jay, Alexander Hamilton, and James Madison—preeminent statesmen among the Framers—wrote 85 essays that appeared in New York newspapers during the ratification debates. The essays were published anonymously under the Latin pseudonym *Publius* (Public Man). The essays' unified arguments sought to convince delegates to the Constitutional Convention of the merits of the federal system. The essays addressed the fundamental question of the proper role of the national and state governments in exercising constitutionally provided authority: Which level of government has the constitutional authority to perform which functions? An issue constantly on the political and legal agenda, the ultimate test came during the Civil War. Although the Founders did not agree as to the proper strength of the national government, all agreed the new national government should be stronger than that under the Articles of Confederation.

In 200 years, the U.S. government has grown from a few hundred people with relatively limited impact on the residents of 13 small states to a government employing millions, affecting the daily lives of most of the population of more than 260 million people today. This transformation is closely related to the changing way in which Americans understand the federal system. We have come to understand the evolution and development of U.S. public policy system in the context of policy eras that have taken place between 1789 and the present. We now discuss the policy eras and some of the leading events that characterized these eras in American politics.

Policy Eras in American Politics

Federalism and the public policy process today are very different from how they appeared in the late eighteenth century, even from the 1960s. *Intergovernmental relations* have taken on a very different look since 1787, when the constitutional ratification process began. During the first policy era (1789–1865, referred to as the era of *vertical federalism* or *nation-centered federalism*), the new government struggled to define itself. The thrust of federalism during this early period was on relations between the national and state governments. As the national government and the states carved out areas of authority and responsibility, many challenges occurred between levels of government. Alexander Hamilton, writing in *The Federalist,* made clear the view that national power was supreme. We call this a nation-centered view of federalism because it rests on the principle that the U.S. Constitution is a document ratified by the people. Although the states retain great powers, the national government has the ultimate responsibility for preserving the nation and, indeed, the very viability of the states. This view of nation-centered federalism was held by Northerners in justifying the Civil War to prevent Southern states from seceding in 1861.

Public policy during this early period had a strong nationalist character, emanating for the most part from national power. The federal courts played an important role during this era, as states were reluctant to grant extensive national powers that might then be unchecked. The federal-state conflict was thus frequently played out in the courts. One example illuminating the tension between national and state authority was *McCulloch v. Maryland,* a classic decision whereby the U.S. Supreme Court fixed the primacy of the national government through Congress to prohibit state banks from taxing national banks, even though such power was not explicitly provided for in the U.S. Constitution. The courts were called upon to interpret national powers, and such powers were defined broadly. Yet the national government was exercising power on a comparatively small scale; during the administration of George Washington, the federal government had only 1,000 employees (this increased to 33,000 during the administration of James Buchanan 70 years later). The government raised little revenue during the early years (there was no income tax yet) and had limited means to engage in policy development (indeed, there was no military to speak of). The states were also relatively weak in their ability to raise money and to exert authority, and there was little federal-state cooperation. Yet the federal government did give land to states to support education, and some joint federal-state-private ventures (e.g., canal construction initiated by states) were initiated.

The early period of the U.S. government was characterized by the growth of nation-centered federalism, in which vertical relations predominated between the national and state governments. The nature of the relationship was thus top-down, whereby the national government made policy overtures to the states by way of offering programs and opportunities for economic growth and resource development. Both the national and state governments operated on a small scale because of the newness of the arrangement and because of the lack of revenue. During the decade that preceded the Civil War champions of state-centered federalism tried to assert the power of the states. Southern leaders feared that the federal government, dominated by the increasingly populous North, would regulate, even abolish slavery. John C. Calhoun, a theorist on popular sovereignty and one of the leading proponents of the state-centered approach, claimed that states could nullify laws of Congress (the so-called doctrine of nullification). Calhoun also argued that a state could withdraw from the Union, and several Southern states seceded in 1861. The Confederate States of America emphasized the supremacy of the states as embedded in the confederate system, but state-centered federalism died along with the Confederacy in 1865.

Following the Civil War, the relationship between the national government and the states changed as a response to urbanization and industrialization. Between 1865 and 1900, *dual federalism* best exemplified the conditions of life between the national government and the states. Under the era of dual federalism, each government type had separate authority and areas of responsibility. The U.S. Supreme Court interpreted the U.S. Constitution as requiring a hands-off relationship between the federal and state governments. As a result, each level of government, with its own responsibilities, was somewhat independent of the others. New policies ushered in the era of regulation of big business and the first meaningful national attempt to assist states in education, agriculture, and economic development. Two regulatory policy schemes crafted by the U.S. Congress early on were the Interstate Commerce Act of 1887 (which created the Interstate Commerce Commission, the first modern regulatory agency) and the Sherman Antitrust Act of 1890 (designed to control the growth and power of monopolies). Congress had already passed the Morrill Land Grant Act of 1862, but its effects in promoting settlement and agriculture were not felt until the post–Civil War westward expansion. The Morrill Act donated land to states to establish education programs in agriculture and mechanical arts. The schools became known as *land grant colleges* (many exist today, some still designated by the "A&M" in their names).

From 1900 to 1937, federalism changed again, whereby national and state relations showed maturity, growth, development, and greater cooperation. The growth of the national regulatory framework continued when Congress created the Federal Trade Commission (FTC) in 1914. The mandate of the FTC was to maintain free and fair competition in business. Ultimately, the FTC was expected to keep consumers from being cheated. Although it did not act forcefully during the first 25 years, the FTC reluctantly carried out its charge. Another area of national involvement in state activities came in the form of child welfare laws and regulation. The child welfare movement took root during the 1880s as a result of the massive influx of immigrants to the United States; young workers needed protection. Lewis Hine, commissioned the official photographer for the Immigration and Naturalization Service (INS) at Ellis Island, developed an interest in the lives of the children of immigrants he had photographed during disembarkation and processing. Hine followed some immigrants and their children into northern sweatshops and factories and found the children laboring for low pay in horrible working and living conditions. As a result of his efforts, and with the assistance of other child welfare advocates, national and state attention was brought to the plight of child workers. Yet child welfare reform waned until after World War I, when child welfare regulations and laws were instituted with renewed vigor.

In 1913 the federal government established the income tax, thereby increasing revenues. State and local governments also discovered new ways to grow revenue streams into their coffers, instituting gasoline and cigarette taxes, higher property taxes, and some state income taxes. By the late 1920s state and local governments still held control over most government services in the states and localities (health and sanitation, police and fire, and meager social-service functions). There was little federal involvement in providing such services or in regulating citizens' behavior. This all changed dramatically with the onset of the Great Depression.

The 1929 stock market crash precipitated the Great Depression; it affected almost every American. During the most troublesome years, one-fourth of the workforce was unemployed, and banks failed daily. There were no national programs to supply unemployment services or other public assistance. Life conditions for many people—for the poor, the newly poor and jobless, the homeless, and anyone confronting the burdens of an uncertain economic and employment future—were extremely discouraging. State and local governments were not capable of assisting those in need.

Democrat Franklin D. Roosevelt was elected president in 1932 amid the crisis. He designed, and Congress passed, several programs that together became known as the New Deal. Its purpose was to stimulate economic recovery and lift up the victims of the Great Depression who were unemployed, hungry, homeless, and in need of government assistance. New Deal programs regulated many activities in business and labor, established the first welfare system, and instituted federal-state cooperation in the funding and administration of programs through federal grants-in-aid. Grants-in-aid provided federal money to states (and, less frequently, to local governments) to create programs to help people.

The relationship between the states and federal government thus changed dramatically. Prior to the New Deal, government touched lives by giving or selling something to citizens—such as land for settlers or subsidies for businesses—thereby helping people develop the western regions. All of a sudden, New Deal programs directly affected the lives of citizens through *regulation* of banks, working conditions, and business practices as well as through *redistributive* policies designed to protect the poor (e.g., Social Security and Aid to Families with Dependent Children).

Following World War II (1941–1945), a new policy era emerged, the era of *creative federalism.* The national government continued to play a significant role in developing policy for states and localities, but the role was not as extensive as that required during the Great Depression. The activity and roles of interest groups within the public policy process expanded tremendously. During the postwar era, national goals included achieving social objectives for states, and congressionally created national goals were implemented and carried out by states. One of these programs was the Serviceman's Readjustment Act of 1946, better known as the G.I. Bill, which provided financial assistance to veterans for education. It served as an investment in an entire generation of Americans, an investment that would benefit the national economy many times over in education, industry, and research and development for decades to come. Other national goals expressed through federal programs include the War on Poverty and associated poverty programs during the 1960s.

During the late 1960s and early 1970s, the era of the *second generation regulatory programs* saw creative federalism whereby the federal government attempted to place on the national agenda programs to solve state and national social, economic, and urban problems. This period also signaled the development of public-interest (i.e., consumer) policies and the rise of public interest groups that mobilized around environmental and consumer issues.

Since 1972 the policies that derived from the era of *new federalism* have taken hold, placing greater emphasis on state and local authority for corrective actions. Pres. Richard Nixon introduced his ideas for new federalism, which shifted power and authority from the national government back to state and local governments. The primary means of returning power back to states was the 1972 State and Local Fiscal Assistance Act (the General Revenue Sharing Act). Its purpose was to restore balance (seen as having been lost under creative federalism) among federal, state, and local governments. The key difference now was that states and cities were given control over resources Washington provided (through revenue-sharing funds); *they* would decide which projects and programs would be funded. During the 1980s this version of new federalism was extended by Pres. Ronald Reagan, who continued decentralizing power and authority but cut much federal support for programs.

The changing nature of federalism since 1789 has affected public policies that are formulated or implemented at the state and local levels. Furthermore, the separation of powers also affects public policymaking within the intergovernmental system. Many entries in this encyclopedia provide a reference to legislation or other entries. Making historical connections gives the needed background for understanding motivations for and influences on policy development.

The Current Political Culture and Public Policy

The willingness of communities, states, or nations to make public policy to solve problems is affected by *political culture,* the distinctive way of looking at and participating in politics. We might also view political culture, as Lucian Pye states, as "the set of attitudes, beliefs, and sentiments that give order and meaning to the political process" (Pye, 1968). Political culture can be understood as a mindset or a way of perceiving and interpreting politics.

In the United States, there are distinct cultural patterns in which people in different regions of the country view and participate in politics. Variations in political culture and attitudes about politics occur at the community, city, state, and regional levels. In some cases, cultural patterns are affected by the presence of ethnic groups or local traditions and the approach that individuals and groups take toward politics and political participation. Ultimately, political culture has to do with how communities and states view the role of government and politics in relationship to everyday life. Some regions see government as the first resort. For example, in the Northeast, heavily urbanized areas frequently call on federal assistance to manage urban problems. Successful elected officials are typically urbanites and demonstrate a clear sense of what cities stand for and face in terms of the challenges confronting urban centers in the Northeast. In the Midwest, traditional patterns of independence and autonomy from government as expressed in the agricultural heartland mean residents do not rely as directly on federal assistance. Elected public officials in Midwestern states are viewed more positively if they reflect the values of agricultural interests and show familiarity with lifestyles associated with agriculture and small-town life. The distinctions among political cultures in communities, states, and regions translate into different perceptions toward the problem-solving role of government. In essence, communities and states in the federal system differ in their expectations as to what governments can or should do on behalf of citizens.

If a problem requires federal action, an appeal is made to the local members of Congress, that is, the U.S. representative or U.S. senator, who may or may not view the problem as requiring national attention. If it does merit congressional action, then the process begins whereby other members of Congress are lobbied on the importance of the problem and the need to create *legislation.* This is an extensive process, whereby members of congressional subcommittees and committees are convinced of a need for legislation.

The local public policy process occurs in counties, cities, and smaller communities (towns, villages, etc.). Local city councils or county boards serve as the local legislative branch of government, making laws, ordinances, and policies. Nonelected boards and commissions (usually with three to seven members appointed by elected bodies for specific terms) also serve a legislative capacity, issuing regulations, restrictions, variances, and permits for services or actions. All of these *public institutions* are policymaking bodies. Each is required to respond to calls for public action, but they need not act upon every request. Rather, they respond to the merit and magnitude of the problem and the likelihood that public action will realistically resolve it.

Public policy is also affected by ideology and the values that predominate in the political arena. We can look at *political ideology* as a means to understand the emergence of competing values. Historically, *conservatism* and *liberalism* (and their variations) have dominated policymaking. Both ideologies are rooted in 19th-century liberalism's commitment to economic, political, social, and religious freedom. In looking at the political perspectives of American policymakers, we find all are some shade of "liberal" or "conservative," even though many in our society believe in different ideologies. Liberals and conservatives thus have a common commitment to freedom, democracy, the free-market system, and individualism, but they disagree on the principles to be used in making and evaluating public policy.

The first disagreement centers on the *principle of freedom* and its proper limits: Conservatives tend to value civil and personal freedoms less and are more willing to limit these freedoms; liberals are more inclined to place limits on economic freedom. As for *political equality*, liberals tend to have a deeper commitment to equality than do conservatives. *Tradition* and *authority* are important to conservatives, whereas liberals favor a commitment to *change* and *individual choice* in moral and social behavior. Liberals feel that the role of government is to make life better; conservatives are more pessimistic about the role and influence of government in the lives of citizens. The values inherent in the liberal and conservative perspectives emerge in policy debates at all levels of government. This is particularly the case when the subject is the role of government itself and the extent to which market forces should be relied upon for economic and social health in society.

A new set of values, one that attracted much attention during the late 20th century, is encompassed in a philosophy known as *communitarianism*. Communitarianism focuses on the interconnection between rights and responsibilities. The thrust of communitarian public policy initiatives is on the revitalization of local neighborhood and city institutions, community policing, family preservation and restoration of family values, individual character formation, and health care reform. In the communitarian belief, well-ordered communities and their inherent virtues are more important than individual freedom. The communitarian philosophy embraces a clear, simple notion of citizenship.

In the following pages we explore the terms, concepts, actors, legislation, and events that make up the world of American public policy. I include a chronology (including major legislation and significant events) of public policy for each of the following policy areas: agriculture, civil rights, commerce and transportation, communications, crime, economics, education, energy, entitlement programs, the environment, health, housing, and labor.

References

Charles Bonser, Eugene McGregor Jr., and Clinton Oster Jr., *Policy Choices and Public Action* (1996).
Thomas Dye, *Understanding Public Policy* (1995).
Charles O. Jones, *Introduction to the Study of Public Policy* (1984).
James P. Lester and Joseph Stewart Jr., *Public Policy: An Evolutionary Approach* (1996).
Dennis Palumbo, *Public Policy in America: Government in Action* (1988).
B. Guy Peters, *American Public Policy: Promise and Performance* (1993).
Lucian W. Pye, *Political Culture and Political Development* (1965).
Susan Welch et al., *Understanding American Government* (1997).

Encyclopedia of American Public Policy

Key Concepts

Accountability

Concern over accountability influences public servants and politicians; indeed it pervades the very atmosphere of public administration. In any democracy, government must be responsive to the needs of citizens, but especially in a democracy as pluralistic and complex as that in the American system. Democratic theorists, not to mention citizens who are impacted by the actions of bureaucrats, are intent on holding public officials accountable for their actions.

An important aspect in operating a public bureaucracy is the problem of accountability or control—getting the bureaucracy to serve agreed-upon goals. Citizens want to know that the government and its bureaucratic structure work on behalf of citizens, whether on the local, state, or national level. In an intergovernmental political system, such as the U.S. system, accountability means that the public is able to control the policies and behaviors of public organizations and to make them answer for what they do. For public policies to have the desired effect and impact intended by policymakers, public officials must act in ways that fulfill the needs of citizens who seek solutions to public problems.

There is a significant degree of mistrust and cynicism among the U.S. public toward government and politicians. The cynicism brings greater attention to the accountability of politicians and public officials, particularly as to their efforts to make and implement public policy. Any degree of mistrust of government challenges public accountability and the efforts of politicians and people who work in the public sector. Violation of ethical responsibilities and scandals involving politicians and public officials also test the accountability of public officials.

See also: Key Concepts: Pluralism; Public Bureaucracy

References: Fred A. Kramer, *Dynamics of Public Bureaucracy: An Introduction to Public Management* (1981); Naomi Lynn and Aaron Wildavsky, *Public Administration: The State of the Discipline* (1990).

Administrative Agencies

Government activities generally result in decisions being made and actions being taken to correct a problem or to provide a solution in an area of governmental authority. Decisions made by governmental entities fall into three categories: legislative decisions made by a representative body like the U.S. Congress; judicial decisions that result from judgments issued in a legal proceeding and establish a rule of law or precedent; and executive decisions that are made by a top elected official like a state governor or the U.S. president. These actions, and the policies that result, must be put into operation. The administrative agency (an organized group or groups of people) applies the rules and regulations that govern a specific public policy area.

Administrative agencies exist at every level of government. Counties, cities, states, and the federal government all use administrative agencies to implement decisions on public actions, which we call public policy. The number of administrative agencies has grown significantly since 1900, and some 3 million civilian employees work for the federal government.

State and local governments employ more than 16 million people, the result of the need for state and local governments to create means for governing and problem-solving. The Tenth Amendment to the U.S. Constitution states that "powers not delegated to the United States by the Constitution, nor prohibited by it to the states, are reserved to the states respectively, or to the people." This delineates the roles of the states and localities in performing functions in their interests that the federal government cannot constitutionally do.

Cities and counties create administrative structures, also called administrative agencies, to administer and implement state and local laws, rules, and regulations. For example, communities typically have rules regarding the maximum height of fences. If a resident wants to build a fence that exceeds the maximum allowed height, then he is required to appeal (or apply) for a variance from the rule establishing the height limits. The variance application is made to the administrative agency responsible for such matters (e.g., the city planning department and/or its advisory commission). In this case, the administrative agency (the planning department) would likely employ experts empowered to decide the issues alone or in cooperation with members of the advisory commission.

Administrative agencies are staffed by expert or knowledgeable individuals in the field. At the federal level, agencies must conform to the standards and procedures established in the Administrative Procedure Act. All U.S. states have adopted model administrative procedure acts or follow administrative plans of some kind. The purpose of state and federal administrative procedure acts is to seek consistency and fairness in administrative processes. As administrative agencies make decisions, hold hearings, and wield their discretion, the goal is to manage such processes within the context of administrative fairness and constitutional protections of due process.

See also: Key Concepts: Administrative Procedure Act of 1946; Public Policy

References: Jay M. Shafritz and E. W. Russell, *Public Administration* (1997); Kenneth F. Warren, *Administrative Law in the Political System* (1988).

Administrative Law

Administrative law comprises many aspects of law and government: laws about the duties and proper operation of an administrative agency as mandated by legislatures and courts; rules and regulations determined by administrative agencies outright; powers and procedures of administrative agencies; laws governing judicial review of administrative action; in short, the legal rules and principles that define the authority and structure of administrative agencies, specify the procedural formalities that agencies use, determine the validity of particular administrative decisions, and define the role of reviewing courts and other elements of government in their relation to administrative agencies.

Administrative agencies such as the Occupational Safety and Health Administration (OSHA) and the Department of Energy regularly apply administrative law in their daily operations. For example, if a paint company finds a new way to manufacture a better paint for consumers, OSHA requires the paint company to make certain that the production process does not cause emissions of harmful odors, gases, or chemicals into the air of the surrounding environment; that employees are not harmed in the manufacturing process by the presence of hazardous fumes; and that the homeowner is not exposed to dangerous fumes or substances during application. OSHA is responsible for administering rules and regulations that govern aspects of occupational health and safety in a fair, responsible, and reasonable way. The paint company is required to make the workplace and production process safe for the worker; it must ensure that the product is safe for the consumer. Courts might be called upon to determine, along with agency experts, acceptable safety and health factors affecting workers and consumers.

In sum, administrative law is a broad area of the law addressing the power and authority of administrative agencies, the way in which agencies use power in implementing public policy, and how private individuals are affected in the application of public policy.

See also: Energy: Department of Energy; Key Concepts: Administrative Agencies; Regulation

References: Leif H. Carter and Christine B. Harrington, *Administrative Law and Politics: Cases and Comments* (1991); Florence Heffron and Neil McFeeley, *The Administrative Regulatory Process* (1983); Kenneth Warren, *Administrative Law in the Political System* (1988).

Administrative Procedure Act of 1946

The Administrative Procedure Act (APA) provides a set of laws and procedures to govern how federal agencies operate with clients and the general public. In general terms, the APA: specifies the conditions under which administrative agencies adjudicate (i.e., hold hearings and decide controversies) and make rules; recognizes the discretion of administrative agencies as defined in the authorizing statute; and establishes judicial review by the court system. Congress authorizes agencies to act in the first instance, providing a legislative mandate; the APA then gives direction for the standards and rules regarding decisionmaking, policymaking, enforcement, and regulation. The APA also requires that notice and hearing guidelines be published with rules of appeal or amendment. The purpose of the APA was to develop a standard rulemaking process throughout the federal system. It was concerned with the most important areas of the administrative process and is the major source for administrative law.

Prior to the 1946 passage of the APA, there existed a maze of procedures and regulations that regulatory agencies developed independently. It was important in the increasingly complex regulatory environment of the late 1940s to standardize and structure the federal regulatory and administrative activities of agencies. The APA also provides for agency discretion in matters of agency responsibility.

See also: Key Concepts: Administrative Agencies; Administrative Law; Judicial Review

References: Leif H. Carter and Christine B. Harrington, *Administrative Law and Politics: Cases and Comments* (1991); Fred A. Kramer, *Dynamics of Public Bureaucracy: An Introduction to Public Management* (1981); Jay Shafritz and E. W. Russell, *Public Administration* (1997).

Advisory Committees

Members of Congress and the president sometimes seek information and assistance from experts and citizens outside the government. Advisory committees or advisory commissions counsel the president and Congress on specific problems or policy areas. One example is the Advisory Commission on Intergovernmental Relations. It was created in 1959 to review the federal system and recommend ways to improve intergovernmental relations. Commissions often conduct studies then publish recommendations.

Advisory committees can operate like interest groups as they attempt to influence the direction and outcome of public policy, bringing in outside views for new policies being considered. Some advisory committees are composed primarily of experts; others (called representative committees) are composed of people representing various competing interests. In 1990 a total of 60 federal departments and agencies supported 1,071 advisory committees with 22,391 members. These committees issued 972 reports and are frequently relied upon as useful sources of opinion and information. A majority of advisory committees have a narrow focus and are used for political purposes.

See also: Key Concepts: Interest Groups

References: David H. Rosenbloom, *Public Administration: Understanding Management, Politics, and Law in the Public Sector* (1998).

Agenda Building

An important, early stage in winning the attention of government officials is to get on the government's agenda. The agenda-building process comprises the decision to review and possibly offer policy solutions and to use public resources to study a problem. It is an indication that a specific course of action will ensue. To get on the government's agenda is to "make the list" for government action. Some public issues take years to get on the public agenda; others may carry high visibility and thus receive immediate attention. This is a feature of government and public policy formulation throughout all levels of government. For example, the Iron Mountain copper mine in northern California creates water and soil pollution, is a potential public health problem, and was designated as a Superfund site under a federal environmental law. Although the mine had been in operation since the 1880s and had been polluting nearby streams and lands for decades, only within the last 20 years was enough public pressure brought to bear to force the government to take action. The potential magnitude of the problem at this Superfund site accorded the Iron Mountain issue high visibility on the government's agenda in 1983.

Not every policy proposal that receives government attention is approved; it is merely a first step. Once an issue is on the agenda, the body responsible for developing policy—the city council, board of supervisors, planning commission, Congress—decides whether the problem has a public solution and should be granted public funds for action. In the case of Iron Mountain, the U.S. Environmental Protection Agency (EPA) was authorized to assign Superfund status. The EPA is the regulatory agency responsible for implementing and enforcing environmental regulations and policies. If the decision is to take action, then public resources are committed to a solution.

See also: Environment: Environmental Protection Agency

References: David H. Davis, *Energy Politics* (1993); Charles O. Jones, *An Introduction to the Study of Public Policy* (1984).

Allocational Policy

There are three general categories of public policy: allocational, developmental, and redistributive. Some policies, like Social Security and welfare benefits, are redistributive in that they satisfy equity concerns in society. Developmental policies aid and encourage state and local economic growth and development. Allocational policy produces and distributes public goods and services to consumers and taxpayers. State and local governments provide the bulk of allocational policy through state and local government services, including education, health, welfare, public works and transportation, public safety and fire protection, and parks and recreation. Many of the efforts of state and local governments reflect the public agenda. Because of the decentralized federal system, state and local governments are better able to fulfill the needs of local citizens than is the federal government. Services at the local level are more easily managed on a localized basis. This is one way that citizens hold public officials accountable within the federal system.

See also: Key Concepts: Accountability; Redistributive Policy

References: Thomas R. Dye, *Understanding Public Policy* (1995); B. Guy Peters, *American Public Policy: Promise and Performance* (1993).

Amendments

Amendments—the way in which laws are changed after original passage—are one of the great challenges within any political system. Laws express the values and character of a people and their government. Laws are codes of conduct and offer a set of behavioral standards to which individuals, states, and the national government are required to comply. The foundation for laws, their values, and indeed the very structure of intergovernmental relations and political authority in the American system is the U.S. Constitution. The people who framed the Constitution realized that it would have to adapt to changing circumstances over the years. Accordingly, they provided formal means to change, or amend, the Constitution. There are two ways to amend the U.S. Constitution: first, Congress can propose an amendment, which must then be ratified by three-fourths of the state legislatures or by three-fourths of the states in special conventions; second, two-thirds of the state legislatures can petition Congress to call a national convention to propose an amendment, which must then be ratified by three-fourths of the state legislatures or by three-fourths of the states in special conventions. Two-thirds of both houses of Congress must pass any proposal to amend the Constitution. Congress then has the power to determine if the proposed amendment will be ratified by state legislatures or by state conventions. Congress can also set a time limit for the discussion and vote of the required number of states. The time that Congress sets can be extended, as happened with the Equal Rights Amendment (ERA).

The ERA was created and sponsored by proponents to resolve inequities for women that had not been remedied by the ratification of the Nineteenth Amendment in 1920, which gave women the right to vote. The proposed ERA would have added a constitutional prohibition against gender discrimination. Congress passed the ERA, but the states failed to ratify it (falling three states short of the thirty-eight needed by the June 30, 1982, deadline).

Amending the constitution is a deliberate, slow process by design given the potential impacts from changing national laws. But there are less formal ways to change laws, whereby the president, Congress, and the courts interpret events in accordance with constitutional principles; in essence they "fill in the gaps" where the Constitution is silent.

While in office, Pres. Richard M. Nixon became embroiled in a constitutional fight over executive privilege. Nixon claimed that executive privilege shielded him from having to turn over the infamous tapes that recorded Nixon talking with his staff and others inside the White House. Congress and the special prosecutor appointed in the Watergate affair had subpoenaed the tapes, but Nixon refused to cooperate. The U.S. Supreme Court thus ordered Nixon to turn them over; in doing so the Court also recognized that presidents possess executive privilege under the Constitution.

See also: Civil Rights: Equal Rights Amendment; Key Concepts: Congress, United States; Supreme Court

References: Susan Welch et al., *Understanding American Government* (1997).

American Values

Values and desires expressed by citizens influence public policy. Thus, public policy reflects societal values; when values change, so does the nature and direction of public policy. A general list of American values include: importance of individual and national financial security and stability; upward economic and social mobility; free-market capitalism; political and social tolerance; public virtue and citizenship; equal opportunity; decentralized political power; the value of the individual; political equality; majority rule; and minority rights. These values are distinctly American in that they represent the ideals of the government and society as embodied in the U.S. Constitution, one of history's most important documents. These ideals can be expressed in many different forms of public policy.

One example is U.S. health care policy, specifically the need for access and equity for all citizens. But the reality is that competing forces define and construct different views of what "equitable" policy means. The American Medical Association, for example, might contend it is not in the interests of physicians to favor health reforms that would guarantee access to health insurance for all Americans. In contrast, proponents of universal access might believe that *their* values should be reflected in public policy. As a result, the outcome might be government inaction or public policy that does not reflect more aggressive reforms. As interest groups provide money (in the form of campaign contribution) to support or defeat legislation, the better their chances for achieving the desired outcome. Values change over time, thus the political, economic, and social interests that encourage policy development require a clear understanding of the strategies necessary to promote public policy.

See also: Key Concepts: Political Culture, Political Socialization

References: James P. Lester and Joseph Stewart Jr., *Public Policy: An Evolutionary Approach* (1996).

Amicus Curiae

Amicus curiae literally means "friend of the court" and refers to legal briefs filed by individuals or groups who are interested in but not party to a legal proceeding (i.e., a lawsuit). Interest groups in American politics use different strategies to influence public policy, the amicus curiae brief being one tactic. *Amici* (the people doing the filing) must obtain court permission to present their arguments, which are usually written but can be in oral argument. The amicus brief frequently represents the viewpoint of a special-interest group, which has a vested interest in seeing one party in the litigation prevail over the other. Thus, in a sense the amicus is a way to "lobby" the Supreme Court by citing legal precedent, law journals, and specific research by legal experts in a field of study. The most important U.S. Supreme Court cases will draw scores of amicus briefs: The 1954 school desegregation case, *Brown v. Board of Education,* had 50; the 1963 case *Gideon v. Wainwright,* which recognized indigents' right to counsel in noncapital and capital offenses, saw 24; and the famous 1978 case *Regents of University of California v. Bakke* on affirmative action in school placement had 57. The amicus brief is one way that interest groups influence policy.

See also: Civil Rights: *Brown v. Board of Education; Regents of the University of California v. Bakke*

References: Ronald E. Pynn, *American Politics: Changing Expectations* (1993).

Annual Budget

Among the responsibilities of the U.S. Congress is passing the annual budget, a difficult task given its size and complexity. The 1993 federal budget totaled some $1.4 trillion. In addition to funding programs and services (the appropriations duties), Congress expends much discussion on reducing the federal budget. The president starts the process by presenting a budget (with each bureau, agency, and department explained in detail), which Congress must then approve. With the passage of the Budget and Impoundment Control Act of 1974, however, Congress changed its procedures. Congress now initiates and conducts its own budget-making process along with the executive branch. This "tentative" budget in Congress is called the First Concurrent Resolution, which is adopted by both houses. Congress then reviews the president's budget, seeks advice from the Congressional Budget Office, and takes recommendations from congressional budget committees before outlining a tentative budget that includes projected income and revenue expenditures. Congress sets targets in spending areas including defense, health, transportation, education, agriculture, energy, and so on. The appropriations committees in the House of Representatives and the Senate review budget recommendations and issue a report on the final budget. The Budget and Impoundment Control Act was designed to give Congress control over the budget process, but it did little to control federal spending.

The Balanced Budget and Emergency Deficit Control Act of 1985 (known as Gramm-Rudman after the bill's sponsors) mandated across-the-board cuts in nearly all federal programs to achieve specified deficit levels and deficit goals. Gramm-Rudman proved cumbersome and did not really help to reduce federal spending and the deficit. The major problem was the setting of realistic deficit targets; thus the 1990 Budget Enforcement Act was devised to make changes. Annual budget activities continue to focus on reducing government spending and the deficit.

See also: Economics: Budget and Impoundment Control Act of 1974; Budget Enforcement Act of 1990; Gramm-Rudman Act of 1985; Key Concepts: Appropriations Committee

References: Susan Welch et al., *Understanding American Government* (1997); Aaron Wildavsky, *The New Politics of the Budgetary Process* (1988).

Appropriations Committee

The U.S. Congress plays an important role in the federal budget process. The Constitution gives Congress the authority to control the federal budget by collecting taxes and spending money. One function of Congress is to appropriate money (an *appropriation* is a congressional act that authorizes public funds for specific purposes) and to grant the formal authority to spend the money. Requests for appropriations come to Congress's standing committees. Almost all standing committees are authorization committees for the agencies whose work the committees oversee. For example, the House Interior and Insular Affairs Committee and the Senate Energy and National Resources Committee review the authorization of the National Park Service in the Department of Interior; the agriculture committees oversee the Department of Agriculture; and so on. Authorization committees have the discretion to alter agency requests for funding. All appropriations are reviewed by the Appropriations Committee, one each in the House of Representatives and Senate; the committees thus make recommendations on the entire budget.

See also: Economics: Budget, Federal; Key Concepts: Committee System, Congressional

References: Susan Welch et al., *Understanding American Government* (1997).

Articles of Confederation

When the Revolutionary War started in 1775, the Second Continental Congress met that May to equip an army. The Continental Congress also called for the states to create regular governments. On July 4, 1776, a unanimous Continental Congress adopted the Declaration of Independence. The war lasted until 1783, which meant that the colonies, all with separate state constitutions, had to govern themselves until a national government could be constructed. The Articles of Confederation and Perpetual Union were thus developed, based on a plan proposed by Benjamin Franklin for a "league of friendship" among the new states. The question of sovereignty that eventually defined the legal relationship between the states and the national government was not resolved by the Articles of Confederation.

The Articles of Confederation contained serious deficiencies and did not provide for a strong national government. One deficiency was a full grant of authority to the national government while the states were yet sovereign. This allowed the states' legislatures to deny national authority whenever they saw fit. No national executive or court system was created, and Congress was denied the powers of taxation and regulation of commerce. The assent of nine states was required on important congressional matters such as war, foreign relations, and money collection and distribution. States ignored the Continental Congress and printed their own paper money.

Unanimous consent of the states was required for constitutional amendments, an impossible prospect for the national government. Financial problems for the national government caused by its inability to raise revenues and problems in foreign affairs due to congressional inability to make and enforce commercial treaties forced a call for a new Constitutional Convention in May 1787. One of the major weaknesses of the Articles of Confederation was that the states, in their distrust of strong central power, did not provide for a Constitution that was both national *and* federal. In 1777, when the articles were accepted, sovereignty of the states was paramount; political chaos and economic ruin were the consequence. The new Constitutional Convention, which would eventually frame the U.S. Constitution, remedied many of the problems in the Articles of Confederation.

See also: Key Concepts: Federalism

References: Ronald E. Pynn, *American Politics: Changing Expectations* (1993).

Backdoor Spending

Some budget decisions in Congress are not carried out through the normal appropriations process. Backdoor spending reflects conflict, uncertainty, and prior spending commitments that require appropriations committees and policy committees to consider adjustments or other funding obligations. This conflict can be resolved in three ways: (1) agencies occasionally borrow public money from the U.S. Treasury in the form of federal loans, which are quickly paid back; (2) agencies enter into contracts that obligate the federal government to pay a certain amount for goods and services without going through the appropriations process; and (3) permanent appropriations are authorized by legislation that is outside of the normal appropriations process, such as federal support for land grant colleges. In some cases of backdoor spending, appropriations committees have little discretion to not fund in these special areas and generally will abide by the standing commitments to spend money. Backdoor spending can be problematic for Congress because it represents uncontrollable spending that is frequently attacked by proponents of reduced government spending. Backdoor spending works against those in Congress who favor a balanced and controlled national budget.

See also: Key Concepts: Appropriations Committee

References: B. Guy Peters, *American Public Policy: Promise and Performance* (1993).

Balance of Payments

Any national economy requires trade with other nations. Some nations are more involved in international trade than others. In U.S. trade, it is important for the nation to regulate the balance of payments (the net result of the cost of imports and the cost of exports). For example, if a country spends more money than it receives from abroad, then it has a negative balance of payments; a country that spends less than it receives from abroad has a positive balance of payments. In the 1980s and 1990s the United States has had a large negative balance of payments. This has been brought on by America's demand for foreign products, including automobiles, electronics, clothing, and other consumer items.

Nations seek to maintain a positive balance of payments because a negative balance of payments indicates that a country's products are not competitive. Entrepreneurs frequently seek cheaper labor markets to produce American-financed goods. Cheaper labor markets exist in other countries with low wage structures. This results in an increasing reliance on foreign-produced goods, which contributes to the negative trade balance. Free-trade agreements are designed to promote unrestricted trade between nations without such impediments as tariffs or import restrictions. Nations often attempt to protect key industries from foreign competition by prohibiting the sale of certain products in their countries. Free-trade agreements are designed to clear away these protections so that nations can engage in restriction-free export and import programs.

See also: Commerce and Transportation: Free Trade; Economics: Economic Policy

References: B. Guy Peters, *American Public Policy: Promise and Performance* (1993).

Bill (Legislative)

The U.S. Constitution specifies certain powers of Congress: to lay and collect taxes, to coin money, to declare war and raise and support a military, and to regulate commerce with foreign governments and among the states. These are referred to as "enumerated" powers. Yet Congress also has "implied" power, which includes the authority to make laws to carry out the enumerated powers. When an item is proposed in Congress that seeks congressional action it is called a bill. A bill becomes law if supporters of the bill can manage the obstacles and gain the support of majorities along the way and the necessary funding to implement the bill.

Bills may be introduced in either the House of Representatives or in the Senate, except for tax measures and appropriations bills, which are required by the Constitution to be introduced in the House. Bills can be introduced only by members of Congress. Interest groups and the president must find congressional sponsors to introduce bills (the president initiates about half of all bills). Bills are assigned to a standing committee by the Speaker of the House or the presiding officer in the Senate. After assignment to a standing committee, the bill is sent to the relevant subcommittee. If the bill receives majority support in the subcommittee, it goes to the full committee; if approved, it is sent to the floor of the House of Representatives for discussion and vote. Most bills die in committee or subcommittee, but those that do manage to get out of committee usually become law. If the bill passes the House and the Senate without modification then it is sent to the president for signature into law. If changes to the bill are made in the House or Senate, a conference committee (composed of members of both houses) meets to resolve differences. When the conference committee reaches agreement, the bill is sent back to both houses for passage, then sent to the president for signature. The president has the power to veto the bill, which can be overcome by supermajority votes in Congress. The presidential "pocket veto" occurs when the executive simply fails to sign the bill before Congress adjourns. The president can also use the line-item veto to veto a particular appropriation item or specific tax break without vetoing an entire appropriations bill. An appropriations bill is one in which Congress allocates money to pay for special projects.

Legislative politics (bargaining and compromise) requires the building of voting majorities through the committee system in Congress.

See also: Key Concepts: Committee System, Congressional; Conference Committee

References: Ronald E. Pynn, *American Politics: Changing Expectations* (1993); Steven Waldman, *The Bill: How Legislation Really Becomes Law—A Case Study of the National Service Bill* (1995); Susan Welch et al., *Understanding American Government* (1997).

Block Grants

The grants-in-aid process is one of the primary methods that the federal government uses to distribute federal revenues to the states. Rather than merely give states money to develop programs or projects, the federal government has chosen different ways to promote state and national policy and programs through grants designed to solve specific problems. One of the first federal grant programs was the Morrill Land Grant Act of 1862. The act granted each Union state 30,000 acres for every senator and representative in Congress to endow agricultural colleges; 69 land grant colleges were established.

In 1916 Congress passed the Federal Road Act, which provided federal grants to state highway departments for building and improving rural roads. Several other grants-in-aid programs were initiated during the 1920s, totaling $163 million by 1931. During the 1970s and 1980s the chief mechanism for distributing federal funds was the block grant, which gives money to states or local units for general purposes instead of for specific projects (e.g., for education programs at the discretion of the state). During the late 1960s the Nixon administration began introducing so-called special revenue sharing to reform existing grant programs, and this eventually became known as block grants. Thus, specific grants were merged into a few general block grants covering law enforcement, education, transportation, rural community development, urban community development, and manpower training. The Community Development Block Grant is an example of this consolidation. The purpose of the Community Development Block Grant is to provide assistance to cities for development and renewal projects. The block grant concept remains an important means to share federal revenue for developing of state and local projects.

See also: Housing: Housing and Community Development Act of 1974

References: Clarke E. Cochran et al., *American Public Policy: An Introduction* (1996); Jay M. Shafritz and E. W. Russell, *Public Administration* (1997).

Cabinet

The cabinet is a standard feature of every U.S. presidential administration. Cabinets in the United States differ from those in parliamentary systems in that they do not have the authority and primary responsibility for policymaking. In the U.S. political system, the cabinet is composed of the president, vice president, the heads of the 14 executive departments, and executive branch officials given cabinet rank. Members of the cabinet (except for the president and vice president) are called secretaries. They are generally prominent politicians who will assist and lend credibility to the president and his administration, selected from policy areas in which they have expertise or influence. For example, the secretary of labor usually has connections to or interest in labor policy. The secretary of defense and secretary of state generally have foreign policy backgrounds. Other factors in selecting cabinet officers include geographic representation, race, and gender.

Each secretary has administrative responsibility for an agency or department. There are two distinct levels of cabinet positions, the inner cabinet and the outer cabinet. The inner cabinet includes the secretaries of defense, state, justice, and treasury. Other cabinet officers are less important and are expected to represent the president's agenda and to not become involved in controversy. The confirmation process of cabinet officers frequently becomes a battle of wills and politics in the U.S. Senate, which has confirmation authority over cabinet officers. Presidents do not rely heavily on secretaries except for members of the inner cabinet. The White House staff has replaced the cabinet as the key advisory group to presidents. Presidents rarely call full cabinet meetings, which are sometimes used simply as photo opportunities.

See also: Key Concepts: Administrative Agencies; President

References: Ronald E. Pynn, *American Politics: Changing Expectations* (1993).

Capitalism

The U.S. economy is based on capitalism. In a capitalist system, prices and profits are determined by competition and the free market, with minimum control exercised by the government. Private ownership of the means of production is one characteristic of a capitalist system. The *free-enterprise system* is synonymous with capitalism. Assumptions underlying the free-enterprise system are private ownership of capital and land and the predominance of the profit motive as the guiding force in markets. In free-enterprise, or laissez-faire, capitalism, competition rather than monopoly or oligopoly prevails; prices, freely formed in the market, guide production and distribution.

In capitalist systems the market itself determines prices based on supply and demand for products. But there is the expectation that an imbalance in supply or demand will be self-corrected, which raises the question whether a capitalist economy can really correct itself. Thus, advocates of free enterprise differ as to whether and how government should correct imbalances. One view stresses a forceful, systematic role for government, whereby government "plans" the economy by coordinating activities in major industries, setting wage, price, and profit levels. This is an unpopular approach in the United States. Moderates suggest government should play a more limited role in the economy, setting some regulation of business and industry. There is widespread support for free enterprise, yet as the national economy has shifted from agricultural to industrial to postindustrial new demands are placed on government to develop technologies that contribute to future economic growth. This is one of the major challenges in developing fiscal policy.

See also: Economics: Economic Policy

References: Jeffrey E. Cohen, *Politics and Economic Policy in the United States* (1996); Paul C. Light, *A Delicate Balance: An Essential Introduction to American Government* (1997).

Casework

One of the duties of members of Congress is to provide service and representation to constituents in home districts. Much of this is accomplished through casework, whereby members of Congress solve constituent problems with government. Constituent service can be performed by the individual member or by staff in the home district. Casework means personal favors, answering questions, intervening on behalf of constituents in their dealings with government agencies. This activity is crucial because it is a direct way for members to show they work on behalf of local constituents.

Most casework requests come in the form of letters or telephone calls. Effective casework and constituent service is important to reelection. A member's *homestyle* refers to the way in which that member establishes trust with constituents and explains votes in Congress. The overarching goal is to build voters' trust and a strong record of service on behalf of home districts.

See also: Key Concepts: Congress, United States

References: Paul C. Light, *A Delicate Balance: An Essential Introduction to American Government* (1997).

Categorical Grants

The federal grant process has changed since the original grant programs that emerged with the Morrill Land Grant Act of 1862. The grant programs popular during the 1960s were categorical grants, which the federal government provided to states and local governments. Categorical grants carried tight rules as to how money would be spent; they frequently required the state or local government to match the funds. Other categorical grants contained formulas that took into account the relative wealth of states.

Most categorical grants during the 1960s and 1970s were designed to provide federal assistance in education, law enforcement, state and local government personnel training and development, pollution control, conservation, recreation, and highway construction and maintenance. Local governments felt that the "strings" attached to categorical grants made them unappealing, eroding local control. As these were project-specific grants, they were numerous and covered a variety of funding areas. As the era of large public-spending programs ended under the Reagan administration, categorical grants were consolidated into much broader grant classifications, called block grants.

See also: Key Concepts: Block Grants

References: Paul C. Light, *A Delicate Balance: An Essential Introduction to American Government* (1997); B. Guy Peters, *American Public Policy: Promise and Performance* (1993).

Cloture

In the U.S. Senate, debate can become endless and not always meaningful. Sometimes members engage in time-consuming debate to thwart proposed legislation, something known as filibustering. Under Senate Rule 22, debate may be closed and the matters under discussion considered for vote if 16 senators sign a petition and if after two days three-fifths of members (60 votes, if there are no vacancies) vote for cloture. Once cloture is called, each senator may speak on a bill for a maximum of one hour before a vote is taken. Cloture has been used most frequently to end filibusters. Cloture was used to end the filibuster of the Civil Rights Act of 1964, marking the first successful call for cloture in a civil rights debate in the Senate.

See also: Key Concepts: Congress, United States; Civil Rights: Civil Rights Acts

References: Steffen W. Schmidt, Mack C. Shelley II, and Barbara A. Bardes, *American Government and Politics Today* (1997).

Coalitions

A common saying in labor is "In unity there is strength." A coalition is a collection of individuals, groups, or networks with similar concerns and interests. Interest groups use networks of other groups to forge and influence public opinion. Coalitions can vary in form: They can be small or large; they can be composed of interest groups that are organized around a common policy issue; they can be political parties in a multiparty system (as in the nation of Israel) that coalesce to govern because of the absence of a numerical voting majority carried by one political party; they can be short-lived groups of neighbors who unite to counter development that would change the character of their neighborhood. Coalitions form to influence policy or create political change, for instance in health care, the environment, and industry. Coalitions allow people to use strengths and resources more efficiently.

See also: Key Concepts: Interest Groups

References: Susan Welch et al., *Understanding American Government* (1997).

Code of Federal Regulations

Public policy is created through congressional action, and programs are created to implement that policy; rules are then promulgated to guide decision-making in implementing programs and policy. All public policy is tied to rules. The federal government categorizes such rules in the Code of Federal Regulations (CFR). The CFR organizes the rules into fifty categories by title and chapter. Titles and chapters correspond to public programs, policies, and agencies in the federal government. Every year, federal administrative agencies create rules that take up 7,500 pages in the Code of Federal Regulations. The CFR is the source for all rules—programmatic and procedural—that apply to the operation of federal agencies.

See also: Key Concepts: Administrative Agencies; *Federal Register;* Rulemaking

References: Cornelius M. Kerwin, *Rulemaking: How Government Agencies Write Law and Make Policy* (1994).

Committee System, Congressional

The U.S. Congress comprises the U.S. House of Representatives (with 435 members) and the U.S. Senate (100 members). Some 2,000 to 10,000 bills are introduced every year, with 250 to 2,000 being passed. To manage the workload and give due consideration to proposed legislation, Congress instituted the committee system. Much as in the business world, committees review, filter, analyze, and make recommendations.

Congress is divided into standing committees and ad hoc committees. Standing committees are permanent, whereas ad hoc committees are temporary. There are 19 standing committees in the House of Representatives and 17 in the Senate. Each standing committee addresses a specific subject, such as defense or education. Standing committees have some subcommittees (84 in the House, 69 in the Senate). Proposed legislation is referred to a subcommittee, which holds public hearings. At subcommittee, the bill may be changed or altered (called the "markup"), then sent to the full committee for review and possibly more hearings. If the bill is approved at the standing committee level it is then sent on to the full House or Senate for vote. Only 10–30 percent of all bills referred to committee are "reported out" to the floor of the House or Senate for a vote; only a fraction of those will pass.

Committee members come from both political parties and vary from ten to as many as 61 members. The majority party determines the party ratio for each committee, usually seating a disproportionate number on key committees to ensure control. Members serve on a committee usually because of an interest or expertise in the subject. Members can thereby become specialists in key areas of legislation (e.g., agriculture or urban affairs). Each committee and subcommittee is led by a chair, who is its most influential member. Chairs have the authority to call meetings, set agendas, and preside over committee funds and staff appointments. Seniority typically applies in selecting the chair: The member of the majority party with the longest service on a committee becomes its chair. Because of the great many bills proposed in Congress, committee assignments are limited. Senators usually sit on 11 committees and subcommittees; representatives sit on seven. Service offers the advantage of influence, expertise, and publicity, all of which can benefit members of Congress.

See also: Key Concepts: Congress, United States; Interest Groups; Public Policy

References: Paul C. Light, *A Delicate Balance: An Essential Introduction to American Government* (1997); Steven Waldman, *The Bill: How Legislation Really Becomes Law—A Case Study of the National Service Bill* (1995).

Communitarianism

The tenet of communitarian philosophy is the need to reestablish communities as the center of moral virtue. Thus, the well-being of communities is at the heart of the communitarian philosophy. Civility, the preservation and preeminence of the social order, and commitment to belief in civic virtue are important elements of communitarianism. Communitarians feel that government, bureaucracy, and citizens should work on behalf of the community. They suggest that the focus on individualism that has taken root in American society threatens the ties and relationships necessary for keeping communities and their virtues intact. Individuals and individualism are welcome within communitarian philosophy, but only insofar as individuals contribute to the whole and do not wander for purposes of polarizing the community. Communitarianism is also founded on the belief that giving to the community is virtuous and leads to the taking of responsibility. Such action strengthens the moral, social, and political foundations of society. Community bonds are important, contributing to the nurturing of rights and responsibilities that are fundamental to civil society.

Communitarianism grew out of the fear of some social and political observers that civility in American society was eroding. The focus on individual rights in the last 30 years has had a troubling effect for academicians such as Amitai Etzioni and Robert Booth Fowler. They point to two critical elements that serve as the core of communitarian thought: the balance between individual rights and social responsibilities; and the roles of social institutions that foster moral values within communities.

Critics of the communitarian philosophy question the diminution of individual rights for the common good. The diverse collection of individuals that makes up communities is important, and different viewpoints and interests add vitality instead of posing a threat to the common good. Ultimately, the dichotomy of communitarianism and individualism merges when we weigh the role of government and the direction of public policy. What defines the public or the public good? How is public policy created to serve the greatest good? These are the leading questions that communitarians face in the development and application of their ideas.

See also: Key Concepts: Community Organizations

References: Amitai Etzioni, *Rights and the Common Good: The Communitarian Perspective* (1995); Robert B. Fowler, *The Dance with Community* (1991).

Community Organizations

During the early 1830s French journalist Alexis de Tocqueville traveled throughout the United States observing the American way of life. One of de Tocqueville's sharpest observations was the associational nature of Americans and American communities. He found Americans to be inclined toward joining groups and seeking associational ties through voluntary local community, town, and village groups. Although preserving rugged individualism befitted the American character in the early 19th century, he noticed how willing Americans were to join groups and organizations. Today, community organizations are a primary means of influencing policy and implementing programs. Public policy that filters down to local communities is typically implemented by advisory boards or commissions that are authorized by federal and state jurisdictions to develop local action plans and procedures. Usually serving as volunteers, they meet regularly and make recommendations to local elected officials, thereby fulfilling civic duties by contributing time to local government service. Local councils rely on citizens' groups and community organizations to mobilize opinion and action toward problem-solving. In some cases, these community organizations can be volunteer, private, nonprofit organizations referred to as nongovernmental organizations. They lend support and expertise to formal government structures.

See also: Key Concepts: Advisory Committees; Interest Groups

References: James P. Lester and Joseph Stewart Jr., *Public Policy: An Evolutionary Approach* (1996).

Conference Committee

When legislation moves through the House of Representatives and the Senate, the Constitution requires that identical bills be passed before going to the president for signature into law. However, if the House and the Senate versions are significantly different, then a conference committee of the two chambers is called to reconcile the bill. The presiding officers of each house, in consultation with the chairs of the standing committees that reviewed and discussed the bill, choose the members of the conference committee (but both political parties are represented). Majorities of each house must then agree to the conference committee's revisions if a bill is to pass. In the process of conference review, the bill may be substantially rewritten; it may or may not pass both houses. Either house can vote to send the bill back to the conference committee (known as "recommitting" the bill), but the bill could die if Congress adjourns without approving a new compromise. Approximately one in four or five bills that become law go before the conference committee; and those that do tend to be the most controversial.

See also: Key Concepts: Committee System, Congressional; Congress, United States

References: David Edwards and Alessandra Lippucci, *Practicing American Politics: An Introduction to American Government* (1998); Paul C. Light, *A Delicate Balance: An Essential Introduction to American Government* (1997).

Congress, United States

The U.S. Congress is the chief policymaking body in the United States. It is divided into two houses, the House of Representatives and the Senate. The House of Representatives has 435 members elected for two-year terms, plus delegates from the District of Columbia, Puerto Rico, Guam, American Samoa, and the Virgin Islands; the Senate has 100 members. Congress derives its powers from the U.S. Constitution.

In its lawmaking role, Congress makes binding rules for all Americans. Members of Congress serve their constituents by engaging in casework, or assisting local constituents. Congress votes on legislation that impacts local constituents. A member of Congress typically votes according to party expectations, but the congressperson may also vote based on the interests of constituents back home. British philosopher Edmund Burke stated that a representative should weigh the interests of constituents but not blindly, that is, vote according to the representative's perception of the best interests of the constituents. In Burke's view, legislators act as trustees of constituents' votes, not as the agent of voters. Most members of Congress employ a trustee-delegate combination in contrast to representatives in a parliamentary system, who vote the strict party line.

Congress engages in oversight by controlling agency budgets throughout the annual budget and review process, by holding committee hearings and investigations, by reviewing and holding hearings on presidential appointees, and by exercising the right to review and vote down legislation that comes before Congress. Congress can also call for investigations of agency action as a form of oversight.

When members debate issues on the floor of the House or Senate, they view it as a way to educate the public, exposing the range of issues and rationales. Members also send constituents educational newsletters that inform and discuss the member's approach to various policy issues. Congressional debates serve as a means to resolve public policy conflicts and differences.

Congress addresses large policy issues: unemployment, health care, energy, public education, tax-and-revenue systems, the environment, communications technology and access, agriculture support and policy, transportation, welfare, poverty. Thus, every member is required to act on the multitude of issues and problems that have significance for the entire nation. Every piece of public policy might not affect the home district, yet each member participates by serving on committees or merely by voting. The work of committees in Congress in the various policy areas is serious business; the committee system is crucial to the success or failure of public policy.

When Congress assigns a bill to a subcommittee, the policymaking process begins. It might end in subcommittee, but the problem has come to the national agenda, which itself can be the most difficult stage in the policy process. Thus, Congress does not act on every policy demand that is made. In 1994 Congress adopted more than 200 laws. Not every law made is new; some are revisions of past bills or amendments to prior legislation. Procedural policy is frequently made to determine how action is to be taken. Substantive policies, in contrast, determine how a policy will evolve or who will be responsible for enacting and implementing policy-related programs. Distributive policies allot national resources to specific groups in society. Redistributive policies shift revenue derived from income, wealth, and property to those in need. Regulatory policies are government attempts to intervene in commerce or in private matters by imposing restrictions or limitations. Another version of regulatory policy, self-regulatory policy, is sought by professions and occupational groups to govern entry to or behavior in certain professions. The regulations come in the form of licensing or quality control and the setting of standards to guide production.

In making public policy, members of Congress rely heavily on staff, lobbyists, and interest groups for information and guidance. Placing an issue on the national policy agenda is a challenge.

See also: Agriculture: Agricultural Policy; Civil Rights: Civil Rights Policy; Communications: Communications Policy; Economics: Economic Policy; Entitlement Programs: Welfare Policy; Environment: Environmental Policy; Health: Health Policy; Key Concepts: Casework; Committee System, Congressional; Distributive Policy; Redistributive Policy; Regulation

References: James E. Anderson, *Public Policymaking* (1997); Donald C. Bacon, Roger H. Davidson, and Morton Keller, eds., *The Encyclopedia of the United States Congress* (1995); Ross K. Baker, *House and Senate* (1995); Roger H. Davidson and Walter Oleszek, *Congress and Its Members* (1994); Thomas R. Dye, *Understanding Public Policy* (1995); David Edwards and Alessandra Lippucci, *Practicing American Politics: An Introduction to American Government* (1998); Charles O. Jones, *An Introduction to the Study of Public Policy* (1984); David E. Price, *The Congressional Experience* (1992); Eric Redman, *The Dance of Legislation* (1973); Steffen W. Schmidt, Mack C. Shelley II, and Barbara A. Bardes, *American Government and Politics Today* (1997).

Conservatism

Conservatism is a political ideology with origins in Great Britain and Europe. During the late 18th century, conservatism was a reaction to the political liberalism embodied by the American Revolution. The American Revolution was supported by the French, and their flirtations with liberalism during the 18th century caused a conservative response in Great Britain. The French experience with liberalism threatened monarchies throughout Europe and caused the British to believe that traditional institutions were doomed if the French succeeded in their own revolution.

Conservatism in America was founded on the belief that rules guide society and that government provides order. The preservation of private property and individual freedom are also central to conservative philosophy. Conservatives and conservatism do not welcome rapid change or reform; they are distrustful of emotion-based action and passionate impulses; they distrust government intervention into private affairs and feel that individuals, not the government, are responsible for their own well-being.

Political conservatives during the 1990s believe that government should increase military spending, that social and welfare programs should be conducted by private or charitable groups, and that fundamentalist religious tenets should be the yardstick for issues such as abortion, school prayer, and family relations. Conservatives also do not generally support affirmative action programs. The Republican Party is considered to be the party of conservatism; many Republicans feel that the party should reflect religious fundamentalism.

The impact of conservatism on public policy is measured by the influence conservatives wield at the local, state, and national levels of government. Public policy is affected by public opinion; public opinion forms around political, economic, and social issues; political majorities heavily influence public policy, and if these majorities are composed of conservatives, then policy will reflect the interests and the opinions of conservatives. Yet political majorities might also be made up of liberals, who will in turn influence policy and public opinion. The activity of interest groups, political parties, members of Congress, and other forces collectively influence public opinion and public policy and turn policy toward either a conservative or liberal direction.

The political conservative prefers to see restrained government action in domestic affairs and promotes military and defense preparedness in international affairs.

See also: Key Concepts: Ideology; Liberalism; Political Socialization; Public Opinion

References: Edwin M. Coulter, *Principles of Politics and Government* (1994); Walter Lippmann, *The Public Philosophy* (1955); Susan Welch et al., *Understanding American Government* (1997).

Corporatism

One of the important dimensions of the public policy process is how issues get placed on the public agenda and how policy—once it is formulated—is implemented. Interest groups alert policymakers to the need for solutions to public problems; they might also serve as the leading agents to implement public policy once formulated. Public officials might recognize some groups as formal representatives of a sector of the economy and rely on those groups to aid in developing and directing policy. The direct involvement of interest groups in public decisionmaking is sometimes referred to as "corporatism." B. Guy Peters stated that interest group activity—for example, labor, management, farmers, students, the elderly—whereby groups represent and implement public policy, is an example of corporatism. Advisory groups are also frequently composed of advocates and interest groups seeking to influence policy development. In this way, interest groups are able to implement public policy.

See also: Key Concepts: Implementation; Interest Groups

References: Jeffrey M. Berry, *Lobbying for the People: The Political Behavior of Public Interest Groups* (1977); B. Guy Peters, *American Public Policy: Promise and Performance* (1993).

Cost-benefit Analysis

When public policy decisions are made, the goal is to maximize value and serve the interests of programs; one way is to analyze the costs and benefits. Cost-benefit analysis requires looking at alternatives according to a quantitative (numerical) value; the alternatives are ranked by highest value. The purpose of ranking in this way is to determine the optimum (best) ratio of benefits to costs, which will lead the decisionmaker to the best choice among all the alternatives.

Cost-benefit analysis requires the decisionmaker to consider "real" costs and benefits. To benefit the consumer, then, costs and benefits must be balanced against resources. If a solution requires funds that are unavailable or creates some sort of crisis, then the costs would far outweigh the benefits. Costs and benefits can also be understood according to pecuniary benefits and costs (referring to changes that might occur in the relative prices in the economy as adjustments are made toward problem-solving). Some people gain from a solution, whereas others might lose. Direct and indirect costs and benefits also factor into cost-benefit analysis. Direct costs and benefits have a clear link to the main program or project; indirect costs and benefits carry secondary effects but must be considered as relevant to decisionmaking overall. These are also referred to as "spillovers" or "externalities" and are the byproducts of problem-solving.

Cost-benefit analysis weighs especially heavily in environmental policymaking and regulation, as they often carry significant expense to industries in helping keep water and air safe for society.

See also: Environment: Environmental Policy; Key Concepts: Decision Analysis

References: George J. Gordon and Michael E. Milakovich, *Public Administration in America* (1998); Fred A. Kramer, *Dynamics of Public Bureaucracy: An Introduction to Public Management* (1981); Grover Starling, *Managing the Public Sector* (1998).

Decision Analysis

In any organization, whether public or private, people in positions of responsibility must make logical decisions that lead to the attainment of that organization's goals. Public officials or agency leaders are expected to base those decisions on goal attainment. Particularly in public-sector decisionmaking, the element of uncertainty as to how a policy might work is key. Decision analysis involves breaking problems down to discover the best solutions, thereby developing public policy that will carry lasting direct benefit. Decision analysis helps decisionmakers to structure complex problems by creating a "decision tree" in order to dissect problems and situations, explore and understand the elements of a problem, analyze consequences of actions proposed, understand the costs, benefits, and effects of outcomes of decisions, and test alternative approaches to problem-solving. Decision trees are composed of a series of lines and situations that are drawn to explore connections, time, costs, probability, and logic.

Decision analysis allows decisionmakers to consider all that is known and to project probable or unknowable factors that might affect the decisionmaking process. Decision analysis helps form judgment in complex policy situations.

See also: Key Concepts: Implementation; Public Policy

References: B. Guy Peters, *American Public Policy: Promise and Performance* (1993); Grover Starling, *Managing the Public Sector* (1998).

Decision Tree

See Key Concepts: Decision Analysis

Democracy

The nature of political systems is the starting point for policy analysis. Political scientists, in analyzing policy, consider many factors: the principles that support that political system's rationale for making laws and public policy; circumstances that guide the behavior of public and elected officials in the system; rules that govern the relationships between the government and its people; how people gain access to political influence and power; how laws are made and who implements them; the conditions of citizenship; and the protections for citizens from their government. These types of issues are fundamental to understanding how political systems operate and how public policy is made. The political history and traditions of a nation are also salient.

The United States is the world's oldest constitutional democracy. The ideals and reality of democracy tend to clash when we talk about the American experience, and so it might be accurate to view the American democracy as an ongoing experiment. Looking back, we see diversions from the democratic ideal throughout American history. Yet what are these democratic ideals, and what do American citizens expect of them?

Democracy has three major characteristics: a definition of membership and an explanation of who "the citizens" are; a method for selecting elected officials who, as agents of the citizens, act on behalf of and represent citizens; and the development and application of the codes of conduct and rules of obligation that spell out how citizens are expected to act, how the rules and codes are made, and who is empowered to apply and adjudicate disputes based on the rules.

The essential elements of any democracy are equality in voting; free competitions for public office; majority or plurality rule when disputes occur or issues need to be decided by free choice and possibly elections; freedom of expression to think, speak, write, worship, and assemble in groups; unfettered distribution of political resources and the right to seek political office; and protection of minority rights amid majority rule. These have been challenged in the American democratic experience, yet the goal remains to seek and apply democratic ideals to all citizens for the purpose of ensuring a strong, representative, constitutional government. Although any nation can call itself a "democracy," the true measure is the extent to which that nation honors the principles and ideals contained in the democratic prescription outlined above.

See also: Key Concepts: Pluralism; Political Culture; Political Socialization

References: Charles Bonser, Eugene B. McGregor Jr., and Clinton V. Oster Jr., *Policy Choices and Public Action* (1996); Robert Dahl, *A Preface to Democratic Theory* (1968); David Edwards and Alessandra Lippucci, *Practicing American Politics: An Introduction to American Government* (1998).

Demographic Change

Public policy is developed for many reasons. One is the change in the structure, size, and characteristics of the population. The first of the baby boomers (those born between 1945 and roughly 1962) are now nearing retirement age and will be in need of services, which will affect Social Security and health care costs. The United States also has a higher proportion of people of Asian and Hispanic heritage than ever before, which will impact the role of government services to communities and states. These are examples of demographic changes.

Political scientists, social scientists, economists, sociologists, and other academics are interested in how populations change in numbers, ethnic characteristics, gender, age, and other economic and social categories to predict and analyze the public policy issues facing government. Local, state, and national governments and policy analysts must understand demographic change in order to respond to and serve changing populations.

See also: Key Concepts: Political Socialization; Public Policy

References: Thomas R. Dye, *Understanding Public Policy* (1995); Ronald E. Pynn, *American Politics: Changing Expectations* (1993); Peter Skerry, *Mexican Americans: The Ambivalent Minority* (1993).

Direct Democracy

The best example of an early state that practiced direct democracy, as described in Aristotle's classification of governments, is the city-state of Athens in ancient Greece. All issues of import for citizens of Athens (not including slaves and certain others) were decided by committees of the ruling council, then offered to the citizens' assembly for vote. Direct democracy is a system whereby legislative decisions are made directly by the people, not elected representatives. The small towns and villages in New England are modern-day examples of direct democracy at work. The New England system is workable in places with small populations.

Yet direct democracy also has a growing role in state politics. In California, for example, the state constitution provides for three forms of direct democracy: initiative, referendum, and recall. Each form allows citizens to vote directly on matters of government at the state and local levels. Using the initiative, voters can propose news laws or change existing ones by petition, that is, obtaining signatures based on a fixed percentage of total votes in the last gubernatorial election. If enough signatures are gathered, and if the proposed initiative meets certain constitutional standards, the item is placed on the ballot. The initiative process in California bypasses the California State Assembly. The referendum is a procedure whereby citizens can approve changes to the state constitution that have already been passed in the state legislature. A referendum also provides citizens with the opportunity to repeal an existing law, or it can serve as a means for voters to accept or reject a legislative or constitutional proposal. In California and some other states, a referendum requires a petition. The recall is a means for citizens, again by petition and vote, to remove from office an elected official.

Direct democracy provides citizens the opportunity to make, affect, and influence public policy.

Twenty-four states have the legislative initiative; thirty-six states have a recall mechanism. Frequently, citizens use direct democracy to bypass legislatures that are slow or refuse to take action on controversial issues.

See also: Key Concepts: Democracy

References: Bruce E. Cain and Roger G. Noll, eds., *Constitutional Reform in California* (1995); Steffen W. Schmidt, Mack C. Shelley II, and Barbara A. Bardes, *American Government and Politics Today* (1997).

Distributive Policy

Political scientist Theodore Lowi described three types of public policy: distributive, redistributive, and regulatory policies. Distributive policy, as the name suggests, distributes benefits or services (e.g., transportation projects, public education programs, and financial aid) to citizens. Although specific segments of the population are often targeted as potential beneficiaries, others can also enjoy benefits. Distributive policy allows government to serve specific client groups, as small or as large as those groups might be.

See also: Key Concepts: Public Policy; Redistributive Policy; Regulation

References: James E. Anderson, *Public Policymaking* (1997); James P. Lester and Joseph Stewart Jr., *Public Policy: An Evolutionary Approach* (1996); Theodore Lowi, *The End of Liberalism: The Second Republic of the U.S.* (1974).

Diversity

In the context of American politics at the end of the 20th century, *diversity* refers to variations and differences in its economy, society, and political system. Diversity has an impact on the formation and implementation of public policy. Diversity speaks to the issue of variety and the wealth and multitude of differences.

There are vast differences in how Americans fit into the American economy. There is extraordinary wealth and substantial poverty. There are widespread social problems caused by disparities in wealth and poverty. Social, political, and economic inequality are the consequence. Much local, state, and national public policy is directed at alleviating these problems. Some of the diversity issues that affect public policy in the 1990s are the concentration of minority groups in urban areas and the need to provide adequate housing, employment opportunities, safe streets, and social support programs; to improve and fund public education; to manage urban crime and create drug-abuse programs; and to provide quality health care and preventive health programs. Diversity in the United States is a matter of urban and rural populations, immigrants and migrant populations, changing demographic characteristics of state populations as a result of immigrant populations, changing age patterns throughout society, and the consequent patterns of economic inequality and inequality of opportunity for diverse groups of people.

Diversity is a characteristic of American society. Throughout the states, education systems are becoming more diverse in race, age, and income. The task for local, state, and national policymakers will be to understand and manage the issues of diversity that confront legislators and engage the private economic sector in meeting the challenges posed by the rich diversity that so characterizes American life in the next century. Since the mid-1960s, with the expansion of voting rights in the United States, there has been a significant increase in the diversity of representation in the American political system in local, state, and national politics. Men and women from various ethnic groups now hold political office throughout the United States.

See also: Key Concepts: Demographic Change

References: B. Guy Peters, *American Public Policy: Promise and Performance* (1993); Susan Welch et al., *Understanding American Government* (1997).

Division of Labor (U.S. Congress)

There are 535 members of the U.S. Congress (435 in the House, 100 in the Senate); 2,000 to 10,000 bills are proposed in Congress annually. Much work is required to review each bill and make decisions on public policy and formal legislation. A process called the division of labor eases the workload facing legislators.

The labor in Congress is divided into committees: There are 19 standing committees in the House and 17 in the Senate, each of them having responsibility for a specific subject (e.g., transportation, defense, natural resources, etc.). Each standing committee has subcommittees (84 subcommittees in the House, 69 in the Senate). All are supported by appointed expert staffs (comprising some 30,000 people) that provide assistance, information, and guidance. Many staff members also work in constituency service for members of Congress, in legislative capacities, or in media work.

The division of labor in Congress is essential for completing the work that American citizens expect from their national elected officials.

See also: Key Concepts: Committee System, Congressional; Congress, United States

References: David E. Price, *The Congressional Experience* (1992); Eric Redman, *The Dance of Legislation* (1973); Susan Welch et al., *Understanding American Government* (1997).

Domestic Policy Council

The president and Congress spend great time and energy designing public policy to serve national interests. The leading domestic policy areas are crime, the economy, social programs, health care, and the environment. During Richard M. Nixon's administration in the late 1960s and the early 1970s, the president merged several offices into the Domestic Policy Council (DPC) to coordinate domestic programs. Later, Pres. Bill Clinton altered the makeup of the DPC and then formed the National Economic Council to focus on national economic policies.

When presidents are evaluated for their effectiveness in office, American voters are most interested in domestic policy and programs. Yet presidents are often more successful with their foreign policy initiatives than they are with domestic issues (e.g., George Bush, who managed U.S. forces during the 1991 Gulf War against Iraq). Bush's effectiveness and approval rating skyrocketed during and immediately after the Gulf War, but he faltered in the domestic policy arena. The DPC and Clinton's National Economic Council function specifically to bolster the president's ability to positively affect domestic and economic policy and programs.

See also: Economics: Economic Policy

References: Jeffrey E. Cohen, *Politics and Economic Policy in the United States* (1996); David Edwards and Alessandra Lippucci, *Practicing American Politics: An Introduction to American Government* (1998); Susan Welch et al., *Understanding American Government* (1997).

Dual Federalism

After the U.S. Constitution was ratified by the states in 1789, the new nation had to set up business and decide pragmatically how the federal government would operate. States feared that a strong federal government might unduly wield power over the states. The early federal-state relationship was a system of dual federalism, that is, the federal and state governments were separate and distinct in terms of authority and jurisdiction. This system of dual federalism prevailed until roughly 1933, as the Great Depression had changed the dynamics of federal-state relations.

Although they embarked on joint programs in railroad development, banking, and education during the early years, the two entities did not widely engage in intergovernmental cooperation. State governments chartered businesses and corporations and generally supported commerce to promote strong economies. But when foreign competition threatened their economic interests, states appealed to the federal government for protection, generally in the form of tariffs on imported goods.

The national government's role as protector of state interests gradually ceased when the 1929 Great Depression set in. The states and the national government had mutual interests in fighting the effects of faltering economies and massive unemployment. Farm programs suffered, and state commercial interests were in jeopardy, conditions that brought about the decline of dual federalism. By 1933 the federal government had created public programs with national application and impact. The Social Security Act of 1935, the Works Progress Administration programs, the Wagner Act (creating the National Labor Relations Board with regional offices), and the Tennessee Valley Authority programs introduced a strong intergovernmental element into the existing federal system. The federal government used grants-in-aid to encourage states to adopt these national programs. The intergovernmental relationship that started with the onset of these New Deal programs has had lasting effects into the 1990s and beyond.

See also: Economics: New Deal; Entitlement Programs: Social Security Act of 1935; Key Concepts: Federalism

References: Robert Goldston, *The Great Depression: The United States in the Thirties* (1968); David B. Robertson and Dennis R. Judd, *The Development of American Public Policy: The Structure of Policy Restraint* (1989); Grover Starling, *Managing the Public Sector* (1998).

Due Process

Due process, the fundamental principle of law and justice in the United States, is found in the Fifth Amendment to the U.S. Constitution. *Due process* means people have the right to be treated fairly and openly if charged with crimes or other violations of the law. In the administrative setting and at the workplace, citizens also have the right to expect fair application of the law in accordance with the rules and customs of the American legal system.

There are two dimensions of due process: procedural and substantive. *Procedural due process* means fairness in the application of procedures, that is, appropriate notice, air hearing, opportunity for defense, an impartial tribunal, and other mechanisms that ensure individuals are not deprived of life, liberty, or property by the government. *Substantive due process* relates to the content or subject matter of a law or rule. It protects against unreasonable acts that might be conducted in an arbitrary or capricious way. Due process requires clarity and definitiveness in laws; the substance of the law has to be reasonable in its application. In the criminal context, due process protects the accused: Individuals are considered innocent until proven guilty and are entitled to the full protection of laws as they go through the criminal justice system.

The Fourteenth Amendment guarantees equal protection of the law for all people. It prohibits the "abridgement of privileges and immunities of citizens of the United States" and proclaims that "no state shall deprive any person of life, liberty, or property, without due process of law; nor deny any person within its jurisdiction the equal protection of the laws." The Fourteenth Amendment thus also guarantees citizens fair treatment under law.

See also: Civil Rights: Fourteenth Amendment; Crime: Criminal Justice Policy

References: Leif H. Carter and Christine B. Harrington, *Administrative Law and Politics: Cases and Comments* (1991); Kermit L. Hall, William M. Wiecek, and Paul Finkelman, *American Legal History* (1991); Cornelius M. Kerwin, *Rulemaking: How Government Agencies Write Law and Make Policy* (1994); Joseph Senna and Larry Siegel, *Introduction to Criminal Justice* (1993).

Econometric Approach

Policy analysts adopt different research strategies that enable them to use a certain method or focus to discover the motivation and the impact of public policy. The econometric, or public choice, approach is based on theories that assume individuals are "rational" and motivated by personal need. The question thus becomes *how* these individuals respond to calls for policy changes in areas important to them. Will they accept policy as long as it benefits them, or will they reject policies that have no effect on them and thus do not fulfill individual needs? The underlying assumption is that people will "economize" their policy preferences based on such self-interest. At the center of this policy approach is the belief that individuals will use reasoned choices that require them to weigh alternatives that will provide them with the most satisfaction.

Understanding this and other approaches to policy analysis helps policymakers obtain the information they need to project reactions and responses to policy initiatives such as health care, law enforcement, land use, and the environment.

See also: Key Concepts: Policy Analysis; Public Choice Theory

References: William N. Dunn, *Public Policy Analysis: An Introduction* (1993); James P. Lester and Joseph Stewart Jr., *Public Policy: An Evolutionary Approach* (1996); David C. Paris and James F. Reynolds, *The Logic of Policy Inquiry* (1983).

Elitist Model

Political scientists create abstract models to visualize how policy will look in real-world application; a model is a simplified representation of an aspect of the real world. Political scientist Thomas Dye has written on the elitist model of public policymaking. Elites are those few individuals or groups who hold or have access to political power and who are the most influential in the policy and government processes. Sociologist C. Wright Mills coined the term *power elite* to describe those who have disproportionate amounts of power.

Thomas Dye's elite model assumes a small number of people have power and many others do not. Politics under this conception is a matter of the allocation (choice) of values that will prevail. Thus, a few people hold power and make political choices while the masses have little or no influence over the choices of values that guide government decisions and behavior. Elite dominance of politics is slow and gradual, in which case elites perpetuate their dominance over policy and politics. Common values that ruling or governing elites share include the importance of private property, limited government, and preservation of individual liberty. Public policy that emerges from elite dominance of politics reflects the values of elites and not of the masses of citizens; public policy is thus imposed in a top-down manner. Studies have shown the elitist model explains community politics and community decisionmaking. A leading critic of the elitist model is Robert Dahl, who has written on the opposing pluralist model. Dahl believes that anyone who has the will and motivation to pursue his or her political interests can be successful. Elite theorists believe that key resources, contacts, and influence are essential, and that money and access to it play a key role.

See also: Key Concepts: Pluralism

References: Thomas R. Dye, *Understanding Public Policy* (1995); Thomas Dye and L. Harmon Ziegler, *The Irony of Democracy: An Uncommon Introduction to American Politics* (1996); James P. Lester and Joseph Stewart Jr., *Public Policy: An Evolutionary Approach* (1996).

Evaluation

Policy evaluation (sometimes called policy analysis or policy science) is concerned with the outcomes or impacts of policy. Were the outcomes or impacts expected and desired? What were the actual results of policy? Political scientists evaluate all stages of the policy process: identifying and clarifying the formulation of policy; discovering what happened when the policy was implemented; determining, at the end of policy, what occurred and why. This information is important because a policymaker might need to know whether the resources committed to a policy were spent wisely. A politician who proposes policy might want to know how the policy worked and whether it clearly affected the people or groups who were the targets or recipients of the policy.

Evaluation addresses appraisal, rating, ranking and assessment, and outcomes. Policy evaluators select criteria for evaluation: effectiveness, efficiency, adequacy, equity (fairness), responsiveness, and appropriateness. With each evaluation criteria there is an indication of how the criteria are satisfied or met. The purpose is to provide reliable information as to policy performance and the extent to which goals were met. Evaluation also helps clarify the how's and why's a policy succeeded or not. Such information allows people to correct or change future policies.

See also: Key Concepts: Policy Outcomes; Public Policy

References: William N. Dunn, *Public Policy Analysis: An Introduction* (1993); Frank Fischer, *Evaluating Public Policy* (1995); Charles O. Jones, *An Introduction to the Study of Public Policy* (1984).

Executive Departments

See Key Concepts: Administrative Agencies

Federal Advisory Committee Act of 1972

The role and influence of interest groups in American politics have changed during the 20th century. At times, interest groups have been seen as unduly influencing political and policy processes. The Federal Advisory Committee Act of 1972 affirmed the role of interest groups as a useful source of opinion and information to policymakers. The purpose of the act was to improve the quality of interest groups in their information-providing capacity to public agencies by assuring that the lobbying process was representative. The act required that official meetings between advisory committees and public administrators be open to the public. The Federal Advisory Committee Act presumes that agencies will be in contact with special interest groups. These groups (or advisory committees) have the resources to gather and provide ordinarily unavailable information to agencies. This law proves that government agencies and legislators rely on special interest and advisory groups to represent perspectives and inform legislators of preferred public policy directions.

See also: Key Concepts: Advisory Committees; Interest Groups

References: Allen Cigler and Burdett Loomis, *Interest Group Politics* (1990); David H. Rosenbloom, *Public Administration: Understanding Management, Politics, and Law in the Public Sector* (1998).

Federal Register

The official acts of the federal government's executive branch must be recorded. The *Federal Register* is a daily publication of the orders, rules, and regulations of the executive branch. Any rule generated by agencies is required to be published in the *Federal Register.* During the 1980s, a time of government deregulation, the number of pages in the *Federal Register* was reduced. But as government regulatory activity, rulemaking, and orders grow, the bulk of the *Federal Register* increases.

See also: Key Concepts: Administrative Agencies; Rulemaking

References: Steffen W. Schmidt, Mack C. Shelley II, and Barbara A. Bardes, *American Government and Politics Today* (1997); Edward Sidlow and Beth Henschen, *America at Odds* (1998).

Federal System

A federal system of government comprises two levels: the national (or central) government and the states (or provinces). In the United States, the U.S. Constitution guarantees equal protection to citizens under the laws of either level of government. In Canada, the federal system comprises the national government (located in Ottawa) and the provincial governments. Within federal systems, the national and state levels have direct legal authority over citizens in certain policy areas. In the United States, such legal authority is based in the Constitution, which cannot be changed by Congress. A third level of government (local) is not mentioned in the U.S. Constitution. Local governments comprise city, county, or other governmental units that derive authority from a state. There are 86,743 governments of all types in the United States.

In discussing the federal system, the focus is on separation of powers. The term *subnational* refers to units of government below or other than the national government. A truly federal system of government is one in which a constitution spells out the powers of the national and the subnational units of government. Countries that have a truly federal system of government include: Argentina, Australia, Austria, Brazil, Canada, Germany, India, Malaysia, Mexico, Switzerland, and the United States.

Federal systems confer specific powers and implied powers. These powers cannot be taken away, and they protect citizens in federal systems. The U.S. federal system resulted from distrust among the Framers of a strong national government. American colonists felt they had no representation in the parliamentary government back in England. When the original thirteen colonies declared independence in 1776, they were acting to preserve their individual, distinct cultures. The new states then wrote their own constitutions, creating a system (the Articles of Confederation) in which sovereignty between states and the national government was shared: The states had sovereign power in their areas of interest, and the national government had a modicum of sovereignty as agreed upon by the states. The Articles of Confederation were eventually replaced due to the weakness of the national government.

Early discussions of the U.S. Constitution focused on the powers of the national and state governments, especially the distribution and supremacy of such powers. There are eight types of powers in the American federal system: (1) enumerated (delegated) federal powers, whereby the national government possesses broad authority to declare war, print currency, and the like; (2) enumerated (delegated) state governments powers, for example, to conduct elections and ratify constitutional amendments; (3) powers reserved to the state governments (those powers not delegated to the national government or denied to the states); (4) concurrent powers, which are shared by state and national governments (e.g., to tax, spend money, and build roads); (5) implied powers of the national government, or appropriate powers not specifically delineated in the Constitution; (6) inherent power in the national government, that is, presidential authority to act in the interests of national defense and security; (7) denied powers to the national government, generally the prohibitions detailed in the first eight amendments; and (8) denied powers to the states (e.g., to make treaties, print currency, and regulate interstate commerce).

The proper distribution of federal power is an issue that continues to challenge the president, Congress, and the states. Our political system is referred to as *federalism,* which has continually evolved in response to changing times and circumstances. One of the advantages of the U.S. federal system is that it preserves regional differences in American culture and political life. Despite regional and other differences in American politics, cooperation among the various political elements in society is important, making it possible to overcome the contentiousness of political differences.

See also: Key Concepts: Federalism

References: David Edwards and Alessandra Lippucci, *Practicing American Politics: An Introduction to American Government* (1998); Paul C. Light, *A Delicate Balance: An*

Essential Introduction to American Government (1997); Ronald E. Pynn, *American Politics: Changing Expectations* (1993); Edward Sidlow and Beth Henschen, *America at Odds* (1998).

Federalism

Federalism refers to the relationship between the states and the national government. The leading question about federalism is this: What did the Constitution's Framers have in mind when they created a political system that had a strong national government and state governments that also wanted to have influence over national policy? The system of government that has evolved since the 1789 ratification of the Constitution comprises state units of government as well as a national government. The Constitution guarantees the independence of the states, reflecting a commitment to self-government and reinforced by the states' election of representatives to Congress. The national and state governments share certain powers, but the national government generally cannot act without authorization from members of Congress. This sharing of power is a reflection of sovereignty, whereby the national government is supreme in some areas but not in others (e.g., where states are supreme).

The "policy era" of American federalism roughly covers the years 1789–1865, characterized by vertical, or nation-centered, federalism. Relations between the states and national government were being defined, with national authority being more prominent. That prominence was affirmed in the U.S. Supreme Court case *McCulloch v. Maryland,* in which the power of Congress to establish a national bank had been challenged. The challenge questioned whether Congress had the right to manage money, to lay and collect taxes, issue currency, and borrow money. Another question was whether a federal bank could be taxed by a state. The Supreme Court decided that Congress did have the power to charter a national bank and that the states did not have the authority to tax the national bank. This important decision established the authority of the national government to tax, collect money, and borrow funds. Moreover, it represented one of the first challenges to the authority of the national government to act in ways defined by the Constitution. This decision added to the top-down nature of the relationship between the national and state governments in the new nation.

After the Civil War, the relationship between the states and the national government was altered in the wake of changing economic, industrial, and social conditions throughout the United States. The era of "dual federalism" (1865–1900) clearly set separate areas of authority. It was characterized by growth in the American economy, and there was an understanding that the federal government had authority over interstate commerce and that the states held authority as to intrastate commerce (allowing states to regulate commerce within their areas of responsibility). The Interstate Commerce Act of 1887 was passed during this period.

The third era of federalism (1900–1937) is referred to as "cooperative federalism," whereby the states and national government resolved commercial matters through regulatory structures to maintain fair and free competition in the national economy. The U.S. economy was in serious trouble as a result of the Great Depression. The role of the national government expanded in response to calls from the states for economic relief and assistance. The administration of Pres. Franklin D. Roosevelt created a series of policies and programs known as the New Deal, designed to lead the United States out of the Great Depression. New Deal programs lasted from 1932 until 1940 (some of the programs ended in 1938); the nation's economic status changed with the onset of World War II in Europe (1939) and U.S. involvement (1941).

The era of "creative federalism" took hold during the postwar years (1945–1969). The federal government developed federal grants-in-aid to states to provide assistance in housing for low income families, highway construction, unemployment and welfare programs, and medical care. Since the early 1970s, the era of "new federalism" has taken flight, whereby states and local governments take on a larger role in managing programs funded by the federal government. This occurred primarily through general revenue sharing programs initiated by the federal government.

Federalism has been a changing process, with each region having a different relationship with the national government that befits regional or state needs. Since the 1930s the national government has been more involved in state and local public policy matters and has attempted to create standards for federal programs. Such standards (in the form of mandated programs and requirements) place the national government in a position of authority over the states in the implementation of public policy.

See also: Key Concepts: Categorical Grants; Federal System; Public Policy

References: Paul C. Light, *A Delicate Balance: An Essential Introduction to American Government* (1997); Susan Welch et al., *Understanding American Government* (1997); James Q. Wilson and John J. DiIulio Jr., *American Government: The Essentials* (1998).

Federalist Papers, The

The Federalist Papers was a series of eighty-five essays written by Alexander Hamilton, James Madison, and John Jay that appeared in New York newspapers from October 1787 to August 1788. They were written in defense of the proposed Constitution and its republican form of government. They were reprinted in other newspapers throughout the states and intended to sway public opinion toward the arguments of the Federalists, who favored a strong central government and the new Constitution. The essays reflected the thinking of three individuals who had given substantial thought to the development of political ideals and structures that broke new ground in political theory.

The Federalist essays discussed separation of powers and the operation of the three branches of government; the need for political tolerance and the case for permitting the development of political factions (*Federalist #10*); and why the representatives to the Constitutional Convention should ratify the new Constitution (that occurred in 1789, with the Bill of Rights amending the original document).

See also: Key Concepts: Federalism

References: Steffen W. Schmidt, Mack C. Shelley II, and Barbara A. Bardes, *American Government and Politics Today* (1997); Susan Welch et al., *Understanding American Government* (1997).

Gerrymandering

Gerrymandering is the process of redrawing an electoral district to make it easier for a political party to win that district. The theoretical purpose of redrawing districts is to reflect population shifts. The practical reason is to ensure that the party in power has an easier time winning an election (moving district lines to accommodate voting patterns in districts favors the party's candidate). The majority parties in state legislatures determine the size of congressional districts as well as the shape of the district boundaries. Such reapportionment (i.e., redrawing districts) is required by the Constitution every ten years to reflect the national census.

Racial gerrymandering occurs when a state legislature redraws districts to ensure the election of candidates of a particular race to Congress. This process was challenged in the 1993 U.S. Supreme Court case *Shaw v. Reno,* whereby the Court ruled that a district was so irregularly drawn that it was designed to segregate the races. The court sent the redistricting decision back to the lower courts for reconsideration.

The term *gerrymandering* originated in the acts of Elbridge Gerry, vice president under George Washington. As governor of Massachusetts, Gerry had redrawn the boundaries of a congressional district for political advantage. It reminded his critics of a salamander, and they coined the term for the new practice of redrawing congressional districts.

See also: Key Concepts: Congress, United States

References: David Edwards and Alessandra Lippucci, *Practicing American Politics: An Introduction to American Government* (1998); James Q. Wilson and John J. DiIulio Jr., *American Government: The Essentials* (1998).

Goal Specification

One of the most important and difficult aspects of the public policy process is the specification of policy goals. What should be done? What is the appropriate role of government in the policy process? How much should be spent to accomplish policy goals? How much public participation should be encouraged or allowed in the setting of goals and in their accomplishment? How are goals implemented and evaluated upon completion? These important questions start with the fundamental question of what should be done to correct a problem that requires public action.

Goal specification becomes important when a problem is placed on the public agenda. If a problem or issue receives the attention of government (at any level of government—national, state, local), the next stage is to decide what to do to solve a problem and to accomplish desired ends. This requires the specification and identification of policy goals. Goal specification is a crucial element of the policy process because if the goals of policy are not realistically established (in a word, "accomplishable"), then the policy effort will fail. Public policymakers frequently struggle to identify realistic goal structures in the policy process. Requirements for accountability in public policymaking and government spending make the issue of goal specification extremely important.

See also: Key Concepts: Accountability; Agenda Building

References: Charles E. Davis, *The Politics of Hazardous Waste* (1993); Frank Fischer, *Evaluating Public Policy* (1995); Charles O. Jones, An *Introduction to the Study of Public Policy* (1984).

Government in the Sunshine Act of 1976

One of the outcomes of Watergate (the scandal that enveloped Pres. Richard M. Nixon during the early 1970s and eventually led to his resignation) was a call for more openness in government activities at the local, state, and federal levels. Congress moved to open the federal bureaucracy to public scrutiny in 1976 when it passed the Government in the Sunshine Act. The act requires all multimember federal agencies to hold regular meetings in public. The definition of *meetings* covered most any gathering or collection, either formal or informal, of agency members, including telephone conference calls. The only restrictions on this degree of openness were court proceedings, personnel matters, and any items specifically mentioned in the bill. This legislation was part of a general reform effort known as "sunshine," or public meeting, laws, representing the idea that pragmatic results of public meetings were a desired goal and that this goal could be met most effectively if executive and closed sessions were eliminated as a standard governmental practice unless absolutely required. The consequence of sunshine laws is that public officials are made accountable for their decisions in a public setting. A related element of sunshine laws is the Freedom of Information Act of 1966, the method by which citizens can request and obtain public documents.

See also: Key Concepts: Accountability

References: Stephen J. Cann, *Administrative Law* (1998); Leif H. Carter and Christine B. Harrington, *Administrative Law and Politics: Cases and Comments* (1991); Steffen W. Schmidt, Mack C. Shelley II, and Barbara A. Bardes, *American Government and Politics Today* (1997).

Government Performance and Results Act of 1993

Public accountability has emerged as an important goal of government programs during the past two decades. The Government Performance and Results Act of 1993 went into effect in 1997, requiring every federal agency to put forth a strategic plan, a mission statement, and a set of priorities by which each agency would meet its tasks.

See also: Key Concepts: Public Bureaucracy; Public Management

References: Edward Sidlow and Beth Henschen, *America at Odds* (1998).

Horizontal Federalism

In the context of federalism in American politics, *horizontal federalism* refers to relations among similar levels of government (e.g., among states or among cities). There are numerous examples of relations between states in separate policy areas (e.g., hazardous waste is an issue that requires states to plan cooperatively for hazardous waste storage). The federal government expects states to agree on solutions for common state policy problems. Cities also work together to coordinate policy in areas such as criminal justice, air quality, and land use and planning. These are examples of horizontal federalism at work, necessary for the successful implementation of public policy.

See also: Key Concepts: Federalism

References: James P. Lester and Joseph Stewart Jr., *Public Policy: An Evolutionary Approach* (1996); Michael G. Reagan and John G. Sanzone, *The New Federalism* (1981).

House of Representatives

See Key Concepts: Congress, United States

Ideology

Ideology is defined as a coherent set of beliefs and values about history, nature, psychology, and society that individuals or groups accept as their way of looking at life, politics, and others in a society. Ideology is also the way that a person or group views the world. The most important components of ideology are the beliefs and values that serve as the foundation of an ideology. Some people believe that ideology is about power and whose beliefs and values should dominate. That is how we see political ideology: in terms of whose values and beliefs will prevail in competition with other sets of values and beliefs.

Ideologies tend to serve as the leading philosophies behind different social forces, and as a source for philosophy ideologies need to be all-encompassing, which means that they must have sweeping answers for a range of activities or issues; they must be consistent, leading to connections between issues and events; they must be plausible and realistically address common perceptions of events in social or political life; and they must be useful, serving the needs of believers, with clear justifications tied to them. Ideologies tend to promote rigid positions or views of people, life, and politics.

The leading ideologies in American politics are "liberal" and "conservative." Liberals tend to believe that the role of government is to promote well-being and to provide assistance when called upon. Conservatives believe that government should be limited, as government is more apt to restrict individual rights than to aid and promote personal freedom. Liberalism and conservatism encompass more than that, of course. In the end, however, ideology represents belief systems that people adopt and hold to be true.

See also: Key Concepts: Conservatism; Liberalism

References: Edwin M. Coulter, *Principles of Politics and Government* (1994); Leslie P. Thiele, *Thinking Politics: Perspectives in Ancient, Modern, and Postmodern Political Theory* (1997).

Implementation

Policy implementation is the penultimate stage in the public policy process. Public policies originate as a result of a problem that affects people in ways that require solutions that can only be provided by government. Once a problem is determined to affect people in extraordinary ways, it is placed on the public agenda. The problem is most likely championed or represented by a public official who is familiar with or who has the resources to attempt to provide a solution. Once a policy or solution is formulated, then resources have to be applied or made available to affect the problem (the policy formulation stage). After the policy is formulated, the next action is the implementation of the policy.

Implementation can be difficult because the people or legislators who formulate the policy are not clear as to how to solve the problem. Nevertheless, the formulators take time to study a problem, gathering information and data to find the solution. Policy implementation is the true test. Policy implementation can be controversial also because the implementation of policy can have unforeseen effects. The implementation of public policy can be difficult, as the process rarely results in consensus on preferred outcomes.

See also: Key Concepts: Agenda Building; Public Policy

References: James E. Anderson, *Public Policymaking* (1997); Charles O. Jones, *An Introduction to the Study of Public Policy* (1984); James P. Lester and Joseph Stewart Jr., *Public Policy: An Evolutionary Approach* (1996); Jeffrey L. Pressman and Aaron B. Wildavsky, *Implementation* (1973).

Incrementalism

Instead of making public policy decisions comprehensively, the U.S. public policy process has been characterized as taking incremental steps toward policy development. American legislators and politicians tend to pursue a measured, cautious approach to problem-solving. Public policy is made in increments—small, measured pieces—rather than in ambitious, grand programs.

The New Deal under Franklin D. Roosevelt was a comprehensive initiative. The nation's large-scale problems called for immediate government action. The New Deal programs that developed over 13 years introduced major changes in the economic and employment environment. Yet they were consistently incremental in nature, and very few had lasting effect. (The programs to protect homeowners from mortgage foreclosures, the banking programs that secured and protected deposits in banks, the Social Security Act, and a few other programs have survived into the 1990s, but these were incremental in that they were not public policy programs that provided comprehensive answers to the problem of unemployment and poverty.)

American politics does not approach problem-solving in comprehensive ways. The incremental approach to policy development is the least costly, most politically expedient way in which American legislators at the local, state, and national levels conduct the business of public policy development.

See also: Economics: New Deal; Key Concepts: Public Policy

References: Charles Bonser, Eugene B. McGregor Jr., and Clinton V. Oster Jr., *Policy Choices and Public Action* (1996); Clarke E. Cochran et al., *American Public Policy: An Introduction* (1996); Charles F. Lindblom, *The Policy Making Process* (1980).

Independent Executive Agencies

See Key Concepts: Administrative Agencies

Independent Regulatory Agencies

Independent regulatory agencies have responsibility for specific areas of public policy. These agencies make and implement rules and regulations in an area of the national economy for the purpose of protecting the public interest. The first regulatory agency in U.S. government was the Interstate Commerce Commission (ICC), created in 1887. The ICC was established to respond to the development of economic monopolies in the business sector, which had a hold over prices, sales, and transport of goods. The ICC created rules and regulations restricting unfair business practices and the transport of goods and commodities between the states.

Independent regulatory agencies can be divided into those that came before World War II and those that came after the war. The agencies that were created after the war are called "second-generation regulators." They include the Environmental Protection Agency, the Equal Employment Opportunity Commission, the Nuclear Regulatory Commission, and the Federal Election Commission.

See also: Civil Rights: Equal Employment Opportunity Commission; Commerce and Transportation: Interstate Commerce Commission; Communications: Federal Communications Commission; Economics: Federal Trade Commission; Environment: Environmental Protection Agency

References: Steven J. Cann, *Administrative Law* (1998); Leif H. Carter and Christine B. Harrington, *Administrative Law and Politics: Cases and Comments* (1991); Ronald E. Pynn, *American Politics: Changing Expectations* (1993); Steffen W. Schmidt, Mack C. Shelley II, and Barbara A. Bardes, *American Government and Politics Today* (1997).

Indirect Costs and Benefits

Public policy is designed to accomplish specific, limited goals. Frequently, indirect and unintended costs and benefits can occur as a result of the implementation stage in the policy process. As a rule, costs and benefits tend to be unforeseen.

See also: Key Concepts: Public Policy

References: Thomas R. Dye, *Understanding Public Policy* (1995); B. Guy Peters, *American Public Policy: Promise and Performance* (1993).

Indirect Democracy

Democratic political systems come with different forms of government, for example, direct or indirect. Direct democracy is a political system whereby citizens can vote and participate on most issues. Some state constitutions give citizens the right to initiate a change to the state constitution by petition, to introduce new legislation through the referendum process, or remove public officials from office through the recall process.

Indirect democracy describes the U.S. (i.e., federal) system of government. Citizens act through elected representatives, who vote and make policy on their behalf. Parliamentary democracies can also have direct or indirect political systems.

See also: Key Concepts: Direct Democracy

References: Ken DeBow and John C. Syer, *Power and Politics in California* (1994); Susan Welch et al., *Understanding American Government* (1997).

Industrialized Nation

An *industrialized* nation is a nation possessing a diverse economy and stable political and monetary systems. An industrialized nation also has the established infrastructure, agriculture, technology, transportation systems, communication systems, waterways, and economic support systems that in combination enable the nation to develop, market, sell, and buy essential goods and services. Industrialized nations compete economically and possess economies of scale in transportation that are profitable and not overdeveloped, economies of scale in production technology, links to population-serving industries, and balanced, supportive production specialization. Industrialized nations typically produce and sell a wide variety of products, goods, and services. Industrialized nations tend to develop militaries to protect interests at home and abroad. The Group of Seven, created in 1975, comprises the seven leading democratic, industrialized nations: the United States, Japan, Britain, France, Germany, Canada, and Italy. Russia was made a "consulting observer" to the Group of Seven in 1997. Australia, Argentina, Brazil, and other nations are included on the list of industrialized nations.

See also: Commerce and Transportation: Industrial Policy; Economics: Economic Policy

References: Karl E. Case and Ray C. Fair, *Principles of Economics* (1989); David E. Edwards and Alessandra

Lippucci, *Practicing American Politics: An Introduction to American Government* (1998).

Informal Rulemaking

See Key Concepts: Rulemaking

Initiative

See Key Concepts: Direct Democracy

Institutional Agenda

Issues that come before local, state, and national government levels for action are said to be placed on the government agenda. There are two types of public agendas: the systemic and the institutional. The systemic agenda is a broad type of agenda in which there is a set of issues that the political system decides to address (e.g., poverty or disease). The institutional agenda is the decision to take action through the creation of public policy in a certain issue or policy area. It is narrowly focused on specific policy or issue areas that agencies manage and act on. An agency as a political institution can have more than one area of responsibility included in its institutional agenda, and so the institutional agenda might be more broadly defined.

See also: Crime: Federal Bureau of Investigation; Health: Acquired Immunodeficiency Syndrome; Key Concepts: Agenda Building

References: James E. Anderson, *Public Policymaking* (1997); B. Guy Peters, *American Public Policy: Promise and Performance* (1993).

Intended Consequences

The purpose of public policy is to solve a problem or to accomplish a goal. Goal attainment is expected to have desired, intended consequences that demonstrate that policy is successful. Consequences and successful goal attainment are not always easy to determine and measure.

See also: Education: G.I. Bill

References: B. Guy Peters, *American Public Policy: Promise and Performance* (1993).

Interest Groups

In the American democratic process, citizens and groups are free to organize based on interests and needs. Interest groups, the common form of organization, attempt to influence government. These groups exist outside the government. Interest groups are also referred to as "pressure groups," as their tactic is to pressure government to bring about the change that they and their clients desire. There are governmental groups that operate in much the same way as private and public interest groups; we call these "intergovernmental lobbies." The key point is that interest groups are voluntary organizations of people who collectively pursue goals to benefit self-interests. The method interest groups use to influence government is called "lobbying."

Interest groups take a variety of forms. Private interest groups organize to influence government policy to promote private ends. Public interest groups influence public policy to create public-oriented benefits. These usually nonprofit groups lobby government for the greater good. Intergovernmental lobbies are governmental bodies with representatives, called lobbyists, in Washington, D.C., who influence public policy to support efforts in local government. Lobbyists contact policymakers at the local, state, and national levels to promote interests. In many ways, interest group activity is a form of government participation. Interest groups pose a problem for democratic systems if they have undue influence over government policy. In advocating policy positions and representing constituents, interest groups frequently make money contributions to political candidates or current officeholders, which raises the question whether legislators are truly independent or merely represent interest groups and their specific needs. For this reason, Americans tend to distrust interest groups and lobbying activities. Political action committees (PACs) are associated with interest groups and provide money to candidates for public office at the local, state, and national levels. Federal campaign finance laws limit the amount of money that PACs can give to candidates.

Interest groups are not always permanent fixtures. For example, a group of neighbors might organize to influence the city council or the county board to enhance their neighborhood's quality of life. Once the issue is resolved, the group will disband. In any event, interests groups will continue to play an important role in the policymaking process.

See also: Environment: Environmental Policy; Key Concepts: Public Interest Research Groups; Public Policy

References: Jeffrey M. Berry, *Lobbying for the People: The Political Behavior of Public Interest Groups* (1977); Jeffrey M. Berry, *The Interest Group Society* (1997); Allen Cigler and Burdett Loomis, *Interest Group Politics* (1990).

Intergovernmental Relations

See Key Concepts: Federalism

Iron Triangle

Iron triangle is the phrase used to describe alliances among interest groups, legislators and their staffs, and government agencies. Such relationships further the interest group's policy goals. Iron triangles begin to form when an interest group identifies a desired goal. Lobbyists representing the interest group will contact the agency to familiarize agency bureaucrats, then let the agency decisionmakers know that it is important to encourage members of Congress to support certain legislation. Lobbyists then contact Congress members to alert and educate them about the group's needs. Each point on the triangle has been contacted, and the network of information, education, persuasion, and conversation has been completed. This is how iron triangles operate to influence the policy agenda.

See also: Key Concepts: Interest Groups

References: Jeffrey M. Berry, *The Interest Group Society* (1997); Thomas R. Dye and L. Harmon Ziegler, *The Irony of Democracy: An Uncommon Introduction to American Politics* (1996).

Isolationism

Congress has struggled with the issue of America's proper role in international affairs. At the turn of the 20th century, isolationism was a contentious issue. The Monroe Doctrine had obliged the United States to concern itself with affairs in the Western Hemisphere. Pres. Teddy Roosevelt even sent a fleet of U.S. warships around the world to "show the flag," but at the time the United States could more easily remain aloof from international affairs and crises. The United States returned to an isolationist approach to world affairs until World War I; thereafter the United States has increasingly engaged in international politics.

After World War II the United States assumed an international peacekeeping role. It entered several military alliances with other nations during the post–World War II era, which furthered U.S. commitments in international politics. Such meddling has created problems. We no longer discuss world affairs strictly in terms of whether the United States should be isolationist in its approach. The United States is regularly called upon to intervene in disputes between and within nations. The United States is a major player in the United Nations and often takes a leading role in disputes around the world. Given advancements in communications and the intertwined nature of the global economy, it is difficult for any industrial nation to isolate itself from international politics.

See also: Economics: Economic Policy

References: James Baker with Thomas M. DeFrank, *The Politics of Diplomacy* (1995); John Prados, *Keepers of the Keys: A History of the National Security Council from Truman to Bush* (1991).

Issue Attention Cycle

In the wake of a policy change, many political scientists and media observers investigate the reasons why the issue was placed on the public agenda. To clarify the way in which issues reach the public agenda, Anthony Downs coined the phrase *issue attention cycle.* It refers to the phenomenon of how objects of great public concern for a short period of time generate a response from government. Downs suggested that initial enthusiasm is followed by sober realism about costs and the difficulties of implementing policy. Public interest in that issue then declines, moving to another issue or set of issues. How issues get on the public agenda has much to do with the severity of the problem and the kinds of policy responses that are rationally required to solve public problems.

See also: Key Concepts: Agenda Building

References: Anthony Downs, "Up and Down with Ecology—The 'Issue Attention Cycle,'" *Public Interest* 28 (1972); B. Guy Peters, *American Public Policy: Promise and Performance* (1993); B. Guy Peters and Brian W. Hogwood, "In Search of the Issue Attention Cycle," *Journal of Politics* 47 (1985).

Issue Networks

Issue networks are groups of individuals who communicate, cooperate, and organize around common policy issues. These groups may act independently or in association to influence action on a specific cause or interest. They educate, inform, organize, and coalesce around public policy issues in which groups have a common interest and agenda.

See also: Key Concepts: Interest Groups

References: Thomas R. Dye, *Understanding Public Policy* (1995).

Judicial Activism

See Key Concepts: Judicial Review

Judicial Restraint

See Key Concepts: Judicial Review

Judicial Review

A function of the constitutional separation of powers among the three branches of government, the power of judicial review allows the U.S. Supreme Court to rule on the constitutionality of congressional and presidential actions. The federal judiciary is itself kept in check by the president and the U.S. Senate, who have the power to appoint and confirm, respectively, federal judges. The federal judiciary does not rule on constitutional matters willy-nilly; justiciable controversies must be brought to it via the filing of a complaint (i.e., a lawsuit).

Marbury v. Madison, an early American case, laid the foundation for judicial review. The dispute involved the appointment of a new judge, William Marbury, who had been named by the outgoing president, John Adams. Marbury never received his appointment papers; Thomas Jefferson, newly elected president, ordered Secretary of State James Madison not to issue the appointment papers to Marbury. Marbury sued, asking the Supreme Court to force the president to issue the appointment papers. Under the Judiciary Act of 1789, the Supreme Court had the power to force the president to comply with Marbury's request. This was the first test of the Supreme Court's legitimacy within the federal structure. The Court, under the leadership of Justice John Marshall, narrowly defined its power to force the president to issue the appointment papers yet declared a portion of the Judiciary Act of 1789 invalid. The Court held that it could not force other branches of government to comply with its rulings, as Congress had given the Court power that was omitted under the Constitution. Since that case was decided, the Court has had many opportunities to rule on the constitutionality of acts by Congress and the executive, two famous cases being Pres. Franklin D. Roosevelt's "court-packing" attempt and Pres. Richard M. Nixon's attempt to withhold White House recordings in the Watergate scandal.

Judicial review is also analyzed in terms of frequency, that is, whether the Court is eager (i.e., "liberal") or restrained (i.e., "conservative") in using its far-reaching power. Some members of the Supreme Court might be anxious to overturn legal precedent that is not in keeping with political and social times; these are judicial activists. In contrast, judicial conservatives shy away from overturning legal precedent or even setting new precedent that expands social, individual, and political rights without a clear constitutional mandate. Sometimes, the Court is the catalyst for dramatic change in America's social and racial climates (for instance, in striking down the separate-but-equal standard for educating African American students). Thus, in the context of American politics, liberals prefer an activist Court, whereas conservatives prefer a Court that demonstrates judicial restraint. The balance between activism and restraint swings back and forth over decades as new justices replace those that have left the bench. Under Chief Justice William Rehnquist, the Supreme Court has been perceived as conservative, or restrained.

See also: Civil Rights: Civil Rights Policy

References: Kermit L. Hall, William M. Wiecek, and Paul Finkelman, *American Legal History* (1991); Harold J. Spaeth, *Supreme Court Policy Making: Explanation and Prediction* (1979); Stephen L. Wasby, *The Supreme Court in the Federal Judicial System* (1988).

Legislative Process

See Key Concepts: Congress, United States

Legislative Staff

State legislators and members of the U.S. Congress rely on staffs to gather information, research bills, schedule hearings, write and amend bills, and work with constituents to serve home districts. Staffs are essential to legislative work. Frequently, staff members are expert in specific policy areas.

In the U.S. Congress there are approximately 30,000 staff members. They work for members of

Congress as well as for special support agencies, including the Congressional Research Office, the Office of Technology Assessment, the Congressional Budget Office, and the General Accounting Office. House members keep an average of 16 personal staff members; senators average more than 40. Staff members gain valuable legislative experience that serves them well if they seek public office. They typically write letters, answer constituent questions, solve constituent problems, and make important contacts with interest groups, agencies, and other members of the legislative branch.

See also: Key Concepts: Casework; Congress, United States; Iron Triangle

References: Thomas R. Dye, *Understanding Public Policy* (1995); David E. Price, *The Congressional Experience* (1992); Eric Redman, *The Dance of Legislation* (1973); Susan Welch et al., *Understanding American Government* (1997).

Legislature

In political systems, the legislature creates laws, policies, and standards for action. Legislatures and legislative activity can be found at the local, state, and national levels of government. The local legislative function is typically performed by city councils, at the county level by county boards (elected supervisors or commissioners). In New England, local legislators are frequently known as selectmen. Across the United States, there are different names for local legislators, such as aldermen, council members, or burgesses. Names for legislators derive from the British political system, which served as the model for many local and state governments.

Legislatures at the state level can exist as bicameral or unicameral structures. A bicameral legislature has two chambers or houses, most frequently an assembly (or state house of representatives) and a senate. Each body has separate functions, defined by state law. A unicameral legislature has one chamber and combines the functions of the more traditional dual-chamber legislature. One of the features of 20th-century legislatures is the idea of professionalization. A professional legislature is authorized to provide resources to members of the legislature, typically for hiring staff members to support the legislative process. Professional legislatures are expected to conduct business on a more than limited legislative schedule.

In the U.S. political system, the federal legislative function is carried out by the U.S. Congress, comprising the House of Representatives and the Senate. Under a parliamentary system, the legislative power is fused into the national legislature, called a parliament. The British and Canadian systems are parliamentary forms of government, also bicameral, but the chief legislative power resides in the House of Commons. Members of the House of Commons in the British and Canadian systems are elected to office; members of the British House of Lords are appointed (members to the Canadian Senate are appointed as well). The Canadians sought to reform this and make the Senate equal to the House of Commons, but the national vote in 1992 failed to bring about these reforms. The situation remains the same in England.

See also: Key Concepts: Congress, United States; Federalism

References: Thomas R. Dye and L. Harmon Ziegler, *The Irony of Democracy: An Uncommon Introduction to American Politics* (1996); Edward Sidlow and Beth Henschen, *America at Odds* (1998).

Legitimacy

Public policy requires the support of legislatures and the public. When legislatures make public policy they need to possess the necessary authority to make decisions that affect some segments of the public and constituents more beneficially than others. Thus, policymakers need legitimacy to make policy. B. Guy Peters defines *legitimacy* as a belief on the part of citizens that the current government represents a proper form of government as legal and authoritative. To be *authoritative* means that the force of law supports the action taken by government or by the government's representatives.

Legitimacy requires the public's acceptance of the role and actions of government, but it also requires that the procedures for making decisions are also acceptable. Decisions result in actions, and those actions must be seen as necessary and acceptable to solve a public problem. Legitimacy is not something that every citizen in the nation gives to government decisions and action. Governments and legislatures require only a majority of citizen support, and therefore many people do not necessarily believe that government decisions or actions are legitimate. As long as legislatures get majority support to make policy and to implement that policy, the substance of government legitimacy is firm. The political culture in a nation or state reflects the character of legitimacy in the political system itself. Political culture and the process of political socialization work to build trust in the political system. The socialization process educates, informs, and molds people in political systems to the politics of that system. Ultimately, political culture and political socialization lead to development of trust in and legitimacy of the political system and its structures for policymaking.

See also: Key Concepts: Political Culture; Political Socialization

References: Edwin M. Coulter, *Principles of Politics and Government* (1994); B. Guy Peters, *American Public Policy: Promise and Performance* (1993).

Liberalism

The modern meaning of the term *liberalism* derives from the concept of classical liberalism. Classical liberalism refers to belief in free enterprise, individualism, support for free trade, and absence of government involvement in the national economy. As we define and apply modern liberalism in the United States, it stands for a belief in civil and political rights; extension and preservation of the rights of women and minorities; support for government involvement in solving the nation's domestic problems; and support for the poor and disadvantaged. Modern liberals have also been identified with promoting strong environmental protection policies. Political democracy and the extension of political rights and political participation across the spectrum of American citizens is important to liberals. Separation of church and state, particularly in politics, is also a major tenet of liberalism. Finally, liberals believe in promoting social tolerance and believe in the importance of inclusiveness in the political system as opposed to exclusion because of social, economic, ethnic, gender, and sexual differences.

See also: Key Concepts: Ideology

References: Edwin M. Coulter, *Principles of Politics and Government* (1994); Edward Sidlow and Beth Henschen, *America at Odds* (1998).

Local Government

Local government comprises governmental systems at the town, city, and county levels, all of which fall under the authority of state governments. City government structures are based on two predominant models: the strong mayor system and the weak mayor/council manager system. A strong mayor system is one in which the mayor is elected to office by citizens of the city; members of city council are elected as well, but the mayor is the chief executive in city government and holds the executive power. The weak mayor/council manager form is one in which the mayor, though elected by the citizens, does not wield significant individual power and authority over city government. In this kind of system, the mayor is an elected council member who serves as mayor on a rotating basis. The mayor is a member of the city council and runs for reelection as such. The executive management function in this system is performed by the city or town manager, who is hired by the city council and works at the pleasure of the city council. In both systems, the city council performs the legislative function for the city.

County governments typically function under a system in which citizens seek election as members of the county board (individual board members might carry the title of supervisor or commissioner). Depending on the county charter, the board can have any number of supervisors (typically three or five), who serve as legislators and policymakers for county issues. Annually, board members elect a president to organize the business and agenda of the board.

In both city and county governments, boards and commissions act in an advisory capacity; they are appointed by the city council or county board as appropriate. Special districts, yet another element of local governments, are governmental bodies formed to provide administrative structures for specific needs, such as irrigation, pest abatement, air quality, and utilities. Local and city governments are creatures of the state; the legal principle that serves as the foundation of this principle is known as Dillon's Rule. Under this rule, city governments must view their power very narrowly; state power is supreme in actions between states and cities. City and local government structures are essential in the process of intergovernmental design and implementation of public policy.

See also: Key Concepts: Federalism; Public Bureaucracy; Public Sector

References: John J. Harrigan, *Politics and Policy in States and Communities* (1984).

Majority Building

Majority rule has been the lasting political rule of decisionmaking in American politics. It pervades almost every aspect of political and community life in American society. The American political culture promotes majority rule as the basic decision rule in committee settings in schools, clubs, churches, nonprofit and for-profit organizations, and local, state, and national politics.

Majority rule has its origins in the distrust that the Founders had in the British political system, which did not allow American colonists to decide matters on their own behalf. Majority rule—or the decisions of numerical majorities—represents community support in American political and social settings. Majority rule also supports the legitimization of political decisions by demonstrating that numerical majorities provide support for decisions and actions. This expression of majority support suggests that discussions have taken place, bargaining and negotiating probably ensued, and issues were discussed in an open forum, which all offer support to the legitimization of the political decisionmaking process. Public policy requires majority-building and majority support for acceptance and implementation.

See also: Key Concepts: Legitimacy

References: Charles O. Jones, *An Introduction to the Study of Public Policy* (1984).

Multiculturalism

The United States is a nation comprising people of many races, ethnic groups, and cultures. During the 1980s and 1990s, the term *multiculturalism* gained favor to describe the variety of cultures that have contributed to the uniqueness of American society. Multiculturalism also promotes the idea that education programs should reexamine traditional influences and intellectual contributions, which previously had been limited to Western European interpretations and contributions. Multiculturalism recognizes that African Americans, Hispanic and Latin Americans, Native Americans, and Asian Americans have made major contributions to American life in education, culture, the arts, and the sciences. Advocates of a strict multicultural perspective do not accept the traditional characterization of America as a melting pot of cultures. They feel the variety of cultures is lost in such a characterization. Multiculturalism has been criticized for its failure to account for the excesses of multiculturalism, as experienced in the ethnic battles in Yugoslavia and the Soviet Union. American life has proven more inclusive during the 1990s, and there is room for Western European thought and intellectual traditions as well as for the multiethnic contributions of African Americans, Hispanics and Latinos, Native Americans, Asian Americans, and all other ethnic and cultural groups.

See also: Education: Education Policy

References: Clarke E. Cochran et al., *American Public Policy: An Introduction* (1996); James P. Lester and Joseph Stewart Jr., *Public Policy: An Evolutionary Approach* (1996).

National Performance Review

The National Performance Review (NPR) was a public management reform effort during the first administration of Pres. Bill Clinton. Vice Pres. Al Gore led the NPR effort and focused on all federal operations. NPR is an offshoot of the so-called reinventing government movement, which introduced government reform during the 1990s. The reinventing government philosophy is based on making government activities more entrepreneurial. The major aims of NPR were to eliminate red tape in government operations, put customers of federal agencies first, empower employees to get results, and encourage agency personnel to cut back to basics and eliminate waste. An NPR survey stated that Americans want the federal government to control immigration, help the needy, improve education, reduce crime, protect the environment, and improve jobs and the economy. NPR sees surveys as consistent with serving American citizens as customers. NPR today is a major government initiative directed at enhancing public management and improvement of government performance in the federal sector. More than a hundred federal agencies have established standards for customer satisfaction and are designing administrative means to meet customer-service models and goals.

See also: Key Concepts: Public Management

References: President Bill Clinton and Vice President Al Gore, *Putting Customers First, 1995: Standards for Serving the American People,* National Performance Review (October 1995); David H. Rosenbloom, *Public Administration: Understanding Management, Politics, and Law in the Public Sector* (1998).

New Federalism

After Pres. Richard M. Nixon was elected to office in 1968, he tried to redefine the relationship between the federal government and the states. Nixon acted on the idea of new federalism and focused on transferring federal power to states as the political subunits. This reflected a shift from a period of national supremacy in public policymaking (a remnant of the New Deal) to state-centered federalism, in which the states would have more authority over implementation of national programs. There was also a shift from categorical grants to block grants, a consolidated and reduced grant regime. The burden of administrative and implementation responsibility for many national programs shifted to states thanks to new federalism. Funding for block grants occurred through revenue sharing, with federal involvement being reduced in the administration of programs.

See also: Economics: Federal Revenue Sharing; Key Concepts: Block Grants; Federalism

References: Michael D. Reagan and John G. Sanzone, *The New Federalism* (1981); Steffen W. Schmidt, Mack C. Shelley II, and Barbara A. Bardes, *American Government and Politics Today* (1997); James Q. Wilson and John J. DiIulio Jr., *American Government: The Essentials* (1998).

Nontarget Groups

Target groups or target populations are the key groups seriously affected by a problem; they are the focus of policy and programs (i.e., the expected recipients of benefits). Nontarget groups are those not designated as the subjects of policy or programs but are impacted by the program or policy. Nontarget groups are affected positively and negatively by policy and programs. Frequently, the effects are economic as certain governmental services become strained or overstretched. Policymakers and policy analysts are interested in the impact of policy on nontarget groups, as they must be understood if policymakers are to understand the effects of policy implementation.

See also: Key Concepts: Public Policy

References: Thomas R. Dye, *Understanding Public Policy* (1995).

Open Society

In an open society, citizens are not constrained in their political participation; the free exchange of ideas and criticism is welcomed, even encouraged, in an open society. Open societies are also characterized by a free press and free elections with a dual- or multiparty political system. An open society can also be characterized as a political democracy, in which: government is conducted by the people in representative fashion; individuals have an equal opportunity to pursue individual goals; feedback from the populace gives direction to government policy; and political participation is encouraged but not forced.

See also: Key Concepts: Political Behavior

References: Edwin M. Coulter, *Principles of Politics and Government* (1997).

Oversight

The concept of political oversight is essential to the checks and balances built into the American political system. Oversight means that one branch of government has legitimate authority to oversee or monitor, as appropriate, actions of another branch. Congress has oversight function as to executive agencies, including the programs and policies they administer. Congressional committees have authority to monitor the execution of laws by administrative agencies under their jurisdiction, holding hearings at which bureaucrats testify and provide information about agency operations. Congress performs another oversight function by requiring regular reports from agencies. Congress also engages in oversight when confirming presidential appointees to ambassadorships, agencies, and the Supreme Court.

The presidential veto gives the president oversight authority in regard to acts of Congress. The Supreme Court performs oversight by passing on the constitutionality of acts of Congress and of actions taken by the president.

See also: Key Concepts: Congress, United States; President; Supreme Court

References: Susan Welch et al., *Understanding American Government* (1997).

Partisan Analysis

Policy analysts gather information on the qualities of public policy to convince others of the importance and value of that policy. Policy analysts inform legislators about the prospects for success of public policy; one method to create support is by engaging in partisan analysis, which involves designing proposed legislation so it will be viewed favorably and be accepted by enough interests inside and outside Congress. Partisan analysis is a form of coalition building.

See also: Key Concepts: Policy Analysis

References: B. Guy Peters, *American Public Policy: Promise and Performance* (1993).

Perception

Political scientist Charles O. Jones applies an interesting and useful framework for understanding public policy. Jones discusses the policy process in its various stages. The first stage is *perception.* Public policy comes as the result of the perception of a problem for a group of people. A problem has to be perceived as such, and it has to be demonstrated that public action and a public solution are required to address and solve the problem. Perception of a problem is an important first step in the policy process.

See also: Key Concepts: Policy Cycle

References: Charles O. Jones, *An Introduction to the Study of Public Policy* (1984).

Picket Fence Federalism

The evolution of federalism and intergovernmental relations has changed the roles and responsibilities of the national government and the states. These changing relationships are affected by the perceptions of presidential administrations and their approaches to establishing proper relationships among the three levels of government. *Picket fence federalism* refers to the evolution and development of policy subsystems that have become elements of the layers of government that are traditionally accepted representing the federal system. Such policy subsystems link the various *vertical* elements of the federal system—the national government and its structures, the state governments and their structures, and local government structures—one to the other; viewed metaphorically, they are the horizontal slats that hold the vertical pickets of a fence. Policy subsystems comprise issue networks supported by interest groups. Such interest groups can be governmental policy experts as well as agency bureaucrats, who link policy issues and discussions to government decisionmakers.

See also: Health: Health Policy; Key Concepts: Dual Federalism; Federalism

References: B. Guy Peters, *American Public Policy: Promise and Performance* (1993).

Pluralism

In a system characterized by pluralism, competing groups vie for political power and resources. All groups are not equally endowed with resources, but they do have the opportunity to make up for such inequality with passion and the desire to achieve goals. Policymaking in American government reflects this pluralist description of a number of separate and competing groups. Interest groups play a major role in American politics and in the understanding of pluralism at work.

Pluralism operates at lower levels of interests and government as well. If members of an urban community need better services, they can organize to present their wishes to the city through the city council, making known their plight, their problems, and their needs. The only resources required for this kind of political activity are will and energy. The response that a community group receives might not satisfy demands, but continued pressure can bring about the results it seeks.

See also: Key Concepts: Interest Groups

References: B. Guy Peters, *American Public Policy: Promise and Performance* (1993); Susan Welch et al., *Understanding American Government* (1997).

Policy Adoption

Policy adoption is the final determination and acceptance of a policy proposal. At the federal level, policy proposals must pass through the congressional committee and subcommittee processes to generate the discussion, review, hearing, and testimony that indicate support and justification (or lack thereof) for policy. Once that policy makes its way out of the House of Representatives and the Senate, appropriations decisions are made to apply resources and funding to the policy to ensure its application and implementation. The president then signs the proposal (by this time a formal law), and it is adopted. The agency responsible for implementing the policy is involved at the committee hearing stage to provide input about possible outcomes.

At the local and state levels of government, the policy adoption process works in much the same way (the state committee process is much the same as at the federal level). At the local level, subcommittees of the city council or county board review a policy proposal, discuss the merits and implications, then decide whether to send it on to the council or board with a recommendation for discussion and further review. Citizen input can occur at any level in the local policymaking process, and citizens can appear before the council or board to provide opinions, support, or opposition to a proposed policy.

See also: Key Concepts: Congress, United States

References: James E. Anderson, *Public Policymaking* (1997); Charles O. Jones, *An Introduction to the Study of Public Policy* (1984).

Policy Advocacy

Policy advocacy means taking a position on a specific public policy or policy area. Policy advocacy is motivated by one's political and ideological point of view. (For example, an environmentalist will most likely favor policy that supports preservation of the environment; an antiabortion activist will favor policy that limits abortions.) Policy advocacy is dominated by ideological principles, preferences, and values. In terms of understanding the dimensions of public policy, advocacy has a limitation in viewing policy strictly in terms of preferences instead of objectively evaluating the quality of policy, whether the policy has served its purpose and accomplished its goals, and whether the target population of the policy has benefited.

See also: Key Concepts: Policy Analysis; Public Policy

References: Clarke E. Cochran et al., *American Public Policy: An Introduction* (1996).

Policy Analysis

Policy analysis is concerned with the extent to which a policy meets its goals. Analysis also involves understanding how policy processes worked and how the implementation of policy has been accomplished. Policy analysis asks the critical questions of what happened, what worked, and whether it was successful.

Techniques for analyzing policy include many different types of analytic approaches, statistical techniques, and social scientific methodologies that focus on modeling the policy process. The techniques can be applied at the beginning of programs and policies as well as at the conclusion of programs to determine the effect and benefits. This is called "preprogram" and "postprogram" analysis. The sophistication of such techniques varies according to the length, size, objectives, and goals of a program.

The people who engage in policy analysis are called policy analysts. Policy analysts are academicians, experts, economists, attorneys, and bureaucrats who are familiar with or expert in policy areas. Their expertise allows them to critically analyze policy proposals, the formulation of policy, and policy in action. Policy analysts are frequently influenced in their interpretations, analyses, and predictions by their political points of view. Therefore, the opinions of policy analysts need to be weighed against their political positions on issues.

Policy advisers also have a role in policy analysis. Political candidates employ policy advisers, who inform and educate candidates about policy issues and predict how constituents will respond to issues. Policy advisers are important to candidates because they have a better understanding of the dimensions and implications of policy than do most candidates.

See also: Key Concepts: Policy Choices

References: Clarke E. Cochran et al., *American Public Policy: An Introduction* (1996); David H. Rosenbloom, *Public Administration: Understanding Management, Politics, and Law in the Public Sector* (1998).

Policy Analysts

See Key Concepts: Policy Analysis

Policy Choices

In any legislature, the decision to draft and support one policy over another has to do with the quality of the policy design, the likelihood that the proposed policy will work effectively to solve a problem, and whether the cost of policy implementation is balanced by the results that implementation is expected to offer. Policy choices in legislative settings focus on whether the proposal is the best course of action and whether the policy can get the required support to be passed and funded.

The committee systems in Congress and in state legislatures work as a filter for reviewing and discussing proposed legislation. During subcommittee and committee sessions, details are analyzed, debated, advocated, and explored. The sponsors of legislation advocate the policy most directly, and legislators will see their names become attached to bills throughout the legislative process. Legislation can thus be seen as a system of policy choices. How that legislation gets on the public agenda is a result of the severity of a problem, the necessity for a solution, and the quality of advocacy throughout the process of policy review in legislatures.

See also: Key Concepts: Policy Cycle

References: Thomas R. Dye, *Understanding Public Policy* (1995); Charles O. Jones, *An Introduction to the Study of Public Policy* (1984).

Policy Cycle

The policy cycle is the route that public policy takes from the time of formulation (and even before the formulation stage) to the time of evaluation or termination. Stages of the policy cycle include the problem stage, when a problem is in need of a solution and must be placed on the public agenda; the problem definition stage, when the problem is defined and a decision made regarding how to affect the problem; the action-in-government stage, when the determination is made whether an agency or program can act on a problem; the policy formulation stage, in which legislative bodies in government discuss, analyze, and debate the options for solving a problem and the prospects for designing a policy to affect the problem; the appropriation stage, in which resources are committed to the problem by the legislative body; and the policy termination stage, which happens after the policy has been implemented and the results of the policy have been studied, evaluated, and interpreted.

Other elements of the public policy cycle are proposed by political scientist B. Guy Peters, who suggests that policy maintenance, policy termination, and policy succession each deserve attention when considering the flow and movement of the policy process. Policy maintenance comes about as a result of inaction and the absence of decisions. Thus, policy is maintained because there is no action to change or adjust policy. Another element of the policy cycle is policy termination. Programs that are created as a result of public policy tend to take on a sense of permanency implying that the programs will always be present. Programs require administrative mechanisms (a bureaucracy) to implement rules and regulations governing the policy, and such administrations serve a "clientele" that relies on the continuation of programs. Termination of policy and programs is infrequent; if it does occur, program clientele still require assistance.

What happens when policy programs end? Should programs be replaced and/or succeeded by other programs, or should they be consolidated and collapsed into other existing programs? Some programs are split and made into different programs with similar goals and funding mechanisms; other programs are subsumed under new areas of government responsibility. This final element of the policy cycle is known as policy succession. Policy succession occurs for a variety of reasons and is frequently the result of the need to continue to satisfy and serve client groups. Once a program has a history of serving such groups, it is difficult to terminate or even change the focus of that program.

See also: Key Concepts: Agenda Building

References: Charles O. Jones, *An Introduction to the Study of Public Policy* (1984); Dennis J. Palumbo, *Public Policy in America: Government in Action* (1988); B. Guy Peters, *American Public Policy: Promise and Performance* (1993); Walter Rosenbaum, *Environmental Politics and Policy* (1998).

Policy Formulation

See Key Concepts: Agenda Building; Policy Cycle

Policy Maintenance

See Key Concepts: Policy Cycle

Policy Outcomes

The results of policy attempts to solve problems are known as policy outcomes. Understanding such outcomes are important, because governments need to know whether a policy has been successful; either way, decisions whether to continue a policy or alter funding, scale back efforts, or terminate the policy are inevitable. Policy outcomes can only be determined by studying the experience and asking what happened and whether what happened was a part of the desired outcomes. The beneficiaries of a program can be interviewed and studied to see if policy positively affected the program's clients.

See also: Key Concepts: Evaluation; Policy Cycle

References: Frank Fischer, *Evaluating Public Policy* (1995);

Charles O. Jones, *An Introduction to the Study of Public Policy* (1984).

Policy Outputs

Much thinking, information gathering, and analysis goes into the design, formulation, and implementation of public policy. For public policy to work and satisfy the goals of policymakers, certain elements must be in place. Policy *inputs* are the essential resources, information, conversations, contacts, and connections that in combination work to create a policy that solves problems. The implementation of policy requires an understanding of what impact the policy has on the target population or problem.

Policy *outputs* are the tangible results of policies. Outputs are observable, real-life consequences resulting from the application of resources and information.

See also: Key Concepts: Policy Outcomes

References: Edward J. Calabrese, Charles E. Gilbert, and Harris Pastides, eds., *Safe Drinking Water Act: Amendments, Regulations, and Standards* (1989); Clarke E. Cochran et al., *American Public Policy: An Introduction* (1996); Walter Rosenbaum, *Environmental Politics and Policy* (1998).

Policy Subsystems

See Key Concepts: Picket Fence Federalism

Policy Succession

See Key Concepts: Policy Cycle

Policy Termination

See Key Concepts: Evaluation; Policy Cycle

Political Behavior

Political scientists are interested in how and why people vote and participate in politics. The study of political participation as such is called "political behavior." Political behavior is affected by demographic issues such as age, race, gender, and income; by the amount of interest people have in politics or political issues; and by how people get information about politics, that is, the role of the media and how media influence politics and behavior.

Political behavior is affected by the process of political socialization. Political socialization is the manner in which people receive information about politics and how they form opinions, feelings, and attitudes toward politics, politicians, and political institutions. These factors in combination affect political participation and ultimately determine how and whether citizens exercise political rights. The clearest form of participation—and an indication of political behavior—is voting. One indicator of voting behavior is voter turnout. How many people voted? Who voted and why? How and why people vote is important, as candidates need to know their chances for being elected to office. They need to know how frequently constituents vote, what makes them vote, and how they will vote. They also need to know how constituents feel about relevant policy issues. Political behavior addresses forms of political participation and the influences on political participation. Other forms of behavior and political participation include working on political campaigns, attending meetings of local political party organizations, attending city council meetings, and taking part in activities in support of political candidates. There are passive and active forms of political participation that are of interest to political scientists. Passive forms include reading newspapers or magazines, watching debates on television, and reading literature from political candidates.

See also: Key Concepts: Political Socialization

References: Edwin M. Coulter, *Principles of Politics and Government* (1994); Thomas R. Dye and L. Harmon Ziegler, *The Irony of Democracy: An Uncommon Introduction to American Politics* (1996).

Political Culture

Political culture is the set of beliefs that people hold about a political system. These beliefs are affected by traditions, customs, values, and symbols connected to the political system. The elements that characterize American political culture are liberty, freedom, political consensus, individualism, equality, and private property. These elements derive from the experiences of the Founders of the nation when they broke away from British political traditions and created a distinct American system. Representative government is also a foundation of American politics and political culture.

Political culture is important to political systems because its beliefs, traditions, and values are centering points for the nation. People celebrate their sense of belonging to the nation. They celebrate and understand the meaning of national holidays such as the Fourth of July and Veteran's Day. Political culture acts as a bond for people in the political system. Immigrants to the United States are invited to participate in political traditions and to embrace those traditions as a part of becoming an American. When new citizens go through the naturalization process conducted by the U.S. Immigration and Naturalization Service, they are required to learn about American history, politics, and political traditions. They swear allegiance to the flag of the United States, then they are sworn in as citizens. The purpose of having symbols and traditions of the political culture is to generate loyalty. Loyalty might lead to participation in the political process, support for the political system, and strong citizenship.

See also: Key Concepts: Political Socialization

References: Steffen W. Schmidt, Mack C. Shelley II, and Barbara A. Bardes, *American Government and Politics Today* (1997); Susan Welch et al., *Understanding American Government* (1997).

Political Machine

A political machine is a strong party organization that dominates local politics over time. The traditional example of an urban political machine is the Democratic Party organization under Mayor Richard J. Daley in Chicago, Illinois. Daley was Chicago mayor from 1955 to 1976; during that time, the Democratic Party controlled elections through the Cook County Democratic Central Committee. A strong system of political patronage in Chicago was dominated by the organization. The patronage system allowed people elected to office to hand out favors and appoint people to government positions because of their loyalty to the party organization. The political machine had direct control over the policy process in city government and created policies that frequently benefited party supporters. Since Mayor Daley's death in 1976, the party machine in Chicago has disintegrated and no longer operates with the power and authority it once had. The party machine was a common feature of urban politics for the first 60 years of the 20th century, but the influence of political parties in urban settings and the decline of partisanship in urban politics have changed the course of machine politics.

See also: Key Concepts: Political Parties

References: John J. Harrigan, *Politics and Policy in States and Communities* (1984).

Political Participation

See Key Concepts: Political Behavior

Political Parties

There are two dominant political parties in the United States, the Democratic Party and the Republican Party. The Framers of the Constitution did not account for the development of political parties, which emerged from the interests developing during the ratification of the Constitution. The leading interests were the Federalists, who supported the Constitution, and the Anti-Federalists, who opposed ratification. The Federalists lost the 1800 election to Thomas Jefferson's Democratic Republicans, who won each election until the party split in 1824. The more modern sense of party ideals came about in the elections of 1824 and 1828, when the Democratic Republicans split with the rest of the party, creating the Democrats and the Whigs.

The Democratic Party that emerged from the split became today's Democratic Party, and the Whigs became the National Republicans. By 1860 a new Republican Party had organized; its presidential candidate was Abraham Lincoln. The Republican Party's stronghold during the post–Civil War years was northern states; the Democrats dominated southern politics. The Republicans dominated presidential elections until 1932, when Franklin D. Roosevelt, the Democratic governor of New York, was elected to the White House.

Political parties serve several functions in the American political system. They recruit candidates to political office, offer campaign support, and stimulate interest among the electorate in the electoral process. Parties are responsible for presenting alternative policies so that citizens can see there are policy possibilities other than those offered by candidates in office. Once a candidate is elected to office at the national level, the candidate and the party are responsible for operating the government. Policies need to be proposed, formulated, discussed, approved, appropriated, and implemented. When parties are out of power, they compose the loyal opposition to the party in power and are expected to organize members both inside and outside of government to propose alternative policies and debate policies presented by the party in power. Political parties were expected to inform voters of policies and issues; they do so now through party platforms during presidential elections. The information process has been taken over by electronic and print media.

Political parties have a structure of operations that reaches the lowest levels of government. The national party organization supports state party organizations. The state party organization provides assistance to local party organizations (usually at the county level). During off-year elections, local and state party organizations hold meetings, raise funds for campaigns, and otherwise remain active.

See also: Key Concepts: Political Behavior

References: Ronald E. Pynn, *American Politics: Changing Expectations* (1993); Steffen W. Schmidt, Mack C. Shelley II, and Barbara A. Bardes, *American Government and Politics Today* (1997).

Political Resources

Political resources comprise several elements. One kind of political resource—essential to getting elected to public office at the national or state levels—is money to run a successful campaign. Another way of viewing political resources is to recognize the support necessary to successfully propose a piece of legislation and have that legislation approved by a legislative body. The required support in this context is a numerical majority of legislative votes to carry a bill through the process. Resources can be essential information and facts that enable a policymaker or decisionmaker to successfully convince others that one point of view or decision is the best. Political resources can also be based on the ability to garner voter approval as a factor of personality and trustworthiness.

Political resources frequently are seen as skills that enable individuals or groups to further their points of view. The essential skills to place an issue on the public agenda are derived from an individual's education, intelligence, and willingness to engage others to seek common solutions. One argument, put forth by proponents of pluralism as an explanation of how people get political power, holds that people who are willing and able to spend the time and energy to organize and mobilize around an issue or problem are the ones who succeed politically and therefore derive benefits. Ultimately, political resources may rely heavily on the will and motivation of an individual or group to bring about political change.

See also: Key Concepts: Pluralism; Political Socialization

References: Jeffrey M. Berry, *The Interest Group Society* (1997); Edwin M. Coulter, *Principles of Politics and Government* (1997).

Political Socialization

Political socialization is the process whereby people learn about politics and values are formed that stimulate citizens to engage in political participation. The traditional agents of political socialization are age, income, gender, race, economic status, education, and family influence. Political socialization is responsible for shaping individual opinions, beliefs, and values about politics. Much of the learning begins during childhood and expands according to demographic factors as a person ages and gains experience that affects one's outlook toward politics. Political culture and the values and symbols attached to that culture also affect political socialization. Political events shape the socialization process as well and have an effect on how an individual approaches the political system and the policy process.

Political socialization is an important part of the political system because it affects how people will participate and develop beliefs in the political process. Citizens need to be socialized so that they can establish beliefs and present those beliefs consistently with what they demand from the political system. Public policy emanates from the needs of constituents, and constituents need to be able and willing to articulate needs in ways that are meaningful to legislators at all levels of government.

See also: Key Concepts: Political Behavior; Political Culture

References: Edwin M. Coulter, *Principles of Politics and Government* (1994); Paul C. Light, *A Delicate Balance: An Essential Introduction to American Government* (1997).

Pork Barrel Legislation

Pork barrel legislation serves legislators' home constituencies through such projects as building construction, new roads and highways, grants to local governments, and highly visible federal commitments that will bring local jobs. The term comes from legislators declaring that they are "bringing home the bacon" to constituents as a result of connections and legislative activity. Pork barrel projects are important for legislators to show home constituents that they are serving their needs with federal funds. Frequently, pork barrel projects are "riders" on larger pieces of legislation, permitted to "ride along" as a favor for the legislator's past support.

See also: Key Concepts: Legislature

References: David Edwards and Alessandra Lippucci, *Practicing American Politics: An Introduction to American Government* (1998); Eric Redman, *The Dance of Legislation* (1973).

President

The U.S. president plays a major role in the public policy process, representing one of three branches in national government. The president is expected to present an agenda to the nation and lead the effort to see his party's policies adopted in the Congress. Presidents are expected to use persuasion, leadership, constitutional authority, and personal will to move the agenda. Some presidents have been more effective than others. In the 20th century, Teddy Roosevelt, Woodrow Wilson (in a qualified way), Franklin D. Roosevelt, Harry Truman, Dwight D. Eisenhower, John F. Kennedy, Lyndon B. Johnson, Ronald Reagan, and Bill Clinton (in terms of reviving the national economy) were effective moving the policy process.

The constitutionally defined roles of the president are commander in chief of the armed forces, chief administrator of the executive branch departments, chief diplomat, chief legislator, and chief of state. The president is also the leader of the party, representative of the people, mobilizer of the government, moral leader, world leader, social reformer, and manager of the economy. Over the years, presidents have used national crises to build on their powers, and such unofficial powers tend to become permanent features of the office. Presidents have used the electronic media during the past 30 years to appeal to the nation, an opportunity that members of Congress cannot match. Presidents have resources that are important to presidential power: jobs, through presidential appointments; money and the use of budgetary allocations; cabinet support; and access to information. The U.S. president is the most powerful person in the world and can produce great change in public policy. The president needs the support of Congress to be a successful policy leader; success depends on leadership skills, party support and majorities in the House and Senate, and the ability to demonstrate moral leadership to the American people. The State of the Union address at the beginning of each year allows the president to present a cogent and realistic policy agenda to the nation.

See also: Key Concepts: Congress, United States

References: James MacGregor Burns, *Leadership* (1978); David Edwards and Alessandra Lippucci, *Practicing American Politics: An Introduction to American Government* (1998); Theodore Lowi, *The Personal President: Power Invested, Promise Unfulfilled* (1984); Richard Neustadt, *Presidential Power: The Politics of Leadership* (1960).

Pressure Groups

See Key Concepts: Interest Groups

Program Evaluation

See Key Concepts: Evaluation

Protectionism

When trading in foreign markets, nations often protect domestic industrial and farm products through pricing. One means is the imposition of tariffs on imported products. Tariffs act as a tax on the sale of foreign products to domestic consumers; this is protectionism. Another form of protectionism is import quotas on foreign goods. Import quotas restrict the quantities of an imported product. During the last decade, some countries have entered agreements with the United States to voluntarily limit the amount of goods exported to the United States. This is an orderly market agreement. Protectionism offers some level of security for domestic producers and manufacturers against foreign competitors, many of whom produce goods at cheaper costs and then lower the prices of goods to undercut domestic producers.

Protectionism, though offering some benefit to domestic producers, has the disadvantage of limiting choices and creating higher prices for consumers. Another problem of American protectionism is that by restricting or limiting sales of foreign products in the domestic market, other nations do not derive the income from the sale of their goods in the American market, and they in turn cannot buy American goods because they do not have the income that is produced by trade. Protectionism can be offset or softened by government subsidies to support domestic products and industries; however, this has its disadvantages because prices of domestically produced goods can be set at artificially high or low levels.

International trade agreements such as the North American Free Trade Agreement (NAFTA) discourage tariffs and other protectionist policies.

See also: Commerce and Transportation: Free Trade; Economics: Economic Policy

References: David Edwards and Alessandra Lippucci, *Practicing American Politics: An Introduction to American Government* (1998).

Public Agenda

See Key Concepts: Agenda Building

Public Bureaucracy

The public bureaucracy is distinguished from the corporate or private-sector bureaucracy in that it depends on government resources for existence. Public bureaucracies exist at the federal, state, and local levels of government. The public bureaucracy is composed of any government agency and its decisionmakers and employees. It creates and implements rules and policy that originate from the president and Congress (at the national level) and governors, state legislatures, mayors, city councils, and county supervisors (at local levels).

Members of public boards and commissions are also considered to be parts of the public bureaucracy. The bureaucracy is bound to the laws and provisions of the U.S. Constitution, and members of the public bureaucracy have a goal of service to client groups served by public agencies. These agencies recruit, hire, and promote employees based on the merit system. The bureaucracy is structured according to hierarchical principles; decisionmaking is based on objective rules.

At the federal level, values expressed in the National Performance Review (NPR) developed by Vice Pres. Al Gore have been disseminated into all executive agencies. The major principles of NPR have to do with client satisfaction and citizen service. The client satisfaction model in the federal bureaucracy is expected to restore citizens' confidence in government agencies.

See also: Key Concepts: Administrative Agencies

References: David H. Rosenbloom, *Public Administration: Understanding Management, Politics, and Law in the Public Sector* (1998).

Public Choice Theory

Public choice theory applies economic analyses to public policymaking. The public choice theorist believes that voters, taxpayers, candidates, interest groups, legislators, and other people involved in politics seek to maximize personal benefits in politics as well as in the economic marketplace. The public choice theorist feels that people engage in political activity—in whatever form—for private gain and self-interest. Interest groups pursue selfish ends by influencing and lobbying.

See also: Key Concepts: Interest Groups

References: Thomas R. Dye, *Understanding Public Policy* (1995); David H. Rosenbloom, *Public Administration: Understanding Management, Politics, and Law in the Public Sector* (1998).

Public Interest Research Groups

Public research interest groups (PIRGs) are affiliated with public interest groups, gathering data and information in support of public interest causes. PIRGs started as a result of the organizing activity of Ralph Nader. PIRGs are active in more than 25 states and initiate public interest causes and other public interest organizations. PIRGs are staffed primarily by young people, typically recent college graduates who visit college campuses to recruit staff members. PIRG staffs research environmental issues, public health issues, consumer protection issues, labor issues, and other areas that affect the poor and disadvantaged. Their purpose, besides gathering information and data, is to educate groups on causes and problems on the public interest agenda. Some staff members are attorneys who have a commitment to public interest law. The ultimate purpose of PIRGs is to contribute to the development of and education about public interest policy throughout the United States.

See also: Key Concepts: Interest Groups

References: Jeffrey M. Berry, *Lobbying for the People: The Political Behavior of Public Interest Groups* (1977); Jeffrey M. Berry, *Interest Group Society* (1997).

Public Management

The process of public management involves people running and having responsibility for public organizations. Running a public organization requires an individual to use the organizational structure, its rules and regulations, and its resources to achieve public goals. Those goals can include the implementation and administration of public policy and programs. The goals of public management are derived from legislatures, presidents, and the courts; in short, they are generated from the process of representative government.

Public management utilizes the principles of organization theory applied to accomplishment of public organizational goals. These principles enable the public manager to lead, organize, direct, use resources, recruit, select, promote personnel, and make decisions that satisfy the requirements for accomplishing public-sector goals. Public management uses administrative doctrine to guide the work of public organizations. This doctrine is made up of rules, procedures, and ways of doing things that reflect the basic values of the public organization. Public managers are at each level of government.

At the federal level, public management includes agency directors and all individuals who hold leadership positions in public bureaucracies. Even those who are not agency supervisors are part of the system of public management. Each person in a public bureaucracy contributes to the attainment of goals that direct the activities of public agencies.

At the state level, executive agencies have public managers in leadership positions. The state court systems are also administered by public managers. The various state attorneys general manage the offices of the state prosecutors, who enforce state laws. At the local level, the mayor's offices retain individuals who administer and lead the local agencies toward local goal attainment. The city manager and the county administrative officer serve the public management functions in cities and counties. Cities and counties also have agencies that are managed by agency directors. Those agencies include chiefs of police, county sheriffs, fire and public safety chiefs and directors, personnel directors, social service agency directors, planning agency directors, and public works directors. Public management positions require knowledge, experience, and educational degrees. Management positions are considered to be professional positions, and the standards for professional public management positions have been established by associations such as the American Society for Public Administration. The education standards for academic content for public administrators and public managers are established by the National Association of Schools of Public Administration and Public Affairs.

The profession and processes of public management are essential to the public policy system.

See also: Key Concepts: Public Bureaucracy

References: George J. Gordon and Michael E. Milakovich, *Public Administration in America* (1998); Fred A. Kramer, *Dynamics of Public Bureaucracy: An Introduction to Public Management* (1981); David H. Rosenbloom, *Public Administration: Understanding Management, Politics, and Law in the Public Sector* (1998); Jay M. Shafritz and E. W. Russell, *Public Administration* (1997).

Public Opinion

Public opinion comprises the political attitudes and beliefs expressed by ordinary citizens. It represents society's policy preferences. Governments and government leaders need to know what people are thinking and feeling about issues and policies. There are several ways to measure public opinion. People write letters to newspaper editors, expressing opinions on issues and politics. Public opinion surveys conducted via telephone are another method (a reasonable survey sample is roughly 1,000 interviews or responses to survey questions). Samples need to be representative—in age, gender, race, income, and levels of education—of society. Such surveys, or public opinion polls, provide information and data about how people think and react to issues and political candidates.

Public opinion polls have become an important part of the political process. Candidates for political office rely on polls to gauge constituents' feelings. Candidates specifically want to measure their chances for being elected to office. There are hundreds of polling companies that do nothing but conduct surveys and polls for political candidates for political purposes. Public relations firms also conduct polling.

The process of political socialization influences and ultimately determines how individuals form opinions. These opinions reflect support, dismay, resentment, anger, or outright acceptance for any given policy. The results of public opinion surveys and polls are important for government decisionmakers, for such opinions represent how constituents will respond to government action or inaction.

See also: Key Concepts: Ideology; Political Culture; Political Socialization

References: Edward S. Greenberg and Benjamin I. Page, *The Struggle for Democracy* (1993); Edward Sidlow and Beth Henschen, *America at Odds* (1998).

Public Opinion Polls

See Key Concepts: Public Opinion

Public Organizations

A public organization is any agency funded by federal, state, or local government. As such, public organizations are institutions of government, meaning that they are created, authorized, and guided by the systems and values of the governments that establish them, created to serve public ends and functions. They operate under public scrutiny and are expected to be open, fair, accountable, and honest in their operations. They are highly structured bureaucracies based on principles of organization theory and administrative hierarchy. They do not operate to make a profit and do not create products for sale or distribution. Public organizations are in the business of providing services, implementing public policy, and accomplishing publicly established and defined goals.

At the local government level, the city manager or mayor's office is considered to be a public organization. A city or county planning department is also a public organization. Such offices review, interpret, and implement rules, regulations, and policy made by local and state governments. At the state level, the state legislative analyst's office conducts research and analysis on policy issues in support of state legislatures. Federal public agencies formulate, implement, and enforce policy and regulations.

See also: Key Concepts: Administrative Agencies

References: Hal G. Rainey, *Understanding and Managing Public Organizations* (1997).

Public Policy

Public policy is a series of government decisions directed at providing a solution or set of solutions to public problems. A policy can be a goal to accomplish something broad in scope or simply to solve an isolated problem. Policy can also be a set of processes to change the outcomes of previous decisions or actions. Policy can be the decision to not act at all and to not commit resources to action. Policy can be lots of things and can involve many participants. The ways in which policy is created, formulated, discussed, and decided comprises the policy process.

Public policy begins with a problem that requires attention or a solution. How government responds to the problem is determined by how large the problem is, how many people are affected by the problem, how seriously they are affected, and what kind of solution is required. The representative process is activated when policy decisions are made in Congress, because members of Congress decide and make policy on behalf of their constituents and in the best interests of the nation. Certainly other factors come into play. They may feel that a policy is not in the public interest and will not receive enough public support to warrant congressional support of a new bill.

Public policy is created at the local level of government as well. Yet a local government decision to not act on a problem would also represent government policy, indicating that government structures might not appreciate the dimensions of a problem. But in the face of government inaction on an issue, citizens can seek relief and policy solutions from other governmental bodies.

Public policy can also be seen as goals, programs, decisions, standards, or proposals. Policy can come in many forms and is the result of government decisions. Policy can be laws, legislation, statutes, regulations, or legal opinions. Public policy decisions will always depend on the nature of a given problem.

See also: Key Concepts: Legislature; Policy Analysis; Policy Cycle

References: James E. Anderson, *Public Policymaking* (1997); Thomas R. Dye, *Understanding Public Policy* (1995); Charles O. Jones, *An Introduction to the Study of Public Policy* (1984); James P. Lester and Joseph Stewart Jr., *Public Policy: An Evolutionary Approach* (1996).

Public Sector

The public sector comprises all public agencies at the national, state, and local levels of government. Public-sector agencies differ from private-sector organizations in that the work and processes of public-sector agencies are governed by the federal and state constitutions. Public agencies exist within a system of separation of powers. At the federal level, Congress has the power to create federal agencies; at the state level, state legislatures are authorized to create state agencies. City councils and county boards have the power to create agencies at the local level.

Public-sector agencies operate in the public interest. Unlike private-sector companies, which operate based on economic self-interest, public agencies serve the public, having the legal obligation to perform functions on behalf of citizens. Thus, public sector agencies provide services and public goods. These agencies are also empowered to regulate private-sector activities to ensure equality and fairness in the marketplace. Public agencies traditionally do not operate to make a profit. This is a frequent complaint by some who claim that public agencies should behave more like private firms.

Resources for public agencies come from tax dollars distributed to specific programs. Public agencies function in a political environment that is open to public scrutiny by citizens and the media. Public decisions must be made in open meetings, which encourages citizen input and participation. Public participation in the affairs of government fosters accountability, a basic requirement in representative government.

See also: Key Concepts: Accountability; Public Management; Public Organizations

References: David H. Rosenbloom, *Public Administration: Understanding Management, Politics, and Law in the Public Sector* (1998); Jay M. Shafritz and E. W. Russell, *Public Administration* (1997).

Recall

See Key Concepts: Direct Democracy

Redistributive Policy

There are different types of public policy, each of which accomplishes different ends. Redistributive policies redirect government revenues to less-affluent segments of society. Welfare policy is an example of redistributive policy. Funds to pay for welfare programs, health care for the poor (Medicaid), unemployment compensation, and public housing programs for low income people are all redistributive programs designed to help the disadvantaged. This kind of public policy strives to promote social equity, making the lives of those less fortunate better in the short term. The underlying philosophy is that the poor will not always remain so and will eventually not require public assistance. This is the central disagreement between liberals and conservatives, as the latter in general do not favor public assistance programs, claiming that beneficiaries of redistributive policy programs rarely stop collecting public assistance. Liberals contend that public assistance in and of itself is the goal. Between these divergent philosophies we sometimes find moderate solutions, such as programs designed to get longtime welfare recipients "back to work."

See also: Entitlement Programs: Welfare Policy; Key Concepts: Distributive Policy

References: Thomas R. Dye, *Understanding Public Policy* (1995); James P. Lester and Joseph Stewart Jr., *Public Policy: An Evolutionary Approach* (1996).

Referendum

See Key Concepts: Direct Democracy

Regulation

During the 19th century, the United States relied on the business, transportation, agricultural, and industrial sectors to develop the national economy and help the nation to spread westward. As a result of such "free reign," businesses, industries, and transportation companies (primarily railroads) developed extraordinary power in comparison to farmers and other important economic groups. Near the end of the 19th century, Congress was reacting to claims of unequal competition and the growth of economic monopolies. The Interstate Commerce Commission (ICC) was created in 1887 to regulate and control the influence of railroads. ICC was the first national regulatory commission, its role to change the way that railroads set rates for shipping goods. This marked the beginning of the use of regulatory power.

During the first two decades of the 20th century, more federal regulatory agencies were established, including: the Federal Reserve, the Federal Trade Commission, and the Federal Power Commission. During the 1930s, the Great Depression created conditions for new regulators to emerge: the Securities and Exchange Commission, the Federal Deposit Insurance Corporation, the Federal Home Loan Bank Corporation, the Federal Maritime Commission, the Federal Communications Commission, the National Labor Relations Board, and the Civil Aeronautics Board. These regulatory commissions and agencies were created to regulate private-sector activities in specific areas; if left unregulated, such activities might have compounded problems in unemployment, farm and home foreclosures, bank failures, and consumer confidence in the economy.

During the 1970s, so-called second-generation regulators were established: the Environmental Protection Agency, the Occupational Safety and Health Administration, the Consumer Product Safety Commission, and the Nuclear Regulatory Commission. These regulatory agencies had a broader focus than did earlier regulators (except for the Nuclear Regulatory Commission). The central issue in regulatory policy is the costs associated with private-sector intervention via regulatory action.

As president, Ronald Reagan led the nation toward deregulation of the national economy. The extensive regulation of private-sector activities was costly for government and required federal staffing to conduct regulatory functions, which sometimes imposed unreasonable costs on regulated businesses and industries. The ICC was disbanded, many of its functions turned over to the Surface Transportation Board. The railroad, trucking, and airline industries were deregulated, unfettered by ICC control. Other industries were deregulated, opening up competition, creating mergers, and prompting many businesses to seek more profitable locations outside the United States. Regulatory policy is controversial because it runs counter to the economic philosophy of laissez-faire capitalism, which prevailed during the 19th century. The federal government found that it could not leave the economy to its own devices and trust that it would adjust itself. Regulation is government intervention, which is necessary when the economy is unable to provide the needed balance in supporting government policy.

See also: Commerce and Transportation: Interstate Commerce Commission; Environment: Environmental Protection Agency

References: Charles Bonser, Eugene B. McGregor, and Clinton V. Oster Jr., *Policy Choices and Public Action* (1996); Leif H. Carter and Christine B. Harrington, *Administrative Law and Politics: Cases and Comments* (1991); David H. Rosenbloom, *Public Administration: Understanding Management, Politics, and Law in the Public Sector* (1998).

Regulatory Agencies

See Key Concepts: Regulation

Representation

Within the public policy process, problems requiring a policy solution must have a link to government action. This formal link, which places the problem on the public agenda, is representation by some government official. Political scientist Charles O. Jones defines *representation* as the link between people, problems, and government. The representative can be a legislative representative, a staff member in an agency, a member of city council or county board, or a public official who knows the dimensions of a problem and understands how to link people to government. Representation is essential to the democratic process; in most cases the representative becomes the champion of the policy problem and carries the policy to government for action.

Many problems do not get enough government support to change public policy. Members of Congress introduce hundreds of bills every legislative session, yet only a small percentage becomes public policy. Some members are very active in introducing legislation and feel that their constituents want them to create policy and serve as policy "champions" on their behalf. Other members of Congress merely vote, rarely designing their own bills for consideration. These tend to be loyal party members who usually vote the party line. Their sense of representation is to offer support to constituents by being low-key players in Washington, providing effective constituent service in home districts through casework.

Representation is an essential early element in the policy process. It also speaks to how issues get to government and how the representative perceives his or her role in the party in Congress. Edmund Burke, the 18th-century British writer and observer of politics, felt that the representative should be an agent of the constituents yet exercise personal judgment when voting on issues before the representative body. In many ways the representative is a delegate, a party member who holds the trust of constituents to act on their behalf. Representation is fundamental to politics and is a crucial element for democracy.

See also: Key Concepts: Agenda Building; Legislature

References: Edwin M. Coulter, *Principles of Politics and Government* (1994); Charles O. Jones, *An Introduction to the Study of Public Policy* (1984).

Rulemaking

Rules are guides of behavior for individuals, groups, and societies. In public agencies, rules serve as the orders and directives that explain how the business of government and its agencies is conducted. Bureaucratic agencies make rules that apply to policy areas and programs those agencies implement. Rules in many circumstances constitute the rule of law. They govern the actions of recipients of policy as well as the implementers of that policy.

The Administrative Procedure Act of 1946 explains that rules have current and future effects. The act established how rules would be made and provided agencies with rulemaking authority. However, true authority to make rules is found in organic statutes, which create agencies and authorize agencies to act.

See also: Key Concepts: Administrative Agencies; Administrative Law

References: Steven J. Cann, *Administrative Law* (1998); Leif H. Carter and Christine B. Harrington, *Administrative Law and Politics: Cases and Comments* (1991); Cornelius M. Kerwin, *Rulemaking: How Government Agencies Write Law and Make Policy* (1994).

Second-generation Regulators

See Key Concepts: Regulation

Senate

See Key Concepts: Congress, United States

Specialization in Congress

See Key Concepts: Committee System, Congressional

Standard Operating Procedures

Standard operating procedures (SOPs) are created and used by organizations to manage policy problems. Organizational or agency SOPs enable agencies to simplify regular, routinized activities and decisions. SOPs mean agencies do not have to approach every situation anew, reducing uncertainty in organizational operations through common forms, standard approaches, and established procedures. SOPs can also promote efficiency and productivity in operations.

Overreliance on SOPs can cause problems in serving the public. Not all situations fit the SOPs, and therefore a different set of responses might be required to address a problem. New problems thus require flexibility, ensuring "clients" that their best interests—not the agency's—are being served.

See also: Key Concepts: Accountability; Rulemaking

References: B. Guy Peters, *American Public Policy: Promise and Performance* (1993).

Subgovernments

See Key Concepts: Iron Triangle; Picket Fence Federalism

Subsidies

See Key Concepts: Protectionism

Sunset Laws

During the era of government deregulation, so-called sunset laws are used to short-circuit public policy that regulates business and industry, requiring that such programs be reviewed after a specified period. The sunset period could be five years, after which the agency or program leaders would have to justify its continuation. Absent such justification, the laws would "sunset" out of existence. Sunset laws were the creation of states in restricting state policies and spending. State regulations sometimes cause businesses to seek greener pastures elsewhere in hopes of finding less regulation and a friendlier business climate. Sunset laws thus have become one way to promote friendly business environments at the statewide level.

See also: Key Concepts: Regulation

References: Clarke E. Cochran et al., *American Public Policy: An Introduction* (1996); John J. Harrigan, *Politics and Policy in States and Communities* (1984).

Supreme Court

The federal judiciary is one of the three branches of the U.S. government; the U.S. Supreme Court is its chief judicial unit, followed by U.S. circuit courts of appeals and then district courts. The Supreme Court is the only court specifically created by the U.S. Constitution (Article III). The Court has nine justices, who are appointed for life by the president with the advice and consent of the U.S. Senate. The Court sits for nine months of the year, from the first Monday in October until the end of June. State supreme or appeals courts serve the same function at the state level. Supreme Court decisions become the law of the land and have the effect of creating policy. The Court also uses the power of judicial review (arising from the 1803 case *Marbury v. Madison*) to decide the constitutionality of actions by other branches of government.

Supreme Court cases, the last stop in the appeals process, are heard on appeal from the other federal courts and from state supreme courts—but only if the Court agrees to hear the case. If the court grants appellate review (through the writ of certiorari), the parties are notified, then submit briefs outlining legal arguments and case precedent. Following oral arguments, the Court renders a judgment in the form of a written opinion written by one of the justices in the majority. If in the majority, the chief justice writes the opinion or assigns it to one of the other justices in the majority. If the chief justice is not in the majority, the senior associate justice in the majority assigns the opinion. But any justice in the majority can write a concurring opinion, which might come to the same conclusion using a different analysis; justices who are in the minority can write dissenting opinions.

The Court is selective in its review of lower court cases. Yet the justices' willingness to interpret the U.S. Constitution is the subject of political debate. Justices can be seen as activist, if willing to update the Constitution to fit the times, or restrained, if unwilling. Such philosophies are debated in the Senate Judiciary Committee whenever a Supreme Court justice is nominated.

See also: Key Concepts: Judicial Review

References: Henry J. Abraham, *Freedom and the Court: Civil Rights and Liberties in the United States* (1988); Kermit L. Hall, William M. Wiecek, and Paul Finkelman, *American Legal History* (1991); Harold J. Spaeth, *Supreme Court Policy Making: Explanation and Prediction* (1979).

Target Groups

Target groups are those groups that are the subjects of a policy or program. Public policy is designed to affect such groups, to provide solutions to problems that specifically involve them. When policy is implemented, the target groups are observed and surveyed to see if the policy or program has been successful. Any evaluation of public policy will focus on the target population. Target groups are the "clients" of programs. They are important in the policy process because they offer support for programs and demonstrate that support by informing decisionmakers about the need for or quality of specific programs.

See also: Key Concepts: Evaluation

References: Charles O. Jones, *An Introduction to the Study of Public Policy* (1984).

Two-party System

The United States has a two-party system at the national level. Although third parties such as the Greens, the Libertarians, and the Reform Party have fielded candidates in major elections, and it is theoretically possible for them to win, the financial cost of running for a national office such as U.S. Representative or U.S. Senator is prohibitive if a candidate is not a member of one of the two dominant political parties. The two major parties—the Democrats and the Republicans—provide campaign and financial assistance to candidates whom they think have a serious chance to win elections. This is especially the case when a candidate for the U.S. presidency is nominated by one of the two major parties. Those candidates can expect to receive campaign finance and staff assistance from the Democrats or Republicans.

Typically, candidates for the U.S. presidency who are not affiliated with one of the two major parties do not stand a significant chance of being elected because the majority of voters tend to vote according to their party identification, or if they stray from their party affiliation, they either vote for candidates in the other major party or fail to vote at all. In the 1992 presidential election, industrialist Ross Perot ran for the presidency under the banner of the Reform Party, which he had organized as an independent political party. Perot received only 19 percent of the national vote. In the 1980 presidential election, John Anderson ran for the presidency as an independent and received only 6.6 percent of the national vote. U.S. Senator Eugene McCarthy ran as an independent candidate for the presidency in 1976 and former governor of Alabama George Wallace ran as an independent in 1968.

There is a greater likelihood that candidates running for state level political office may not necessarily be affiliated with either the Democrats or Republicans. The majority of state representatives do have ties to the two dominant parties but this is not a precondition for election to state offices. In some states, candidates for state offices are better off not to be associated with one of the two major parties. The presence of third parties in these states is influenced by the state's political culture and history of independent party movements being supported by voters. For example, the state of Minnesota has had a tradition of third-party candidates being elected. Jesse Ventura, who was elected as governor of Minnesota in 1998, is a member of the state's Reform Party, which has traditionally been a significant force in Minnesota politics.

The Republican Party grew out of the Whigs in the 1850s and was seen as the antislavery party. In the presidential election of 1860, the Republican Party's candidate was Abraham Lincoln. In the early twentieth century, the Republican Party adopted a conservative ideology, promoting individualism and the protection of private property rights. It favored small government and deregulation of the marketplace. The early part of the twentieth century was dominated by Republican administrations in the White House. Woodrow Wilson was the only Democratic president during the first three decades of the twentieth century.

After the stock market crash of 1929 and the resulting Great Depression, the Republican Party and the Republican president, Calvin Coolidge (succeeded by Herbert Hoover in 1929), were reluctant to use federal power to relieve the growing effects of the Depression; the party was voted out of the White House in 1932. Democrat Franklin D. Roosevelt held office until his death in 1945. The Republicans did not regain the White House until General Dwight D. Eisenhower was elected in 1952. The 1960s were dominated by Democratic presidents until Richard M. Nixon was elected to the presidency in 1968.

The Democratic Party emerged as a viable national party in the elections of 1824 and 1828. They were originally affiliated with Thomas Jefferson's Democratic Republicans. Since the 1960s, the Democratic Party has had a liberal national policy agenda that has stressed government spending to solve social and economic problems. Democrats have also been advocates of reproductive freedom for women. Democrats have been more inclined to favor and extend civil rights to women and minorities in American political, economic, and social life since the 1960s. The Democratic Party prefers to view itself as the party of working class Americans and the party has had a strong connection to labor unions in the United States.

In the 1990s, the Republican Party has been identified with conservatism. Republicans believe in reduced government activity in the economy, a strong sense of personal morality, and principles of "family values" as the basis for sound communities. The party is heavily influenced by Christian and religious conservatives, who have tried to move the party away from moderate positions toward the far right of the political spectrum. During the Reagan administration (1981–1989), the Republican Party led the fight for deregulation of the private economy; this had positive effects in some major industries, particularly transportation, but has also been blamed by liberals for increasing the poverty of some populations such as women and children. The party expanded its voter base during the Reagan administration by appealing to blue-collar and middle-class voters affected by economic inflation. During Reagan's two terms in office, these so-called Reagan Democrats switched over to the Republican Party. In 1992, many of them returned to the fold, helping elect Democrat Bill Clinton to the White House and reelecting Clinton in 1996.

See also: Key Concepts: Political Culture; Political Parties

References: Edward S. Greenberg and Benjamin I. Page, *The Struggle for Democracy* (1993); Edward Sidlow and Beth Henschen, *America at Odds* (1998).

Typologies

In studying public policy, scholars attempt to create models that illustrate how policy works and what factors and forces affected the successful implementation of policy. A useful device is typology. Typologies are ways to organize information into separate, related categories for systematic analysis. For example, the Greek philosopher Aristotle created a typology of political systems centuries ago that explained his perception of the characteristics of political systems in accordance with the different types of systems. Aristotle's typology still has utility, although our approach to understanding the intricacies and realities of political systems in the late 20th century is more sophisticated and accounts for the complexities of political behavior and political culture. Political scientist

Lewis Froman offered his examples of the essential qualities that a sound typology should have: inclusiveness (are all possibilities considered?); mutual exclusivity (are the categories distinct?); validity (are there accurate measures in the stated concepts?); reliability (can the typology be used effectively in other settings and for other examples?); operationalization (can the concepts in the typology be measured?); and differentiation (are the concepts in the typology important and significant for development of theory?).

A typology works best if it has a combination of these qualities, but it still is only a mechanism for generating theory and discussion. Policy studies place issues into an abstract dimension for purposes of analysis and discovery. The creation of typologies of public policy facilitates the understanding of how the policy process works and can predict what will happen upon formulation and implementation.

See also: Key Concepts: Policy Analysis

References: Lewis Froman, "The Categorization of Policy Contents," in *Political Science and Public Policy,* ed. Austin Ranney (1968); James P. Lester and Joseph Stewart Jr., *Public Policy: An Evolutionary Approach* (1996).

Vertical Federalism

Throughout the development of the federal system in the United States, the federal government has grown, taking on changing roles and responsibilities in relation to states (intergovernmental relations). Vertical federalism represents the interaction of the three levels of government in the U.S. system, that is, national, state, and local. During the early years of the American republic, the federal system reflected vertical intergovernmental relations, with limited interaction between the three levels, the federal and state levels with their own areas of authority and responsibility as evolving local governments formed governing structures. As the nation developed and expanded, the roles of the states and national government expanded with it. The national government in Washington took on increasing responsibilities, creating policies that supported national development and increased the national government's role in the affairs of the states. During the 19th century, the system and nature of intergovernmental relations changed as industrialization and economic growth characterized progress in American society. When the nation faced economic crisis during the 1930s, the role of the national government grew into a cooperative one with states to help them manage the consequences of the Great Depression.

The idea and era of vertical federalism ended with the New Deal. The states began to play a greater role in national affairs, thus ending the top-down policy role played by the federal government. With the development of New Deal policies in the Roosevelt administration, the era of cooperative federalism emerged and the relationship between the states and the national government moved into another phase that emphasized a partnership and sharing of policy authority and implementation.

See also: Key Concepts: Federalism

References: James E. Anderson, *Public Policymaking* (1997); James P. Lester and Joseph Stewart Jr., *Public Policy: An Evolutionary Approach* (1996).

Agriculture

Chronology

1862 Morrill Land Grant Act passed, setting aside land for states to develop land grant colleges and universities.

1862 Pres. Abraham Lincoln signed a law creating the U.S. Department of Agriculture.

1887 Hatch Act passed, encouraging state legislatures to establish an Agricultural Experiment Station in their land grant colleges.

1913 Federal Reserve Act passed, creating the Federal Reserve Bank to help farmers.

1914 Smith-Lever Act passed; it sponsored the development of county farm bureaus and created the American Farm Bureau Federation and a nationwide agricultural extension service.

1916 Federal Farm Loan Act passed; it created public credit institutions for providing farmers with long-term and short-term loans.

1917 National Milk Producers Association formed; it is one of the oldest commodity programs and represents milk producers.

1929 Agricultural Marketing Act passed; it established the Federal Farm Board, the federal government's first step toward subsidizing commercial agriculture.

1933 Agricultural Adjustment Act (AAA) passed, creating a price-support system for farmers.

1936 Soil Conservation and Domestic Allotment Act passed to find a way to give financial assistance to farmers after the AAA was declared unconstitutional. Soil conservation was important but secondary to getting financial assistance to farmers.

1938 Second Agricultural Adjustment Act passed.

1949 Farm Act imposed severe production cutbacks on agricultural production and required the USDA to boost price supports for major crops by 50 percent or more, resulting in a serious setback for export of American crops.

1954 Public Law 480 passed to promote and increase foreign demand for U.S. agricultural commodities. This was also called the Food for Peace Program.

1956 Agricultural Act established an acreage reserve and a conservation reserve for farm lands for the purpose of reducing the supply of farm products by limiting availability of U.S. farm land for production.

1967 Food Stamp Program went into effect encouraging increased domestic food consumption.

1973 Agriculture and Consumer Protection Act passed establishing direct payment subsidy programs in wheat, corn, rice, cotton, and barley.

1985 Food Security Act provided agricultural price supports for five crop years through target prices, loan rates, and deficiency payments. The act also authorized the Secretary of Agriculture to require reductions in acreages planted for farmers to participate in the price support program.

1985 Export Enhancement Program instituted an export subsidy program that allowed U.S. exporters to compete with the European Community in specifically targeted markets.

1987 Agricultural Credit Act passed reorganizing the Farm Credit System and provided up to $4 billion in assistance to the Farm Credit System through the sale of 15-year bonds guaranteed by the U.S. Treasury.

1990 Farm Bill passed to offer more price supports to farmers.

1996 Freedom to Farm Act passed to provide more extensive crop insurance coverage, planting flexibility, and flexibility to supplement insurance from private providers.

Agribusiness

Agribusiness includes commercial activities related to the food industry: fuel for farming, feed, fertilizer, financing food production, transporting food products, processing of food, and the sale of food and food products. Examples of agribusiness industries include meatpacking plants, egg producers, makers of agricultural chemicals, and producers and packagers of convenience foods. The major change in agriculture during the 20th century United States was the shift from family-owned operations to large, nonfamily farms and resulting massive industrialization. Corporate farms are managed by a hired employee. In 1997 slightly more than 3.4 percent of all U.S. farms were corporate farms, controlling approximately 25 percent of total land farmed. Family corporations held 90 percent of the land in corporate farms in 1997. Since 1940 the trend is toward increasing the size of farms and greater concentration of production. Farms have commercialized in order to compete in a changing agricultural economy.

See also: Agriculture: Agricultural Policy

References: Charles C. Geisler and Frank J. Popper, *Land Reform, American Style* (1984); Don Paarlberg, *Farm and Food Policy: Issues of the 1980s* (1980).

Agricultural Adjustment Act of 1933

The Agricultural Adjustment Act (AAA), passed by Congress on May 12, 1933, as part of Pres. Franklin D. Roosevelt's New Deal, established the Agricultural Adjustment Administration to restore the purchasing power of farmers to parity with the years 1909–1914. The plan also encouraged farmers to reduce acreage of crops in return for benefit payments supported by a processing tax levied on processors of farm products. Federal land banks were sources of refinancing for farm mortgages. The principal goal of the AAA was to reduce the farm surplus and to provide price supports for farmers, working principally to the advantage of large farmers. During the 1930s, the people who farmed the land were not the landowners but renters, or tenant farmers. The benefits went to the landowner, to be distributed fairly to tenants according to their interest in the land. This encouraged fraud and deception on the part of landowners as southern black tenants and black landowners were excluded from the benefit programs. This legislation was also designed to encourage soil conservation practices.

In 1936 the Supreme Court decided in *United States v. Butler* that the Agricultural Adjustment Act of 1933 was unconstitutional because the processing tax was not a proper use of the taxing power and because regulation of agriculture was the function of the states.

See also: Agriculture: Agricultural Policy

References: Charles C. Geisler and Frank J. Popper, *Land Reform, American Style* (1984).

Agricultural Adjustment Act of 1938

The Agricultural Adjustment Act (AAA) of 1938 was the second attempt to lend support to farmers through the New Deal programs. The act authorized the Secretary of Agriculture to set marketing quotas for export crops on the condition that two-thirds of the farmers in a given area approved the quotas. This act was similar to the 1933 AAA except that the benefit payments to farmers for surplus crops were to be paid out of the federal treasury rather than through a processing tax. The act also created the Federal Crop Insurance Corporation to insure crops. This was a major benefit, as crop insurance protected farmers in the case of lost crops due to weather, pests, or other disasters. The goal of reducing the surplus was not satisfied by this New Deal program, but prices did rise. The language in this legislation still stands as the basic price-support provisions for American farmers.

See also: Agriculture: Agricultural Policy

References: Charles C. Geisler and Frank J. Popper, *Land Reform, American Style* (1984); Judith I. de Neufville, ed., *The Land Use Policy Debate in the United States* (1981).

Agricultural Credits Act of 1923

The Agricultural Credits Act established 12 intermediate credit banks for farm loans. This act was a congressional response to counter declining farm revenues, prices, and land values. Most agricultural policy efforts at this time were caused by urban growth and the increasing use of farmlands for recreational and transportation purposes. Urban use of what was quickly coming to be seen as surplus land was deemed more valuable than agricultural use. The farm crisis deepened during the early 1920s, and Congress attempted, through public policy, to control overproduction, as the market was overstocked and overdeveloped.

See also: Agriculture: Agricultural Policy

References: Charles C. Geisler and Frank J. Popper, *Land Reform, American Style* (1984); Judith I. de Neufville, ed., *The Land Use Policy Debate in the United States* (1981).

Agricultural Marketing Act of 1929

In response to Pres. Herbert Hoover's call for farm relief, Congress passed the Agricultural Marketing Act, establishing the Federal Farm Board, its goal to stimulate marketing of farm products via loans to farm cooperatives. A serious problem during the late 1920s was declining prices for farm commodities, especially after the stock market crash of 1929. The Federal Farm Board was authorized to establish stabilization corporations to buy surplus crops. These corporations were created in cotton, wheat, and other areas to control crop prices. Despite government efforts to ease the plight of farmers during the onset of the Great Depression, farmers' economic power lagged behind that of the rest of the country.

See also: Agriculture: Agricultural Policy

References: Charles C. Geisler and Frank J. Popper, *Land Reform, American Style* (1984); Judith I. de Neufville, ed., *The Land Use Policy Debate in the United States* (1981).

Agricultural Policy

The history of U.S. agricultural policy is one of change, seen in approaches to farming, research and education, commodity programs, and the emergence of issues raised by nonfarmers. The first agricultural policy initiatives were in development, research, and education. Policy goals were tied to maintaining a prosperous, productive farm sector with the family farm at the center. Farm policy shifted remarkably over time. The first failures were a consequence of overproduction, increasing complexity, and specialization. During the Great Depression, farm policy initiatives swung toward reducing production and stabilizing price structures. A series of congressional acts set into motion legislation to offset decreasing prices: the Smith-Lever Act (1914), the Federal Farm Loan Act (1916), the Cooperative Marketing Act (1923), and the Agricultural Credits Act (1923).

New Deal proposals limited output to increase prices and raise net incomes for farmers, encouraging farmers to reduce the acreage planted. Price supports were central to the New Deal programs, bolstering parity requirements that characterized commodity programs (which were developed in wheat, corn and other feed grains, cotton, rice, peanuts, tobacco, dairy products, wool, and sugar). The Agricultural Adjustment Acts of 1933 and 1938 were the primary laws that provided price supports and production controls on major American crops. (Today we call such programs "farm subsidy programs"). Yet legislation could not stem declines in family farms. In 1910, 35 percent of the American population lived on farms, compared to 3 percent in 1992. Farms in the 1990s average more than three times the acreage and use six times the mechanized power and machinery as they did in 1910.

Another factor, one with a significant impact on agriculture and agricultural policy, was the rise of the consumer movement during the 1970s. Consumer activists focused on the use of chemicals in agriculture and the presence of chemical residue on food, issues of food and nutrition, and more diligence in food and meat grading and inspection. Issues that continue to affect agricultural policy are food additives, chemical residue, and other agents that act as protective shields to meat and food.

The U.S. Department of Agriculture is the federal agency with authority to affect agriculture, food, and farmland. Congress created the Department of Agriculture in 1862 in a series of measures designed to stimulate the Civil War economy. The Morrill Land Grant Act was passed just two months later. The act granted each Union state 30,000 acres for each senator and representative in Congress to endow an agricultural and mechanical college. This act led to the establishment of 69 land-grant colleges and provided much-needed training and education in agriculture in states. As a result of the act, between 1870 and 1880 an area equal to the land mass of Great Britain came under cultivation.

The Department of Agriculture has played a significant role in gaining government support for American farmers. The leading political constituencies in agriculture are farmers, the chemical companies that serve agriculture, and people engaged in large-scale farming, the agribusiness interests. There are also the general farm organizations such as the American Farm Bureau Federation, National Council of Farmer Cooperatives, National Farmers Organization, National Farmers Union, and the National Grange. There are also commodity associations such as the National Milk Producers and the Soybean Council of America. Marketing and trade organizations such as the National Livestock Producers Association also have an interest in agricultural policy. During the early years of the New Deal, the American Farm Bureau sought intervention and assistance from the national government to sustain agriculture with government programs. The New Deal years brought together the interests of the Farm Bureau and the Department of Agriculture. Traditionally, these two groups rarely agreed on approaches to serving the interests of farmers.

Technology, science, increasing industrialization, the presence of chemical residue on food, food quality and nutrition, the power of agribusiness, and the proper balance of agricultural exports were the leading issues in agricultural policy during the 1990s. The Federal Agriculture Improvement Acts of 1996 ended the traditional structure of commodity programs. The bill is characterized as legislation that will bring a more market-oriented focus to U.S. agriculture. By this act, government support payments are divorced almost completely from planting decisions. Proponents of the bill project slightly higher income levels as a result. Major policy goals for agriculture in the 1990s have been to preserve family farms, promote parity in prices and farm income, and improve the bargaining power of agricultural producers in the food industry.

See also: Agriculture: Agribusiness; Agricultural Adjustment Act of 1933; Agricultural Adjustment Act of 1938; Agricultural Credits Act of 1923; Agricultural Marketing Act of 1929; Cooperative Marketing Act of 1923; Federal Farm Loan Act of 1916; Economics: New Deal

References: Don E. Albrecht and Steve H. Murdock, *The Sociology of U.S. Agriculture* (1990); Willard W. Cochrane and Mary E. Ryan, *American Farm Policy: 1948–1973* (1976); Gail J. Cramer and Clarence W. Jensen, *Agricultural Economics and Agribusiness* (1991); Charles C. Geisler and Frank J. Popper, *Land Reform, American Style* (1984); Judith I. de Neufville, ed., *The Land Use Policy Debate in the United States* (1981); Ross Talbot and Don F. Hadwiger, *The Policy Process in American Agriculture* (1968).

Bankhead-Jones Farm Tenant Act of 1937

During the Great Depression of the 1930s, small farmers, many of them tenant farmers, suffered most directly. (Tenant farmers lease land from landowners to cultivate.) One solution was to relocate farmers, many of whom were destitute, allowing them to "homestead" land as a means of training them to raise food for their own survival. Homesteaders did not own the land, rather working it at the pleasure of state directors of the federal Resettlement Administration, which grew out of the National Industrial Recovery Act of 1933. In 1937 Congress abolished the Resettlement Administration with the Bankhead-Jones Farm Tenant Act. The act provided for loans to assist tenants, sharecroppers, and farm laborers to become owner-operators. Other provisions of the act included the creation of a rural rehabilitation loan program; a program that set up plans for submarginal land retirement and development; and the establishment of the Farm Security Administration in the Department of Agriculture to administer new programs under Bankhead-Jones. As a part of the federal agricultural policy of the time, the new Farm Security Administration deferred to local autonomy and local practices.

Although the Bankhead-Jones Act was designed to consolidate various agriculture programs that directly aided poor and tenant farmers, black families and farmers were excluded from receiving benefits. This contributed to the displacement of southern black farmers by restricting access to capital to purchase equipment and machinery to cultivate land. By allowing local customs and practices to prevail, states and rural communities (particularly in the South) could continue to disregard federal goals of nondiscrimination in the implementation of agricultural policy.

See also: Agriculture: Agricultural Policy; Economics: National Industrial Recovery Act of 1933

References: Don E. Albrecht and Steven H. Murdock, *The Sociology of U.S. Agriculture* (1990); Charles C. Geisler and Frank J. Popper, *Land Reform, American Style* (1984).

California Veterans' Farm and Home Purchase Act of 1921

U.S. housing policy during the early 20th century focused on providing low cost rental housing. After World War I, populations shifted from rural to urban areas, and most states and cities were incapable of providing housing to accommodate new urban dwellers. Severe housing shortages created pressure for government action. The major problem in urban areas was the increasing number of evictions, especially in New York City. Tenants appealed to courts for legal assistance and engaged in rent strikes to bring public attention to their problem.

Thus, some postwar programs were created to enable veterans to purchase homes with government assistance. One such program was the California Veterans' Farm and Home Purchase Act of 1921. The American Legion put pressure on California legislators to provide low-interest, amortized loans to families of veterans. State action was necessary because private financial institutions were hesitant to relieve the housing crisis by increasing low-interest loans. It was not in their interest; they were afraid of tampering with the laws of supply and demand. Eventually private business groups, including chambers of commerce and building and real estate associations, came to rely on federal subsidies to encourage building of low-cost homes for working-class families. In 1931 Pres. Herbert Hoover's Conference on Home Building and Home Ownership cited 14 divisions of federal agencies that were engaged in housing-related research. In 1932 the first federal housing legislation was passed, creating federally supervised home loan banks to offer housing assistance. The Federal Home Loan Bank Act of 1932 contributed to the health of the national economy, demonstrating the viability of cooperative efforts with business interests; such indirect legislation was preferable to direct intervention. The California Veterans' Farm and Home Purchase Act of 1921 set the stage for federal and state legislation that would emerge from the New Deal programs in housing policy.

See also: Housing: Housing Policy

References: Gail Radford, *Modern Housing for America* (1996).

Chavez, Cesar Estrada (1927–1993)

The history of U.S. agricultural policy was directly influenced by Cesar Chavez. Agricultural policy is more than legislation about production, land use, commercial development, and marketing. Agricultural policy is also about harvesting crops, the people who harvest them, and the conditions under which they live and work. The U.S. agriculture industry has relied heavily on migrant and/or foreign workers as farm laborers during the 20th century. The man most responsible for exposing the plight of agriculture laborers is Cesar Chavez, who founded and led the first successful farm workers' union in U.S. history. Chavez was the president of the United Farm Workers of America, AFL-CIO.

Chavez was born near Yuma, Arizona, on land homesteaded by his grandfather during the 1880s. Chavez began life as a migrant farm worker when he was ten years old, as his father had lost the family land during the Depression. Chavez spent his teenage years migrating throughout the Southwest with his family, laboring in fields and vineyards. He left school after the eighth grade. He served in the U.S. Navy at the end of World War II. He began his training in labor organizing in 1952 with Fred Ross, who was an organizer for the Community Service Organization, which was a barrio-based (neighborhood-based) self-help group sponsored by Chicago community organizer Saul Alinsky. By the end of 1952 Cesar Chavez was a full-time organizer with Community Service Organization, organizing voter registration drives and battling racial and economic discrimination.

Chavez founded the National Farm Workers Association (NFWA) in 1962. NFWA engaged in its first major strike in 1965 in the Delano, California, area against grape growers. NFWA merged with the fledgling United Farm Workers of America (UFW) in 1966 and then affiliated itself with the AFL-CIO. Cesar Chavez came to be seen as the leader of farm workers in the United States. In 1991 he received the Aguila Azteca (Aztec Eagle), Mexico's highest award, presented to people of Mexican heritage who have made major contributions outside Mexico. He received the presidential Medal of Freedom in August 1994, the highest civilian honor in the United States. Pres. Bill Clinton presented the award posthumously.

See also: Agriculture: Agricultural Policy; Labor: American Federation of Labor–Congress of Industrial Organizations

References: Peter Skerry, *Mexican Americans: The Ambivalent Minority* (1993).

Cooperative Marketing Act of 1923

Also known as the Capper-Volstead Act, the Cooperative Marketing Act of 1923 exempted agricultural cooperatives from antitrust laws, which regulated trusts and monopolies in the U.S. economy. Farm cooperatives began forming in earnest during the 1920s. These marketing cooperatives were preceded in the late 19th century by so-called Grange cooperatives, but they lacked effective leadership and loyalty to the concept of the Grange cooperative. The most effective cooperatives were in the South, but they also suffered from poor business practices and internal dissension.

The notion of the staunch, individual farmer is part of American mythology. However, with overproduction and the decline of farm product prices during the 1920s, centralized producer cooperatives seemed to be the answer to controlling supply and improving the increasingly disadvantageous position of individual farmers. The Cooperative Marketing Act of 1923 was an early move toward promoting the formation of farm cooperatives during a time when farmers were reluctant and distrustful of government regulation and assistance in agriculture.

See also: Agriculture: Agricultural Marketing Act of 1929; Agricultural Policy

References: Don E. Albrecht and Steve H. Murdock, *The Sociology of U.S. Agriculture* (1990); Ross Talbot and Don F. Hadwiger, *The Policy Process in American Agriculture* (1968).

Farm Bill of 1996

The Farm Bill of 1996 (the Federal Agriculture Improvement and Reform Act), was created to divorce government support payments from planting decisions. The bill was also designed to increase agricultural income and to tie together previous legislation. This comprehensive farm legislation focused on agricultural market changes and introduced flexible contracts for farmers through 2002. It also relaxed the restrictions on farm practices in the areas of conservation of land, wetlands protection, and planting flexibility requirements. The bill provided marketing assistance loans through 2002 to producers of wheat, feed grains, cotton, rice, and oilseeds. The legislation also provided guaranteed price support programs for dairy farmers and guaranteed loans for peanut and sugar producers. The bill was seen as an important set of proposals in support of farmers and the agricultural industry.

See also: Agriculture: Agricultural Policy; Farm Subsidies

References: Charles Bonser, Eugene B. McGregor Jr., and Clinton V. Oster Jr., *Policy Choices and Public Action* (1996).

Farm Credit Act of 1933

The Farm Credit Act of 1933 authorized the Farm Credit Administration to extend credits to refinance farm mortgages. The act simplified credit activities for farmers in need of credit from the federal government. During the Great Depression, farmers faced ruin. The Roosevelt administration proposed the Agricultural Adjustment Act of 1933 to stabilize farm prices and raise incomes for American farmers. The Farm Credit Administration bought farm mortgages away from private banks and insurance companies, which stopped the rapid pace of farm foreclosures in the early 1930s. Price supports in the Agricultural Adjustment Act, the security offered by the Farm Credit Act, and the prospect of profits were important for getting American agricul-ture back on track after years of decline and federal disinterest.

See also: Agriculture: Agricultural Adjustment Act of 1933; Agricultural Adjustment Act of 1938; Agricultural Policy

References: Robert Goldston, *The Great Depression: The United States in the Thirties* (1968); Ross Talbot and Don F. Hadwiger, *The Policy Process in American Agriculture* (1968).

Farm Subsidies

Agricultural production and price stability are important aspects of government support for agriculture. Agricultural subsidies, or farm subsidies, usually come in the form of price support programs, developed during the mid-1930s. Their purpose is to keep agricultural prices high to increase farm income. One-half of total agricultural output receives significant support and protection: Wheat, cotton, corn, peanuts, rice, wool, sugar, tobacco, and dairy products are commodities in the Untied States that receive the most price support. Government protection in this form allows farmers to maintain production and receive steady, if not increasing, income.

Government also buys commodities as a way to protect against oversupply. Through Commodity Credit Corporation loans, farmers put crops up as collateral, with a complex set of agreements for repaying the loan or sale of the crop if necessary. The government also limits agricultural output, largely by restricting the amount of land used for production. Other options include deficiency payments, in which the government makes direct payments to farmers to make up for differences between market and support prices. Import restrictions on farm commodities keep domestic production levels and prices high.

In 1997 U.S. farmers received approximately 30 percent of income via subsidies.

See also: Agriculture: Agricultural Policy

References: Don E. Albrecht and Steve H. Murdock, *The Sociology of U.S. Agriculture* (1990); Charles Bonser, Eugene B. McGregor Jr., and Clinton V. Oster Jr., *Policy Choices and Public Action* (1996); Willard W. Cochrane and Mary E. Ryan, *American Farm Policy: 1948–1973* (1976); Don Paarlberg, *Farm and Food Policy: Issues of the 1980s* (1980).

Federal Agriculture Reform

See Agriculture: Agricultural Policy

Federal Farm Loan Act of 1916

In a growing nation that relied heavily on the development of agriculture, the late 19th century was a challenging and uncertain time. The nation's farmers were sorely in need of agricultural credits to support crop development and sales and to maintain livelihoods. Crop failures were common, and for many Americans agriculture was the sole source of family income. In 1916 Congress passed the Federal Farm Loan Act, creating mechanisms for the development of many of today's farm organizations. The act built a credit system that was unique in serving the needs of agriculture. It created 12 land banks in different regions of the country, which were authorized to make long-term real estate loans to farmers. Federal land banks are a major source of real estate credit to farmers. This act of Congress was important because it made it possible for farmers to obtain long-term loans through means other than commercial banks.

See also: Agriculture: Agricultural Policy

References: Don E. Albrecht and Steve H. Murdock, *The Sociology of U.S. Agriculture* (1990); Charles C. Geisler and Frank J. Popper, *Land Reform, American Style* (1984); Ross Talbot and Don F. Hadwiger, *The Policy Process in American Agriculture* (1968).

Frazier-Lemke Farm Bankruptcy Act of 1934

Farm bankruptcies and foreclosures plagued American agriculture during the 1930s. Congress passed the Frazier-Lemke Federal Farm Bankruptcy Act in 1934, providing a five-year moratorium on foreclosures, during which time a farmer could buy back a farm at a reappraised price. The act was declared unconstitutional in 1935 by the Supreme Court and was replaced by the second Frazier-Lemke Act (1935), which called for a three-year moratorium but only with a court order. This foreclosure moratorium legislation was an important development in support of American farmers during the New Deal era.

See also: Agriculture: Agricultural Policy

References: Don E. Albrecht and Steve H. Murdock, *The Sociology of U.S. Agriculture* (1990); Charles C. Geisler and Frank J. Popper, *Land Reform, American Style* (1984).

LaFollette, Robert M. (1855–1925)

Sen. Robert LaFollette was a leader in the Progressive movement during the late 19th century, becoming a major national political leader. Known as "Fighting Bob," LaFollette was a Republican who served as governor of Wisconsin from 1900 to 1906.

He was an advocate of farming interests in the Midwest and enjoyed the support of farmers, small businesses, professionals, and intellectuals who saw him as their champion against big business.

LaFollette was elected to the U.S. Senate in 1905 and he was seen as a progressive Republican. He pursued the Republican nomination for president in 1908 and 1912 but was unsuccessful. He founded the National Progressive Republican League in 1911. LaFollette favored isolationism over American involvement in World War I and joined Congress in voting against membership in the League of Nations.

See also: Key Concepts: Isolationism

References: David P. Thelen, *Robert LaFollette and the Insurgent Spirit* (1996).

McNary-Haugen Bill

After a 1921 recession that resulted in a decline in prices for farm products, American farmers began receiving government support. The McNary-Haugen bill was a farm relief bill that was introduced by two members of Congress who represented farming areas, Charles McNary of Oregon and Gilbert Haugen of Iowa. The goal was to support product prices by relieving the burden of farm surpluses, which drove prices down. The bill called for the federal government to purchase the annual surplus of corn, wheat, cotton, and other commodities at relatively high prices and to sell the commodities abroad. Farmers had an obligation to pay an equalization fee, which would make up for government losses in the buying and selling of surplus farm commodities. It failed to pass in Congress in 1924 and 1926; it finally passed in 1927, but Pres. Calvin Coolidge vetoed the legislation. Other farm bills did succeed in helping farmers with price supports later during the 1920s.

See also: Agriculture: Agricultural Marketing Act of 1929

References: Don E. Albrecht and Steve H. Murdock, *The Sociology of U.S. Agriculture* (1990); Ross Talbot and Don F. Hadwiger, *The Policy Process in American Agriculture* (1968).

Smith-Lever Act of 1914

The Smith-Lever Act of 1914 granted federal funds to the states for farm extension work. The program engaged the Department of Agriculture and state agricultural colleges in cooperative attempts to create agricultural experiment stations to develop new agricultural sciences, increase efficiency of agricultural production, and add to the total supply of food and fiber products. This legislation was a key aspect of the government's agricultural development policy, giving tremendous support to agricultural development in the states. The Morrill Land Grant Act had established the system of land grant colleges throughout the country, and the creation of the agricultural extension service was instrumental in laying the foundation for the current system of agricultural extension services available to farmers.

See also: Agriculture: Agricultural Policy

References: Don E. Albrecht and Steve H. Murdock, *The Sociology of U.S. Agriculture* (1990).

Civil Rights

Chronology

1787 Northwest Ordinance passed; it forbade slavery in new states between the Ohio and Mississippi Rivers.

1857 Supreme Court ruled in *Dred Scott v. Sanford* that African Americans, slave or free, were not citizens and had no rights; slavery could extend into the territories Congress had declared free.

1862 First Emancipation Proclamation was issued by Pres. Abraham Lincoln to end slavery in southern states.

1865 Thirteenth Amendment to the Constitution passed, prohibiting slavery.

1868 Fourteenth Amendment passed, providing citizenship to African American men; it also established the equal protection clause.

1870 Fifteenth Amendment passed, guaranteeing voting rights for African American men.

1896 The Supreme Court decided in *Plessy v. Ferguson* that the separate-but-equal doctrine of legal segregation was valid.

1920 The Nineteenth Amendment passed, granting women the right to vote.

1954 Supreme Court decided in *Brown v. Board of Education* to end the separate-but-equal doctrine as it applied to education facilities.

1964 Civil Rights Act of 1964 passed, prohibiting discrimination on the basis of race, color, sex, religion, and national origin.

1965 Voting Rights Act passed, prohibiting state and local measures designed to keep African Americans from voting.

1968 Civil Rights Act of 1968 passed, prohibiting discrimination in housing and employment.

1986 Supreme Court in *Meritor Savings Bank v. Vinson* found that sexual harassment was a form of job discrimination prohibited by the Civil Rights Act of 1964.

1990 Americans with Disabilities Act of 1990 passed, mandating that public facilities must be accessible to people with disabilities.

1991 Civil Rights Act of 1991 passed, outlawing the use of quotas in programs to eliminate discrimination on the basis of race and gender.

Affirmative Action

Generally speaking, affirmative action is an equal employment opportunity policy characterized by goals and timetables for hiring and promoting women and minorities. The concept grew out of public pressure on the federal government to correct previous discriminatory employment practices commonplace in federal, state, and local governments. The pressure came initially from pioneers in the civil rights movement. In March 1961 Pres. John F. Kennedy stated in Executive Order 10925 that affirmative action would be required to implement the policy of nondiscrimination employment by the federal government and its contractors.

The first targets were "artificial barriers" to employment of women and minorities. Training programs were created to bring in these previously denied groups. In the Civil Rights Act of 1964, the Equal Employment Opportunity Commission (EEOC) was created; equal employment opportunity became federal policy. Enforcement under the Equal Employment Opportunity Act of 1972 was given to the EEOC. The "goals and timetables" of affirmative action were contained in an executive order issued by Pres. Richard M. Nixon in 1969. The Civil Rights Act of 1964 created protected classes of groups that would receive preferential treatment in hiring and employment, such as veterans, the elderly, disabled Americans, and others perceived as disadvantaged.

Much has been made of the arguments for and against affirmative action. Some affirmative action programs did offer advantages to certain groups and individuals. The legislation created protected classes of people who would receive preferential treatment in hiring. The issue of preferential treatment has antagonized opponents of affirmative action because of the claim that the establishment of preferences is discriminatory. Affirmative action did not and has not eliminated racism and discrimination. Affirmative action has not leveled the playing field. Some women and minorities obtained jobs that otherwise would have been kept from them due to gender or race. The opponents of affirmative action claim that this policy is unfair, and there are examples of such unfairness. Yet proponents for continued affirmative action have a strong claim considering the impact of decades of traditional, ritual, official, and degrading policies and acts of discrimination in public and private employment against women and minorities. Public opinion polls during the early 1990s demonstrated a widespread decline of support for continuing affirmative action.

See also: Civil Rights: Civil Rights Acts; Civil Rights Policy

References: Clark E. Cochran, et al., *American Public Policy: An Introduction* (1996); David H. Rosenbloom, *Public Administration: Understanding Management, Politics, and Law in the Public Sector* (1998); Jay M. Shafritz and E. W. Russell, *Public Administration* (1997).

American Association of Retired Persons

U.S. public policy is heavily influenced by interest groups that have a stake in government. One of the most influential and powerful interest groups is the American Association of Retired Persons (AARP), founded in 1947 as an association for retired teachers. AARP found prosperity in selling life and health insurance to the elderly. With some 35 million members, AARP was not always active in influencing public policy. In 1970 Pres. Richard M. Nixon held the White House Conference on Aging, and AARP saw its interests at stake, and a dispute regarding control of the conference surfaced.

AARP is a leading advocate for its aging membership; well funded from the sale of insurance and other services (it also receives federal grants), it sponsors policy research and relies on many lobbyists and policy analysts. Their chief goal is to generate information about health and aging issues to share with legislators, legislative committees, and agencies during their deliberations. One of the most important policy areas is elderly health care. AARP has favored stronger national legislation that would benefit the low-income elderly, as well as catastrophic health insurance under Medicare.

See also: Health: Health Policy; Key Concepts: Policy Analysis

References: Theodore Litman and Leonard S. Robins, *Health Politics and Policy* (1997).

American Civil Liberties Union

Two founding principles of the American political system are: a majority of people, through democratically elected representatives, governs the country; and the power of the majority must be checked to safeguard individual rights. The American Civil Liberties Union (ACLU) works to secure civil liberties and individual rights. Founded in 1920, when individual rights of Americans were less secure, by Roger Baldwin, ACLU was the first public interest law firm of its kind. Its initial goal was to work through the law and courts to transform ideals contained in the

Bill of Rights into reality for Americans. ACLU takes on popular and unpopular causes. It has office affiliates in all 50 states and most major cities, totaling 300 U.S. chapters. Projects include AIDS and the rights of AIDS/HIV patients, arts censorship, capital punishment, children's rights, education reform, lesbian and gay rights, immigrants' rights, national security, privacy and technology, prisoners' rights, reproductive freedom, voting rights, women's rights, and workplace rights. ACLU employs more than 60 staff attorneys who work with 2,000 volunteer attorneys in managing 6,000 cases per year. ACLU is a nongovernmental organization that relies on annual dues, contributions from members, and grants to support its activities.

See also: Civil Rights: Civil Rights Policy

References: Kermit L. Hall, William M. Wiecek, and Paul Finkelman, *American Legal History: Cases and Materials* (1991).

Americans with Disabilities Act of 1990

The Americans with Disabilities Act of 1990 (ADA) is the most comprehensive U.S. law addressing the rights of disabled persons. Under its provisions, persons have a disability if they meet one or more of the following criteria: a physical or mental impairment that substantially limits one or more of the major life activities of such individuals; a record of such an impairment; or being regarded as having such an impairment. There are 43 million Americans with disabilities covered under ADA.

The workplace, education facilities, and other public and private places carry challenges for disabled people. ADA, as amended, prohibits discrimination against persons with disabilities in employment, transportation, and access to services in the public and private sectors. ADA also provides income support and rehabilitation opportunities.

The impetus for ADA was an umbrella organization, the National Council on Disability. Groups lobbied Congress and state legislatures to protect persons with disabilities. ADA received strong support in the U.S. Senate from Sen. John Kerrey and Sen. Robert Dole, both of whom live with disabilities, and from Sen. Edward Kennedy, who led the Democratic Party in supporting the bill. Groups such as United Cerebral Palsy, the National Head Injury Foundation, the National Easter Seal Society, and the Chicago Lung Association, led by the National Council on Disability, helped to carry through this important piece of legislation.

See also: Key Concepts: Interest Groups

References: Theodore Litman and Leonard S. Robins, *Health Politics and Policy* (1997).

Anthony, Susan B.

In 1869 Susan B. Anthony, a leader in the temperance movement and the women's suffrage movement, made her initial proposal for an amendment to the Constitution to provide equal political privileges to men and women. In 1878 an amendment was proposed to the Congress. It languished until 1919, when Congress passed the amendment and referred it to the states for ratification. The Nineteenth Amendment to the U.S. Constitution, giving women the right to vote (suffrage), was ratified in August 1920 thanks to suffrage leaders like Susan B. Anthony, Elizabeth Cady Stanton, Anna Howard Shaw, and Carrie Chapman Catt. Susan Anthony used popular demonstrations to illustrate the inequality of women in politics. Her tactics eventually helped to guarantee women the right to vote.

See also: Civil Rights: Nineteenth Amendment; Women's Movement

References: Susan Welch et al., *Understanding American Government* (1997).

Brown v. Board of Education

After years of arguing school desegregation cases before the nation's courts, Thurgood Marshall, the director of the legal division of the National Association for the Advancement of Colored People (NAACP), learned that the U.S. Supreme Court would hear the case of *Brown v. Board of Education of Topeka, Kansas.* The NAACP had fought for school desegregation since the 1930s, seeking an end to discriminatory admissions policies and practices in colleges, universities, and professional schools. The NAACP also attacked the separate-but-equal doctrine established in *Plessy v. Ferguson* in 1897, which set the groundwork for discrimination and Jim Crow laws for public facilities. The NAACP challenged the separate-but-equal policy as it applied to public education. In *Brown v. Board of Education,* the Supreme Court ruled that racial segregation in state public schools was unconstitutional. The Court decided that the separate-but-equal doctrine had no place in public education. Thurgood Marshall had demonstrated that discriminatory policies meant unequal opportunities for black students. The Court agreed, finding that black students were deprived of equal protection under the Fourteenth Amendment to the U.S. Constitution. Justice Earl Warren wrote that the separate-but-equal doctrine resulted in unequal educations and made black children feel inferior. The Supreme Court thereafter ruled that schools would be required to desegregate "with all deliberate speed."

Marshall had argued in a series of prior cases that there was no semblance of equal education for black students in elementary and high schools and in admissions to colleges, universities, and professional schools. *Brown v. Board of Education* was the culmination of years work. In 1954 seventeen states still required racially segregated schools; four other states permitted legal segregation. *Brown* provided the momentum for civil rights challenges yet to come throughout the 1950s and 1960s.

See also: Civil Rights: Civil Rights Policy; De Facto Segregation; De Jure Segregation

References: Lucius J. Barker and Mack H. Jones, *African Americans and the American Political System* (1994); Susan Welch et al., *Understanding American Government* (1997).

Civil Rights Act of 1991

Sensitive to the possibility that civil rights legislation might contain language supportive of quotas, the Civil Rights Act of 1991 (formally the Civil Rights and Women's Equity Act of 1991) consists of amendments to Title VII of the Civil Rights Act of 1964 and other bills that prohibit discrimination. This legislation states that quotas are not required, encouraged, or permitted in protecting against acts of discrimination by employers. The act has three major provisions: (1) The presence of statistical imbalances in an employer's workforce would not, by itself, serve as evidence to prove discrimination, but statistical imbalances in employment might indicate evidence that a "disparate impact" was felt by women or minorities; (2) employers are required to show proof that statistical imbalances in the workforce that result in the possibility of "a disparate impact" might be necessary and are related to job performance; (3) victims of discrimination can receive both compensating money awards (in the form of back pay and attorney's fees) and punitive money awards that have no limit for racial discrimination and a limit of $150,000 for sex discrimination.

The Supreme Court, in *Adarand Constructors, Inc. v. Peña* (1995), held that an affirmative action program could not make use of quotas or preferences for unqualified persons. Specific remedies designed to correct past racial discrimination in narrow areas were constitutional but would receive strict judicial scrutiny. In 1996, in *Hopwood v. State of Texas,* the Supreme Court let stand a federal appellate court decision that the use of race as a means of achieving diversity on college campuses undercuts the Fourteenth Amendment. The Civil Rights Act of 1991 worked toward the goal of assuring a "colorblind" society by not requiring business firms and other institutions to use race and ethnic differences in hiring and promotion decisions.

See also: Civil Rights: Civil Rights Policy

References: Thomas R. Dye, *Understanding Public Policy* (1995); Steffen W. Schmidt, Mack C. Shelley II, and Barbara A. Bardes, *American Government and Politics Today* (1997).

Civil Rights Acts

Civil rights are fundamental, protected by government from the unlawful actions of others (including government itself). Social, legal, political, and economic forces give rise to discrimination against a particular class or group. In the U.S. political system, discrimination takes form in segregation (whether de facto or de jure), that is, artificial barriers between individuals or groups. De facto segregation is imposed by informal social, economic, and political practices. Denying opportunities to individuals because of their age, appearance, and gender are examples of de facto segregation. De jure segregation occurs through the force of law. Jim Crow laws, enacted in the South at the end of the 19th century, prohibited black citizens from owning property, voting, or using public facilities, such as restaurants and restrooms; these are examples of de jure segregation. The civil rights acts were intended to correct the injustices caused by segregation.

The first civil rights act was passed by Congress on March 16, 1866, and granted citizenship to former slaves. Pres. Andrew Johnson vetoed the act, declaring it an invasion of states' rights. Congress overrode the president's veto.

The Civil Rights Act of 1964 was directed at removing vestiges of discrimination and segregation that remained throughout American society, particularly in the South. The act had five main elements: it expedited lawsuits over voting rights; it barred discrimination in public accommodations; it authorized the U.S. attorney general to institute suits to desegregate schools; it barred discrimination in any program receiving federal assistance; and it set up the Equal Employment Opportunity Commission and established the right to equality of opportunity in employment. The two most important provisions, voting rights and discrimination in public accommodations, were serious problems for African Americans, primarily in the South. Civil rights activists traveled to the South to challenge state public accommodation laws and to register African American voters, who had been barred from voting by state law. These were dangerous, volatile times, but through concerted action and strong leadership the activists prevailed.

The Civil Rights Act of 1964 is one of the most important pieces of legislation of the 20th century because it speaks directly to discrimination in the workplace. Racial discrimination happened throughout the United States, not just in the South. The extent of racial discrimination in railroads, the steel industry, heavy manufacturing, and other industries was debilitating to African American workers. The Civil Rights Act of 1964 offered hope for correcting past wrongs. The act did not bring about immediate changes, but it set in motion mechanisms (e.g., affirmative action policies in state and federal employment) that would work against future discrimination.

Title VII of the Civil Rights Act of 1964 contains a key provision on equal opportunity. It was unlawful for employers to refuse, fail to hire, discharge, or otherwise discriminate against a person because of race, creed, or religion; it is also unlawful to limit, segregate, or classify employees or applicants for employment in any way to deprive them of employment opportunities. Preferential treatment or the use of quotas is forbidden. Supreme Court cases have bolstered the provisions of Title VII: *Griggs v. Duke Power Co.* (1975) establishes that job requirements needed to be tied to successful job performance and that job requirements should not have a disparate racial impact; *United Steelworkers of America v. Weber* (1979) determines that racial preferences are allowed by the Civil Rights Act because the purpose of the act was to breakdown barriers to black employment, barriers that for decades favored white employees to the disadvantage of blacks; and *Johnson v. Transportation Agency, Santa Clara County* (1987) makes clear that Title VII covers group entitlement provisions, meaning that managers, when making promotion decisions, are permitted to consider whether an employee is a minority, a woman, or a disabled person.

The Civil Rights Act of 1968 focuses on discrimination in housing. It forbids discrimination in most housing and imposes penalties on individuals or groups who attempt to interfere with individual civil rights. The 1968 act also strengthens government enforcement procedures in fair housing and discriminatory mortgage lending practices.

See also: Civil Rights: Affirmative Action; Civil Rights Movement; Civil Rights Policy; King, Martin Luther, Jr.

References: Clarke E. Cochran et al., *American Public Policy: An Introduction* (1996); David Edwards and Alessandra Lippucci, *Practicing American Politics: An Introduction to American Government* (1998).

Civil Rights Movement

The civil rights movement was initially directed at improving the plight of African Americans during the 1950s. Although the nation was founded as a democracy emboldened with the ideals of freedom, justice, and equality for all citizens, African Americans, Native Americans, Asians, and other ethnic minorities did not benefit equally. After slaves were freed by the first Emancipation Proclamation (1862, applying in areas under Union control, which meant that no slaves were actually freed), Pres. Abraham Lincoln encouraged Congress to pass the Thirteenth Amendment to the U.S. Constitution on December 18, 1865, which prohibits slavery in the United States. Subsequent amendments to the Constitution made former slaves citizens and guaranteed due process of law (Fourteenth Amendment) and the right to vote. These laws were momentous and laid the groundwork for including former slaves and their descendants into American political, economic, and social systems. However, hopes were dashed with the creation of Jim Crow laws in the South; acts of de facto and de jure segregation were prevalent by the end of the 19th century.

In 1896 the Supreme Court, in *Plessy v. Ferguson,* set back equality for African American citizens. In *Plessy,* the Supreme Court upheld the separate-but-equal doctrine under the Fourteenth Amendment. Homer Plessy, an African American resident of Louisiana, challenged a local ordinance that required African Americans to sit in separate railcars. The decision to uphold such segregation in this case allowed acts of racial discrimination and segregation to continue for decades. But a passionate protest movement began in the 1940s after World War II, reaching its zenith during the 1950s and 1960s.

The U.S. civil rights movement had its origins in legal battles fought by Thurgood Marshall, chief legal counsel for the National Association for the Advancement of Colored People (NAACP). He had been a victim of racial discrimination while seeking admission to the University of Maryland Law School. Marshall studied under the tutelage of Charles Hamilton Houston, professor of law at Howard University. Houston encouraged Thurgood Marshall to attack racial segregation by way of targeting the separate-but-equal doctrine of *Plessy.* Marshall and the NAACP argued a series of cases throughout the South and Midwest, challenging admissions policies to colleges and professional schools that denied admission or maintained separate facilities for minorities. Marshall and his associate attorneys also challenged the separate-but-equal doctrine as it applied to high school facilities. In 1954 Marshall argued the case of *Brown v. Board of Education* before the Supreme Court. The Court ruled unanimously that segregation in Topeka's elementary schools violated the Fourteenth Amendment, ending the separate-but-equal doctrine. The decision set into motion school integration "with all deliberate speed."

In December 1955 Rosa Parks, a 43-year-old African American resident of Montgomery, Alabama, challenged a local ordinance that required her to move to the "colored section" of public buses when buses became crowded. She refused to move, was arrested, and was fined $10. Her refusal to honor the local segregation code was the beginning of a year-long boycott and protest led by Dr. Martin Luther King Jr., a 27-year-old Baptist minister. In 1956 the federal district court issued an injunction prohibiting segregation on buses in Montgomery. This marked the beginning of an era of civil rights protests throughout the United States.

Dr. King led nonviolent protests. Much of the activity was directed at desegregation of public facilities; tactics included sit-ins, freedom rides, and freedom marches. In August 1963 approximately 250,000 African Americans and sympathetic white Americans attended the Freedom March on Washington. Dr. King made his famous "I Have A Dream" speech, calling for racial unity, harmony, and an end to racial discrimination and segregation. These efforts led to the passage of the Civil Rights Act of 1964, which forbids discrimination on the basis of race, color, religion, gender, and national origin. Before his assassination, Pres. John F. Kennedy had set the tone for Congress as to civil rights legislation. After Kennedy's death in November 1963, Pres. Lyndon B. Johnson continued the drive for civil rights legislation. It did not come easy; the 1964 act was passed in Congress only after overcoming the longest filibuster in Senate history (83 days) and only after cloture was imposed for the first time in Congress.

Activists in the civil rights movement demonstrated bravery, courage, and extraordinary commitment to the ideals of American democracy in the face of life-threatening danger and personal challenges. Many activists traveled to the South on freedom rides to protest laws that protected segregated facilities. Others participated in voter registration activities in Mississippi, a violent place for voting rights activists. Many organizers and activists were college students (black and white) armed only with a passionate commitment to end racial discrimination. After the assassination of Dr. Martin Luther King Jr. in spring 1968, some used more militant means to correct racial injustice. The Black Panther Party and the Nation of Islam called for "black power" to wrest freedom and justice from the American political system. The Nation of Islam (the Black Muslims) called for separation of races and the establishment of self-help strategies for African Americans. The Nation of Islam was led by Elijah Muhammad and Malcolm X. Malcolm X believed in policies of self-determination and that African Americans should fight injustice by "any means necessary." Malcolm X was assassinated in 1965 allegedly by followers of Elijah Muhammad, who saw Malcolm X as a rival in the Nation of Islam. The Black Panther Party frequently engaged in violent altercations with urban police departments as a way of challenging the justice system.

After 1968 the civil rights movement became more inclusive of the rights of women, Mexican Americans, Native Americans, and gays and lesbians. The popular "melting pot" characterization of America was found lacking (some recent observers use a "salad bowl" metaphor to more accurately describe racial identity and inclusion in the America of the 1990s). The goals of the civil rights movement focused originally on racial equality and the end of racial discrimination. Discrimination still occurs, but the widespread, state-supported forms of segregation and discrimination are things of the past. Yet initiatives to preserve the rights of all Americans will be a focus of public policy during the 21st century.

See also: Civil Rights: Affirmative Action; Civil Rights Acts; King, Martin Luther, Jr.

References: Lucius J. Barker and Mack H. Jones, *African Americans and the American Political System* (1994); Stokeley Carmichael and Charles V. Hamilton, *Black Power: The Politics of Liberation in America* (1967); John Hope Franklin and Isidore Starr, eds., *The Negro in 20th Century America* (1967); Paul C. Light, *A Delicate Balance: An Essential Introduction to American Government* (1997); John T. McCartney, *Black Power Ideologies* (1992); Steffen W. Schmidt, Mack C. Shelley II, and Barbara A. Bardes, *American Government and Politics Today* (1997).

Civil Rights Policy

U.S. civil rights policy comprises legislative acts as well as decisions by the U.S. Supreme Court directed at protecting fundamental rights of citizens and groups from the unlawful actions of others, including the government itself. The major legislative acts include the series of civil rights acts (1866, 1964, 1968, and 1991); Supreme Court decisions run the gamut from *Dred Scott v. Sanford* (1857) to *Plessy v. Ferguson* (1896) to *Brown v. Board of Education of Topeka* (1954). Other government actions, such as the 1948 executive order of Pres. Harry Truman prohibiting segregation in the U.S. Armed Forces and discrimination in federal employment, had a major impact.

Charles Hamilton Houston and Thurgood Marshall, prominent civil rights attorneys, led the drive. Through efforts such as theirs, school segregation under the separate-but-equal doctrine was rolled back through the courts. Dr. Martin Luther King Jr. personally challenged the U.S. government to enact laws barring discrimination and racial segregation. King led a quarter-million people during the Freedom March on Washington in August 1963. He had organized the Montgomery, Alabama, bus boycott to protest racial segregation. Dr. King, a minister in Montgomery, encouraged Montgomery's black citizens to violate a city law that required them to sit in the backs of buses. In 1955 Rosa Parks, a black seamstress from Montgomery, boarded a bus from work. The bus was full, and when a white man boarded, the driver told four black people sitting behind the white passengers to move to the back. Rosa Parks refused to move, declaring she was sitting in "no-man's-land" (the term for the section of seats behind the rows designated for whites; if the bus was not full, then black passengers could sit in this section, but if filled, then the black passengers were required to move to the back, standing if necessary). Rosa Parks was exhausted after a full day's work and chose to defy the driver's order. The driver was authorized to enforce the law, and Parks was arrested. Dr. King organized and led the successful boycott of the Montgomery bus system. The bus line was losing money because of the boycott, and the city demanded that the boycott leaders either settle their dispute and abide by the law or face arrest. The leaders of the boycott surrendered to police, and more than 100 were arrested.

This event drew national attention, and a year later the U.S. Supreme Court struck down Alabama state and local laws requiring segregation on buses. The city of Montgomery eventually complied, and the boycott ended. Such nonviolent protests were instrumental in changing civil rights policy.

Later, Congress passed the Voting Rights Act of 1965, which abolished literacy and other tests used to keep African Americans from voting (primarily in the South). Congress expanded the Voting Rights Act in 1970, 1975, and 1982. In 1964, passage of the Twenty-Fourth Amendment abolished the poll tax for national elections, and in 1966 the Supreme Court ruled the poll tax illegal in all elections.

Civil rights include issues of gender discrimination. During the 19th century, many state laws restricted women from holding property and from voting. The women's suffrage movement that would emerge at the end of that century, led by Susan B. Anthony and Elizabeth Cady Stanton, among others, eventually conferred the full benefits of citizenship, including the right to vote (with the 1920 passage of the Nineteenth Amendment). During the 1960s there was a resurgence to promote the equality of women. Betty Friedan, a women's movement leader, counted on the emergence of the National Organization for Women (NOW) in 1966 as a vehicle for improving the conditions of women in politics, employment, and society at large. These efforts built upon the success and tactics of the labor movement of the 1930s and 1940s and the civil rights movement of the 1950s and 1960s.

The Civil Rights Act of 1964 forbids discrimination hiring, promoting, and firing on the basis of gender. The Equal Pay Act of 1963 requires that women and men receive equal pay for equal work. A continuing issue is sexual harassment in the workplace. Sexual harassment involves harassment of women (or men) by the commission of acts involving unwanted touching, propositions for sex in exchange for a job or promotion, and unwarranted and inappropriate comments or conduct of a sexual nature. The U.S. Supreme Court ruled in *Meritor Savings Bank v. Vinson* (1986) that sexual harassment was a form of job discrimination prohibited by the Civil Rights Act of 1964.

Civil rights policy has expanded since the activism of the 1950s and 1960s to include public policies that protect the rights of women, Mexican Americans, Native Americans, gays and lesbians, and disabled people. The equal rights movement crystallized in attempts by NOW and the National Women's Political Caucus (NWPC) to add an Equal Rights Amendment (ERA) to the U.S. Constitution to guarantee equal treatment for women and men; ERA ratification failed twice. Activism by groups such as NOW and NWPC has raised awareness of issues relating to women and their political and economic power; it has resulted in policies that help level the playing field for women in America.

See also: Civil Rights: Affirmative Action; Anthony, Susan B.; Civil Rights Acts; Equal Rights Amendment; King, Martin Luther, Jr.; *Meritor Savings Bank v. Vinson*

References: David Edwards and Alessandra Lippucci, *Practicing American Politics: An Introduction to American Government* (1998); John Hope Franklin and Isidore Starr, eds., *The Negro in 20th Century America* (1967); Ronald E. Pynn, *American Politics: Changing Expectations* (1993).

Confiscation Act of 1861

To create chaos in the South and among Confederate forces, Congress passed the Confiscation Act of 1861, which freed all slaves working or fighting for the Confederates. The act also provided for the seizure of all property used for "insurrectionary purposes" (i.e., that was used to assist the Southern rebellion). Later that year, Congress passed a more radical confiscation act, promising to punish treason by Southerners, confiscate property, and emancipate slaves. Pres. Abraham Lincoln was reluctant to sign the bill and considered a veto, but Congress wrote a statement of explanation of its intent, and the president eventually signed the bill (even though he disagreed with the broad language of forfeiture of property "without personal or criminal hearing"). The act had limited effect, and widespread confiscation never took place. The 1861 emancipation of slaves had little impact; Southern states did not abide by the act, and the emancipation provisions were unknown to many slaves.

See also: Civil Rights: Emancipation Proclamation

References: J. G. Randall and David Donald, *The Civil War and Reconstruction* (1961).

De Facto Segregation

De facto ("according to reality") segregation is private, personal discrimination directed at individuals or groups. It occurs as a result of individual decisions to deny rights. Such discrimination is debilitating, degrading, and humiliating. Private discrimination in renting housing and hiring workers because of their race, gender, or physical disability are examples of de facto discrimination. De facto segregation was found throughout the United States after the Civil War and into the 1970s and was not just a matter of tradition in the South.

See also: Civil Rights: Civil Rights Policy; De Jure Segregation

References: Lucius J. Barker and Mack H. Jones, *African Americans and the American Political System* (1994); John Hope Franklin and Isidore Starr, eds., *The Negro in 20th Century America* (1967).

De Jure Segregation

De jure segregation is based in law, whereas de facto segregation is based on private behavior. Any discrimination relegates minorities to second-class citizenship, but de jure segregation lent segregation the imprimatur of government. Jim Crow laws and other forms of de jure segregation were eliminated during the last half of the 20th century thanks to the efforts of civil rights leaders, the government, and courts.

See also: Civil Rights: *Brown v. Board of Education;* Civil Rights Policy; De Facto Segregation

References: Lucius J. Barker and Mack H. Jones, *African Americans and the American Political System* (1994); John Hope Franklin and Isidore Starr, eds., *The Negro in 20th Century America* (1967).

DuBois, W. E. B. (1868–1963)

At a time of racial discrimination and segregation, W. E. B. DuBois argued for equal treatment and dignity for all African Americans. He did not accept the notion that African Americans could not fit easily into American social and economic systems, whereas another contemporary, the influential African American Booker T. Washington, advocated that African Americans should focus on the trades and vocational education as the route to eventual, gradual acceptance by American society. DuBois countered that if African Americans were granted the same opportunities as the dominant population in America, then they could succeed and prosper.

DuBois was born in Great Barrington, Massachusetts, in 1868. His Puritan New England upbringing fostered education and hard work. DuBois excelled in high school and college. He graduated from Fisk University, a traditional black school in Tennessee, and went on to earn a Ph.D. from Harvard. DuBois was a part of the Niagara Movement, a coalition of African Americans and white intellectuals seeking racial harmony and the elimination of discrimination. DuBois was also one of the founders of the National Association for the Advancement of Colored People (NAACP) in 1909. DuBois wrote several books on African Americans. He lived his final years in Africa after losing hope that America would ever truly embrace an open and free society. He died in 1963.

See also: Civil Rights: Civil Rights Policy

References: W.E.B. DuBois, *The Souls of Black Folk: Essays and Sketches* (1961); W.E.B. DuBois, *The Autobiography of W.E.B. DuBois: A Soliloquy on Viewing My Life from the Last Decade of Its First Century* (1971).

Emancipation Proclamation

On January 1, 1863, Pres. Abraham Lincoln issued the Emancipation Proclamation, granting slaves in the Confederate states their freedom. The common misconception is that it was the ultimate antislavery message, meant to free all slaves. Yet Tennessee and the Union slave states (Delaware and Kentucky) were not included, for the proclamation applied only to "rebellious" states (thus, in the areas of Virginia and Louisiana under Union control, slavery continued). Lincoln saw the proclamation as a necessity of war, and it had no force of law. The emancipation of slaves through government authority came on December 18, 1865, when the Thirteenth Amendment to the Constitution was ratified.

See also: Civil Rights: Civil Rights Acts; Civil Rights Policy

References: Joseph R. Conlin, *The American Past: A Survey of American History* (1993); J. G. Randall and David Donald, *The Civil War and Reconstruction* (1961).

Equal Employment Opportunity Commission

The Equal Employment Opportunity Commission (EEOC) was established under Title VII of the Civil Rights Act of 1964. The five-member EEOC is responsible for enforcing federal statutes that prohibit employment discrimination. These statutes include: Title VII of the Civil Rights Act of 1964, which prohibits employment discrimination on the basis of race, color, religion, sex, or national origin; the Age Discrimination in Employment Act of 1967, which prohibits employment discrimination against individuals 40 years old or older; the Equal Pay Act of 1963, which prohibits discrimination on the basis of gender in compensation for substantially similar work under similar conditions; Title I of the Americans with Disabilities Act of 1990, which prohibits employment discrimination on the basis of disability in both the public and private sectors; and Section 501 of the Rehabilitation Act of 1973, which prohibits employment discrimination against federal employees with disabilities.

The basic mission of the EEOC is to administer EEOC policy and various judicial actions related to that policy and to educate and provide technical assistance to promote equal opportunity in employment. Activities include investigation, adjudication, settlement, and conciliation of charges; resolving claims using other forms of alternative dispute resolution; litigation; and provision of policy guidance and information about implementation of federal nondiscrimination policy.

The principles under which the EEOC operate serve as the foundation of affirmative action in U.S. hiring practices.

See also: Civil Rights: Affirmative Action; Americans with Disabilities Act of 1990; Civil Rights Acts; Labor: Equal Pay Act of 1963

References: Leif H. Carter and Christine B. Harrington, *Administrative Law and Politics: Cases and Comments* (1991); Thomas R. Dye, *The Irony of Democracy: An Uncommon Introduction to American Politics* (1996); Steffen W. Schmidt, Mack C. Shelley II, and Barbara A. Bardes, *American Government and Politics Today* (1997).

Equal Protection

The Fourteenth Amendment to the U.S. Constitution provides that no person shall be denied the equal protection of the laws. Equal protection is a pillar of any democratic system and, along with due process, provides the basis for preserving the civil rights and liberties for all citizens.

See also: Civil Rights: Fourteenth Amendment

References: Kermit L. Hall, William M. Wiecek, and Paul Finkelman, *American Legal History* (1991); Alfred H. Kelly, Winfred A. Harbison, and Herman Belz, *The American Constitution: Its Origins and Development* (1983); Steffen W. Schmidt, Mack C. Shelley II, and Barbara A. Bardes, *American Government and Politics Today* (1997).

Equal Rights Amendment

On August 26, 1920, the Nineteenth Amendment to the Constitution was ratified, granting women's suffrage (full voting and political rights). This was a watershed event toward fully incorporating women into the political process. Yet many women, especially in the South and Southwest, could not exercise their right to vote. The Equal Rights Amendment (ERA), first considered by Congress in 1923, did not receive serious attention until the 1970s. It states: "Equality of rights under the law shall not be denied or abridged by the United States of any State on account of sex." The amendment was passed by Congress in 1972 and sent to the states for ratification. Every president since Harry Truman had endorsed the amendment, but state support was lacking. During the first year of the ratification process, 22 states passed the ERA; 38 were needed. Despite an extension of time, only 35 states ratified ERA; the amendment died by 1982.

Opponents feared it would prompt the drafting of women for military service. Another concern was that passage would rescind laws protecting women in the workplace. The National Organization for Women, able to organize widespread support for ERA during the 1970s, could not overcome the opposition and fear. Yet the failure of the ERA did not deter women's organizations from pursuing a women's rights agenda. Many shifted attention to expanding women's economic opportunities and rights and to protecting abortion rights.

See also: Civil Rights: Civil Rights Policy; Friedan, Betty; Women's Movement

References: Ronald E. Pynn, *American Politics: Changing Expectations* (1993); James Q. Wilson and John J. DiIulio Jr., *American Government: The Essentials* (1998).

Equality of Opportunity

See Civil Rights: Equal Employment Opportunity Commission

Fifteenth Amendment

The Fifteenth Amendment to the U.S. Constitution was one of several amendments passed soon after the Civil War. The Thirteenth Amendment prohibited slavery; the Fourteenth Amendment granted citizenship to blacks (overruling the 1857 *Dred Scott* Supreme Court decision and establishing equal protection); and the Fifteenth Amendment provided the right to vote to African American men: "The right of citizens to vote shall not be denied . . . by the United States or by any State on account of race, color, or previous condition of servitude."

Much of the opposition to African American suffrage during the late 1860s came from congressmen from Northern states, who felt that former slaves were unable to intelligently exercise voting rights. The issue of suffrage for former slaves and free African Americans initially focused on a bill before Congress that granted suffrage in the District of Columbia, one-third African American. Pres. Andrew Johnson originally vetoed the suffrage bill, declaring suffrage was not necessary for protecting African American rights. Congress overrode Johnson's veto, setting the stage for passage of the Fifteenth Amendment.

See also: Civil Rights: Civil Rights Policy

References: J. G. Randall and David Donald, *The Civil War and Reconstruction* (1961); Susan Welch et al., *Understanding American Government* (1997).

Fourteenth Amendment

Known as the equal protection amendment, the Fourteenth Amendment attempts to define American citizenship and the rights belonging to citizens of the United States. The important language of the first section of the amendment prohibits "a state from abridging the privileges and immunities of citizens of the United States, depriving any person of life, liberty, or property, without due process of law, or denying to any person the equal protection of the law." Thus, when it was ratified in 1868, it prohibited states from denying equal protection of the laws to millions of former slaves. The equal protection clause of the Fourteenth Amendment was a rallying point for the civil rights movement during the 1960s.

See also: Civil Rights: Civil Rights Policy

References: David Edwards and Alessandra Lippucci, *Practicing American Politics: An Introduction to American Government* (1998); J. G. Randall and David Donald, *The Civil War and Reconstruction* (1961).

Friedan, Betty (b. 1921)

Betty Friedan has been an important voice and influence in the women's movement. In 1966 she and several other women started the National Organization for Women (NOW) to push for the adoption of the Equal Rights Amendment (ERA). Friedan was the first president of NOW and advocated for women's rights in general. Friedan and others felt that the status of women was not improving if they did not aggressively seek to further the women's cause in employment, government, and discrimination. NOW membership has grown to some quarter-million. Since founding NOW, Friedan and other advocates for women's rights have pursued issues of gender discrimination, equal pay for equal work, sexual harassment, and expanded opportunities for women in management and leadership positions.

See also: Civil Rights: Equal Rights Amendment; Labor: Equal Pay Act of 1963

References: Barbara Sinclair Deckard, *The Women's Movement* (1979); Susan Welch et al., *Understanding American Government* (1997).

Gay and Lesbian Rights

During the late 1960s and early 1970s homosexuals aggressively asserted claims for equal rights and fair treatment. The watershed was the 1969 Stonewall incident, a confrontation between members of the New York City Police Department and gays at a predominantly gay bar, the Stonewall Inn. The Gay Activist Alliance and the Gay Liberation Front were formed to champion the rights and equal treatment of gays and lesbians.

The gay rights movement has helped create many organizations to further the cause and raise visibility of issues that affect gays and lesbians. As a result of organizing and campaigning, more than half the states with laws prohibiting sodomy have repealed them. Civil service laws banning the hiring of gays and lesbians have also been eliminated, and there are new laws prohibiting discrimination against gays and lesbians in government, banking, housing, and public accommodations. Cities across the country have also passed legislation to prohibit discrimination against gays and lesbians.

The emergence of gay rights and gay activism has been an important element of public policy. As a matter of public policy, the issue of gay rights moved toward the mainstream in American politics during the 1990s; tolerance toward all Americans is the major goal in this area of public policy.

See also: Civil Rights: Civil Rights Policy

References: Mark Blasius, *Gay and Lesbian Politics: Sexuality and the Emergence of a New Ethic* (1994); Steffen W. Schmidt, Mack C. Shelley II, and Barbara A. Bardes, *American Government and Politics Today* (1997); Edward Sidlow and Beth Henschen, *America at Odds* (1998).

Glass Ceiling

The term glass ceiling describes the invisible barrier facing women and people of color in the corporate world to reach positions of leadership. Women and minorities are often prevented, for whatever reason, from attaining positions of power and authority in organizations. The barriers are subtle, the reasons ambiguous.

See also: Civil Rights: Friedan, Betty; Women's Movement

References: Barbara Sinclair Deckard, *The Women's Movement* (1979); Steffen W. Schmidt, Mack C. Shelley II, and Barbara A. Bardes, *American Government and Politics Today* (1997).

Jackson, Jesse (b. 1941)

The Rev. Jesse Jackson is a leading figure in African American politics and has been a candidate for the presidency during the 1980s and 1990s. Jackson was an associate of Dr. Martin Luther King Jr.; he was with King at a motel in Memphis, Tennessee, in 1968 when King was assassinated. Jackson has emerged as the foremost champion of African American political rights during the 1970s, 1980s, and 1990s. He advocates an economic independence and development agenda for African Americans.

During the 1980s, Reverend Jackson created the Rainbow Coalition, which brings together women, gays and lesbians, and various ethnic and minority groups to advocate a political agenda more sensitive to the issues important to women, gays, and minorities. Although Jackson's presidential campaigns have not led to the White House, he remains a leading advocate on behalf of economically and politically disadvantaged people.

See also: Civil Rights: Civil Rights Policy; King, Martin Luther, Jr.

References: Michael Barone and Grant Ujifusa, eds., *Almanac of American Politics* (1995).

Jim Crow Laws

Although the constitutional amendments that followed the Civil War guaranteed citizenship and voting rights to African Americans, Southern states created new laws that restricted the rights of African Americans; these laws were not successfully challenged and abolished until the 1960s. So-called Jim Crow laws were designed to prevent equal treatment for blacks under law. They led to the separate-but-equal doctrine, an unfair system for facilities (in transportation, education, etc.) that was upheld by the U.S. Supreme Court at the end of the 19th century.

The first Jim Crow law was passed in Florida in 1877, and other states followed suit. Soon enough, Jim Crow laws restricted the movement, access, and education opportunities of African Americans. The Supreme Court reaffirmed the constitutionality of the separate-but-equal doctrine in the 1897 decision *Plessy v. Ferguson,* and it wasn't until the landmark 1954 decision in *Brown v. Board of Education* that the Supreme Court outlawed segregated education facilities. Slowly thereafter, Jim Crow laws were abolished.

See also: Civil Rights: Civil Rights Policy

References: Lucius J. Barker and Mack H. Jones, *African Americans and the American Political System* (1994); Paul C. Light, *A Delicate Balance: An Essential Introduction to American Government* (1997).

King, Martin Luther, Jr. (1929–1968)

Martin Luther King Jr. was the civil rights champion for African Americans and the poor during the 1950s and 1960s. King was a Baptist minister from Montgomery, Alabama, who led the first major challenge to Montgomery's Jim Crow laws with a boycott protesting segregation on city buses. His leadership earned him national and international prominence, and he would go on to lead demonstrations, marches, and protests. His was the foremost voice of reason and nonviolence during the civil rights movement.

King was awarded the Nobel Prize in 1964. His leadership led directly to the passage of the Civil Rights Act of 1964 and the Voting Rights Act of 1965. He was known for his eloquence, for his ability to move people through the power of speech. In August 1963 King led the Freedom March on Washington; more than 200,000 people joined King and other civil rights leaders in nonviolent demonstration at the Lincoln Memorial. Dr. King gave a stirring speech that invoked principles of civil disobedience, human rights, and equality for all Americans. King also wrote several books in which he argued the cause of civil rights for African Americans. In *Letter from a Birmingham Jail* King makes the case for direct nonviolent action against racial discrimination to a group of white ministers who criticized his aggressive stance against racism and injustice.

In 1968 King was preparing to lead the Poor People's March to Washington, D.C., to elevate the plight of the poor. He was assassinated in Memphis, Tennessee, by James E. Ray on April 4, 1968. King also spoke out against the war in Vietnam, which brought about intense government scrutiny of his life, including surveillance by the Federal Bureau of Investigation under its director, J. Edgar Hoover.

See also: Civil Rights: Civil Rights Policy

References: Lucius J. Barker and Mack H. Jones, *African Americans and the American Political System* (1994); Coretta Scott King, *My Life with Martin Luther King* (1969); C. Eric Lincoln, ed., *Martin Luther King Jr.: A Profile* (1970).

Meritor Savings Bank v. Vinson

One of the issues affecting social and economic progress for women is sexual harassment in any form. *Meritor Savings Bank v. Vinson* (1986) established the legal standard for a "hostile work environment," an important element for proving sexual harassment at the workplace. If successful in proving sexual harassment, women are entitled to seek damages in addition to back pay, job reinstatement, and other remedies.

See also: Civil Rights: Civil Rights Policy

References: Edward Sidlow and Beth Henschen, *America at Odds* (1998); Sheila Tobias, *Faces of Feminism: An Activist's Reflections on the Women's Movement* (1997).

Motor Voter Act of 1993

An essential component of political participation in a democracy is voting. Although the American system has few rules regarding eligibility to vote in elections, some citizens find it difficult to register to vote. The Motor Voter Act of 1993 (officially the National Voter Registration Act) requires states to provide all eligible citizens with the opportunity to register to vote when they apply for or renew a driver's license. States are also required to make mail-in registration available to eligible citizens by providing registration forms at certain public assistance agencies. Millions of people have registered to vote since the law went into effect on January 1, 1995.

The two major political parties disagreed on the need for such a bill. Traditionally, Republicans have not favored expanding opportunities for political participation and voter registration, as party leaders perceive that registration efforts typically target people favoring the Democratic Party and its candidates. Throughout the 20th century, Democratic leaders have encouraged widespread voter registration and political participation.

See also: Key Concepts: Political Behavior

References: Edward Sidlow and Beth Henschen, *America at Odds* (1998).

National Association for the Advancement of Colored People

The National Association for the Advancement of Colored People (NAACP) is an interest group founded in 1909 by W.E.B. DuBois and other advocates for equal treatment of African Americans. The founders were a racially integrated group known as the Niagara Movement; their purpose was to elevate the status of African Americans in the political and economic systems. Since its founding, the NAACP has been the primary group to further the causes and interests of African Americans.

During the 1930s and 1940s, the NAACP relied on its Legal Defense Fund to challenge segregation and discrimination. Thurgood Marshall, who would later be the first African American to sit as a justice on the U.S. Supreme Court, led the Legal Defense Fund in challenging laws that prohibited equal rights and equal treatment of African Americans. Marshall's foremost success was the 1954 U.S. Supreme Court case *Brown v. Board of Education,* which struck down the separate-but-equal doctrine as it applied to public education facilities.

Throughout the 1950s and 1960s the organization remained an important advocate for equal rights and justice. More recently it has focused on promoting economic equality for African Americans. Several leadership changes during the 1990s affected the direction and purpose of the NAACP.

See also: Civil Rights: Civil Rights Policy; DuBois, W. E. B.

References: Lucius J. Barker and Mack H. Jones, *African Americans and the American Political System* (1994); C. Vann Woodward, *The Strange Career of Jim Crow* (1957).

National Organization for Women

See Civil Rights: Friedan, Betty

Nineteenth Amendment

The Nineteenth Amendment to the Constitution was passed on August 18, 1920. Following years of public organizing and demonstrations by citizens promoting women's suffrage and full political rights, Congress passed—and the states ratified—the measure that granted all citizens the right to vote regardless of gender. Leaders of the suffrage movement included Susan B. Anthony, Elizabeth Cady Stanton, and Amelia Jenks Bloomer. Women who marched on behalf of women's voting rights during the early 20th century were known as suffragettes.

See also: Civil Rights: Anthony, Susan B.; Civil Rights Policy; Women's Movement

References: Barbara Sinclair Deckard, *The Women's Movement* (1979); Eleanor Flexner, *Century of Struggle: The Women's Rights Movement in the U.S.* (1975).

Plessy v. Ferguson

See Civil Rights: Civil Rights Policy

Preferential Treatment

See Civil Rights: Affirmative Action

Pro-choice Groups

The Supreme Court's 1973 decision in *Roe v. Wade* established a right to privacy that has been applied to issues ranging from birth control to abortion. The Court majority decided that because doctors, theologians, and philosophers could not agree when life begins, judges should not assert that life begins at conception. The Court's decision was that a woman's right to privacy of her body was paramount. Under this decision, women have the right to abortion during the first three months of pregnancy and, subject to reasonable regulations for health, during the middle trimester of pregnancy. States were given the authority to prohibit abortions during the final trimester. This ruling invalidated abortion rulings in 45 states.

Since *Roe v. Wade,* abortion opponents have appealed to Congress and state legislators to "reverse" the Supreme Court decision through legislation. In response to the opposition, pro-choice groups have formed to educate people on abortion rights and lobby against antiabortion groups. Some antiabortion zealots have engaged in terrorism by murdering abortion doctors and bombing abortion facilities. Abortion rights groups include the Planned Parenthood Federation of America and the National Abortion Rights Action League, among others. An active antiabortion group is Operation Rescue; it regularly pickets Planned Parenthood centers around the United States and has aggressively opposed abortion rights.

See also: Key Concepts: Interest Groups

References: David J. Garrow, *Liberty and Sexuality: The Right to Privacy and the Making of* Roe v. Wade (1994); Susan Welch et al., *Understanding American Government* (1997).

Pro-life Groups

See Civil Rights: Pro-choice Groups

Protected Classes

See Civil Rights: Affirmative Action

Regents of the University of California v. Bakke

A common argument against affirmative action is that it promotes reverse discrimination. In providing a broader representation of minorities and women through their hiring and admissions policies, academic institutions might discriminate against qualified whites. In the controversial 1978 case *Regents of the University of California v. Bakke,* the U.S. Supreme Court struck down a special admissions program for minorities at the medical school of the University of California–Davis on the grounds that it excluded a white applicant, Allan Bakke, because of his race and violated his rights under the equal protection clause of the Constitution. Bakke applied to the medical school during two successive years and was denied admission on both occasions. During both years black applicants with lower grade point averages and lower admissions scores were accepted through a special admissions process, which was designed to reserve 16 places (out of 100) for minority students. Throughout the admissions process, the university did not deny that it based admissions decisions on race. The university argued that its use of race was "benign" and meant to assist minority applicants, not hinder them. The Supreme Court held that the objectives of the race-based admissions program were legitimate but that it was a violation of the equal protection clause to have a separate admissions process for minorities with a specified quota of openings unavailable to white students. The Court ordered Bakke be admitted to the medical school and the minority special admissions program be discontinued.

The Supreme Court does not perceive all race-based programs as unconstitutional. The Court has been willing to approve affirmative action programs targeted at past discriminatory actions. The Court believes that the nation has an obligation to eliminate "the disabling effects of identified discrimination." The question still remains whether affirmative action programs adversely affect populations not served by the goals of race-based policies and programs. Claims of reverse discrimination continue into the 1990s. Although the Supreme Court agreed that minority groups were aided at the expense of white people, the Court's divided opinion was made on narrow grounds.

See also: Civil Rights: Affirmative Action; Key Concepts: Supreme Court

References: Thomas R. Dye, *Understanding Public Policy* (1995); Ronald E. Pynn, *American Politics: Changing Expectations* (1993).

Roe v. Wade
See Civil Rights: Pro-choice Groups

Separate-but-Equal Doctrine
See Civil Rights: Civil Rights Policy

Sexual Harassment
See Civil Rights: *Meritor Savings Bank v. Vinson*

Thirteenth Amendment
The Thirteenth Amendment to the Constitution abolished slavery in 1865, rejecting the cultural and economic institution that predominated in southern states. Although this amendment was not a cure-all, it devised a new foundation for social relations that could lead to equality for all Americans.

See also: Civil Rights: Civil Rights Policy

References: Joseph R. Conlin, *The American Past: A Survey of American History* (1993).

Voting Rights Act of 1964
See Civil Rights: Civil Rights Policy

Women's Movement
The inspiration for the women's movement that emerged during the late 1960s and early 1970s was the organization, passion, and experiences of women during the early-20th-century suffrage movement that led to the 1920 passage of the Nineteenth Amendment; it also had origins in the hard work and commitment of women in the labor movement during the 1930s and 1940s. These experiences gave women the impetus for asserting equal rights during the post–World War II years. Women were a vital element in the wartime workforce. This introduced a new dimension for the role of women in American life. Many progressives soon held egalitarian goals that were inclusive of women and did not exclude them because of their gender.

The civil rights movement of the 1960s provided women another forum to express political ideas and to gain important organizing experience. Many university-educated women from the northern states joined the freedom marches and freedom rides to push integration of public facilities in the South. They also were important to voter registration efforts in Mississippi and throughout the South. Young, progressive-minded women saw the realities of poverty and social conditions for the first time; they used this experience while asserting their own demands for equal treatment during the late 1960s and early 1970s. The Vietnam War era was also a testing ground for women engaged in political organizing; all of this contributed to their readiness to begin and maintain the women's movement in the years to come.

The Equal Rights Amendment (ERA) was the focal point of the women's movement during the 1970s. Women were discriminated against in employment throughout the United States, as women were not welcome in certain business and professional environments. The Equal Pay Act of 1963 requires that women and men receive equal pay for equal work. The pay disparities between men and women did not change immediately as a result of this bill, but there was more activity to close the pay gap during the 1990s. The Civil Rights Act of 1964 forbade discrimination on the basis of gender as well as race in hiring, promoting, and firing. The law prohibited discrimination but did not necessarily eliminate discrimination where it existed. The Equal Rights Amendment did not get the required three-fourths support in the states to amend the Constitution. The final blow to ERA came in 1980, when the Republican Party refused to endorse ERA; in 1982 Pres. Ronald Reagan came out against the amendment.

During the 1990s, women were successful in moving other important issues onto the public agenda, like sexual harassment and affirmative action. Betty Friedan played a major role during the 1970s and 1980s as president of the National Organization for Women (NOW). Friedan and her colleagues worked to get women elected to public office, organized to promote reproductive freedom for women, and attempted to introduce programs to improve the economic and political statuses of women. NOW continues to have a sizable membership in all 50 states. Women have used political organization to assert their rights and interests, much like other interest groups. Women's groups organize and lobby at the local, state, and national levels of government. The National Women's Political Caucus has become a major force in encouraging women to run for public office.

See also: Civil Rights: Civil Rights Movement; Equal Rights Amendment; Friedan, Betty; Nineteenth Amendment

Commerce and Transportation

Chronology

1887 Act to Regulate Commerce of 1887 created the Interstate Commerce Commission (ICC) and set rules and policy to regulate interstate commerce and railroads.

1906 Hepburn Act passed, strengthening the Interstate Commerce Commission and Interstate Commerce Act (Act to Regulate Commerce of 1887).

1910 Mann-Elkins Act expanded the Act to Regulate Commerce to include telephone and telegraph lines, strengthened the long haul–short haul clause of the act, and gave the ICC power to suspend high interstate shipping rates.

1914 Federal Trade Commission Act passed, establishing the Federal Trade Commission.

1920 Esch-Cummins Transportation Act passed after World War I to return railroads to private ownership instead of nationalizing them. The act also created a Railroad Labor Board to adjust wage disputes in the industry.

1933 Emergency Railroad Transportation Act placed railroad holding companies under the Interstate Commerce Commission and created the position of Federal Coordinator of Transportation to make railroads more efficient.

1953 Small Business Administration was established to provide support, loans, and grant assistance to small businesses.

1956 Interstate and Defense Highway Act passed to fund building of 41,000 miles of interstate highway and improve urban roadways.

1966 National Transportation and Motor Vehicle Safety Act passed, creating the National Highway Traffic Safety Administration (NHTSA) to establish "crashworthiness" standards for U.S. automobiles.

1971 National Railroad Passenger Corporation established Amtrak as a government supported national passenger railroad service in the United States.

1976 Railroad Revitalization and Reform Act reformed regulatory practices that had the previous effect of financially strangling railroad freight carriers and promoting inefficient operations.

1980 Staggers Act passed to limit the impact of excessive regulation on the railroad industry.

1995 Interstate Commerce Commission abolished; replaced by Surface Transportation Policy Board of U.S. Department of Transportation.

Act to Regulate Commerce of 1887

This act (known as the Interstate Commerce Act) created the Interstate Commerce Commission (ICC) as a response to railroad monopolies. In 1886 the U.S. Supreme Court had decided that state regulation of interstate railroad traffic was unconstitutional. Congress in 1887 responded by creating the Interstate Commerce Commission, the first modern regulatory agency in the U.S. government. In performing its constitutional function, Congress regulates certain kinds of economic activities. And though Congress promotes a strong economy through legislation, it also protects against questionable business practices and abuses.

During the late 1800s railroads, thanks to huge government subsidies, had become the central mode of transportation and freight movement. Railroads engaged in abusive practices that had harmful effects on midwestern farmers and small businesses. The Interstate Commerce Act prohibited discriminatory and unfair pricing practices in matters of interstate commerce and railroad activity. Under the new law, railroads were required to make their rates and charges for transporting freight public and to report the rates and charges to the five-member ICC.

During the early development of administrative law and policy, many agencies like the ICC were not granted enforcement powers in their areas of authority. Their recourse was to the courts, ultimately the U.S. Supreme Court, for enforcing agency orders. Of the first 16 cases to reach the Supreme Court challenging ICC authority, railroads won 15. Thus, agencies had to "earn" their power and authority through judicial review. Much of the activity of the ICC focused on public policies addressing business practices; the buying, selling, and merging of businesses and corporations; and the setting of rates and prices for hauling, transporting, storing, and selling of commodities and goods. In 1996 the U.S. Congress disbanded the Interstate Commerce Commission, placing many of its functions under other federal agencies.

See also: Commerce and Transportation: Interstate Commerce Commission; Key Concepts: Administrative Law; Regulation

References: Charles Bonser, Eugene B. McGregor Jr., and Clinton V. Oster Jr., *Policy Choices and Public Action* (1996); Leif H. Carter and Christine B. Harrington, *Administrative Law and Politics: Cases and Comments* (1991); Florence Heffron and Neil McFeeley, *The Administrative Regulatory Process* (1983).

Elkins Act of 1903

During the early 20th century, business monopolies held sway over consumers and government and resisted regulation. The Interstate Commerce Act of 1887 created the Interstate Commerce Commission (ICC), which was given power to investigate railroads. The major purpose of the act was to ensure that reasonable shipping rates were established by the railroads for shipping common goods. The ICC was powerless, however, to regulate railroads, and subsequent legislation was required to empower the ICC. In 1903 Congress passed the Elkins Anti-Rebating Act, making the published shipping rate (prices for shipping goods by rail) the legal rate. The rates were filed with the ICC, and any departure from the published rates—rebates, drawbacks, or general rate cutting—was a criminal violation with fines up to $20,000 for shippers and railroads.

The Elkins Act strengthened the ICC but did not go far enough to regulate railroads or secure fair rates. The act had the effect of lending some credibility to the Interstate Commerce Act, but not enough to have an impact on regulation of railroads by means of establishing reasonable shipping rates.

See also: Commerce and Transportation: Interstate Commerce Commission

References: Ari Hoogenboom and Olive Hoogenboom, *A History of the ICC: From Panacea to Palliative* (1976).

Esch-Cummins Transportation Act of 1920

This legislation called for the return of the railroads to private ownership, instead of the nationalization of the railroads, as proposed by Glenn E. Plumb of the Railroad Labor Brotherhoods. The Interstate Commerce Commission was given the power to develop plans for consolidating railroads into a number of groups exempt from antitrust laws and to set minimum and maximum shipping and transportation rates. The act also created the Railroad Labor Board to respond to wage disputes. The early 1920s was a period of change and labor strife in the railroad industry. Although passenger service and ridership was on the rise, major shippers and producers were locked in battles with railroads, which controlled shipping rates and schedules to the disadvantage of other companies. The railroads consolidated 50 years later, but not under government leadership.

See also: Commerce and Transportation: Act to Regulate Commerce of 1887; Transportation Policy

References: Joseph R. Conlin, *The American Past: A Survey of American History* (1993).

Federal Maritime Commission

To promote free trade on oceans and waterways used by American shipping interests, Congress created in 1961 the Federal Maritime Commission. Its five members are appointed by the president with the advice and consent of the Senate. The purpose of the commission is to administer the nation's shipping laws and policy. It is an independent regulatory commission that regulates rates, shipping services, and trade agreements of American shipping companies. The commission protects shippers, carriers, and others engaged in foreign commerce from restrictive rules and regulations of foreign governments. Much like the former Interstate Commerce Commission (which regulated overland transport of goods and commodities), the Federal Maritime Commission reviews maritime shipping routes and rates for transport of goods to ensure fair and reasonable rates to individuals and companies that contract with maritime shippers that engage in domestic offshore commerce. The commission also regulates the shipping of goods that are potentially hazardous to ocean environments and administers the Shipping Act of 1984 and the Foreign Shipping Practices Act of 1988.

See also: Commerce and Transportation: Interstate Commerce Commission; Key Concepts: Regulation

References: Charles Bonser, Eugene B. McGregor Jr., and Clinton V. Oster Jr., *Policy Choices and Public Action* (1996).

Free Trade

Free trade means absence of tariffs, subsidies, and restrictions on trade between nations. Such restraints cause higher prices and tend to reduce profits and sales of goods. British economist David Ricardo developed the theory of comparative advantage, which claims that trade enables countries to specialize in producing the products that they produce best. Furthermore, specialization and free trade will benefit all trading partners (real wages will rise), even those that may be absolutely less efficient producers. Thus, Ricardo's theory is at the heart of arguments favoring free trade. Free trade makes it possible for markets to expand, for more products to be produced at lower cost, and for consumers to benefit from increased competition, variety, and quality and from lower prices.

See also: Economics: Economic Policy

References: Charles Bonser, Eugene B. McGregor Jr., and Clinton V. Oster Jr., *Policy Choices and Public Action* (1996); Clarke E. Cochran et al., *American Public Policy: An Introduction* (1996).

Hepburn Act of 1906

The Hepburn Act came at a time when monopolies challenged the political and economic policies of the nation. Railroads were supreme and controlled many state economic decisions. Railroads resisted government regulation, and railroads had "captured" public officials that were supposed to apply the few regulations that governed railroad activities. Yet the combination of public pressure, particularly in rural areas, and constituencies within government made it possible to pressure Congress for rate regulation.

The Hepburn Act strengthened the Interstate Commerce Act of 1887, giving the Interstate Commerce Commission (ICC) the power, on appeal of the shipper, to set maximum rates and by placing the burden of proof on the carrier. The act also enlarged the commission to seven members; allowed it to examine railroad books; extended its jurisdiction to include pipelines, express companies, bridges, and ferries; and prevented railroads from carrying most items produced by companies in which they held an interest. The Hepburn Act was important because it allowed the ICC to review rates and make rate adjustments. The Hepburn Act made the ICC, not courts, the dominant government entity that regulated the railroads.

See also: Commerce and Transportation: Act to Regulate Commerce of 1887; Key Concepts: Regulation

References: Leif H. Carter and Christine B. Harrington, *Administrative Law and Politics: Cases and Comments* (1991); Ari Hoogenboom and Olive Hoogenboom, *A History of the ICC: From Panacea to Palliative* (1976).

Industrial Policy

Industrial policy is determined by a nation's ability to produce and sell goods and products at costs that will return a profit to manufacturers and producers. Agriculture-based nations are restricted to selling agricultural products to other nations if the infrastructure for agricultural production is sound and supports development, transportation, and packaging of those products. If the harvesting mechanisms, transportation systems, and marketing means are not sufficient for export or sale of agricultural goods, then agricultural production will not bring revenues other than the sale of the products and goods to meet the needs of the national population.

Some nations have diverse national economies, possessing well-developed agricultural sectors with sound marketing, transport, development, and export mechanisms to sell products inside the country as well as to consumers in other countries. These nations might have the capacity for industrial development of machinery, electronics, minerals, and textiles for sale and export. A nation's industrial policy can depend on the availability of agricultural land for production and sound production standards that ensure quality in agricultural products; the presence of minerals in the natural environment and the capacity to extract and process those minerals for production into usable and saleable goods and products; infrastructure to transport, develop, and market goods; and a stable political system that provides opportunities for economic growth. The United States is recognized as the world's most developed economy, with a mixture of agricultural production, electronic product development, mineral industries, textile industries, and a free-market system that promotes product development and sales.

See also: Economics: Economic Policy

References: Joseph R. Conlin, *The American Past: A Survey of American History* (1993); Karl E. Case and Ray C. Fair, *Principles of Economics* (1989).

Interstate and Defense Highway Act of 1956

After World War II, the United States experienced substantial economic growth. Thus came the need for economic development to accommodate changing needs. During the early 1950s the mobility of Americans grew, spurred by increased use of the automobile, a necessary means of transportation. People moved to the areas that offered the best economic advantages, in many cases to the suburbs. New roads and highways were needed.

Congress therefore passed the Interstate and Defense Highway Act of 1956, appropriating $27 billion to build 41,000 miles of interstate highway; $15 billion was committed to constructing 8,000 urban interstate miles to improve urban roadways and provide access to areas being developed outside the cities. Federal expenditure would cover 90 percent of construction costs financed by a federal gasoline tax. The projected completion date was set at 1972.

The goal was to relieve highway congestion and improve the national highway system. Another aspect related to the Cold War; the Defense Department requested that some interstate roads be developed to serve as landing strips for military aircraft in case of national emergency. Highway congestion remains a fact of life in the United States, particularly around urban areas, but the national highway system allows Americans to be the most mobile people in the world.

See also: Commerce and Transportation: Transportation Policy

References: Charles Bonser, Eugene B. McGregor Jr., and Clinton V. Oster Jr., *Policy Choices and Public Action* (1996); John R. Meyer and Clinton V. Oster Jr., *Deregulation and the Future of Intercity Passenger Travel* (1987); Roy J. Sampson, Martin T. Farris, and David L. Shrock, *Domestic Transportation: Practice, Theory, and Policy* (1985).

Interstate Commerce Commission

The Interstate Commerce Commission (ICC) was created by the Interstate Commerce Act of 1887, before the federal government engaged in substantial regulatory activity. The railroads were dominant, protecting their interests by placing their advocates on federal and state commissions constructed to regulate and control them. The ICC was no different, and it proved ineffective in its regulatory role for the first 20 years of operation. The Hepburn Act of 1906 strengthened the ICC as to rate setting and its regulatory role, but its authority was frequently challenged in the nation's courts. The ICC derived its authority to regulate interstate commerce from the commerce clause of the U.S. Constitution, but such authority was applied only to the railroads (later to the trucking industry).

By the 1950s and 1960s the ICC was accused of regulatory excess. Much of the regulatory activity focused on three areas: rates and value of service pricing in competition with trucking services; excess route mileage, in which the ICC was reluctant to allow railroads to abandon service on unprofitable routes; and freight car utilization, which resulted in poor utilization of freight cars and excess costs for freight car usage. The passage of the Motor Carrier Act of 1980 changed the regulatory environment for the trucking industry, opening it to deregulation (also increasing the number of carriers) and reducing costs. During the era of government deregulation in the 1980s, the commission found itself obsolete. The ICC was abolished in 1995 and replaced by the Surface Transportation Policy Board within the U.S. Department of Transportation.

See also: Commerce and Transportation: Act to Regulate Commerce of 1887; Elkins Act of 1903; Hepburn Act of 1906

References: Charles Bonser, Eugene B. McGregor Jr., and Clinton V. Oster Jr., *Policy Choices and Public Action* (1996); Ari Hoogenboom and Olive Hoogenboom, *A History of the ICC: From Panacea to Palliative* (1976); John R. Meyer and Clinton V. Oster Jr., *Deregulation and the Future of Intercity Passenger Travel* (1987).

Mann-Elkins Act of 1910

The Mann-Elkins Act expanded the Interstate Commerce Act to include telephone and telegraph lines, strengthened the long haul–short haul clause of the act, and gave the Interstate Commerce Commission the power to suspend high interstate shipping rates. This act attempted to further regulate the railroads, requiring railroads to show clear reasons for raising shipping rates. Railroads claimed that increases in the costs of wages, materials, and in the general activity of running the railroads required rate increases. The railroad industry during the early 20th century was made up of large and small railroads with varying degrees of power within geographical regions. In many cases, railroads were free to charge anything they desired.

See also: Commerce and Transportation: Act to Regulate Commerce of 1887

References: Ari Hoogenboom and Olive Hoogenboom, *A History of the ICC: From Panacea to Palliative* (1976).

National Association of Manufacturers

The National Association of Manufacturers (NAM) represents the interests of goods manufacturers for domestic sale and export. NAM lobbies members of Congress in support of public policy. In 1996 NAM, the National Chamber of Commerce, the National Federation of Independent Business, the National Association of Wholesale Distributors, and the National Restaurant Association created a coalition of business groups to raise money and engage in lobbying. The coalition raised millions of dollars for television and radio advertising in support of conservative congressional candidates.

See also: Key Concepts: Interest Groups

References: Theodore J. Lowi and Benjamin Ginsberg, *American Government: Freedom and Power* (1998).

National Railroad Passenger Corporation

Rail passenger service in the United States ceased to be a profitmaking enterprise during the 1930s Depression, but World War II softened the blow as millions of soldiers and sailors needed transport across the country. After the war, the automobile replaced the passenger train, and the growth of the national highway system put rail passenger service in serious jeopardy.

By the 1950s and 1960s many of the nation's railroads were consolidating or going out of business. Passenger service proved to be the least profitable use of railroad equipment, and many railroads known for regional and cross-country passenger service discontinued their service. In 1971 rail passenger service took a new direction. The federal government worked with the remaining railroads that offered passenger service and created the National Railroad Passenger Corporation. The original name of the new corporation was Railpax, but a more appropriate name was chosen, and in 1971 Amtrak came into existence. Amtrak did not operate as a commuter railroad but did maintain passenger service along traditional routes. Pres. Richard M. Nixon signed the legislation that created the National Railroad Passenger Corporation (Railpax) in October 1970. The legislation authorized, through the Interstate Commerce Commission, a semipublic corporation to run passenger trains, with an initial grant of $40–60 million. The semipublic corporation was expected to become a profitmaking enterprise. On May 1, 1971, Amtrak took over the nation's intercity passenger train service. Amtrak began service with the best equipment from the remaining passenger railroads that existed.

During the late 1990s Amtrak has not achieved profitable status, and government support has diminished since the early 1970s. Many original routes have been discontinued; new equipment has been developed and put into service. The future of Amtrak is unclear. Without federal assistance, the railroad will not survive. Each year in Congress, opponents threaten to cut off funding, yet Amtrak supporters manage to get annual funding. Many Americans have a romantic vision of passenger trains, but such vision does not translate into the financial support needed to be profitable. Most Western democracies wholly subsidize passenger rail service, but U.S. travelers have come to rely on the automobile and airlines to serve travel needs.

See also: Commerce and Transportation: Transportation Policy

References: Harold Edmondson, ed., *Journey to Amtrak: The Year History Rode the Passenger Train* (1972); John R. Meyer and Clinton V. Oster Jr., *Deregulation and the Future of Intercity Passenger Travel* (1987).

National Transportation and Motor Vehicle Safety Act of 1966

During the 1960s public interest activism focused on consumer issues, especially automobile safety. In 1966 Congress passed the National Transportation and Motor Vehicle Safety Act, creating the National Highway Traffic Safety Administration (NHTSA) to develop standards of "crashworthiness" for autos sold in the United States. Crashworthiness means that car bumpers meet a reasonable degree of shock absorbency, and by 1972 all autos sold in the United States had to have passive restraints (seatbelts). Congress placed limits on safety and crashworthiness standards applied by the NHTSA in response to lobbying and pressure from automakers. Since 1966 seatbelts and airbags have become standard safety features.

See also: Health: Nader, Ralph; Key Concepts: Interest Groups

References: Dennis J. Palumbo, *Public Policy in America: Government in Action* (1988).

Railroad Revitalization and Reform Act of 1976

One of the factors that hastened the demise of the regulatory role of the Interstate Commerce Commission was its practice of setting unreasonable rates and usage requirements for railroad freight hauling. When Congress passed the Railroad Revitalization and Reform Act of 1976, the railroad industry was in need of more freedom to set rates, abandon unprofitable routes, and seek mergers with other railroads. This legislation was designed to reform regulatory practices, which caused severe financial problems for freight haulers. Regulations were strangling the industry and promoted inefficient operations. By 1980 the Staggers Act was passed to further limit the impact of excessive regulation on the railroad industry. The act also ended the belief that railroads were a monopoly in need of regulation. Both the Railroad Revitalization and Reform Act and the Staggers Act were products of the push for deregulation that prevailed during the late 1970s and early 1980s.

See also: Commerce and Transportation: Interstate Commerce Commission

References: Charles Bonser, Eugene B. McGregor Jr., and Clinton V. Oster Jr., *Policy Choices and Public Action* (1996); John R. Meyer and Clinton V. Oster Jr., *Deregulation and the Future of Intercity Passenger Travel* (1987); Roy J. Sampson, Martin T. Farris, and David L. Shrock, *Domestic Transportation: Practice, Theory, and Policy* (1985).

Small Business Administration

The Small Business Administration (SBA) was established in 1953 to provide support, loans, and grant assistance to small businesses. The Eisenhower administration had abolished the Reconstruction Finance Corporation and decided to replace some of its functions with SBA. Some members of Congress preferred to see SBA as an independent agency instead of placing it within the Department of Commerce, which they felt was oriented toward big business. Thus SBA became an independent executive agency. Its very existence was threatened during the Reagan administration, as the president felt that SBA wasted money with its loans and played favorites. Small business groups complained to Congress, and President Reagan backed off from plans to abolish the agency. SBA provides a variety of technical and informational services to small businesses, and the agency today enjoys the general support of Congress.

See also: Key Concepts: Administrative Agencies

References: James E. Anderson, *Public Policymaking* (1997).

Tariffs

See Commerce and Transportation: Free Trade; Key Concepts: Protectionism

Trade Policy

See Commerce and Transportation: Free Trade

Transportation Policy

Transportation policy first focused on the railroad industry. The railroads were the first transcontinental transport system, bringing goods and services to the far reaches of the nation. During the late 19th century railroads dominated local and state economies and needed controls. Freight hauling became the issue, and setting rates for freight became the target of regulation. With the Interstate Commerce Act of 1887, Congress intended to control the rate-setting practices of railroads. But the act had little real enforcement power, and the railroads prevailed. During the 1920s and 1930s railroads again became the subject of interest, and the federal government kept rates high enough to make the industry economically viable.

The trucking industry developed during the 1930s and came under the regulations of the Motor Carrier Act of 1935, which was stimulated by the trucking industry to control the growth and entry of new companies entering the freight-hauling business. Congress passed the Civil Aeronautics Act in 1938, which created the Civil Aeronautics Board to regulate and promote air transportation. These three industries dominated transportation into the 1960s. Rail passenger service declined during the early 1960s, and many railroads merged or sold out and abandoned passenger service.

The 1970s and 1980s were decades of deregulation. The Airline Deregulation Act of 1978 gave rate freedom to airlines. The Staggers Rail Act of 1980 removed regulatory restrictions on railroads, and the Bus Regulatory Reform Act deregulated intercity bus transportation.

When the Interstate Commerce Commission was disbanded in the early 1990s, regulations for surface transportation were administered by the Surface Transportation Policy Board. Deregulation of the transportation industry was the major feature of transportation policy during the 1990s. Deregulation has made these industries more profitable and better able to compete in a demanding economy.

See also: Commerce and Transportation: Act to Regulate Commerce of 1887

References: Charles Bonser, Eugene B. McGregor Jr., and Clinton V. Oster Jr., *Policy Choices and Public Action* (1996); John R. Meyer and Clinton V. Oster Jr., *Deregulation and the Future of Intercity Passenger Travel* (1987); Roy J. Sampson, Martin T. Farris, and David L. Shrock, *Domestic Transportation: Practice, Theory, and Policy* (1985).

Communications

Chronology

1920 Federal Radio Act passed, creating rules for regulating the airwaves.

1927 Radio Act provided for the Federal Radio Commission to license stations and place controls on commercial radio.

1934 Federal Communications Act passed, creating the Federal Communications Commission; empowered the commission to regulate and monitor use of the airwaves.

1959 The Supreme Court ruled in *Garland v. Torre* that First Amendment rights must be weighed against other interests—those of prosecutors—when deciding information in trials and compelling journalists to testify.

1967 Public Broadcasting Act passed, providing government funding for public broadcasting networks and creating the Public Broadcasting Corporation.

1969 Supreme Court decided in *Red Lion Broadcasting Co. v. Federal Communications Commission* that individuals should have the right to rebut opposing views or personal attacks that occur on television.

1970 Supreme Court decided in *Caldwell v. United States* that the government had the right to subpoena testimony of journalists, including testimony concerning names of particular individuals in criminal cases.

1996 Telecommunications Reform Act passed, overhauling the original telecommunications law.

Communications Act of 1934

The Communications Act of 1934 established the Federal Communications Commission (FCC) to regulate interstate and foreign communication by telephone, telegraph, cable, and radio. The regulation of radios in the United States originated in 1912, when the first federal law regulating radio communications was enacted. Comprehensive radio regulation began with the Radio Act of 1927, designed to correct the problems of electronic interference in the radio broadcast industry that came as a result of the failure of the 1912 legislation. The Radio Act of 1927 created the Federal Radio Commission and granted it full regulatory powers, including the power to classify radio stations, to assign frequencies to various classes of and individual stations, and to determine hours of operation, power, and geographical service areas. The Communications Act of 1934 retained the powers of the previous 1927 Radio Act but also created the FCC, a permanent independent agency that would regulate all forms of electrical communication. The FCC assumed the functions previously held by the Federal Radio Commission and the Interstate Commerce Commission (which had regulatory authority over telephones and telegraphs). The structure, role, and statutory authority of the FCC has remained relatively unchanged since the 1934 legislation. The advent of television, cable television systems, and satellite communications means the range of regulatory authority of the FCC has expanded. The Communications Act of 1934 represents a broad delegation of authority to a federal agency in technical and nontechnical areas. This legislation was reformed by the Telecommunications Reform Act of 1996.

See also: Communications: Communications Policy; Federal Communications Commission

References: Ronald Berkman and Laura W. Kitch, *Politics in the Media Age* (1986); Glen O. Robinson, Ernest Gellhorn, and Harold H. Bruff, *The Administrative Process* (1979).

Communications Decency Act of 1996

Pres. Bill Clinton signed into law on February 8, 1996, the Communications Decency Act, making it a criminal offense to transmit "indecent" speech or images to minors (people under the age of 13) or to make such speech or images available online (via the internet) to minors. Penalties include fines up to $250,000 and imprisonment for up to two years. This legislation represents the first attempt by Congress to regulate content in cyberspace. Groups in favor of the legislation included the Christian Coalition, the Family Research Council, and the National Coalition for the Protection of Children and Families. Among the groups opposing the legislation were the American Civil Liberties Union (ACLU), the Electronic Frontier Foundation, and Planned Parenthood. The basis of the opposition was that users of the internet choose what images and words to view.

The legislation opened the debate over free speech in cyberspace. In 1996 the ACLU filed suit in federal court (*American Civil Liberties Union v. Reno*) and the court ruled that part of the act was unconstitutional due to its vagueness; the court prohibited the government from enforcing the section that pertained to indecent materials. In 1997 the Supreme Court affirmed the federal court decision, ruling that the act was unconstitutional under the First Amendment.

See also: Communications: Communications Policy

References: David Edwards and Alessandra Lippucci, *Practicing American Politics: An Introduction to American Government* (1998); Steffen W. Schmidt, Mack C. Shelley II, and Barbara A. Bardes, *American Government and Politics Today* (1997).

Communications Policy

Freedom of press and freedom of speech are the foundations of U.S. communications policy. Under the First Amendment to the Constitution, Congress is prohibited from making any law that restricts freedom of the press and of speech. Newspapers conveyed news, information, and opinion in early America, and they have been, for the most part, free of government regulation. With the introduction of radio technology during the early 20th century, the government was compelled to regulate the growing radio broadcast industry. The airwaves were perceived as public property subject to regulation. In 1927 Congress passed the Radio Act in response to requests from the developing radio industry for controls on commercial use. The Radio Act created the Federal Radio Commission, which later became the Federal Communications Commission (FCC). The provisions of the Radio Act were not altogether helpful in controlling the industry, but the act did establish some ground rules. The industry understood that government regulation was essential to stability. Stations were granted temporary and renewable licenses to operate.

On June 19, 1934, Congress passed the Communications Act, which established the FCC. Its purpose was to regulate interstate and foreign communication by telegraph, cable, and radio. Regulation of television came in 1948 and was placed under FCC jurisdiction. As communications technology improved and expanded, the work of the Federal Communications Commission went beyond the early focus on licensing. The FCC had to promote regulatory policy that supported competition in the communications marketplace. Along with the developing regulatory role of assuring competition, added concerns of fairness and access became a part of the regulatory environment.

In 1969 the Supreme Court, in *Red Lion Broadcasting Co. v. Federal Communications Commission,* affirmed the constitutionality of the fairness and rebuttal rules. Known as the fairness doctrine, these rules required broadcasters to provide reasonable time for the expression of opposing views on controversial issues that are discussed on the public airwaves. A rebuttal provision is also included in the rule, providing any person or group that is attacked or ridiculed in a broadcast free airtime to respond. The fairness doctrine was vague in establishing standards, and the rebuttal provision was generally used when television and radio networks granted time to the "other" political parties after major presidential addresses. By 1985 the Federal Communications Commission sought alternatives to the fairness doctrine because of fears that the doctrine would squelch the airing of controversial views in the first place. The Federal Communications Commission ceased enforcing the fairness doctrine in 1987.

In 1967 Congress passed the Public Broadcasting Act, establishing the Corporation for Public Broadcasting. This nonprofit organization receives funds from Congress and distributes the money to public radio and television stations throughout the United States. The Public Broadcasting Service (PBS) produces television programming; National Public Radio (NPR) produces radio programming. The members of the Corporation for Public Broadcasting are appointed by the president. Government funding for PBS and NPR has declined during the 1990s as a consequence of criticism from members of Congress that PBS and NPR are decidedly liberal in their programming and viewpoints. These attacks originated during the Reagan administration and continue to come from conservative members of Congress.

The leading policy issues in communications policy during the 1990s centered on the content and access issues related to the internet and the regulation/deregulation of the cable television industry. The Communications Decency Act of 1996 and the Internet Freedom and Family Empowerment Act directly regulate content on the internet and access to pornographic material. These policy issues will continue to be addressed into the next century.

Another technological development that will come under FCC jurisdiction will be high-definition television (HDTV), which will enable broadcasters to transmit multimedia signals, including voice, video, data, and software. The FCC is in the process of sorting out the issues. The future of communications policy will involve regulatory activity in the rapidly expanding cellular telephone industry and a movement from regulated monopoly to deregulated competition.

See also: Communications: Communications Act of 1934; Communications Decency Act of 1996; Fairness Doctrine; Public Broadcasting Act of 1967

References: Dean E. Alger, *The Media and Politics* (1989); Ronald Berkman and Laura W. Kitch, *Politics in the Media Age* (1986).

Corporation for Public Broadcasting

The 1967 Public Broadcasting Act created the Corporation for Public Broadcasting. A nonprofit organization, it is funded by Congress and distributes money to public radio and television stations throughout the United States. The purpose of the Corporation for Public Broadcasting was to provide assistance for broadcasting in subject and content areas that commercial broadcasters were reluctant to engage. National Public Radio, the Public Broadcasting System, American Public Radio, and Public Radio International are the umbrella organizations for public broadcasting in radio and television. Congressional funding for public broadcasting declines each year amid complaints by conservative members of Congress about the content and liberal direction of public radio and television programming. Much of the congressional attention to public broadcasting borders on government censorship. Dwindling support from Congress compels public radio and television stations to seek corporate and other funds to supplement meager allotments from the government.

The Corporation for Public Broadcasting is governed by a ten-member board of directors appointed by the president. Since 1967 some appointments have been made to satisfy political favors. Some media observers question whether there truly is public broadcasting in the United States.

See also: Communications: Communications Policy

References: Ronald Berkman and Laura W. Kitch, *Politics in the Media Age* (1986); Steffen W. Schmidt, Mack C. Shelley II, and Barbara A. Bardes, *American Government and Politics Today* (1997).

Fairness Doctrine

In 1949 the Federal Communications Commission required broadcasters to operate in the public interest by devoting a reasonable amount of time to controversial issues and to cover these issues fairly by offering contrasting viewpoints. It was left to broadcasters to determine how and when contrasting views on controversial issues would be presented. Television stations during the 1970s and 1980s adopted the practice of offering on-air editorials about issues of the day. Under the fairness doctrine opposing views would have the chance to provide their analysis. Although the fairness doctrine was never legislated, it became common practice. By 1985 the Federal Communications Commission sought alternatives to the fairness doctrine because of fears that the doctrine would squelch the airing of controversial views in the first place. The Federal Communications Commission ceased enforcing the fairness doctrine in 1987.

With the proliferation of cable television and public access stations, there is no firm indication that controversial issues have been more freely aired or discussed since the demise of the fairness doctrine in 1987. The issue for broadcasters remains one of appropriate content and balanced coverage of controversial subjects.

See also: Communications: Communications Policy; Federal Communications Commission

References: Dean E. Alger, *The Media and Politics* (1989); Ronald Berkman and Laura W. Kitch, *Politics in the Media Age* (1986).

Federal Communications Commission

The Communications Act of 1934 established the Federal Communications Commission (FCC) to regulate interstate and foreign communication by telegraph, cable, and radio. The development of the radio as an increasingly commercial communication medium and the commensurate growth of radio programs required regulation of the airwaves. The new FCC had to manage competition for limited radio frequencies. When it was created in 1934, the FCC had seven members (reduced to five in 1984). It enforces laws passed by Congress that affect the communications industries. The charge granted to the FCC by Congress in 1934 was to regulate the broadcast media in the public interest. The FCC was responsible for creating rules and regulations that would guide broadcasters in licensing and public interest broadcasting requirements.

A major function of the FCC is the licensing of radio and television broadcasters. All radio and television stations require a license to operate. Licenses are granted for five years, and the process of licensing became quite controversial during the late 20th century. The matter of license renewal has raised questions of broadcast ownership, the extent of regulation, and the nature of the "free press" in broadcasting.

Issues facing the FCC during the 1990s included the continuing problem of how much regulation is sufficient; the limits of free speech and free press as affected by government regulation; and the role of the FCC given rapidly expanding and changing communications technologies.

See also: Communications: Communications Policy; Fairness Doctrine

References: Dean E. Alger, *The Media and Politics* (1989); Ronald Berkman and Laura W. Kitch, *Politics in the Media Age* (1986).

Freedom of Information Act

The Freedom of Information Act (FOIA) was passed by Congress in 1966 and has expanded access to information about the U.S. government. The act allows citizens to request copies of government documents or information from an executive branch agency. The Administrative Procedure Act (APA) also contains a version of the Freedom of Information Act. Any citizen, by following FOIA procedures, can request copies of documents or other information. If that information is not otherwise protected from public scrutiny (e.g., for reasons of national security), then the agency is obligated to provide it.

Information on specific individuals is available under the Privacy Act of 1974. After the Vietnam War, many individuals suspected that the Federal Bureau of Investigation (FBI) kept records or files on their political activities, and FOIA allowed these individuals to view such information.

The Freedom of Information Act places nine categories of documents beyond the scrutiny of the general public, including internal personnel rules and practices, law enforcement records, interagency memoranda, banking records, and geological and geophysical data related to mineral wealth.

See also: Key Concepts: Administrative Procedure Act of 1946

References: Steven J. Cann, *Administrative Law* (1998); Leif H. Carter and Christine B. Harrington, *Administrative Law and Politics: Cases and Comments* (1991); Steffen W. Schmidt, Mack C. Shelley II, and Barbara A. Bardes, *American Government and Politics Today* (1997).

Internet

The internet is an electronic communication and information system that evolved from a U.S. Defense Department project designed to solve the problem of a potential breakdown of the military communications system during time of war. The Defense Department created the Advance Research Projects Agency Network to serve as a survivable communications network for organizations engaged in defense-related research. If a nuclear attack occurred, this new communications network could survive thanks to an information storage system called the store and forward procedure. This original network was enhanced in 1982 when the National Science Foundation and some university researchers expanded it into the Computerized Science Network.

Today a vast high-speed information network, aided by National Science Foundation research in 1988, is used by all segments of the population and is now an integral part of the national economy. It is a computer-based series of networks that revolves around the World Wide Web (the Web), which serves as the predominant information retrieval service system of the internet. People use the internet to send electronic mail (e-mail), gather information for personal and commercial use, engage in discussion groups, and find information for a variety of personal, business, and other uses. The primary source of information on the internet is homepages, which are personal or professional links to information. The internet is a major enterprise and information retrieval and disseminating system that is used in politics, economics, medical affairs, and in a wide variety of other areas in the expanding information economy.

See also: Communications: Communications Decency Act of 1996

References: Katie Hafner and Matthew Lynon, *Where Wizards Stay Up Late: The Origins of the Internet* (1996); Edward Sidlow and Beth Henschen, *America at Odds* (1998).

Media Power

The media—television, radio, newspapers, magazines, journals, and the internet—is the means of communication or transmission of information. The media comes in the form of electronic media (the internet and online computer information sources), the print media (newspapers, magazines, and journals), and the broadcast media (television and radio). The media in all of its forms has extraordinary power to influence public opinion and public policy in the United States. The media informs citizens about politics, candidates, and public policy, a task formerly held by political parties.

The primary source of news information is network television broadcasts; 98 percent of Americans have a television set in their homes. Television, newspapers, and magazines are owned by corporations, and concentrated ownerships wield a significant amount of power and ability to influence American voters. The media has also taken on the role of investigative reporting on important and obscure political issues and has served as the champion and chief information provider around controversial issues.

The media is in the business of making profits. The media in the United States has been accused of presenting biases in news coverage that favor the interests and views of media owners. The owners deny being biased, but they do shape the news that Americans consume. The Federal Communications Commission has the authority to regulate the electronic media and applies guidelines to promote fairness in electronic communications in the area of personal attacks (personal attack rule); the equal time rule, which requires broadcasters to provide equal time to candidates with dissenting views; the reasonable access provision, which guarantees candidates for federal office reasonable access to unedited airtime; and the political editorializing rule, requiring stations that give public endorsements of candidates to offer other candidates for that office a chance to reply on air. The media in various forms does have power to influence, but the media also plays an important role in American politics by introducing and publicizing candidates and setting the policy agenda.

See also: Communications: Federal Communications Commission

References: Dean E. Alger, *The Media and Politics* (1989); Ronald Berkman and Laura W. Kitch, *Politics in the Media Age* (1986); David Edwards and Alessandra Lippucci, *Practicing American Politics: An Introduction to American Government* (1998).

National Association of Broadcasters

The National Association of Broadcasters (NAB) is composed of corporate executives who run member television and radio stations in the American broadcasting industry. The purpose of NAB is to lobby and influence legislators in Washington, D.C., so that congressional decisions favor the industry.

See also: Key Concepts: Interest Groups

References: Jeffrey M. Berry, *The Interest Group Society* (1997).

National Cable Television Association

The National Cable Television Association (NCTA) is made up of owners and executives in the cable television industry. NCTA operates to protect the interests of its members and of the cable television industry as a whole. Cable has been a growth industry, and public policy affecting costs, subscriptions, access, and licensing has been an area of controversy. NCTA lobbies members of Congress to inform and educate them about issues affecting the industry. As an interest group, NCTA is in a unique position, because it does not have the "natural" allies that more common interest groups possess.

See also: Key Concepts: Interest Groups

References: Jeffrey M. Berry, *The Interest Group Society* (1997).

National Endowment for the Arts

The National Endowment for the Arts (NEA) is a federally supported agency that offers grants and resources to support the arts. NEA and the National Endowment for the Humanities were established by the National Foundation of the Arts and Humanities Act of 1965. NEA has a chair and national governing council with 26 members appointed by the president and confirmed by the Senate. Congress sets policy guidelines and funding levels for NEA (funding is based in three-year cycles). Those engaged in the arts seek federal funding for projects and programs to promote education and development of artists. NEA came under attack by the Republican-led Congress in 1995 for promoting and funding art considered to be indecent. The agency withstood the attacks; its diminished funding continues to come under criticism by some conservative members of Congress.

See also: Economics: Federal Revenue Sharing

References: James Q. Wilson and John J. DiIulio Jr., *American Government: The Essentials* (1998).

New York Times v. Sullivan

The 1964 Supreme Court decision in *New York Times v. Sullivan* broadened media protection from libel suits. In order to collect damages, a public official had to prove that a falsehood resulted from actual malice on the part of a news organization. Under this decision, public officials assumed a special status, their actions open to public scrutiny. The Court would continue to protect the media against unwarranted libel cases, yet it began to change its narrow view of public officials in subsequent cases; by 1979 the Court broadened the category of individuals who could bring libel suits against the media.

See also: Communications: Communications Policy; Media Power

References: Ronald Berkman and Laura W. Kitch, *Politics in the Media Age* (1986).

Public Broadcasting Act of 1967

The Public Broadcasting Act of 1967 established the Corporation for Public Broadcasting (CPB), a nonprofit corporation that receives federal funds and distributes these funds to public radio and televisions stations. The amount of government money that goes to CPB is limited, requiring public radio and television stations to solicit contributions from citizens and corporate donors. Oil companies have funded public broadcasting stations, but the public broadcasting system prefers to not rely too heavily on corporate gifts.

CPB has a ten-member board appointed by the president. Public radio and television have increased in popularity during the 1990s; public broadcasting offers some of the most intelligent and diverse programming available.

See also: Communications: Communications Policy

References: Dean E. Alger, *The Media and Politics* (1989); Ronald Berkman and Laura W. Kitch, *Politics in the Media Age* (1986).

Red Lion Broadcasting Co. v. Federal Communications Commission

Red Lion Broadcasting Co. v. Federal Communications Commission (1969) established the right of rebuttal to personal attacks on television. A conservative member of the clergy made an on-air attack on station WGCB against an author and his book. In response, the author asked the television station for free reply time to rebut the remarks. The station owner refused, and so the author filed a lawsuit, seeking free reply time; the case eventually went to the U.S. Supreme Court. The Court ruled that the station was obligated to supply free airtime for rebuttal.

Red Lion established the precedent for the right of rebuttal. Some media observers and critics felt this was a serious restriction on broadcasters' interest in covering controversial issues on television. How free time for rebuttal would be granted or managed became the issue, and so broadcasters avoided controversial issues in the first place. With the advent of cable television, the control of content and the right of rebuttal became less significant as issues of public policy. Public access channels are common features in the cable television industry; regulating the content of broadcasting has become very controversial and does not invite the controls attempted during the first decades of television.

See also: Communications: Communications Policy

References: Dean E. Alger, *The Media and Politics* (1989); Ronald Berkman and Laura W. Kitch, *Politics in the Media Age* (1986).

Crime

Chronology

1908 FBI was created by Congress. J. Edgar Hoover was appointed director in 1924.

1914 Harrison Act passed by Congress to control and regulate the supply and use of narcotics.

1931 Wickersham Commission created by President Herbert Hoover to investigate the status of the nation's police forces. Commission's findings indicated that there was inadequate police training and police officers were ill-prepared to conduct their law enforcement duties.

1961 *Mapp v. Ohio,* U.S. Supreme Court decision making the exclusionary rule applicable in unwarranted searches and seizures of a person's home.

1963 *Gideon v. Wainwright,* U.S. Supreme Court decision establishing the right to counsel for all state defendants facing felony trials.

1966 *Miranda v. Arizona,* U.S. Supreme Court extended constitutional protections to criminal defendants by requiring police to inform defendants of their rights to counsel and to remain silent.

1968 Federal Gun Control Act passed banning interstate and mail-order sales of handguns and prohibiting sale of firearms to felons, fugitives, or people judged to be mentally insane.

1970 Racketeer Influenced and Corrupt Organization Act (RICO) passed, authorizing seizure of money, bank accounts, personal property, and other assets held by people involved in organized crime and racketeering.

1972 *Furman v. Georgia,* U.S. Supreme Court placed the first constitutional restraints on capital punishment by considering the application of cruel and unusual punishment.

1993 Brady Handgun Violence Prevention Act passed, requiring a five-business-day waiting period before an individual can buy a handgun.

1994 Comprehensive Crime Control Act passed, banning assault weapons; gave additional funding to states to build more prisons and hire police officers; required registration of sex offenders upon setting up residence in new communities; introduced the federal "three strikes" requirement for life sentences for convictions in the commission of three federal crimes.

Brady Handgun Violence Prevention Act of 1993

Gun control legislation highlights passionate differences of opinion among Americans. Proponents of gun control believe gun control will bring down crime, yet some studies have shown Americans possess more than 200 million guns. Opponents of gun control believe guns offer personal protection. The Brady Handgun Violence Prevention Act of 1993 requires handgun dealers to send police agencies a form completed by the gun purchaser. Police agencies have seven days to check whether the purchaser is a convicted felon, fugitive, drug addict, or mentally ill person. It is seen as a small step toward preventing the wrong people from buying handguns. The National Rifle Association, the leading gunowners' lobby, uses its vast resources to counter or defeat most handgun legislation.

This law was named after James S. Brady, the former press secretary to Pres. Ronald Reagan; Brady was shot in a Reagan assassination attempt in 1981. He suffered serious brain and motor function damage. The Brady Bill was championed by Brady and his wife, Sarah. After several years of lobbying from gun control advocates, Congress passed the bill. It is difficult to pass federal legislation because of the strength of the gun lobby. State and local laws also regulate gun ownership; Illinois, Massachusetts, New Jersey, and New York have the most restrictive laws that prohibit handgun ownership except by people licensed by law enforcement officials. Gun control will continue to be a volatile issue in American politics.

See also: Crime: National Rifle Association

References: Thomas R. Dye, *Understanding Public Policy* (1995).

Capital Punishment

Cultural issues affect how societies punish serious crimes such as murder and treason. The death penalty—the ultimate sentence—is known as capital punishment, a controversial issue in American politics. The major question is whether it serves as a deterrent to others. Some people believe in the theory of deterrence, which suggests that people are rational actors who would avoid the unpleasant consequences of their actions (the death penalty) if they do not commit murder. Others suggest that the death penalty does not deter crimes and is cruel and unusual punishment. They believe society should reflect the highest standards of moral conduct and that the death penalty is merely retribution for a heinous crime. Still others believe that the death penalty, whether it deters crimes or not, serves as a symbolic measure for society.

Some states allow capital punishment, yet studies have shown that some crimes are unaffected by the existence of the death penalty. There is evidence, however, showing a relationship between the death penalty and a reluctance to commit murder. Opponents of the death penalty argue that the higher moral ground that befits an advanced society should be sought in sentencing murderers.

In 1972 the Supreme Court placed the first constitutional restraints on capital punishment in *Furman v. Georgia.* A majority of the Court rejected the idea that capital punishment was inherently cruel and unusual, but five justices agreed that it was cruel and unusual as then practiced in the United States. The Court chose to hear arguments on the propriety of the death penalty in 1976 and 1977, deciding capital punishment is not cruel and unusual punishment if administered fairly. Many today contend that application of the death penalty varies according to the defendant's age, gender, race, and status in society.

See also: Key Concepts: Supreme Court

References: Clarke E. Cochran et al., *American Public Policy: An Introduction* (1996); Herbert Jacob, *Law and Politics in the United States* (1986); Ronald E. Pynn, *American Politics: Changing Expectations* (1993); Richard Quinney, *Class, State, and Crime* (1977); Susan Welch et al., *Understanding American Government* (1997).

Comprehensive Crime Control Act of 1994

In U.S. politics, a strong anticrime position is a popular position. During the 1990s violent crime was an issue in most local, state, and national campaigns for office. Much of the attention has been directed at street crime and drug-related crime. Pres. Bill Clinton signed into law the Comprehensive Crime Control Act of 1994 to address the crime problem. The act had several key provisions: a ban on assault weapons; additional funding to states to build more prisons and to hire policemen; the registration of sex offenders upon their leaving prison and taking up residence in communities; an automatic life sentence for the commission of three felony crimes with convictions in federal crimes; and the allocation of federal funds to develop social programs (midnight and evening basketball programs) for crime prevention in inner cities. The Comprehensive Crime Control Act of 1984 preceded the 1994 legislation but targeted similar crime-control issues: increased funding for law enforcement, prison construction, and state victim-compensation programs. The 1994 bill was broader in design and in the application of federal funds.

See also: Crime: Criminal Justice Policy

References: Clarke E. Cochran et al., *American Public Policy: An Introduction* (1996); Thomas R. Dye, *Understanding Public Policy* (1995); Richard Quinney, *Class, State, and Crime* (1977).

Correctional Policy

The proper role of prisons in a democracy is hotly debated. Should prisons rehabilitate convicted criminals or instead be harsh centers for punishment? Should they train and educate or merely warehouse people who have broken the law?

The United States has the highest incarceration rate of any country in the world. In 1994 the state prison population was approximately 900,000 and the federal prison population was 95,000. Some 1,500 new prison beds are needed each week as the states and federal government arrest and convict more offenders. The annual nationwide cost of building, maintaining, and operating prisons in 1998 was approximately $35 billion. Some states, like California and Texas, commit more money to building prisons than to public education. A recent complicating factor is the introduction of "three-strikes" legislation, adopted first by California and Washington. Under three-strikes legislation any person thrice convicted of a felony is sentenced to life in prison. Three-strikes bills compound overcrowding in prisons.

Corrections is the third phase of the criminal justice process. Police identify suspects, make arrests, and bring the defendants to the courts, where trials by jury determine guilt or innocence. If found guilty, offenders are sentenced to be punished or rehabilitated for their crimes. The function of correctional prisons may be retribution, which involves restitution to the state and society; deterrence, a means of warning people against engaging in criminal activity; treatment and rehabilitation, with opportunities while in prison to learn skills or receive an education; or incapacitation, or locking up criminals to prevent them from committing crimes.

The costs of incarcerating criminals and the failure of the philosophical approaches to changing criminal behavior pose great challenges to the system. The states and federal government are unwavering in their fight against crime and in their willingness to build more prisons and incarcerate offenders. Yet many contend that criminal corrections policy suffers when legislators focus primarily on putting criminals away while ignoring the apparent critical early life factors such as support for public education, families, and crime prevention.

See also: Crime: Crime Control Bill of 1994; Criminal Justice Policy

References: Lee H. Bowker, *Corrections: The Science and Art* (1982); Steffen W. Schmidt, Mack C. Shelley II, and Barbara A. Bardes, *American Government and Politics Today* (1997).

Crime Control Bill of 1994

In September 1994 Congress passed the Violent Crime Control and Law Enforcement Act (known as the Crime Control Bill). The bill funded $30.2 billion over six years for more than 60 law enforcement, prison construction, and crime prevention programs. The bill also increased penalties for federal crimes and added new law enforcement personnel. Funding under the bill ends in fiscal year 2000, although the federal appropriations process determines actual funding levels. Funding is based on awards to states and local governments through formulas or competitive project grants. Local governments are the primary recipients of the cops-on-the-beat law enforcement grants, which are authorized for $8.8 billion. State governments have been authorized to receive federal grant money for prison construction.

Other provisions of the bill include implementation of the Brady Gun Control Bill; undocumented alien felon incarceration grants; drug courts; family and community endeavor grants; and violent crimes against women grants. A "three-strikes" provision for federal crimes is also contained in the bill, mandating life in prison for people convicted of three felonies. The bill also extended the death penalty to more than 50 federal crimes. In 1998 funding authorization came under intense scrutiny, and many of the programs originally listed stand to be eliminated. This legislation was a focus of the Republican Party's 1994 "Contract with America" as its attempt to strengthen the Crime Control Act of 1990.

See also: Crime: Criminal Justice Policy

References: Steffen W. Schmidt, Mack C. Shelley II, and Barbara A. Bardes, *American Government and Politics Today* (1997).

Criminal Justice Policy

Federal and state constitutions grant authority to legislatures to pass laws on criminal behavior. Legislatures define criminal behavior and establish penalties. As in most public policy areas, laws that are targeted at criminal behavior begin with private citizens, interest groups, local communities, agencies, public officials, and members of legislatures. Legislatures are then expected to respond by designing bills, establishing procedures, funding programs, defining crimes, and fixing sentences. After the legislatures enact the laws, courts apply the laws according to constitutional standards.

The agents of the American criminal justice system are the police, courts and judges, prosecutors and defense attorneys, correctional officials, probation and parole officers, counselors, and various staffs. All are concerned about the origins of crime, crime patterns, the collection of crime data, issues related to victimization, and crime trends. Race, gender, age, and other demographic factors are important in dealing with crime and creating criminal justice policy. One of the most important areas is juvenile crime and justice. The focus of the juvenile justice system is delinquent children. Without proper treatment and attention, delinquent children can become a future statistic. There has been an alarming increase in antisocial behavior among juveniles, and more professionals are making efforts to ensure that job opportunities are present for young people; that improved family relationships receive programmatic attention and funding; and that school systems are more effective in educating and preparing young people for life after graduation.

See also: Crime: Correctional Policy; Crime Control Bill of 1994

References: Joseph Senna and Larry Siegel, *Introduction to Criminal Justice* (1993); L. Thomas Winfree Jr. and Howard Abadinsky, *Understanding Crime: Theory and Practice* (1996).

Decriminalization

There are several ways that criminal justice academics, practitioners, and commentators view the function of criminal justice policy in the United States: Some believe that a strict approach should be taken to deter criminal conduct through punishment and other sanctions; others advocate rehabilitation, that caring for and treating people should be the goal of criminal justice policy; another perspective is the due process approach, introduced by Herbert Packer in *Limits of the Criminal Sanction,* which calls for fair and equitable treatment of offenders by the criminal justice system (with impartial hearings, competent legal counsel, equitable treatment); finally, the nonintervention approach seeks to decriminalize certain forms of conduct and treat offenders (e.g., in victimless crimes, marijuana possession, public drunkenness, and vagrancy). The decriminalization argument is limited to first offenders, minor offenses, and attempts to keep offenders out of the criminal justice system by diversion programs. This approach to criminal justice policy has become commonplace in the management of certain offenses, especially given the problem of overcrowded prisons.

See also: Crime: Criminal Justice Policy

References: Herbert Packer, *Limits of the Criminal Sanction* (1968); Joseph Senna and Larry Siegel, *Introduction to Criminal Justice* (1993); James Q. Wilson, *Thinking about Crime* (1975).

Department of Justice

The U.S. Department of Justice (DOJ) is an executive department that was established in 1870. The department's principal duties are to furnish legal advice to the president; enforce federal crime laws; and supervise the federal corrections system. It is considered to be the largest law firm in the nation, with some 100,000 employees. Its more general role is to serve as counsel for American citizens by enforcing the law in the public interest with attorneys, investigators, and agents. Its other duties are to provide protection against criminals and subversion, provide safeguards for American consumers, and enforce drug, immigration, and naturalization laws.

The department represents the government in legal matters and provides legal advice to the heads of executive departments. The department is lead by the U.S. attorney general, who is appointed by the president with the advice and consent of the Senate. The attorney general directs department activities and supervises U.S. attorneys and U.S. marshals in the various judicial districts.

The department is divided into four branches: the executive direction and management offices; the litigation organizations; investigatory and law enforcement offices; and legal and policy offices. Other agencies located within the Department of Justice include the Federal Bureau of Investigation (FBI); the Drug Enforcement Administration (DEA); the Bureau of Prisons; and the Immigration and Naturalization Service (INS).

During the 1980s and 1990s DOJ became heavily involved in the nation's war on drugs, primarily in stopping the transport of illegal drugs into the United States; the agency has had mixed success in drug interdiction. DOJ and the FBI have also been active in prosecuting white-collar crimes. The DOJ has benefited from advanced computer technology to gather data and information on crime and criminals.

See also: Crime: Federal Bureau of Investigation; Labor: Immigration and Naturalization Service

References: Steffen W. Schmidt, Mack C. Shelley II, and Barbara A. Bardes, *American Government and Politics Today* (1997); Joseph Senna and Larry Siegel, *Introduction to Criminal Justice* (1993).

Drug Enforcement Administration

In 1914 the Congress passed the Harrison Act, the federal government's first attempt to control and regulate the supply and use of narcotics. In 1973 the various federal level drug enforcement units were consolidated into the Drug Enforcement Administration (DEA), an agency within the Department of Justice. DEA operates through agents who assist local and state law enforcement agencies and governments in investigating illegal drug use, surveillance, and enforcement; its goal is to carry out drug enforcement policy for the federal government. Much DEA activity is devoted to working with foreign governments and their agencies (especially in Mexico and Latin America) to interdict drugs brought into the United States.

The government's efforts have been characterized as the nation's war on drugs. DEA has very direct methods in place to stop the flow of drugs, but critical scrutiny has been steady, and the success of DEA efforts has been the subject of continuing inquiry. The Federal Bureau of Investigation coordinates with DEA in the administration of drug interdiction and enforcement programs.

See also: Crime: Criminal Justice Policy; Department of Justice

References: Joseph Senna and Larry Siegel, *Introduction to Criminal Justice* (1993)

Drug Policy

See Crime: Drug Enforcement Administration

Exclusionary Rule

Under the exclusionary rule, based in the Fourth Amendment to the Constitution, all evidence obtained by illegal search or seizure is inadmissible in criminal trials; illegal confessions (protected against under the Fifth Amendment) are also excluded from criminal trials. It is a means of restricting police from engaging in unlawful searches and seizures.

The exclusionary rule is based on Fourth Amendment guarantees that individuals have the right to be secure in their persons (unlawful bodily searches), homes, papers, and effects from unreasonable searches and seizures. The U.S. Supreme Court made the exclusionary rule applicable to the states in the 1961 decision *Mapp v. Ohio. Mapp* involved an unwarranted search and seizure of a person's home, whereby police broke into a home without a proper search warrant looking for evidence that would link the individual to a bombing and possession of police paraphernalia; the police found pornographic material, for which the suspect was arrested and convicted in state court. The material found by police was not the original subject of the search, and the U.S. Supreme Court overturned the state court conviction, declaring the original police search unconstitutional. In the 1990s the exclusionary rule is being applied more narrowly, meaning that evidence is more easily admissible in court proceedings.

See also: Crime: Criminal Justice Policy

References: Joseph Senna and Larry Siegel, *Introduction to Criminal Justice* (1993); L. Thomas Winfree Jr. and Howard Abadinsky, *Understanding Crime: Theory and Practice* (1996).

Federal Bureau of Investigation

The Federal Bureau of Investigation (FBI) is the elite law enforcement organization in the United States. The FBI grew out of a need for an investigative arm within the Department of Justice. Pres. Theodore Roosevelt was set on busting the trusts and monopolies in American industry, and he wanted to expose members of Congress who supported the trusts surreptitiously. Roosevelt first sought aid from Congress when, in 1907, he asked it to fund a detective force for the Department of Justice. Congress would not grant funding, fearing the creation of a secret police force. Roosevelt's attorney general, Charles J. Bonaparte, appealed to Congress on the president's behalf, but it refused to budge. Bonaparte persisted, and in 1908 the Bureau of Investigation was created.

The early efforts focused on antitrust prosecutions, bankruptcy and fraud cases, prostitution, and commercial vice operations. It made a national reputation in pursuing white slavery; the next big issue was the apprehension and prosecution of radical aliens. Subversive bombings were on the increase in the United States in the years following World War I; the leader of the General Intelligence Division was a young Justice Department lawyer named J. Edgar Hoover. Hoover's unit was successful and made an estimated 10,000 arrests in early 1920.

J. Edgar Hoover was appointed as director of the Bureau of Investigation on May 10, 1924. He set about professionalizing the FBI with a training regimen for agents and the creation of career service for all agents. The name of the agency was changed in 1935 to the Federal Bureau of Investigation. Its role changed during the 1950s and 1960s, and the FBI became the nation's chief law enforcement agency. It investigated the activities of suspected Communist Party members, the assassinations of civil rights workers in the South, and suspected political radicals and antiwar activists during the Vietnam War era. The final years of J. Edgar Hoover's directorship were filled with criticism, as accusations flew that the FBI was disrupting American lives and denying fundamental rights under the guise of pursuing criminals. Hoover died in 1972, succeeded by Patrick Gray. One of the most damaging investigations that the FBI engaged in was the COINTELPRO effort, a domestic counterintelligence program intended to discredit Martin Luther King Jr. and other political activists.

The new FBI maintains its reputation as the nation's elite law enforcement group, its advanced technology and criminal profiling becoming the standards for fighting crime. The agency is responsible for fighting domestic federal crimes, particularly white-collar crime, public corruption, terrorism, and espionage. The FBI provides other law enforcement agencies with cooperative services such as fingerprint identification, laboratory examinations, police training, uniform crime reports, and the National Crime Information Center.

See also: Crime: Criminal Justice Policy

References: Nelson Blackstock, *COINTELPRO: The FBI's Secret War on Political Freedom* (1976); Fred J. Cook, *The FBI Nobody Knows* (1964); James A. Inciardi, *Criminal Justice* (1984).

Federal Gun Control Act of 1968

Many Americans feel strongly about their right to own guns and believe that the Second Amendment to the U.S. Constitution guarantees them the right to own guns. The amendment states that "a well regulated militia" may be kept and that the people have a "right . . . to keep and bear arms." States are authorized to regulate the control and sale of guns. Because of the amount of violence in the United States, especially that due to the use of guns, gun control legislation is common and controversial. The FBI reported that 29 percent of all aggravated assaults, 40 percent of all robberies, and 64 percent of all murders were accomplished with guns.

In 1968 Congress passed the Federal Gun Control Act in response to the assassinations of Sen. Robert F. Kennedy and civil rights leader Martin Luther King Jr. These two murders were devastating for many Americans and caused American citizens to seek legislation to control the sale and spread of guns in American society. The Federal Gun Control Act had five major provisions: (1) the law banned interstate and mail-order sales of handguns; (2) it prohibited the sale of any firearms to a convicted felon, fugitive, or person who was judged mentally insane; (3) it required all firearms dealers to be licensed by the federal Bureau of Alcohol, Tobacco, and Firearms of the Department of the Treasury; (4) it required gun manufacturers to record the serial numbers of all firearms and dealers to record all sales of firearms (dealers were also required to have proof of identity and residence of purchasers of guns); and

(5) it continued restrictions on private ownership of automatic weapons, military weapons, and heavy ordinance.

See also: Crime: Brady Handgun Violence Prevention Act of 1993

References: Thomas R. Dye, *Understanding Public Policy* (1995); Steffen W. Schmidt, Mack C. Shelley II, and Barbara A. Bardes, *American Government and Politics Today* (1997); U.S. Bureau of the Census, *Statistical Abstract of the United States* (1997).

Furman v. Georgia

See Crime: Capital Punishment

Gideon v. Wainwright

Until 1963 indigent criminal defendants were not guaranteed the right to counsel. That changed with the Supreme Court decision in *Gideon v. Wainwright,* establishing the right to counsel for all state defendants facing felony trials. Clarence Gideon was a 51-year-old Floridian who had been in and out of prison much of his life. He was charged with breaking and entering a poolroom in Panama City, Florida. Ordinarily, this would have been a case of petty larceny, but under Florida law it was a felony. Gideon was a harmless, likable individual who was without a means of living and who couldn't pay for a defense attorney. Gideon claimed that the Supreme Court guaranteed him the right to be represented by counsel (the Court at that time made no such guarantee). Gideon defended himself; he was found guilty and sentenced to five years in prison.

While in prison Gideon filed a petition in forma pauperis (a "poor man's petition"), seeking review of his case by the U.S. Supreme Court. The Court agreed to review the case and assigned Washington attorney Abe Fortas to argue Gideon's case. The Court unanimously decided to overturn a 1941 case (*Betts v. Brady*) and ruled that Gideon was entitled to a new trial. The Court felt that indigent defendants could not be ensured a fair trial without the assistance of proper counsel. On retrial, Gideon was acquitted. This case established the precedent that every criminal defendant was entitled to counsel in the conduct of a felony trial. Abe Fortas was later appointed to the Supreme Court by Pres. Lyndon B. Johnson.

See also: Crime: Criminal Justice Policy

References: James A. Inciardi, *Criminal Justice* (1984); Anthony Lewis, *Gideon's Trumpet* (1966).

Mapp v. Ohio

The exclusionary rule was introduced by the U.S. Supreme Court in 1914; evidence obtained as a result of an unreasonable search and seizure is inadmissible as evidence in federal cases as a violation of the Fourth Amendment to the Constitution. The exclusionary rule was extended to the states in the 1961 Supreme Court case *Mapp v. Ohio.* The case involved an unreasonable arrest, search, and seizure in a Cleveland, Ohio, home by police without a search warrant. The Supreme Court extended the exclusionary rule to the states, making illegally obtained evidence inadmissible in any courtroom. This expansion of the exclusionary rule was disheartening to police and other law enforcement organizations because they felt it ultimately protected criminals. The *Mapp* decision has been modified since the 1960s; there is currently a more relaxed interpretation of the exclusionary rule in the states.

See also: Crime: Criminal Justice Policy

References: James A. Inciardi, *Criminal Justice* (1984); Joseph Senna and Larry Siegel, *Introduction to Criminal Justice* (1993).

Miranda v. Arizona

The Supreme Court's 1966 decision in *Miranda v. Arizona* is considered important for the constitutional protections it extends to criminal suspects. To "Mirandize" a criminal suspect is to notify the suspect as to certain rights, for example, the right to counsel and the right to remain silent. All citizens are protected by the Fifth Amendment, which guarantees that no person shall be compelled to be a witness against himself. Confessions obtained by police without the appropriate *Miranda* notification to the confessor will be deemed inadmissible in later court proceedings as a violation of the Fifth Amendment. The *Miranda* warning has become a part of the American popular lexicon ("You have the right to remain silent; anything you say can and will be held against you") and is a standard element of police procedures.

See also: Crime: Criminal Justice Policy

References: Joseph Senna and Larry Siegel, *Introduction to Criminal Justice* (1996).

Mothers Against Drunk Driving

A good example of a group organizing around a common problem is Mothers Against Drunk Driving (MADD), whose members have had loved ones killed or injured by drunk drivers. Organized in 1982, MADD's activism has led to better awareness of and harsher penalties for drunk driving. Strengthened state laws for drunk driving have surfaced throughout the United States.

See also: Key Concepts: Agenda Building

References: Dennis J. Palumbo, *Public Policy in America: Government in Action* (1988).

National Rifle Association

The National Rifle Association (NRA) is one of the most powerful interest groups in the United States. NRA was founded in 1871 and is dedicated to providing shooting instruction, but the organization tackles much more than that. During the 1960s and early 1970s, when gun control legislation was introduced in the states and Congress, NRA took the lead in protecting rights under the Second Amendment, which guarantees citizens a right to bear arms.

Between 1982 and 1993 NRA spent more than $8 million in support of candidates running for Congress, and NRA remains one of the most powerful lobbying groups in the country, with more than 2.6 million members. NRA typically supports politically conservative candidates who support the unrestricted purchase and sale of firearms. During the 1990s NRA actively supported legislation that permits the sale of automatic weapons. Gun-control supporters organized during the 1980s and 1990s to counter the influence of groups like NRA.

See also: Crime: Brady Handgun Violence Prevention Act of 1993; Key Concepts: Interest Groups

References: James Q. Wilson and John J. DiIulio Jr., *American Government: The Essentials* (1998).

Plea Bargaining

In criminal proceedings, government prosecutors often give defendants the opportunity to plead guilty to a lesser criminal charge. Pleading guilty before trial (plea bargaining) often leads to a lesser sentence, such as probation rather than hard time in prison. Prosecutors are willing to enter plea bargains to save time and costs for the court by avoiding trial. The victims of crime are sometimes put off by plea bargaining, perceiving that the defendant is getting away with lesser punishment, yet the practice is a common tool in the criminal justice system.

See also: Crime: Criminal Justice Policy

References: Herbert Jacob, *Law and Politics in the United States* (1986); Richard Quinney, *Class, State, and Crime* (1977).

Police Culture

Police departments must demonstrate a clear sense of responsibility to the communities they serve. During the first fifty years of the 20th century, urban police forces typically selected members from Irish or Italian stock, those who were white, male, and perhaps the son of an officer. This perpetuated ethnic, racial, and family ties to the system, meaning all others were seen as outsiders. This created distrust between urban police forces and the communities they served, leading to resentment, even hatred for police in general. Urban police departments have changed their ethnic and racial makeup during the past 20 years; African Americans, Latinos, and Asians are now important components of police forces nationwide.

The police culture is the notion that police departments have beliefs, traditions, and behaviors that isolate them from the mainstream elements of the communities they serve. These carry features that further the bond among police officers, like secrecy, or the promise not to "rat" on a fellow officer regardless of the circumstances. Due to the dangerous nature of police work, officers tend to associate with other police officers outside the job, believing that only other officers can understand the pressure police officers endure. Sociologist Jerome Skolnick calls this the "occupational personality" of police, whereby they develop a "hardness" that protects them from the pressures of intense and dangerous duties. The police culture is based on codes of conduct, secrecy, and a feeling of isolation. Progressive police leaders encourage officers to seek friendships and associations outside the job. Police are also encouraged to seek education opportunities for personal and intellectual growth. Perpetuation of the police culture can be seen as detrimental to effective police work.

See also: Crime: Criminal Justice Policy

References: Egon Bittner, *The Functions of Police in Modern*

Society (1980); Jerome Skolnick and David Bayley, *Community Policing: Issues and Practices around the World* (1988); James Q. Wilson, *Varieties of Police Behavior* (1968).

Police Discretion

The criminal justice process begins the moment a police officer stops a suspect or makes an arrest. At that moment, the officer is exercising discretion. That decision might lead to nothing more than a stern warning, but it can also mean arrest, incarceration, criminal trial, and harsh penalties. Thus, police must be careful when exercising discretion, and the U.S. Supreme Court over decades of case law has set constitutional boundaries to prevent abuse and protect citizens.

See also: Crime: Criminal Justice Policy

References: Herbert Packer, *Limits of the Criminal Sanction* (1968); Joseph Senna and Larry Siegel, *Introduction to Criminal Justice* (1993).

Racketeer Influenced and Corrupt Organization Act of 1970

In the battle against organized crime, Congress passed the Racketeer Influenced and Corrupt Organization Act (RICO) in 1970. This act differed from other anticrime legislation by authorizing the seizure of money, bank accounts, personal property, and other assets held by people involved in organized crime and racketeering. The Federal Bureau of Investigation, the Drug Enforcement Administration, the U.S. Customs Service, and the Treasury Department are authorized to seize property of members of organized crime who are arrested. The rationale was that assets—real property, boats, airplanes, and homes—were acquired as a result of criminal activity. RICO was different because the government seized assets before criminal defendants were brought to trial, needing only to prove "probable cause" to seize a defendant's property and assets. As long as the government could meet this standard, property could be seized. This is an extraordinary government measure to fight organized crime.

See also: Crime: Criminal Justice Policy

References: George F. Cole and Marc G. Gertz, *The Criminal Justice System: Politics and Policies* (1998); Thomas R. Dye, *Understanding Public Policy* (1995); L. Thomas Winfree Jr. and Howard Abadinsky, *Understanding Crime: Theory and Practice* (1996).

Right to Bear Arms

See Crime: National Rifle Association

Economics

Chronology

1913 Sixteenth Amendment passed, creating federal income tax.

1932 Revenue Act imposed federal sales tax on gasoline, electricity, refrigerators, and telephone messages. It raised the personal and corporate income tax across the board and imposed the largest peacetime tax increases in the nation's history.

1933 Emergency Banking Act passed, giving the president power to reorganize failed banks.

1933 Glass-Steagall Act passed, creating the Federal Deposit Insurance Corporation.

1934 Securities Exchange Act passed, creating the Securities and Exchange Commission.

1938 Revenue Act, championed by conservatives in Congress, reversed tax reform efforts and changed corporate income tax requirements.

1974 Congressional Budget Act passed, requiring annual publication of tax expenditure budget.

1981 Economic Recovery Tax Act passed, a massive reduction of taxes. The tax cut was intended to reduce the deficit and encourage private spending and investment.

1985 Gramm-Rudman Act passed, mandating caps on the federal deficit and reducing spending on new programs.

1987 Tax Reform Act passed, sponsored by a bipartisan group in Congress to reform taxes to broaden the tax base with a reduced rate structure and encourage development of economic enterprise.

1993 Earned Income Tax Credit was established to reduce the tax burden on low-income families.

1997 Taxpayer Relief Act reduced federal income taxes.

American Dream Restoration Act

In September 1994 Republican members of Congress proposed the "Contract with America," a covenant with voters, who then elected a Republican Party majority in the Congress in the November 1994 elections. One of the ten proposals was the American Dream Restoration Act, which proposed a $500-per-child tax credit to families and a repeal of the so-called marriage penalty in the U.S. tax code. Congress passed the bill, but its major provisions were funded in the Balanced Budget Act of 1995. Pres. Bill Clinton vetoed the legislation. Like other elements of the "Contract with America," the American Dream Restoration Act met with limited success and substantial resistance in Congress; some of its tax-cutting provisions were included in later legislation. President Clinton signed the Taxpayer Relief Act of 1997, which provides a $500-per-child tax credit and education credits.

See also: Economics: Tax Policy

References: Charles Bonser, Eugene B. McGregor Jr., and Clinton V. Oster Jr., *Policy Choices and Public Action* (1996).

Balanced Budget Amendment

Sometimes members of the U.S. Congress call for a balanced budget amendment to the Constitution, but such appeals often receive little attention. A constitutional amendment of this sort would require Congress to pass a balanced budget every year unless a supermajority of Congress declared that a sufficient economic emergency existed to justify running a deficit. Congress would be required to more closely monitor budget development, account for the money that it appropriates, and clearly control spending.

Although the balanced budget amendment has strong appeal to some members of Congress, the national budget process is so complex, so time consuming that it does not fit easily into routine schedules of activity, and annual budgeting is subject to the variations in the national economy. Thus, it is unclear whether a balanced budget amendment would actually fix the U.S. deficit problem.

See also: Economics: Budget Deficit; Budget, Federal

References: B. Guy Peters, *American Public Policy: Promise and Performance* (1993); Ronald E. Pynn, *American Politics: Changing Expectations* (1993).

Balanced Budget and Emergency Deficit Control Act of 1985

This legislation, also known as Gramm-Rudman (after its congressional sponsors), mandates across-the-board cuts in nearly all federal programs by a uniform percentage to achieve specified deficit levels if regular budget and appropriations actions fail to achieve those deficit goals. One of the aspects of the act was that the General Accounting Office (GAO) could sequester funds (impose automatic spending cuts). In *Bowsher v. Synar,* the U.S. Supreme Court ruled Gramm-Rudman unconstitutional because it violated the Constitution's separation of powers (an encroachment on the president's authority to execute the laws). The Court found that investing GAO and the comptroller general with executive authority to sequester funds by estimating, allocating, and ordering spending cuts to meet deficit targets violated the separation-of-powers doctrine. Since the comptroller general is subject to removal by the Congress, the Court determined that the comptroller general, as an officer answerable only to Congress, gave Congress control over execution of the laws, powers that are reserved to the president.

This bill was revised in 1987 by the original authors, replacing the comptroller general with the Office of Management and Budget (OMB), an executive agency under the authority of the president. OMB now had the responsibility for determining the deficit size and the need for automatic cuts. Controlling the budget deficit by legislative action like the Gramm-Rudman was not as easy as sponsors expected. Controlling the federal deficit, the budget, and spending proved difficult. Across-the-board cost-cutting was found lacking as a solution; a new budget plan was introduced in 1990 (the Budget Enforcement Act), altering the setting of deficit targets.

See also: Economics: Budget Deficit; Budget, Federal; Gramm-Rudman Act of 1985

References: Ronald E. Pynn, *American Politics: Changing Expectations* (1993).

Banking Act of 1935

In 1935 Federal Reserve Board Gov. Marriner S. Eccles and U.S. Sen. Carter Glass collaborated to revise the Federal Reserve Act of 1913. The Federal Reserve is the central bank of the United States; the Federal Reserve System was created to implement monetary policy decisions. The original Federal Reserve was created in 1913 in response to a banking panic that exposed the weakness of the national banking system. The Board of Governors and the Federal Open Market Committee play a major role in the Federal Reserve System in their power to make monetary decisions.

The Banking Act that Eccles and Glass wrote changed the composition of the Federal Reserve's Board of Governors to be a seven-person body. The act gave the reconfigured board greater powers over the 12 regional banks and greater control of rediscount rates, reserve requirements, and open-market purchase of government bonds. This new Banking Act greatly increased federal power over the banking system.

See also: Economics: Economic Policy; Federal Reserve Board

References: Jeffrey E. Cohen, *Politics and Economic Policy in the United States* (1997).

Budget and Accounting Act of 1921

In 1921, in the wake of World War I, the United States faced a severe recession. U.S. involvement in the war resulted in huge budget deficits; Congress's response to the impending budget and economic crisis was to pass the Budget and Accounting Act, which established the Bureau of the Budget (now called the Office of Management and Budget) and required the president to submit an estimate of receipts and expenditures to each regular session of Congress. Budget reformers in Congress wanted to find ways to promote fiscal prudence. This legislation was designed to concentrate federal budget responsibilities in the presidency and therefore create an executive budget without giving all budget authority to the president. Congress still reserved its authority over the budget through the Appropriations Committees and the Ways and Means Committees.

See also: Economics: Budget, Federal; Office of Management and Budget; Key Concepts: Appropriations Committee

References: Allen Schick, *Congress and Money: Budgeting, Spending, and Taxing* (1980); Aaron Wildavsky, *The New Politics of the Budgetary Process* (1988).

Budget and Impoundment Control Act of 1974

This act was an attempt by Congress to regain its role in budgetmaking, as its role had been declining since the 1940s. The act created the Budget Committee and the Congressional Budget Office. It was designed to reform the budget-building process and impose restrictions and guidelines on presidential authority to impound funds. A president engages in impoundment by refusing to spend money Congress has appropriated. Pres. Richard M. Nixon frequently impounded funds, and many members of Congress felt that he had overstepped his bounds. The act gave the Budget Committee the task of setting spending targets based on revenue projections, established needs, and national economic considerations. It also required that a presidential decision of permanent impoundment was not valid unless both houses of Congress concurred within 45 days. If the president decided temporarily to not spend appropriated funds, the action would stand unless either house of Congress passed a resolution requiring the president to spend the money. This act took control away from the Appropriations Committees to set overall spending limits; the Budget Committee would control those decisions. Thus, spending limits were now in the hands of the Budget Committee and the entire Congress rather than the Appropriations Committees.

See also: Economics: Budget, Federal

References: Jeffrey E. Cohen, *Politics and Economic Policy in the United States* (1997); Ronald E. Pynn, *American Politics: Changing Expectations* (1993).

Budget Deficit

If a government is running a budget deficit, it is spending more than it is receiving in revenue. To finance a deficit, a government must borrow money. The opposite of a deficit is a surplus, which means that the government takes in more revenue than it is spending. Governments can create deficits by cutting taxes or by increasing spending. The issue of controlling or managing the deficit is a matter of fiscal policy whereby a government attempts to influence the national economy. During the Great Depression, people looked to the government to solve economic problems. Pres. Franklin D. Roosevelt thus used the government to influence the economy in order to affect the business cycle and provide economic stability by increasing government spending to stimulate demand, redistributing income, and regulating the economy and the financial markets.

The United States had a serious budget deficit at the end of World War I and World War II. At the end of each war the government attempted to control spending and stabilize the national economy by creating budget-control mechanisms. After World War II the government institutionalized fiscal policy with the passing of the Employment Act of 1946, designed to promote full-employment goals and policy. Although that never happened (due to the absence of clear policy and mechanisms to create new jobs), this law marked a major change for the U.S. government in influencing the national economy. The United States confronted another period of deficits following the Vietnam War during the mid-1970s. Since that time, controlling the deficit has been an annual issue for U.S. political parties, resulting in calls for a balanced budget and reduced government spending, popularly known as fiscal conservatism.

The budget deficit is important to fiscal policy because it can undermine financial markets' confidence in government. Investors look to government to control spending in order to safeguard investments and protect against inflation. Deficit borrowing also restricts opportunities for private borrowing, which is important to maintaining reasonable interest rates. A deficit also means that a nation is consuming more than its economy is producing. This causes an imbalance in imports from other nations to meet the demand for goods and services required by American consumers and entrepreneurs. The result is that jobs are exported, dollars leave the national economy, and government is encouraged to spend more, which makes the deficit problem even worse.

See also: Economics: Budget, Federal; Economic Policy; Labor: Employment Act of 1946

References: Jeffrey E. Cohen, *Politics and Economic Policy in the United States* (1997); Allen Schick, *Congress and Money: Budgeting, Spending, and Taxing* (1980); Aaron Wildavsky, *The New Politics of the Budgetary Process* (1988).

Budget Enforcement Act of 1990

In the ongoing battle to control government spending during the 1980s and 1990s, the 1985 Balanced Budget and Emergency Deficit Control Act (known as Gramm-Rudman for its congressional sponsors) was designed to restrict government spending by imposing mandatory deficit reductions. The 1990 Budget Enforcement Act made several changes to Gramm-Rudman to help Congress develop a rational budget process in the face of these deficit-reduction mandates. The act changed the budget calendar by including three sequester orders instead of one, as mandated by Gramm-Rudman; limited discretionary spending in the annual appropriation process; and created a pay-as-you-go process, requiring that legislative spending or tax cuts be revenue-neutral (i.e., accompanied with tax increases or spending cuts). The Budget Enforcement Act of 1990 was meant to offset some of the problems in across-the-board cuts and budget management issues brought on by the original 1985 Gramm-Rudman. The 1990 act grants a five-year period for managing the budget and deficits.

See also: Economics: Balanced Budget and Emergency Deficit Control Act of 1985; Budget Deficit; Budget, Federal

References: Ronald E. Pynn, *American Politics: Changing Expectations* (1993).

Budget, Federal

The annual federal budget sets forth the president's proposals for government spending and taxation and estimates how much all proposals will cost. The budget is a statement of the president's economic and political views. It specifies how the president wants the government to be involved in American households and businesses. Taxation, inflation, unemployment, and assorted economic problems are items of concern in developing the national budget. As an instrument of fiscal policy, it determines national spending priorities.

The federal budget operates in the framework of the fiscal year, which runs from October 1 through September 30. Planning for annual budgets begins about 18 months before the start of a new fiscal year. The first step in the budget process involves the president and the Office of Management and Budget (OMB) setting budgetary parameters. The key questions are: What should be the size of the budget? How large or small should the deficit be? What should be the balance between spending for defense and for social programs? These decisions are based on predictions about probable levels of revenue, inflation, economic growth, and interest rates. All are political decisions that reflect the priorities, preferences, and goals of an administration. The OMB then takes the budget outline and presents the priorities and goals to agencies for preparing agencies' requests for funds. The president reviews the requests, adjusts them to meet administration goals, then prepares the formal budget request and submits it to Congress no later than the first Monday in February.

Congress is required to adopt a budget resolution by April 15. It sets congressional priorities in 13 broad categories of spending in policy areas such as defense, transportation, agriculture, and social programs; each category has an appropriations bill. Congress projects available revenues, overall spending levels, and the size of the deficit. The House and Senate budget committees must review and agree upon the budget resolution. If there are changes, then Congress is required to engage in reconciliation, whereby congressional leaders and budget committees negotiate new provisions. Subcommittees of the respective Appropriations Committees hold hearings to provide agencies their last opportunity to influence allocations. If the appropriations bills are passed by October 1, the new fiscal year can start under a new budget. If the bills are not all passed, then "continuing resolutions" are offered and signed by the president to allow the federal government to continue spending as if the previous annual budget was still in effect.

The size of the federal budget in the United States is some $1.7 trillion. The government now spends twice as much as it did during the early 1980s, with spending commitments in national defense, human resources, physical resources, and paying off the interest on the national debt. The primary challenges are to reduce the federal deficit and maintain or increase government services without increasing taxes.

See also: Economics: Budget Deficit; Economic Policy

References: Jeffrey E. Cohen, *Politics and Economic Policy in the United States* (1997); Susan Welch et al., *Understanding American Government* (1997); Aaron Wildavsky, *The New Politics of the Budgetary Process* (1988).

Clayton Antitrust Act of 1914

During the late 19th century the federal government responded to pressures exerted by the antimonopoly movement, which attacked the growing power of large corporations. Victims of corporate power included farmers, who felt that corporate power lowered prices for agriculture products; consumers also complained that corporations controlled markets and charged exorbitant prices for goods. Reining in corporate power would not be easy, however. Corporations received their charters from the states, and so corporations conducted business across state lines relatively free from regulation. Federal courts had also shown leniency toward corporations, interpreting the Fourteenth Amendment to the Constitution liberally to ensure that state legislation did not deprive corporations of life, liberty, or property without due process of law.

Congress restrained corporate power in 1890 by passing the Sherman Antitrust Act, intended to restrict the creation of trusts (combinations and mergers of corporations) and monopolies, which restrained trade. The belief at the time was that the act would control conspiracies to restrain trade and commerce. The act was vague and was enforced only 18 times between 1890 and 1901, four of the enforcements being directed at labor unions.

The Clayton Antitrust Act of 1914 put teeth in the Sherman Antitrust Act, defining illegal practices such as price discrimination aimed at monopoly, tying contracts, interlocking directorates of competing firms, and holding companies. The act authorized remedies in the form of court injunctions, private suits, and Federal Trade Commission cease-and-desist orders. The act made clear that its provisions were not intended to forbid labor or agricultural organizations; it also forbade the use of injunctions in labor disputes unless necessary to prevent irreparable injury to property. Unlike the Sherman Act, the Clayton Act was enforceable, and the Federal Trade Commission brought 92 antitrust suits over eight years. This legislation marked a departure from previous positions and the philosophy expressed in the Sherman Act toward labor organizations. The Clayton Act represented meaningful change in the posture of the federal government toward labor organizations, recognizing the right of labor to organize and act in the interests of workers.

See also: Economics: Federal Trade Commission; Labor: Labor Policy

References: Leif H. Carter and Christine B. Harrington, *Administrative Law and Politics: Cases and Comments* (1991); Kermit L. Hall, William M. Wiecek, and Paul Finkelman, *American Legal History* (1991).

Congressional Budget Office

Many of the unseen actors in the American political process are support staff members and committees in Congress. Congress draws on professional staffs to provide information during decisionmaking. The Congressional Budget Office (CBO) advises Congress on the anticipated economic effect of government expenditures and provides cost estimates for proposed policies. CBO serves both political parties and is more neutral in budget forecasting than is the presidential administration. CBO began operations in 1975 (authorized by the Congressional Budget Act of 1974) and was looked upon as Congress's own budget agency. The president's budget office is the Office of Management and Budget; members of Congress, particularly during the 1970s, felt that the legislature was at a disadvantage in challenging the executive branch in budget matters. Alice Rivlin was named the first CBO director in 1975, after seven months of haggling in Congress over the role and purpose of the budget director.

CBO was meant to be an independent agency that would undertake budget-related studies requested by Congress. The expertise provided by CBO is essential to budget and appropriations decisions in Congress. Accused of acting too independently, CBO has learned to seek political support through committee sponsorship of studies to pursue analysis in areas not originally requested by Congress.

See also: Economics: Budget and Impoundment Control Act of 1974; Budget, Federal; Economic Policy

References: Allen Schick, *Congress and Money: Budgeting, Spending, and Taxing* (1980); Susan Welch et al., *Understanding American Government* (1997); Aaron Wildavsky, *The New Politics of the Budgetary Process* (1988).

Council of Economic Advisers

In 1946 Congress passed the Full Employment Act, designed to make government responsible for promoting maximum employment, production, and purchasing power. The act also created the Council of Economic Advisers. Members of the council (one chair and two others, appointed by the president and confirmed by the Senate) are expected to be nongovernmental personnel, who provide the president with information and perspectives unaffected by special interests. Most council members are academic economists; their role has been strictly advisory to the president. The council is supported by a professional staff of economists who act as the senior staff economists. These staff members are drawn from academics who are on one- or two-year leaves of absence from universities; the senior staff is assisted by junior staff economists.

The formal duties and functions of the Council of Economic Advisers are: to assist and advise the president in the preparation of the national economic report; to gather data regarding economic developments and trends and offer this data as it assists in policymaking; to assess government programs and activities to make certain that the programs and activities are consistent with the achievement of economic policy of the president; to develop and recommend national economic policies that support and promote free enterprise and maintain employment, production, and purchasing power in the national economy; and to provide studies, reports, and recommendations on matters of federal economic policy and legislation.

In recent years the council has focused on advising the president on unemployment, inflation, economic growth, levels of government spending, taxation to affect the cost of living and employment, and productivity issues. The council has used a macroeconomic approach, looking at the whole economy, whereas the Office of Management and Budget emphasizes budget and deficits. The Council of Economic Advisers recommended that cost-benefit analysis be applied to federal environmental regulations. The council, along with the Department of the Treasury, provides information on the national budget, which is then passed along to the Office of Management and Budget for consideration by the president.

See also: Economics: Economic Policy; Office of Management and Budget; Labor: Employment Act of 1946

References: Jeffrey E. Cohen, *Politics and Economic Policy in the United States* (1997); Sven Steinmo, *Taxation and Democracy* (1993).

Deficit Reduction Act of 1984

During the late 1970s and early 1980s the federal government was saddled by recession and a huge budget deficit. In response to pressure to reduce the deficit, Congress sought to increase tax revenues without raising personal income taxes. New taxes were imposed on airports, cigarettes, telephones, gasoline, and fuel oil. Congress passed the Deficit Reduction Act in 1984, designed to increase taxes on alcohol (distilled spirits), extend the telephone excise tax, and repeal interest exclusion (a provision of the Economic Recovery Tax Act of 1981). The 1984 act was a part of a series of federal attempts to raise taxes through "revenue enhancements"; not meant to look like new taxes, they were in fact tax increases that would not burden every American citizen. These efforts did not generate enough revenues to offset the federal deficit.

See also: Economics: Budget, Federal; Economic Policy

References: Jeffrey E. Cohen, *Politics and Economic Policy in the United States* (1997); David G. Davies, *U.S. Taxes and Tax Policy* (1986); Sven Steinmo, *Taxation and Democracy* (1993).

Department of Treasury

The U.S. Treasury Department was created by Congress in 1789. Its functions are to pay all federal bills, collect federal taxes, mint coins and print paper currency, secure government credit, borrow money, administer the nation's balance of payments with other nations, operate the Secret Service, and supervise the national banks. This executive department is composed of the Internal Revenue Service (IRS); the Bureau of Alcohol, Tobacco, and Firearms; the U.S. Secret Service; the U.S. Mint; and the U.S. Customs Service. The department helps determine U.S. economic policy.

The department secretary generally exhibits a fiscally conservative role and is responsible to the president. In recent years, the secretary has been the chief opponent of expanding the government deficit and has worked toward a stable and sound dollar. The secretary is usually chosen from individuals who have backgrounds in business, banking, or finance and is often seen by the nation's business community as its emissary to the president. The secretary sits on the National Economic Council along with seven other cabinet secretaries. This body was created by Pres. Bill Clinton to coordinate economic policymaking with attention to domestic and international economic issues; to coordinate economic advice to the president; to ensure that policymaking decisions and programs are consistent with the president's perceptions of economic policy in action; and to monitor implementation of the president's economic policy agenda.

See also: Economics: Economic Policy

References: Jeffrey E. Cohen, *Politics and Economic Policy in the United States* (1997); Steffen W. Schmidt, Mack C. Shelley II, and Barbara A. Bardes, *American Government and Politics Today* (1997).

Deregulation

During the late 19th century the leading economic philosophy in the United States was laissez faire, meaning the economic marketplace existed on its own without government intrusion. The assumption of laissez faire was that the market and economy could correct themselves if imbalances in supply and demand occurred. This proved to not be the case, and the government intervened, albeit infrequently, to correct some of the imbalances that affected American consumers.

Regulatory activity took hold with the passage of the Interstate Commerce Act in 1887 and the Sherman Antitrust Act in 1890. In both cases, the government found it necessary to control the growth of monopolies and take action against the formation of trusts. During the Depression years, the Roosevelt administration's New Deal policies attempted to right the faltering U.S. economy. Congress and the government thus began a pattern of regulating activities in the private sector to correct imbalances in the national economy.

The next major era of regulatory activity came in the 1960s and 1970s, when so-called second-generation regulators were created, such as the Environmental Protection Agency, the Occupational Safety and Health Administration, and the Nuclear Regulatory Commission. These agencies and their activities have been controversial, as they are required to issue regulations in areas that have competing interests; interest groups and lobbyists counter the other in areas targeted for regulatory action. When regulations are created, they generally require an agency to administer and enforce the regulations, which involves a commitment from government to fund these regulatory activities. Regulations are sometimes costly for those being regulated, typically industries.

Since the 1970s, particularly during the Reagan and Bush administrations, deregulation has been the watchword in government. The initial target for deregulation was the transportation industry: trucking, airlines, buses, and railroads. The impact of deregulation has been to open competition, meaning that smaller businesses sometimes do not survive. Consumers have benefited from deregulation through lower prices and increased choices, yet some services declined or disappeared, leaving some communities with few or no choices at all. A consequence of deregulation is mergers and the buyouts of smaller companies. Mergers caused many industries to reduce workforces for purposes of streamlining.

Economic goals tend to prevail over social or moral goals in the debate over regulation versus deregulation. When governments considered creating new regulations in the 1990s, they weighed the costs against the benefits. Critics of regulation claim that American society is overregulated. The late 1990s have been described as an era of deregulation; the approach of the Clinton administration toward government regulation has been cautious.

See also: Commerce and Transportation: Act to Regulate Commerce of 1887; Economics: Economic Policy; Environment: Environmental Protection Agency; Key Concepts: Regulation

References: Leif H. Carter and Christine B. Harrington, *Administrative Law and Politics: Cases and Comments* (1991); Clarke E. Cochran et al., *American Public Policy: An Introduction* (1996); David Edwards and Alessandra Lippucci, *Practicing American Politics: An Introduction to American Government* (1998).

Dingley Tariff Act of 1897

In the wake of the late-19th-century depression, Pres. William H. Taft attempted to increase tariffs (taxes on imported goods) to protect infant American industries against foreign competitors. Taft's first maneuver was to revise the Dingley Tariff of 1897, which raised tariff rates to an all-time high of 57 percent. The use of the tariff was considered an element of fiscal policy in the growing industrial nation during the latter half of the 19th century. President Taft was encouraged in 1907 to lower tariff rates, but his efforts were unsuccessful. He supported the revision and reduction of tariffs proposed in the Payne-Aldrich Tariff of 1909, which was passed in Congress, but the Progressives in the House managed to keep tariff rates at the level established by the Dingley Act of 1897.

See also: Economics: Economic Policy

References: Jeffrey E. Cohen, *Politics and Economic Policy in the United States* (1997).

Earned Income Tax Credit

The 1993 earned income tax credit is a small policy step to reduce the income tax burden on poor families. This tax credit was an extension and expansion of legislation passed in 1975, which reduced payroll taxes for people with small incomes; it offered rebates of Social Security taxes to low-income workers. During the Reagan and Bush administrations, the earned income tax credit was expanded from 10 percent to 14 percent of payroll earnings (via the 1986 Tax Reform Act). It was increased in 1990 with an accommodation for family size. The purpose of the earned income tax credit is to provide the working poor with a more generous tax credit. For families with two or more children in 1994, the tax credit was 25 percent. Individuals are required to apply for the earned income tax credit, which applies to families with two or less children to the exclusion of large families who may have a greater need. Heads of families must be working to be eligible for the credit.

The tax credit was designed to reduce the poverty rolls and family reliance on welfare. It is uncertain whether poor families can truly take advantage of tax and welfare policies like the earned income tax credit.

See also: Economics: Tax Policy; Entitlement Programs: Welfare Policy

References: Charles Bonser, Eugene B. McGregor Jr., and Clinton V. Oster Jr., *Policy Choices and Public Action* (1996); Jeffrey E. Cohen, *Politics and Economic Policy in the United States* (1997); David G. Davies, *U.S. Taxes and Tax Policy* (1986); Steffen W. Schmidt, Mack C. Shelley II, and Barbara A. Bardes, *American Government and Politics Today* (1997).

Economic Development Administration

The Economic Development Administration (EDA) is an agency within the U.S. Department of Commerce that serves as the federal government's economic development branch. EDA was created under the Public Works and Economic Development Act of 1965. The original goal was to generate new jobs, help retain existing jobs, and stimulate industrial and commercial growth in economically depressed areas. The agency provides assistance to rural and urban areas that suffer from high unemployment, low income levels, or sudden and severe economic distress. EDA works in partnership with state and local governments, regional economic development districts, public and private nonprofit organizations, and Native American tribes. The primary focus of EDA assistance is distressed communities that have long-term economic deterioration. Thus, EDA activity has taken place in communities that have undergone closures of military bases and other federal facilities. The various EDA programs include public works programs, regional economic development programs, technical assistance programs, and related university economic development centers.

Since 1965 EDA has engaged in more than 40,000 development projects. During the 1990s the primary areas of EDA activity were in trade adjustment programs, defense economic adjustment, postdisaster economic recovery, local technical assistance, and sustainable development. Trade adjustment programs are designed to assist communities in which companies have suffered from shifts in trade activity. These are referred to as trade-injured firms. Defense economic adjustment programs have been extensive in the wake of some 150 military bases since

1995. EDA helps communities by demolishing old military structures, constructing new buildings, and rehabilitating old buildings. Given the natural disasters that occurred during the 1990s, EDA has been busy with postdisaster economic recovery assistance. Local technical assistance comes in the form of expertise to formulate economic development strategies. EDA activity in sustainable development is an ongoing enterprise, particularly in regions that rely heavily on natural resources for employment and economic activity. EDA efforts have been directed at the Northwest and the Northeast fishing communities as well as in Appalachia, where coal communities have suffered economic decline.

EDA activity is important for national economic development and communities in need of assistance. Communities gain EDA support by submitting proposals for grants or loans to aid economic development plans. Economic development is essential to communities and states to provide employment and a reasonable standard of living for citizens.

See also: Economics: Economic Policy

References: Jeffrey E. Cohen, *Politics and Economic Policy in the United States* (1997); Jeffrey L. Pressman and Aaron B. Wildavsky, *Implementation* (1973).

Economic Policy

The U.S. economy is based on capitalism and free enterprise. The economy is also more realistically characterized as a mixed economy, in which the government controls and regulates how private property may be used and how private enterprises may function. In American capitalism, private individuals and corporations own the means of production. The writers of the U.S. Constitution provided for an economic system based on free enterprise, a system whereby people could invest in any enterprise or choose any job they preferred. One of the purposes of government is to create the economic and political environment for the economy to prosper. Historically, the U.S. government has stimulated the economy through public investment, subsidization of economic development, and occasional intervention, regulating some of the large corporations that appeared to have monopoly control of certain industries.

During the 19th century the government's philosophy of laissez faire was adjusted to account for inequities that developed through unfettered economic competition. In 1887 the Interstate Commerce Commission was formed, and in 1890 the Sherman Antitrust Act was passed. These signaled the end of the classical period of laissez faire capitalism. Progressives in Congress during the later part of the 19th century prompted government to intervene in the marketplace. During the early part of the 20th century, the federal government was reluctant to intervene in the national economy. It was not until the 1930s that the federal government assumed a greater role in influencing the national economy. During the Great Depression, Pres. Franklin D. Roosevelt permanently increased the federal government's involvement in the economy by providing government jobs; stabilizing the banking system to restore confidence in financial institutions; creating a massive public works program in the form of the Civilian Conservation Corps; funding state welfare programs through the Federal Emergency Relief Act; passing the National Industrial Recovery Act to regulate wages, collective bargaining, and work hours; creating the Agricultural Adjustment Administration to support agricultural production and prices; and creating the Securities and Exchange Commission to protect investors. Much of the activity that came out of the New Deal programs was targeted at promoting employment, maximum production, and economic stability.

The President's Council of Economic Advisers was created out of the Employment Act of 1946. The economic philosophy that guided the New Deal and efforts thereafter was based on Keynesian economics, a theory developed by John Maynard Keynes calling for increased public spending during periods of production slowdown and high unemployment and decreased spending during periods of inflation. This approach to taxing and spending is called fiscal policy. Under fiscal policy, the national government allocates goods and services necessary to the nation; distributes national revenue through an income redistribution plan to help people in need; and stabilizes the economy by controlling inflation, unemployment, and recession.

Today there is little doubt that the national government has some role to play in managing the national economy, as government intervention has become an accepted approach. The discussion centers around the *extent* of government activity in the economy. During the 1990s such government activity meant providing an economic environment that stimulates international trade. The United States, Canada, and Mexico signed in 1993 the North American Free Trade Agreement (NAFTA), promoting free trade with neighbors. The General Agreement on Tariffs and Trade (GATT) had originally been entered after World War II, when national tariffs squelched free trade among nations during a time when it was necessary to rebuild national economies and infrastructures. GATT provisions took years to go into effect; in 1994, the most recent round of agreements and discussions, GATT members focused on continued reduction of tariffs in international trade.

Economic policymaking is an ongoing activity that requires government attention particularly during times of economic fluctuation. The global economy is merely the newest dimension of public policy, and it will be up to Congress to position the United States for success through ratification of international trade agreements.

See also: Agriculture: Agricultural Adjustment Act of 1933; Agricultural Adjustment Act of 1938; Commerce and Transportation: Act to Regulate Commerce of 1887; Economics: Council of Economic Advisers; Keynesian Economics; National Industrial Recovery Act of 1933; New Deal; Key Concepts: Capitalism; Labor: Employment Act of 1946; Federal Emergency Relief Act of 1933

References: Clarke E. Cochran et al., *American Public Policy: An Introduction* (1996); Jeffrey E. Cohen, *Politics and Economic Policy in the United States,* 1997; Robert Goldston, *The Great Depression: The United States in the Thirties* (1968); Richard Harris and Sidney Miklis, *The Politics of Regulatory Change* (1996); Fred A. Kramer, *Dynamics of Public Policy* (1981); Steffen W. Schmidt, Mack C. Shelley II, and Barbara A. Bardes, *American Government and Politics Today* (1997).

Economic Recovery Tax Act of 1981

In 1980 the Reagan administration introduced a series of economic policy initiatives designed to reduce personal income taxes and stimulate investment. The strategy was based on the theory of supply-side economics: If the supply of labor and capital are increased, then economic growth will follow. The supply-side argument does not favor government intervention in the economy, particularly through high taxes. The Economic Recovery Tax Act of 1981 was the primary means for implementing tax reform through supply-side economics. Tax reform and tax reduction were popular themes during the 1980 presidential campaign, and Ronald Reagan presented himself as the champion of tax cuts for Americans. The tax act favored taxpayers in higher income brackets, particularly those most likely to invest additional after-tax income. Lower-income taxpayers received a modest tax cut. Reagan's policy advisers felt that the focus of economic and tax reform had to be those who would invest and save; therefore, incentives would be needed to encourage investment to spur economic growth. This tax legislation was the largest tax cut in U.S. history.

The act brought about a massive increase in the federal deficit. Although taxes were reduced, federal expenditures were not reduced as much. The Reagan policy team expected lower taxes to generate more revenue for the economy, a suggestion founded upon the Laffer Curve, named for economist Arthur Laffer's theory; but the increased revenue was not realized. The economic deficit continued, and a stopgap measure called the Tax Equity and Financial Responsibility Act of 1982 was passed to close some of the loopholes in the tax laws and to increase some indirect taxes. The budget deficit was still something of a mystery for national economic advisers during the 1990s. The provisions of the Economic Recovery Tax Act did nothing to stimulate economic growth, but it did reduce taxes in a meaningful way for some taxpayers. The Clinton administration was on course toward deficit reduction in the strong national economy of the late 1990s.

See also: Economics: Economic Policy; Tax Equity and Financial Responsibility Act of 1982; Tax Policy

References: Jeffrey E. Cohen, *Politics and Economic Policy in the United States* (1997); David G. Davies, *U.S. Taxes and Tax Policy* (1986); Sven Steinmo, *Taxation and Democracy* (1993).

Economic Stagnation

A healthy, active economy generally does not require new policy formulation. In contrast, a stagnant economy—one that is not robust and does not have significant activity in buying, selling, and manufacturing, the result of inadequate aggregate demand—calls out for new policy. In 1932 unemployment in the United States reached 14 million and was on the increase. National income had declined by 50 percent (from $87.5 to $41.7 billion) since 1929. Manufacturing declined by more than 50 percent. The Depression economy was at a standstill.

Economic stagnation is a serious matter for policymakers and government; it has deep political and social implications. Massive unemployment places a tremendous burden on a nation's ability to fight poverty. Historically, American policymakers have used mixed approaches to overcome economic stagnation. Such policy has favored a mix of government and private-enterprise involvement to create jobs. Many of the New Deal programs during the Depression engaged unemployed workers in public works projects and opportunities. The problem with the public-works solution is that government becomes the employer and therefore must provide the funds to pay workers. If tax revenues are down during tight economic times, then it is difficult for government to find the money to pay workers. This does not have the same potential positive impact that private-sector employment would have on stimulating economic growth. The solution to economic stagnation is the infusion of activities and policies that stimulate economic growth. The greatest stimulus to economic growth is expansion of employment opportunities.

See also: Economics: Economic Policy; New Deal

References: Thomas R. Dye, *Understanding Public Policy* (1995); Robert Goldston, *The Great Depression: The United States in the Thirties* (1968).

Enterprise Zones

Since the late 1960s large and medium-size cities have had to adjust to the decline of traditional downtown shopping and business centers. With the failure of urban shopping districts has also come the displacement and shifting of urban manufacturing centers. The national response has been the economic development plan for urban areas. Most cities and towns now have active economic development strategies to help local economies adjust to changing conditions and technologies.

The concept of enterprise zones became a leading element of economic development strategy during the 1980s. An enterprise zone (known as empowerment zones under the Clinton administration) is a targeted geographical area (usually economically depressed) in which local government and private and nonprofit organizations collaborate to stimulate economic development opportunities. Local governments are encouraged to provide incentives for business development with tax breaks to new businesses and industry, technical assistance, reduction or relaxation of regulations, and assistance in the purchase of land. Another goal of enterprise zones is to improve the social conditions of economically depressed areas by creating areas in cities and communities that are free of crime, that offer low-cost housing opportunities, and that reduce unemployment. Federal agencies play a large part in enterprise zones, providing resources to generate programs.

See also: Economics: Economic Development Administration

References: Clarke E. Cochran et al., *American Public Policy: An Introduction* (1996); Jeffrey E. Cohen, *Politics and Economic Policy in the United States* (1997).

Executive Budget

See Economics: Budget, Federal

Family Reinforcement Tax Relief Act of 1996

The Republicans' 1994 "Contract with America" was designed in part to support the American family. The Family Reinforcement Tax Relief Act of 1996 would strengthen enforcement for child support payments; provide tax incentives for adoption in the form of $5,000 tax credits; strengthen parental control of children's education; strengthen child pornography laws; and authorize elderly dependent care tax credits. This act was passed in August 1996.

See also: Economics: Tax Policy

References: Charles Bonser, Eugene B. McGregor Jr., and Clinton V. Oster Jr., *Policy Choices and Public Action* (1996); Thomas R. Dye and L. Harmon Ziegler, *The Irony of Democracy: An Uncommon Introduction to American Politics* (1996).

Federal Deposit Insurance Corporation

The problem of the nation's banks was so acute during the early 1930s that Pres. Franklin D. Roosevelt developed emergency legislation to regulate the banking industry. Roosevelt issued two presidential proclamations: the first declared a national bank holiday, which closed the few banks that were still functioning; the second forbade the exporting of gold.

In 1934 Congress passed the Glass-Steagall

Banking Act, directed act separating commercial banking from investment banking. The act also expanded the power of the Federal Reserve Board to end widespread speculation caused by instability during the banking industry in the 1930s. The act created the Federal Deposit Insurance Corporation (FDIC), which would insure bank deposits of private citizens up to $10,000. This provision of the Glass-Steagall Act became one of the most popular of the New Deal reforms. Americans lost confidence in the banking industry during the early days of the Great Depression due to bank failures and the consequent run on banks, which led customers to withdraw money from the nation's banks. The creation of a system that insured bank deposits for individuals made bank failures nearly impossible and restored Americans' confidence in the banking system. The creation of FDIC was a bold step in the face of certain financial collapse for the American banking industry.

See also: Economics: New Deal

References: Jeffrey E. Cohen, *Politics and Economic Policy in the United States* (1997); Robert Goldston, *The Great Depression: The United States in the Thirties* (1968).

Federal Reserve Board

The Federal Reserve Act of 1913 created a new banking system comprising 12 Federal Reserve Banks, which were owned by member banks distributed throughout the United States. Each Federal Reserve Bank was required to maintain a 40 percent gold reserve. The Federal Reserve is presided over by the seven-member Board of Governors, including the secretary of the treasury and the comptroller of currency. Initially, the Federal Reserve System was designed to regulate credit in the United States by raising or lowering the rediscount rate (the prices or interest rates that the Federal Reserve charges banks and savings and loan companies when it loans them money) or by manipulating the sale of government securities. The Board of Governors and the Federal Open Market Committee decide policy that influences money and credit conditions, supervise and regulate the banking industry, and act to maintain stability of the U.S. financial system. Members of the Board of Governors are appointed by the president with the advice and consent of the Senate; the members serve 14-year terms.

The Federal Reserve system has major influence over monetary policy.

See also: Economics: Economic Policy

References: Jeffrey E. Cohen, *Politics and Economic Policy in the United States* (1997); Allen Schick, *Congress and Money: Budgeting, Spending, and Taxing* (1980).

Federal Revenue Sharing

One of the goals of Pres. Richard M. Nixon's administration during the early 1970s was to reduce federal grants-in-aid programs. Much of federal aid to state and local governments during the 1960s came in the form of categorical grant programs, which provided state and local governments financial assistance for economic development, crime, social problems, poverty, and education. Many categorical grants were transformed into broad grant categories, called block grants. Block-grant programs fell under the general heading of general or federal revenue sharing. General revenue sharing was adopted as policy in 1972 with the passage of the State and Local Fiscal Assistance Act. The act authorized $30.2 billion over five years for 38,000 state and local governments.

The underlying philosophy of block grants and revenue sharing was that money would be given to states and cities, with considerable freedom in spending. Another feature kept required matching funds from states and local governments to a minimum. This grant system came to be called the intergovernmental grant system. Many grants were directed at social programs, and Republicans and Democrats in Congress disagreed as to how the grant money should be spent. Democrats favored spending grant money in cities and industrial states, whereas Republicans believed that the grant funds should be directed at rural and suburban areas in the Republican-controlled Sunbelt states.

In retrospect, revenue sharing was not very successful. Democrats and Republicans abolished revenue sharing in 1986 due to wasteful spending in many of the grant programs.

See also: Key Concepts: Federalism

References: Michael D. Reagan and John G. Sanzone, *The New Federalism* (1981); David B. Robertson and Dennis R. Judd, *The Development of American Public Policy: The Structure of Policy Restraint* (1989); James Q. Wilson and John J. DiIulio Jr., *American Government: The Essentials* (1998).

Federal Savings and Loan Insurance Corporation

The Federal Savings and Loan Insurance Corporation (FSLIC) is operated by the Federal Home Loan Bank Board. In 1933 Congress passed the Federal Home Loan Bank Act, which established home loan banks to rediscount home mortgages held by savings banks and insurance companies. The original Home Loan Corporation was created to refinance home mortgages for people who had lost their homes beginning in 1930 and for those who had difficulty getting mortgages through banks or savings and loan companies. The original Home Loan Bank Board was designed to protect homes from being foreclosed. During the 1990s FSLIC protects savings accounts in FSLIC-insured savings and loan associations.

During the 1980s FSLIC's credibility was challenged when the savings and loan industry suffered a major collapse. Many institutions went out of business, and the FSLIC was obligated to insure the lost money of depositors. In many cases, depositors were not able to recover their deposits, as the FSLIC was beyond its capacity to insure lost funds.

See also: Economics: Federal Deposit Insurance Corporation

References: Charles Bonser, Eugene B. McGregor Jr., and Clinton V. Oster Jr., *Policy Choices and Public Action* (1996); Robert Goldston, *The Great Depression: The United States in the Thirties* (1968).

Federal Trade Commission

Congress passed the Federal Trade Commission Act in 1914 to replace the Bureau of Corporations with the Federal Trade Commission (FTC), which was given the power to investigate corporations (except banks and carriers of freight), receive reports, and issue cease-and-desist orders to prevent unfair business practices. Today FTC enforces federal antitrust and consumer protection laws. The commission also ensures that the nation's economic markets function competitively, efficiently, and free of undue restrictions. FTC performs economic analyses in support of policy deliberations that originate from the executive branch of the national government. The creation of FTC is an example of Congress acting to stem unfair economic practices that restricted trade and free-market competition.

See also: Economics: Economic Policy

References: Edward Sidlow and Beth Henschen, *America at Odds* (1998).

Fiscal Policy

See Economics: Economic Policy

Flat Tax

Tax equity is a major issue in the debate over taxation. Under a flat tax, everyone pays the same tax rate; in contrast, progressive tax rates (the standard during the late 1990s) increase with income—the more one earns, the higher rate one pays. Under a flat tax, anyone who earns less than a set minimum during the tax year would pay no income tax at all; a flat tax would apply to all families and corporations (but a progressive element would require the tax paid to be divided by total income). Variations include whether families would be granted personal allowances and dependent deductions. The appeal of the flat tax is simplicity and fairness; it would require less time and money to file compared to filing current tax returns, which often require the assistance of tax attorneys, accountants, and other tax services. There is widespread support in the United States for a simplified, fairer tax plan that would reduce the ability of the Internal Revenue Service to disrupt the lives of American taxpayers through audits and reevaluation.

See also: Economics: Economic Policy; Tax Policy

References: Charles Bonser, Eugene B. McGregor Jr., and Clinton V. Oster Jr., *Policy Choices and Public Action* (1996); Jeffrey E. Cohen, *Politics and Economic Policy in the United States* (1997).

Galbraith, John Kenneth (b. 1908)

A Canadian-born, Harvard-educated economist, John Kenneth Galbraith introduced Americans to a unique view of economics that looked at corporate power, economic competition, the nature of public goods versus free enterprise, and the role of the individual in the national economy. Galbraith introduced the idea of public goods and the development of a national economy by providing things such as highways and parks that had lasting benefits yet still enabled Americans to purchase private consumer goods. Galbraith was one of the first economists during the 1950s and 1960s to look critically at the impact of big government and corporate power on the lives of Americans. Galbraith felt that corporate power needed to be restrained through organized labor and broader economic competition.

Galbraith came to Washington, D.C., during the 1930s and was among the New Deal liberal corps that worked in federal agencies created to relieve the effects of the Depression. As a result of his experience in the New Deal government under Franklin D. Roosevelt, Galbraith formed ideas about politics, economics, the role of the state, and private economic power that would later be transformed into his major works, such as *American Capitalism* (1952), *The Affluent Society* (1958), and *The New Industrial State* (1967), an all-important work on interaction among private industry, the national government, and individuals in the economy. Galbraith's work is significant in the context of public policy because he raised questions about the appropriate role of regulation and restraint in the national economy. He introduced the idea of countervailing power as a means of using regulation to redress disparities in bargaining power between corporations and workers.

See also: Economics: Economic Policy; Key Concepts: Regulation

References: John K. Galbraith, *The Affluent Society* (1958); John K. Galbraith, *The New Industrial State* (1967).

General Accounting Office

The General Accounting Office (GAO) is responsible for federal government auditing and accounting. It audits the spending of money by federal agencies, investigates agency practices with regard to spending and use of federal money, and makes spending and impact recommendations to Congress, particularly in the area of government financial activities. GAO produces information and studies on the impact of economic activity in the national economy, reporting on the performance of government agencies to Congress, to the public, and to the media. Thus, GAO performs a variety of functions that support economic policy proposed by Congress and others. Its oversight role assures that government money is spent properly; the GAO and its director—the comptroller general—are semi-independent, operating relatively free from political pressure.

See also: Economics: Economic Policy; Key Concepts: Oversight

References: Jeffrey E. Cohen, *Politics and Economic Policy in the United States* (1997); Allen Schick, *Congress and Money: Budgeting, Spending, and Taxing* (1980); Steffen W. Schmidt, Mack C. Shelley II, and Barbara A. Bardes, *American Government and Politics Today* (1997).

General Revenue Sharing

See Economics: Federal Revenue Sharing

General Services Administration

The General Services Administration (GSA) was created in 1949 as an independent executive agency to monitor federal government spending. The agency is responsible for overseeing federal procurement, which requires the agency to create and maintain procedures for the government's purchase of products and services. GSA has had a reputation for being rule- and procedure-bound in its operations. It has many rules determining how items and products can be purchased; this manner of doing business has been the target of criticism by people interested in reforming the federal bureaucracy. GSA practices have come under scrutiny thanks to the National Performance Review, led by Vice Pres. Al Gore under the Clinton administration.

See also: Key Concepts: Administrative Agencies; National Performance Review

References: President Bill Clinton and Vice President Al Gore, *Putting Customers First, 1995: Standards for Serving the American People*, National Performance Review (October 1995); Theodore J. Lowi and Benjamin Ginsberg, *American Government: Freedom and Power* (1998).

Gramm-Rudman Act of 1985

Also known as the Balanced Budget and Emergency Deficit Control Act of 1985, Gramm-Rudman was designed to attack the federal deficit levels for fiscal years 1986–1991. Reducing the federal deficit (debt) meant that Congress and the president would be restricted in their ability to spend federal money on new and existing programs. The act required a maximum federal deficit of $472 billion for 1989 and $436 billion for 1990 and a balanced budget by 1991. The act also called for automatic spending cuts in all budget categories if the targeted budget deficit levels were exceeded. This requirement for automatic spending cuts, called "sequestration," was modified in 1987. The provisions of Gramm-Rudman were modified in 1990, and new deficit targets were set for 1990 and 1991.

Gramm-Rudman encountered significant opposition. Many provisions were impractical, and it proved ineffective given massive federal spending obligations during the early 1990s (such as the Gulf War).

See also: Economics: Balanced Budget and Emergency Deficit Control Act of 1985; Deficit Reduction Act of 1984; Economic Policy

References: Clarke E. Cochran et al., *American Public Policy: An Introduction* (1996); B. Guy Peters, *American Public Policy: Promise and Performance* (1993).

Grants-in-Aid

See Key Concepts: Federalism

Great Depression

See Economics: New Deal

Income Tax of 1894

During the late 19th century Congress passed tariff bills to increase revenues to pay for national expenditures. Congress found itself dealing with budget deficits periodically after the Civil War and sought ways to increase revenue flow. A tariff bill was passed in 1893; an added provision to that bill was the Income Tax of 1894. A 2 percent tax on all incomes above $4,000, the tax was supported by Populists in the Midwest, who viewed it as a more egalitarian tax measure directed at wealthier elements. The Supreme Court struck down the tax in *Pollock v. Farmers Loan and Trust Company,* declaring the direct tax unconstitutional because it was not apportioned equally among the states. Congress thus increased gift and estate taxes, but that did little to solve the looming financial crisis. Politically, the use of tariffs (rather than taxes) was the preferred policy.

See also: Economics: Tax Policy

References: Carolyn Webber and Aaron Wildavsky, *A History of Taxation and Expenditure in the Western World* (1986).

Internal Revenue Service

The Internal Revenue Service (IRS) is a division of the U.S. Department of Treasury and oversees the federal revenue collection structure of the national government. The Office of Internal Revenue was originally created to pay for the costs of the Civil War; the first income tax was levied in 1862 but was discontinued after ten years. In 1894 a second income tax was established but was declared unconstitutional by the Supreme Court. In 1913 Congress passed the Sixteenth Amendment to the Constitution, which allowed Congress to levy income taxes. The IRS enforces the tax laws and collects estate, excise, gift, and other taxes. The money collected by the IRS is the major source of revenue for the federal government.

The current income tax structure was established in 1943. Americans have been critical of the IRS for its overbearing ways. Reform efforts in Congress have surfaced, but they have not changed the tax structure. Continuing issues are tax equity and tax cuts. Among Western industrialized democracies, U.S. taxpayers are taxed the least.

See also: Economics: Economic Policy; Flat Tax

References: Jeffrey E. Cohen, *Politics and Economic Policy in the United States* (1997); David G. Davies, *U.S. Taxes and Tax Policy* (1986); Allen Schick, *Congress and Money: Budgeting, Spending, and Taxing* (1980); Sven Steinmo, *Taxation and Democracy* (1993).

Kemp, Jack (b. 1936)

Jack Kemp is a former Republican member of the Congress who represented Buffalo, New York; he was a professional football quarterback for 13 seasons prior to coming to Congress. He served nine terms in the House of Representatives, from 1971 to 1989. Kemp made his mark in Congress as a tax expert and was an early proponent of the flat tax. Kemp also served as U.S. secretary of housing and urban development, becoming an advocate for enterprise zones to encourage entrepreneurship and job creation in impoverished neighborhoods. Kemp was seen as a moderate who held the respect of members of both political parties in Congress and is highly regarded for his thoughts on tax reform.

See also: Economics: Flat Tax

References: Michael Barone and Grant Ujifusa, eds., *Almanac of American Politics* (1995).

Keynesian Economics

The leading economic philosophy among Western democracies during the first part of the 20th century was classical theory, which suggested that a market economy was a self-adjusting mechanism that would achieve a balance or equilibrium in demand, supply, full employment, and production if left alone from government interference. The 1929 stock market crash and the resulting 1930s Great Depression challenged classical economic theory. A new approach was offered by British economist John Maynard Keynes, who believed that economic instability was the consequence of fluctuations in product demand. Demand for consumer goods was affected by unemployment, lower wages, cuts in business production, and layoffs of employees; all of these factors continued in a downward economic spiral. The spiral would continue unless government spent money and lowered taxes (to make more money available for spending) to stimulate demand. Keynes recommended that governments, if necessary, borrow money to stimulate demand and increase the supply of money available to consumers.

Keynes published his "general theory" in 1936 amid the international economic depression. He focused on income as the chief problem affecting consumption and production. Keynes's ideas encouraged deficit spending; the United States adopted this economic philosophy to relieve problems caused by the Great Depression. Many of the New Deal programs of the Roosevelt administration embodied the Keynesian approach. The 1946 Full Employment Act also reflected the tenets of Keynesian theory, proposing full employment programs to stimulate consumer spending. During the 1980s legislators took a different course, toward the reduction of government spending and deregulation of the economy.

See also: Economics: Deficit Reduction Act of 1984; Economic Policy; Labor: Employment Act of 1946

McCulloch v. Maryland

The issues in the 1819 Supreme Court case *McCulloch v. Maryland* were whether the federal government had the power to establish a national bank and whether the State of Maryland had the power to tax the national bank. The Court decided that the federal government had the right to create a national bank and that the State of Maryland did not have the right to tax it. The underlying issue was implied powers in the Constitution, specifically whether implied powers could legitimately be derived from enumerated powers. Justice John Marshall in his opinion ruled that national supremacy forbids states from interfering in the constitutional operations of the federal government. This case led to the federal government's dominant role.

See also: Key Concepts: Federal System

References: David Edwards and Alessandra Lippucci, *Practicing American Politics: An Introduction to American Government* (1998).

National Banking Act of 1864

The National Banking Act of 1864 created national charter banks. Charter banks could issue government bonds to help pay the costs of the Civil War. The banks also issued national bank notes, which became the national currency, nicknamed "greenbacks." The new banknotes were significant, as the United States did not have a uniform system of banking and banknote currency during the Civil War. A national banking system based on uniform currency promoted a stable financial system for post–Civil War reforms.

See also: Economics: Economic Policy

References: Jeffrey E. Cohen, *Politics and Economic Policy in the United States* (1997).

National Debt

The national debt (the amount of money owed by the federal government) increases when the government spends more than it receives in revenues; this is known as deficit spending. The national debt peaked during World War II, fell steadily until the mid-1970s, then proceeded to increase thereafter. Controlling federal spending has been a major political issue since the late 1970s. The government's primary source of revenue is personal income taxes and corporate taxes. Yet tax receipts do not always balance with federal payouts, including interest payments on the national debt itself. Large national debts occur when the federal government runs up budget deficits year after year. The government finances debt by issuing U.S. Treasury bonds to corporations, individuals, pension plans, foreign governments, foreign businesses, and foreign individuals (known as public debt financing, which merely adds to the public debt). This circular process makes it difficult to ever reduce the national debt.

Since the early 1980s some members of Congress have called for a balanced budget amendment to reduce the national debt; such attempts have failed. The 1985 Gramm-Rudman bill required Congress to reduce the size of national budget deficits, but it was only mildly successful. Reducing federal spending for domestic and international programs is another way to reduce debt, and after the Cold War ended in 1989 many felt that the United States could decrease its international military spending, but that failed to materialize. In 1990 Congress passed a deficit reduction act that negated the provisions of Gramm-Rudman. The issue of reducing the national debt is complex in light of U.S. commitments to domestic and foreign programs.

See also: Economics: Balanced Budget Amendment; Budget, Federal; Economic Policy; Gramm-Rudman Act of 1985

References: Jeffrey E. Cohen, *Politics and Economic Policy in the United States* (1997); Steffen W. Schmidt, Mack C. Shelley II, and Barbara A. Bardes, *American Government and Politics Today* (1997); Sven Steinmo, *Taxation and Democracy* (1993).

National Industrial Recovery Act of 1933

When the U.S. stock market crashed in 1929, a worldwide crisis devastated national economies. Democrat Franklin D. Roosevelt, former governor of New York, was elected president in 1932 based on a "New Deal" for Americans. Part of the New Deal was the series of programs contained in the National Industrial Recovery Act (NIRA), which created the National Recovery Administration to supervise a program of industrial self-regulation. The nation's industrial and trade associations were encouraged to develop fair-competition codes, which would help stimulate production, and establish worker and employer agreements, which would promote industrial growth and economic recovery. Section 7 of NIRA guaranteed labor the right to collective bargaining, and millions of workers would organize and strike. The American Federation of Labor (AFL), previously considered a craft union that ignored the needs of unskilled workers, began organizing workers but urged patience on the issue of collective bargaining. Other unions thus led the fight for better wages, improved working conditions, and the right to bargain collectively. Hundreds of strikes and labor actions surfaced after passage of NIRA.

NIRA created the Public Works Administration, which put people to work on public construction projects. Among the nation's business community, the National Recovery Administration was extremely unpopular, considered to represent socialist attempts by the government to impose industrial programs on the economy. The work programs created by the act eventually employed 2 million people and jump-started a minor economic upswing in 1933.

NIRA was declared unconstitutional by the Supreme Court in *Schecter Poultry Corporation v. United States* in 1936. The Court ruled that the act delegated too much power to the president. Although Roosevelt enjoyed some support from the Supreme Court for his New Deal policies, all nine justices voted against NIRA. The act addressed the illegal shipment of oil across state lines, and many felt that Roosevelt and the Democrats were overcentralizing government authority. The Court also objected to the creation of the labor codes that established collective bargaining and to the price controls and price-fixing powers in NIRA. The National Recovery Administration was dismantled, some of its projects being placed in other programs. NIRA set the stage for national economic recovery through public works projects and created the industrial, public, and transportation infrastructures that Americans today take for granted. The programs that followed also relieved unemployment and put Americans to work.

See also: Economics: New Deal

References: Robert Goldston, *The Great Depression: The United States in the Thirties* (1968); T. H. Watkins, *The Great Depression: America in the 1930s* (1993).

New Deal

In 1932 Franklin D. Roosevelt was elected president based on a "New Deal" for the American people. That year there had been 1,456 bank failures, with untold millions in lost deposits. In March 1933 approximately 14 million Americans were unemployed. In response, President Roosevelt created a series of programs designed to relieve pressure on the banks, prevent farm and home foreclosures, create employment and public works programs, and engage in a national building effort to stimulate the national economy He received wide support to do what was necessary.

A series of "alphabet agencies" was created, and Roosevelt gave his approval to vast social and technological programs. The Tennessee Valley Authority

(TVA), just one program among many, brought electric power and economic development to an impoverished region. TVA had opponents at the outset, as it displaced longtime residents from their lands to make way for reservoirs. Other New Deal programs brought the federal government into people's lives through massive relief efforts. Conservative critics saw a giant welfare state, but President Roosevelt persevered, and the New Deal programs helped to raise Americans out of the Depression.

The "first" New Deal began in 1933 upon Roosevelt's inauguration and included the Emergency Banking Act of 1933; the Unemployment Relief Act, which created the Civilian Conservation Corps; the Federal Relief Administration, led by Harry Hopkins; the Agricultural Adjustment Act; the Tennessee Valley Authority; the Home Owners Refinancing Act and the Glass-Steagall Banking Act, which created the Federal Deposit Insurance Corporation; the Farm Credit Act, which created the Farm Credit Administration; the National Industrial Recovery Act, which established the National Recovery Administration; Civil Works Emergency Relief Act, which created the Civil Works Administration (this program became the Works Progress Administration in 1935); the Securities Exchange Act, which created the Securities and Exchange commission; the Communications Act, which created the Federal Communications Commission; and the National Housing Act, which created the Federal Housing Administration. All were established in 1933.

The "second" New Deal came during 1935 and 1936 and included: the Emergency Relief Appropriation Act, which established the Works Progress Administration; the National Labor Relations Act, which created the National Labor Relations Board; the Social Security Act; the Banking Act; the Revenue Act, which increased the maximum surtax on incomes to 75 percent; and the Soil Conservation and Domestic Allotment Act, which provided farmers with payments for soil conservation.

A liberal corps of policymakers came to Washington to work on New Deal programs and ventured to cities and rural areas nationwide to administer and implement the programs. These committed individuals developed a common set of beliefs, and were important to the success of many of the New Deal programs; many went on to serve in World War II, other government agencies, and universities.

The New Deal programs were controversial and created resentment among the business community. President Roosevelt appealed to the American people to work with him in creating federal programs that would be administered through the states. This was the era of cooperative federalism, whereby all branches of the government were engaged in public program development and implementation as a result of the Great Depression. During this time Roosevelt used the radio to reach the American public in his "fireside chats." The Depression ended with the beginning of World War II, but the New Deal programs introduced a lasting legacy of federal government involvement in the lives of Americans.

See also: Agriculture: Agricultural Adjustment Act of 1933; Agricultural Adjustment Act of 1938; Communications: Communications Act of 1934; Economics: Banking Act of 1935; Entitlement Programs: Social Security Act of 1935; Labor: Emergency Relief Appropriations Act of 1935; National Labor Relations Act of 1935

References: Irving Bernstein, *Turbulent Years: A History of the American Worker, 1933–1941* (1970); Robert Goldston, *The Great Depression: The United States in the Thirties* (1968); Rhonda F. Levine, *Class Struggle and the New Deal: Industrial Labor, Industrial Capital, and the State* (1988); T. H. Watkins, *The Great Depression: America in the 1930s* (1993).

Office of Management and Budget

The Office of Management and Budget (OMB) was created in 1921, when it was called the Bureau of the Budget, under the Budget and Accounting Act. The functions of OMB have changed over the years, but its major task is to help the president construct the annual budget. Each agency reports its budget requests to OMB, which then makes recommendations to the president about the size, nature, and reality of a proposed budget. OMB employs more than 500 career civil servants who hold skills as economists, accountants, and budget analysts.

See also: Economics: Budget Deficit; Budget, Federal

References: Jeffrey E. Cohen, *Politics and Economic Policy in the United States* (1997); Allen Schick, *Congress and Money: Budgeting, Spending, and Taxing* (1980).

Omnibus Budget Reconciliation Acts

During the late 1980s and early 1990s deficit reduction legislation came at a rapid pace in response to calls in Congress and the executive branch for controlling federal spending. The Omnibus Budget Reconciliation Act of 1990 was one of a series of tax increases and deficit reduction bills designed to reduce the deficit by $500 million between 1991 and 1995. The purpose of tax increases was to raise federal government revenues and to impose a 5-cents-per-gallon tax on motor fuels. Entitlement program cuts were mandatory; $57 million was cut from Medicare and other federal health programs. Although the bill targeted key spending areas for cuts, the deficit was not reduced to target levels by 1992.

Pres. Bill Clinton introduced a new Omnibus Budget Bill in 1993 to reduce the budget deficit by $500 billion between 1993 and 1998. More tax increases, reductions in spending on entitlement programs, and increased taxes on gasoline for cars, trucks, and airplanes were features of this new deficit reduction bill. The federal deficit has been reduced, and the national economy registered excellent marks for the 1997–1998 budget year. A welfare reform bill passed in 1997 further reduced federal expenditures in entitlement programs.

See also: Economics: Budget Deficit; Budget, Federal

References: Clarke E. Cochran et al., *American Public Policy: An Introduction* (1996); Jeffrey E. Cohen, *Politics and Economic Policy in the United States* (1997).

Planning, Programming, Budgeting System

The planning, programming, budgeting system (PPBS) was a model of policy development and program planning brought to the federal government by Robert McNamara when he served as secretary of defense to Pres. John F. Kennedy. The PPBS model was based on operations research techniques used in private sector program planning. The focus of PPBS was on concrete objectives and the application of resources to accomplish those objectives. McNamara wanted to replace traditional line-item budgeting techniques with a system that had a broader, more comprehensive program perspective. PPBS was seen as a rational decisionmaking model that used mathematical and computer simulation approaches to forecasting success of operations. Attempts to institutionalize PPBS throughout federal agencies failed after several years of experimentation.

The goal of PPBS was to get policy and program decisionmakers to think comprehensively about program planning. The PPBS technique required decisionmakers to gather as much information as possible about a problem or proposed program, establish policy-based solutions to the problem, then allocate resources that would enable the program to function, with attention paid to the need for adjustments in techniques and budgeting as necessary. The PPBS technique required constant monitoring of program activities; such attention to detail was not common practice under traditional planning approaches in the federal government. The PPBS experiment did have a legacy of attempting to make federal program planning more rational.

See also: Economics: Budget, Federal

References: William N. Dunn, *Public Policy Analysis: An Introduction* (1994); Dennis J. Palumbo, *Public Policy in America: Government in Action* (1988).

Program Budgeting

Program budgeting was an important reform in the agency budgeting and planning process during the Johnson administration. Program budgeting allocates resources on the basis of the activities of government and the services that government supplies to society. The emphasis of program budgeting is on the analysis of programmatic expenditures and efficient use of resources. Program budgeting is an element of the Planning, Programming, Budgeting System, which takes a comprehensive approach to policy development and implementation. Program budgeting seeks strategies that link interactions among policy areas and efficiencies that represent logical connections to policy objectives. In a program budgeting system, problems are identified; programs are developed around specified goals; resources are allocated among programs; budgeting may occur across program lines, which accounts for various program actors; budgeting may be longer than the typical one year budgeting period; and alternative programs are systematically analyzed for the possibility of finding more efficient and effective alternatives.

Program budgeting assumes that data collection about program success is readily available; necessary adjustments can be made if required. As programs operate, it is difficult to be as comprehensive in planning, budgeting, and data-gathering as this model suggests. Decisions on program outcomes would be left to agency leaders who frequently are not involved in the intricacies of a program.

See also: Economics: Planning, Programming, Budgeting System

References: Charles F. Lindblom, *The Policy Making Process* (1980); B. Guy Peters, *American Public Policy: Promise and Performance* (1993).

Proposition 13

California voters in 1978 changed the state constitution by passing an initiative that restricted the ability of local governments to increase the assessment of property taxes based on previous assessment formulas. The initiative hamstrung local governments' traditional taxing power. This started a national movement to reform property taxes at the local level, and other states have adopted their own reform policies.

See also: Key Concepts: Direct Democracy

References: Bruce E. Cain and Roger E. Noll, eds., *Constitutional Reform in California* (1995).

Public Corporations

Public corporations carry out economic and service functions throughout the United States. Public corporations provide revenue to the government, provide transportation services, engage in regional economic development, and engage in banking. A public corporation can be a public utility company; there are also quasi–public corporations like Amtrak, which operates the national passenger rail service.

See also: Key Concepts: Administrative Agencies

References: B. Guy Peters, *American Public Policy: Promise and Performance* (1993).

Rational Comprehensive Approach

See Economics: Planning, Programming, Budgeting System

Revenue and Expenditure Control Act of 1968

In an era of massive government spending to fund the war effort in Vietnam and domestic social programs, the Revenue and Expenditure Control Act of 1968 was an attempt to control government spending in the coming fiscal year 1969. It restricted budget outlays to protect some spending categories from the imposition of spending limits: Vietnam War costs, interest payments, veterans' benefits, and Social Security expenses. This legislation placed spending limits and a ceiling on budget outlays, but it was not successful, as spending continued to soar.

See also: Economics: Budget Deficit; Budget, Federal

References: Jeffrey E. Cohen, *Politics and Economic Policy in the United States* (1997); Allen Schick, *Congress and Money: Budgeting, Spending, and Taxing* (1980).

Tax Equity and Financial Responsibility Act of 1982

During the Reagan administration, a major theme of fiscal policy was to reduce the deficit by cutting taxes, which did not help to raise revenues for government operations. The Tax Equity and Financial Responsibility Act of 1982 was directed at increasing revenues by eliminating some tax loopholes and increasing some indirect taxes. The bill was one of a failed series of measures (based on a philosophy once referred to as "voodoo economics" by George Bush in the heat of a campaign battle) to increase revenues.

See also: Economics: Budget Deficit; Budget, Federal

References: David G. Davies, *U.S. Taxes and Tax Policy* (1986); B. Guy Peters, *American Public Policy: Promise and Performance* (1993).

Tax Policy

Governments need to pay for public policy initiatives; taxes are the government's main generator of revenues. The three main types of taxes in the United States are income taxes, consumption taxes, and property taxes. Income taxes comprise personal income taxes, corporate income taxes, and social security taxes. Consumption taxes include sales tax on items bought in business transactions in the private economy. (Import taxes and excise taxes are also forms of consumption tax and are applied to goods and services brought into the United States as well as goods produced in the United States.) Property taxes are taxes on real estate, automobiles, and gifts and inheritances.

There are four requirements for a successful tax policy: (1) taxes should provide revenue while not exacting undue harm on people and the economy; (2) taxes should be neutral, that is, not be directed to benefit some while harming others; (3) taxes should have buoyancy, meaning that the tax should have the same value during strong and weak economic cycles; and (4) taxes should have a fair distribution effect so that no economic group feels that the taxes are applied inequitably. Many Americans feel that they are overtaxed, but compared to taxpayers in other nations Americans pay the least.

Since the beginning of the 20th century, the U.S. government has dramatically increased its role in American lives, and taxes have increased as a result. Although very few politicians favor raising taxes, Democrats, more so than Republicans, have been traditionally more inclined to raise taxes. Tax reform is an ever-present political issue in American politics, directed mainly at cutting taxes and making taxes more equitable. Tax cuts have not proven to be the answer to deficit reduction.

See also: Commerce and Transportation: Free Trade; Economics: Economic Policy

References: Jeffrey E. Cohen, *Politics and Economic Policy in the United States* (1997); David G. Davies, *U.S. Taxes and Tax Policy* (1986); B. Guy Peters, *American Public Policy: Promise and Performance* (1993).

Unemployment Relief Act of 1933

See Economics: New Deal

Education

Chronology

1785 The Land Ordinance of 1785 passed, requiring some American territories to be surveyed into townships of 36 sections, each section containing 640 acres; one section (number 16) was reserved for the support of public schools.

1787 The Northwest Ordinance of 1787 passed, reserving lands for public schools in new territories.

1852 Compulsory education began in Massachusetts (it was eventually adopted by Mississippi in 1918).

1862 Morrill Land Grant Act passed, providing land for the establishment of colleges that would specialize in agriculture and mechanical arts.

1867 Congress established the U.S. Office of Education.

1917 The Smith-Hughes Act established the first program of federal grants-in-aid to promote vocational education.

1944 Serviceman's Readjustment Act (G.I. Bill) was passed to provide subsidies for veterans pursuing education and training programs.

1946 National school lunch and milk programs began to provide federal grants and community donations for low-cost lunches in public and private schools.

1950 Congress passed the Federal Impacted Area Aid Program to assist areas in which federal activities created a substantial increase in school enrollments or a reduction in taxable resources because of a federally owned facility.

1958 National Defense Education Act was passed, providing financial aid to states and public school districts to improve instruction in science, math, and foreign languages.

1965 Elementary and Secondary Education Act passed, establishing the single largest federal aid to an education program.

1975 Education for All Handicapped Children Act passed to promote equal opportunity of handicapped children in the nation's education system.

1981 Reagan administration sponsored the Education Consolidation and Improvement Act, which consolidated other education programs into block grants and gave local school districts greater discretion.

1994 Goals 2000: Educate America Act was passed to offer education reform that creates a "world-class education" for every child.

"America 2000: An Education Strategy"

In 1990 Pres. George Bush proposed a plan for national education reform called "America 2000: An Education Strategy." The underlying assumption was that schools would improve if standards were set and incentives created to force school professionals to abide by those standards. A departure from previous efforts, the plan emphasized choice through a voucher plan and national testing with school scores tied to the allocation of federal grant money to states and local school districts. America 2000 proposed creating 535 new schools—one for each congressional seat—to serve as competitive alternatives for education opportunities. The Bush strategy was embraced by Pres. Bill Clinton and signed into law as the Goals 2000: Educate America Act in 1994. The strategy came in response to a growing problem in public education in the United States: how to improve public schools and make them more capable of educating people for changing, more competitive, more demanding technological and economic markets.

See also: Education: Education Policy

References: Charles Bonser, Eugene B. McGregor Jr., and Clinton V. Oster Jr., *Policy Choices and Public Action* (1996); James P. Lester and Joseph Stewart Jr., *Public Policy: An Evolutionary Approach* (1996).

American Federation of Teachers

The American Federation of Teachers (AFT) is a national labor union that represents the interests of public school teachers. In 1916 a group of teachers began organizing what was to become the American Federation of Teachers in Winnetka, Illinois. The teachers determined that they needed a national organization that would represent the interests of teachers, not just the interests of school administrators. Delegates to this first meeting in Illinois decided to form the AFT. There are more than 2,100 local unions throughout the United States. The AFT has been a champion of the right to organize, collective bargaining, civil rights legislation, and school desegregation. The AFT is currently engaged in supporting education reform in public education as well as promoting fair pay and improved benefits and working conditions for its members.

The AFT is a powerful lobbying force and interest group. AFT membership is located primarily in big-city school districts; it is an affiliate of the American Federation of Labor–Congress of Industrial Organizations (AFL-CIO). AFT national leadership has traditionally favored government assistance to public education. The AFT was led for 22 years by Albert Shanker as president. Shanker brought a levelheaded but still militant brand of teacher unionism. He won election as president initially in 1974 and was reelected to two-year terms 11 times thereafter. The AFT currently has some 940,000 members. The other organization that represents the interests of teachers is the National Education Association (NEA), which has approximately 2 million members. Both the NEA and the AFT have achieved collective bargaining status in most states and large urban school districts.

See also: Education: National Education Association; Labor: American Federation of Labor–Congress of Industrial Organizations

References: Thomas R. Dye, *Understanding Public Policy* (1995); Dennis J. Palumbo, *Public Policy in America: Government in Action* (1988).

Basic Education Opportunity Grant

The federal government's commitment to higher education has taken on a variety of forms, one being to provide indirect federal subsidies to individual students to attend colleges and universities. The Basic Education Opportunity Grant, also known as the Pell Grant, was designed to assist qualified students to obtain postsecondary education. This grant program originated in the 1972 education amendments to the National Defense Education Act of 1958. The grant provided a minimum income for college students. The centerpiece of the 1972 education amendments was the Pell Grant, which was based on a student's family income. During the Reagan administration, federal support for higher education was cut significantly; there were approximately 100,000 fewer Pell Grant recipients in 1983 than in 1981. Pres. George Bush continued to reduce federal support for higher education, but not at as drastically as Reagan. In 1992 the federal government paid $3.7 billion in Pell Grants to students attending college. With the increasing costs of higher education during the 1990s, the continuing availability of grants is a growing concern.

See also: Education: Education Policy; National Defense Education Act of 1958

References: Charles Bonser, Eugene B. McGregor Jr., and Clinton V. Oster Jr., *Policy Choices and Public Action* (1996); B. Guy Peters, *American Public Policy: Promise and Performance* (1993).

Bilingual Education

Many ethnic groups make up the American population. Thus, it is important to provide quality education experiences and opportunities for people of all ethnic and cultural backgrounds. An example of "education for all" is the obligation to meet the needs of non–English speaking students. The origins of bilingual education are Title VI of the Civil Rights Act of 1964 and the Equal Educational Opportunities Act of 1974. Both mandate that states and local school districts create programs to correct language deficiencies of non–English speaking students. The specific programs were left to the states and local school districts to devise. In 1974 Congress passed the Bilingual Education Act, which provided federal funds to address the language needs of non–English speaking students. During the 1970s bilingual education programs were the seen as the most effective way to remediate problems for non–English speaking students.

Critics of bilingual education programs claim that funds are spent on noncitizens and that education efforts should be singularly targeted at teaching English proficiency in schools. In addition, many in government are intent on reducing the federal role in national education policy. Bilingual education programs, originally funded by federal revenues, are under challenge at the state level as well, particularly in California, where bilingual education was the subject of a ballot proposition. The measure, to eliminate state funding of bilingual education in California, passed in June 1998.

See also: Civil Rights: Civil Rights Acts; Education: Education Policy

References: Clarke E. Cochran et al., *American Public Policy: An Introduction* (1996).

Boards of Education

Public education is characterized by broad participation of local citizens to assist in the formulation of education policy. In most American communities, an appointed or elected board of education has the formal responsibility for making education policy. Boards of education are expected to formulate the policy that is implemented by superintendents and school staffs. People who are elected or appointed to boards of education tend to be well-educated professionals with better-than-average income levels. Local boards do not wield as much power over education policy as most Americans suspect; school and local district staffs tend play a more influential role.

See also: Education: Education Policy

References: Dennis J. Palumbo, *Public Policy in America: Government in Action* (1988).

Charter Schools

During the 1990s parents sought alternative choices in education opportunities. A charter school is an experimental school that operates independently of state authority to blunt the perceived monopoly power of local educators. School districts create charter schools by offering a written agreement, referred to as a charter, to a public school, establishing an agreed curriculum with stated goals, objectives, and purposes.

The charter school is authorized to hire teachers and other employees, hold property, make legal agreements, and operate the programs as it sees fit. The principles of public education still bind charter schools: There is no tuition; religion is not a part of the curriculum; there are no restrictive admissions policies; and access to the school is in keeping with all public education. Minnesota was the first state to charter public schools, in 1991; California has chartered schools since 1992. More than half the states now have some form of charter schools. Chartering schools in disadvantaged urban areas is a huge challenge.

Some critics claim that charter schools create another opportunity that benefits a few to the disadvantage of the majority. The charter school concept represents another attempt at local control and reform in public education.

See also: Education: Education Policy; Vouchers

References: Charles Bonser, Eugene B. McGregor Jr., and Clinton V. Oster Jr., *Policy Choices and Public Action* (1996); David Edwards and Alessandra Lippucci, *Practicing American Politics: An Introduction to American Government* (1998).

Department of Education

In 1867 Congress established the U.S. Office of Education; in 1979 the cabinet-level U.S. Department of Education was created out of the previous Department of Health, Education, and Welfare. It is headed by a secretary, has some 5,000 employees, coordinates federal programs and policies for education, administers aid to state and local education programs, and promotes research in education. The various subagencies are the Office of Special Education and Rehabilitation Services; the Office of Elementary and Secondary Education; the Office of Postsecondary Education; and the Office of Vocational and Adult Education.

The major thrust of education policy has always remained at the state and local levels. The focus there is on upgrading and maintaining the infrastructure that exists. When the Department of Education was created, federal involvement in education was supposed to be limited and not directed at curriculum development unless authorized by law. However, much national legislation addresses curricular issues. The national debate about education during the 1990s centered on the issue of tax breaks for middle-class parents paying college tuition and the requirement for increasing standards in kindergarten through high school by establishing national standards with testing programs in math and reading.

The role of the Department of Education in creating and influencing national education policy continues to be reserved, limited to larger issues like the need for more technical schools and improving technical training after high school. The changes in the training, skills, and workforce needs of employers during the 1990s will continue to be the focus of policy development in the Department of Education.

See also: Education: Charter Schools; Education Policy; G.I. Bill; Vouchers

References: Charles Bonser, Eugene B. McGregor Jr., and Clinton V. Oster Jr., *Policy Choices and Public Action* (1996); Chester E. Finn Jr., *We Must Take Charge: Our Schools and Our Future* (1991); Shoshana Zuboff, *In the Age of the Smart Machine: The Future of Work and Power* (1988).

Education Consolidation and Improvement Act of 1981

Federal education policy during the 1970s and 1980s was directed at improving education opportunities for students, with a specific focus on providing assistance to poor students and students with special needs. The Education Consolidation and Improvement Act of 1981 was the Reagan administration's attempt to focus on compensatory education for deprived students across the country; the aid was directed at school districts with the highest numbers of poor students. The act was also designed to create programs in adult education, education for the handicapped, and school districts with large federal installations. This federal aid program provides 80 percent of federal assistance to elementary and secondary education; block grants to state and local governments account for the remainder.

The Education Consolidation and Improvement Act of 1981 was consistent with the Elementary and Secondary Education Act of 1965, which provided federal assistance to elementary and secondary education through direct general subsidies.

See also: Education: Education Policy; Elementary and Secondary Education Act of 1965

References: Chester E. Finn Jr., *We Must Take Charge: Our Schools and Our Future* (1991); B. Guy Peters, *American Public Policy: Promise and Performance* (1993).

Education for All Handicapped Children Act of 1975

In keeping with education policy developed during the 1960s and 1970s, the Education for All Handicapped Children Act of 1975 targeted a specific population in need of federal assistance. This legislation, unlike the later Education Consolidation and Improvement Act of 1981, required that all handicapped or exceptional students be educated according to their special needs. The targets were children with learning disabilities and physical handicaps as well as educationally gifted children in public schools. School districts were required to provide special programs and were expected to bear the costs.

See also: Education: Education Policy

References: Chester E. Finn Jr., *We Must Take Charge: Our Schools and Our Future* (1991); B. Guy Peters, *American Public Policy: Promise and Performance* (1993).

Education Policy

Leading issues in education policy include how public schools should be funded; what should be included in the curriculum; how education opportunities can be best defined; and how education services are best delivered. Historically, education was a community responsibility, but over the years the states have assumed a greater role.

One of the initial purposes of school systems during the 19th century was to equalize differences in wealth and circumstances so that all children would have equal opportunity to advance according to their abilities. Public education was seen as a liberating force in our national political, social, and economic lives. The Land Ordinance of 1785, passed by the U.S. Congress under the Articles of Confederation (the first formal constitution and legal arrangement, 1781–1789, between the American states that preceded the adoption and ratification of the U.S. Constitution) called for land to be surveyed into townships of 36 sections, each section containing 640 acres. One section (number 16) was reserved for the support of public schools. Because Congress had no power to tax under the Articles of Confederation, newly acquired land became a revenue generator. In the Northwest Ordinance of 1787, Congress offered land grants for public schools in the new territories and established the notion that a strong education was essential to good citizenship. If people were to be granted the right to vote, they must be educated for the task, meaning public education must be universal, free, and compulsory. Compulsory education began in Massachusetts in 1852 and was eventually adopted by Mississippi in 1918.

Early federal aid to education came in the form of grants of federal land to each state. The Morrill Land Grant Act of 1862 provided land for the establishment of colleges that would specialize in agriculture and mechanical arts. These became known as land-grant colleges, which brought university research and technical assistance to family farmers. The result was an enormous expansion in farm productivity.

In 1867 Congress established the U.S. Office of Education; in 1979 the cabinet-level U.S. Department of Education was created. The Smith-Hughes Act of 1917 established the first program of federal grants-in-aid to promote vocational education, enabling schools to provide training in agriculture, home economics, trades, and industries. The national school lunch and milk programs began in 1946 to provide federal grants and community donations for low-cost lunches in public and private schools.

National policy in postsecondary education after World War II turned toward assisting veterans in their college educations. The Serviceman's Readjustment Act of 1944 (also known as the G.I. Bill) stated that for each 90 days of service, military personnel were guaranteed one year of education, plus one month of education for each month of active duty up to a maximum of 48 months. Tuition, fees, and books were paid for, and the government would pay a subsistence allowance of $50 a month for single veterans and $75 a month for married veterans. Out of 14 million eligible veterans, 2.2 million took the opportunity, at a cost of $5.5 billion. The result was that the federal government sponsored education for enough American veterans to power the postwar economic expansion. This is an excellent example of an American public policy that worked well.

The Federal Impacted Areas Aid Program of 1950 was designed to assist areas of the country in which federal activities (such as the presence of a military base) created a substantial increase in school enrollments or a reduction in taxable resources. In response to the Soviet Union's success in launching the Sputnik satellite into space in 1957, Congress passed the National Defense Education Act of 1958, which provided financial aid to states and public school districts to improve instruction in science, math, and foreign languages to make American education more competitive in science and technology. This legislation also established a system of loans to undergraduates, fellowships to graduate students, and funds to colleges to improve teacher training.

In 1965 the Elementary and Secondary Education Act (ESEA) established the single largest education aid program. It targeted "poverty-impacted" schools by offering instructional materials and education research and training. In 1981 the Reagan administration sponsored the Education Consolidation and Improvement Act, which consolidated ESEA and other federal education grant programs into single block grants for states and communities. The goal was to give states and local school districts greater discretion in using federal aid. President Reagan attempted to reduce federal government involvement in education. His administration even proposed the elimination of the Department of Education, emphasizing that education should be a local and state responsibility. During the 1980s the federal government did limit spending in education, and the federal percentage of education funding decreased gradually.

Over the years the most popular federal education aid program has been Head Start, a component of Pres. Lyndon B. Johnson's War on Poverty during the 1960s. Head Start was designed to provide special preschool preparation to disadvantaged children before kindergarten or first grade. The program has had widespread support among Democrats and Republicans, but evidence has been inconclusive regarding the value of the program. Another piece of legislation aimed at a specific population group was the Education for All Handicapped Children Act of 1975. Its intent was to promote equal opportunities for handicapped children and those with special academic needs.

Public schools are financed mainly through property taxes levied by school districts. School financing reflects the values of the types of property located within the district boundaries. Therefore, school districts across the nation vary tremendously in their ability to raise money and support education functions. The issue of funding for public education continues to focus on the role of the federal government. The issue of "school choice" has introduced the voucher concept as a means for parents to determine education opportunities for their children. Finally, the battle over religion in schools continues within the public policy debate, with the U.S. Supreme Court playing an important role.

See also: Civil Rights: *Brown v. Board of Education;* Education: Education Consolidation and Improvement Act of 1981; Education for All Handicapped Children Act of 1975; Elementary and Secondary Education Act of 1965; Head Start; Land Ordinance of 1785; National Defense Education Act of 1958; Key Concepts: Articles of Confederation; Labor: Smith-Hughes Act of 1917

References: Thomas R. Dye, *Understanding Public Policy* (1995); Chester E. Finn Jr., *We Must Take Charge: Our Schools and Our Future* (1991); Dennis J. Palumbo, *Public Policy in America: Government in Action* (1988); B. Guy Peters, *American Public Policy: Promise and Performance* (1993).

Elementary and Secondary Education Act of 1965

The focus of education policy during the 1960s was on equal opportunities for all American children. The Elementary and Secondary Education Act (ESEA) was the largest federal aid to an education program of its time. The act made funds available to all but 5 percent of American school districts and set aside $1.3 billion in federal funds for compensatory education. The concept of compensatory education was new; it meant that the federal government intended to lay a groundwork of education programs to relieve the impact of poverty in school districts. The ESEA targeted "poverty-impacted" schools by providing instructional materials, education research information, and support for teacher training programs. Educationally deprived children and school districts with many low-income families were supposed to be the chief beneficiaries of this legislation.

The Elementary and Secondary Education Act of 1965 was composed of six separate sections or titles. Title I provided federal funds to poverty-impacted school districts. Amendments to the original legislation were passed in 1967 and 1974. The 1967 amendments attempted to equalize funding to help poorer states; the 1975 amendments favored rural education programs in southern states.

See also: Education: Education Policy

References: John E. Chubb and Terry M. Moe, *Politics, Markets, and America's Schools* (1990); Thomas R. Dye, *Understanding Public Policy* (1995); Dennis J. Palumbo, *Public Policy in America: Government in Action* (1988).

G. I. Bill

The Serviceman's Readjustment Act of 1944, popularly known as the G.I. Bill, offered education opportunities to veterans and members of the armed forces for their service to the United States. The original bill paid up to $500 each academic year to pay for college tuition, books, and other supplies and offered a monthly living allowance to veterans, determined by a marital status and income. More than 2 million people eventually obtained a college education as a result; nearly 6 million veterans used the bill for vocational training or to attend other technical or trade schools.

The G.I. Bill has been hailed as one of the most successful pieces of public policy in American history. For many veterans, college was beyond their incomes, as college was traditionally the reserve of children from wealthier families. The G.I. Bill changed all that, making it possible for most any young man or woman to seek a college education.

The G.I. Bill thus created the educational, business, scientific, and intellectual foundation for economic prosperity during the 1950s and 1960s.

See also: Education: Education Policy

References: Edward S. Greenberg and Benjamin I. Page, *The Struggle for Democracy* (1993); Paul C. Light, *Forging Legislation* (1992); Paul C. Light, *A Delicate Balance: An Essential Introduction to American Government* (1997).

Goals 2000: Educate America Act of 1994

See Education: "America 2000: An Education Strategy"

Head Start

Federal aid to urban schools increased dramatically during the late 1960s. Head Start received $103 million as one of the programs in Pres. Lyndon B. Johnson's War on Poverty. The program provided special preschool preparation to disadvantaged children. Head Start has been popular, but critics claim its benefits have not been proved. Studies have shown that students who participated in Head Start do not fare better than other students when they reach their middle-school years.

See also: Education: Education Policy

References: Thomas R. Dye, *Understanding Public Policy* (1995); Dennis J. Palumbo, *Public Policy in America: Government in Action* (1988); David B. Robertson and Dennis R. Judd, *The Development of American Public Policy: The Structure of Policy Restraint* (1989).

Higher Education

Public higher education is the planning and development of education policy in U.S. colleges and universities. There are several important elements: Boards of trustees (chosen or elected to represent interests and set broad policy directions in higher education); state governors and lawmakers (setting budgets); college and university presidents (playing a public relations role externally and gaining the acceptance of faculty internally for state and trustee policy in higher education); faculty, and faculty and staff unions and associations (faculty by designing curricula, unions by protecting the interests of faculty and staff and representing issues of quality on campuses); and students and their parents (demonstrating the effect of policy in meeting the projected outcomes of education goals). All influence higher education in one way or another.

See also: Education: Education Policy

References: Thomas R. Dye, *Understanding Public Policy* (1995).

Land Ordinance of 1785

The Land Ordinance of 1785 divided land in the old Northwest Territory (land north of the Ohio River and east of the Mississippi River) into six-square-mile townships of 36 sections (640 acres each); section 16 was set aside for the support of public schools. This highlighted America's commitment to public education.

See also: Education: Education Policy

References: Joseph R. Conlin, *The American Past: A Survey of American History* (1993).

Lemon v. Kurtzman

The U.S. Constitution forbids the establishment of a state or official religion and guarantees the free exercise of religion. In the context of education policy, prayer in public schools is an ongoing issue. In *Lemon v. Kurtzman,* the U.S. Supreme Court struck down a Pennsylvania law whereby the state paid part of parochial school teachers' salaries. The Court stated that the state was conferring a direct benefit to the church, creating excessive entanglement between the church and state. State aid to public schools is legitimate, but states cannot offer financial support to parochial or other church-affiliated schools. This is consistent with the doctrine of separation of church and state.

See also: Education: Education Policy

References: B. Guy Peters, *American Public Policy: Promise and Performance* (1993).

National Defense Education Act of 1958

When the Soviet Union in 1957 launched Sputnik, the first unmanned space satellite, the U.S. scientific and education communities became determined to excel in science and technology education. Congress passed the National Defense Education Act in 1958, appropriating $1.6 billion to states and public school districts to bolster instruction in science, mathematics, and foreign languages. The bill targeted students seeking undergraduate and graduate degrees to improve teacher training programs. This bill was designed to further the connection between education and the nation's defense needs as a matter of public policy. In a bipartisan effort, Democrats and Republicans in Congress saw it as a way to support both education and national defense. Prior to the Sputnik episode, many conservatives in Congress showed little interest in funding education programs.

See also: Education: Education Policy

References: Thomas R. Dye, *Understanding Public Policy* (1995); B. Guy Peters, *American Public Policy: Promise and Performance* (1993); David B. Robertson and Dennis R. Judd, *The Development of American Public Policy: The Structure of Policy Restraint* (1989).

National Education Association

The National Education Association (NEA) was formed in 1870 to promote the goals of education and educators in the states. NEA represents teachers, education administrators, and faculty in higher education. An interest group with more than 2 million members, NEA influences education policy in the United States through a main office in Washington, D.C. State organizations hold annual conventions, and a national convention sets the national program and goals. NEA has a significant amount of political influence in Congress and state legislatures, providing monetary support to political candidates.

See also: Education: American Federation of Teachers; Education Policy; Key Concepts: Interest Groups

References: Thomas R. Dye, *Understanding Public Policy* (1995); B. Guy Peters, *American Public Policy: Promise and Performance* (1993).

National Endowment for the Humanities

The National Endowment for the Humanities (NEH) is a federal agency that offers grant and research support to scholars who conduct research and engage in projects in the humanities. University and high school teachers are encouraged to submit grant proposals to NEH for funds to investigate issues and subjects in history, the English language, social science, and literature. These funds are the basis for many research projects. The National Foundation of the Arts and Humanities Act of 1965 established NEH, setting the governing structure and funding mechanism. It has a 26-member governing board appointed by the president and confirmed by the Senate.

See also: Key Concepts: Federalism

References: Susan Welch et al., *Understanding American Government* (1997).

National Science Foundation Act of 1950

During the early 1950s the federal government committed to funding education programs in support of science research and development. One of the early efforts was the National Science Foundation Act of 1950, which created the National Science Foundation (NSF) to promote scientific research and to fund grants and fellowships to students for graduate education in the sciences and social sciences. NSF also established institutes for training elementary and secondary school teachers and offers education opportunities through its fellowship and grant programs to enable university and secondary education teachers to do research important to science.

See also: Education: Education Policy

References: Dennis J. Palumbo, *Public Policy in America: Government in Action* (1988).

Northwest Ordinance of 1787

See Education: Education Policy

Public Education

See Education: Education Policy

Serrano v. Priest

One of the tougher issues for public school districts is disparate financing between districts. Poorer school districts that might not enjoy the same financial assistance as affluent ones must rely more on state aid. In 1971 the California Supreme Court decided, in *Serrano v. Priest,* that education is a fundamental right under the state constitution and cannot be a condition of the wealth of a child's parents or neighbors. School districts traditionally relied on property taxes to fund local schools; there are major disparities in property tax revenues between urban and suburban school districts. *Serrano v. Priest* prompted some states to reform school finance. The decision publicized the problem of inequitable school financing.

See also: Education: Education Policy

References: Clarke E. Cochran et al., *American Public Policy: An Introduction* (1996); B. Guy Peters, *American Public Policy: Promise and Performance* (1993).

Serviceman's Readjustment Act of 1944

See Education: G.I. Bill

Vocational Rehabilitation Acts

The first federal Vocational Rehabilitation Act was passed in 1920; it provided vocational rehabilitation for handicapped persons. This was the first time the federal government acknowledged a role in vocational training and specifically for handicapped people. The 1973 amendments to the act eliminated discrimination of handicapped people under programs that received federal funds. This legislation was designed to extend education opportunities to disabled people. Congress went further toward extending protections to people with disabilities with the passage of the Education of the Handicapped Act of 1974, which required that free appropriate public education be provided to all handicapped children.

See also: Education: Education Policy

References: Dennis J. Palumbo, *Public Policy in America: Government in Action* (1988).

Vouchers

Choice in education opportunities is a continuing issue in the public policy debate. Vouchers give parents a choice; a voucher is a money order of sorts that can be used to pay for education anywhere. The voucher would equal the cost of attending public school to cover the costs of schooling elsewhere (e.g., at a private or parochial school).

The voucher concept is a response to varying quality of schools throughout the United States. One problem is that it could potentially increase stratification in education quality and experience. Vouchers help wealthier families that have the ability to send their children to expensive schools, whereas poorer families have little option but to send their children to public schools (in which case the voucher doesn't apply). Accordingly, vouchers do little to improve education for children of families with limited financial resources.

See also: Education: Education Policy

References: John E. Chubb and Terry M. Moe, *Politics, Markets, and America's Schools* (1990); Thomas R. Dye, *Understanding Public Policy* (1995); Chester E. Finn Jr., *We Must Take Charge: Our Schools and Our Future* (1991); B. Guy Peters, *American Public Policy: Promise and Performance* (1993).

Energy

Chronology

1884 U.S. Department of Interior established the Bureau of Mines to work with the mining industry and provide scientific and technical advice to the coal industry.

1916 Pres. Woodrow Wilson created the Petroleum Advisory Committee to coordinate the nation's industrial effort, survey American oil production capabilities, and allocate supplies between domestic civilian needs and military needs during World War I.

1917 When the United States entered World War I, the Petroleum Advisory Committee became the National Petroleum War Service Committee.

1917 President Wilson created the U.S. Fuel Administration to coordinate the supply of fuel in the United States.

1919 National Petroleum War Service Committee became the American Petroleum Institute.

1933 National Industrial Recovery Act was passed, establishing the government's role in petroleum production and the setting of quotas in production.

1933 In May 1933 Pres. Franklin D. Roosevelt signed the Tennessee Valley Authority Act, which provided for the total development of the Tennessee Valley.

1935 President Roosevelt created the Rural Electrification Administration to supply electricity to rural areas throughout the United States.

1937 The Bonneville Power Administration was established, offering power in the Pacific Northwest. The Southwestern Power Administration (1943) and the Southeastern Power Administration (1950) were later created by the Department of Interior to supervise distribution of power from hydroelectric dams.

1938 Congress passed the Natural Gas Act, defining the government's role in natural gas development and defining the authority of the Federal Power Commission in setting and regulating natural gas rates.

1946 Atomic Energy Act was passed, creating the Atomic Energy Commission.

1953 The Submerged Lands Act was passed, giving states clear title to lands within three miles of the Atlantic and Pacific Coasts.

1953 The Outer Continental Shelf Act was passed,

giving the national government exclusive jurisdiction over the ocean bottom beyond the three-mile boundary.

1954 The Atomic Energy Act of 1954 established new procedures for supplying fuel to nuclear reactors. The Atomic Energy Commission would lease fuel to utilities, and utilities were given the opportunity to build and operate nuclear reactors under licensing by the Atomic Energy Commission.

1957 President Eisenhower signed the Price-Anderson Act, which encouraged utilities to invest in nuclear power facilities and set liability limits for private producers of nuclear power in times of accidents.

1960 The Organization of Petroleum Exporting Countries (OPEC) was formed. By 1973 OPEC included Saudi Arabia, Kuwait, Iraq, United Arab Emirates, Qatar, Libya, Algeria, Iran, Venezuela, Indonesia, Nigeria, Gabon, and Ecuador.

1969 The National Environmental Policy Act was passed.

1970 The Clean Air Act was passed, the first comprehensive clean air legislation passed by Congress.

1973 The Environmental Protection Agency suspended clean air standards so that electrical utility plants could convert to coal.

1973 The Emergency Petroleum Allocation Act put a ceiling on oil prices.

1973 On October 17, OPEC announced its oil embargo, creating oil shortages in the United States and increasing the price of oil.

1973 In December Pres. Richard M. Nixon established the Federal Energy Office, which later became the Federal Energy Administration.

1974 The Energy Reorganization Act was passed, eliminating the Atomic Energy Commission and splitting off licensing functions to the Nuclear Regulatory Commission.

1975 The Strategic Petroleum Reserve was established, enabling the federal government to store crude oil for emergency purposes.

1977 National Energy Plan was presented to Congress by Pres. Jimmy Carter.

1977 Congress passed the Surface Mining Control and Reclamation Act, which established nationwide standards on strip-mine reclamation that would be enforceable by the states.

1977 Congress created the Department of Energy.

1978 The National Energy Act was passed; one of the provisions required utilities to shift from oil and gas to coal.

1978 The Natural Gas Policy Act was passed, fixing prices and formulas for pricing.

1980 The Low Level Waste Policy Act was passed, giving states the responsibility to create compacts for waste disposal.

1980 The Uranium Mill Tailings and Reclamation Act was passed, providing money to identify and move or bury uranium mine tailings near residences.

1990 The Clean Air Act amendments addressed the problem of global warming and focused on limiting the use of fossil fuels.

Atomic Energy Act of 1946

After the United States developed and exploded the atomic bomb in 1945, the question for the U.S. government became how to manage the use of atomic energy and weapons. The Atomic Energy Act of 1946 created the Atomic Energy Commission (AEC). A five-member commission of civilians led the agency to ensure against military control of atomic power. An important element, because of the national security implications of atomic energy, was a strict government monopoly over atomic power. The 1946 legislation was a culmination of debates in Congress over the control and administration of atomic power.

In 1954 amendments were made to account for advances in science and to accommodate the need to share information for the commercial research and develop of atomic energy. The 1954 act laid the groundwork for the commercial nuclear power industry.

See also: Energy: Atomic Energy Commission; Nuclear Energy Policy

References: David H. Davis, *Energy Politics* (1993); Earl R. Kruschke and Byron M. Jackson, *Nuclear Energy Policy: A Reference Handbook* (1990).

Atomic Energy Commission

The Atomic Energy Commission (AEC) was created by the Atomic Energy Act of 1946. AEC was originally given responsibility for overseeing the development of civilian and military atomic programs. The commission was authorized to exercise the government monopoly over all nuclear materials, facilities, and experimental projects. The Joint Committee on Atomic Energy was also created as an oversight body for AEC activities. AEC had the task of managing the network of laboratories and facilities that were left over from the Manhattan Project (the secret U.S. project to develop the atomic bomb, which was dropped on Japan in August 1945 to end World War II). David Lilienthal, former chair of the Tennessee Valley Authority, was appointed by Pres. Harry Truman as the first AEC chair. The other original members were Lewis L. Strauss, former aide to Pres. Herbert Hoover; former Securities and Exchange Commission Chair Sumner Pike; scientist Edward U. Condon; Frank P. Graham, president of the University of North Carolina; and Chester Barnard, president of New Jersey Bell Telephone and author of the major work on organizational leadership *Functions of the Executive.*

When the Atomic Energy Act of 1954 was passed, the path to private development of nuclear energy was open. The role of the AEC became one of promoting the commercial uses of nuclear power as well as regulating the new and growing industry. AEC was also responsible for issuing licenses to private firms to build and operate commercial nuclear power plants and to adopt regulations to protect the health and safety of the public in the development of commercial nuclear enterprises. Over the years AEC's charge changed, in response to increasing public concerns about environmental issues, to one of greater regulation of the nuclear power industry. In 1974 Congress passed the Energy Reorganization Act, which gave the new Nuclear Regulatory Commission (NRC) the licensing functions of the old AEC. Other AEC functions in research and development of geothermal and solar programs went to a new agency, the Energy Research and Development Administration (ERDA). The Joint Committee on Atomic Energy was dissolved along with the AEC under the 1974 legislation. The Department of Energy was created in 1977 after public scrutiny, which continued to shadow the industry through the 1990s, peaked.

See also: Energy: Atomic Energy Act of 1946; Lilienthal, David

References: David H. Davis, *Energy Politics* (1993); Earl R. Kruschke and Byron M. Jackson, *Nuclear Energy Policy: A Reference Handbook* (1990); Steven M. Neuse, *David Lilienthal: The Journey of an American Liberal* (1996); Allan M. Winkler, *Life under a Cloud: American Anxiety about the Atom* (1993).

Corporate Average Fuel Economy Standards

The Corporate Average Fuel Economy (CAFE) standards were developed as a result of the threatened reduction of U.S. oil imports during the early 1970s. In 1973 and 1974 the Arab oil embargo exposed America's dependence on foreign oil; the situation would reach crisis stage if international supplies became unavailable or even threatened. In a measure designed to reduce oil imports and lessen American dependence on foreign oil, Congress proposed a law to improve fuel consumption of automobiles in the United States. U.S. automobile manufacturers were able to develop smaller, fuel-efficient cars at lower prices and still make profits on larger automobiles, which were still an important market. The Energy Policy and Conservation Act of 1975 required companies that produced more than 10,000 automobiles annually to meet the average fuel economy standard for their fleet of cars. In 1975 General Motors produced more than 4 million cars. The fuel efficiency standards were set to go into effect in 1978, with the fuel efficiency standard set at 18 miles per gallon and increasing to 27.5 miles per gallon by 1985. If a company exceeded that standard in automobile production, the company could receive credits for succeeding production years. U.S. auto manufacturers had an advantage in meeting the CAFE standard policy because of their broad production lines, whereas foreign auto manufacturers had more limited production ability. The CAFE standard was more easily met by American companies because they could modify all production lines. Foreign manufacturers had more difficulty modifying prodution lines because they were not held to their own domestic fuel efficiency standards. Therefore the CAFE standards were more costly to meet for foreign producers. As an energy conservation effort, the CAFE standards worked favorably toward reinforcing the need for more fuel efficient cars; it also preserved industry jobs a time when the industry was threatened by growing consumer preferences for smaller, cheaper, more reliable foreign autos.

See also: Energy: Energy Policy; Energy Policy and Conservation Act of 1975

References: Charles Bonser, Eugene B. McGregor Jr., and Clinton V. Oster Jr., *Policy Choices and Public Action* (1996); David H. Davis, *Energy Politics* (1993).

Department of Energy

In 1977 Pres. Jimmy Carter signed the Department of Energy Organization Act. The act abolished the Federal Energy Administration and the Energy Research and Development Administration and created a new executive agency, the U.S. Department of Energy, the 12th cabinet-level department in the federal government. The agency housed various agencies, commissions, and offices related to nonnuclear energy policy: energy research, development, regulation, pricing, and conservation. This marked the federal government's first attempt to coordinate these activities. But the new agency also coordinated government activities in the field of nuclear energy.

All this came at a time when the nation's future was threatened by the energy crisis of the early 1970s. Prior to the 1970s energy resources were seen as boundless, and the extent of federal involvement in coordinating energy policy, research, and activities reflected this belief. Thus a comprehensive national energy strategy was not a priority—until the uncertainty and challenges brought on by the energy crisis. As early as 1971 Pres. Richard M. Nixon began building support for coordinating energy research, development, and policy. He established the Special Energy Committee, composed of senior White House advisers, representatives in domestic, foreign, and economic policy areas, and the National Energy Office. The task of the committee was to identify issues and coordinate energy analysis between various offices and agencies.

The Nixon overtures gained momentum in 1973 when the Yom Kippur War broke out, involving Israel, Egypt, Syria, and Jordan. The Organization of Petroleum Exporting Countries (OPEC) placed an embargo (a prohibition on sale) on crude oil shipped to the United States because of its support of Israel. President Nixon created the Federal Energy Office in response to the energy crisis in 1973 and pursued "Project Independence," charting a course for energy independence. In 1974 Congress passed legislation creating the Federal Energy Administration, a two-year temporary agency responsible for gathering energy information and engaging in analysis, managing petroleum allocation and pricing, creating a strategic reserve of fuel and energy supplies, coordinating energy conservation, and promoting the more efficient use of energy resources. Congress passed legislation extending the agency's operations until the end of 1977.

In October 1974 Pres. Gerald Ford signed the Energy Reorganization Act, establishing the Energy Research and Development Administration and the Nuclear Regulatory Commission (NRC), which took over the licensing and regulatory functions of the previous (and now abolished) Atomic Energy Commission. Jimmy Carter was elected president in November 1976; the winter of 1976–1977 was harsh, and the nation faced a shortage of natural gas supplies. President Carter appointed his special assistant, James R. Schlesinger, to head a team that would shape the president's energy policy and reorganization plans, which included a new cabinet-level department. The winter was unrelenting, and on February 2, 1977, President Carter declared a national emergency and with congressional approval created the Emergency Natural Gas Act of 1977. The Department of Energy was created and signed into law on August 4, 1977; Schlesinger was the first secretary. The major subagencies of the DOE today are the Office of Radioactive Waste Management; Bonneville Power Administration; Office of Nuclear Energy; Energy Information Administration; and Office of Conservation and Renewable Energy.

See also: Energy: Atomic Energy Act of 1946; Atomic Energy Commission; Energy Policy; Energy Policy and Conservation Act of 1975

References: Frederick R. Anderson, Daniel Mandelker, and A. Dan Tarlock, *Environmental Protection: Law and Policy* (1984); Lynton K. Caldwell, *Environment as a Focus for Public Policy* (1995); David H. Davis, *Energy Politics* (1993); Francis Sandbach, *Environment, Ideology, and Policy* (1980); Jacqueline V. Switzer, *Environmental Politics: Domestic and Global Dimensions* (1994); Donald T. Wells, *Environmental Policy* (1996).

Energy Crisis

See Energy: Energy Policy

Energy Policy

Given the long-held view that America's energy resources (predominantly coal, oil, and natural gas, mostly in the hands of private industry) were inexhaustible, their availability was not a serious concern until a 1973 oil embargo by the Organization of Petroleum Exporting Countries (OPEC) disrupted international oil supplies and caused an energy crisis. Suddenly, policymakers realized U.S. vulnerability to threats to shut off American access to oil resources. And little thought had been given to the day when energy supplies might run out.

Coal was the chief energy source prior to the late 1920s, accounting for as much as 75 percent. Oil replaced coal during the 1930s as the primary source, which spelled doom for the coal industry, which had overproduced and was oversupplied. In 1932 more than 4,000 coal companies went out of business; those that remained were less than profitable.

Texas was the primary source for American oil during the early 20th century; oil production there was regulated by both the Texas Railroad Commission and the federal government (in the area of interstate transport of oil). A federal depletion allowance was devised, essentially a tax break allowing oil companies to deduct 27.5 percent of gross income from taxable income if the total amount deducted did not exceed 50 percent of net income.

Natural gas was usually found alongside a large pocket of oil, which made for efficient exploration opportunities. The Federal Power Commission (FPC) served as the federal agency that would regulate pricing of gas. The Natural Gas Act of 1938 designated FPC as the regulator for gas, but the agency was never very aggressive in regulating the industry, in keeping with the general regulatory philosophy of the 1930s.

Nuclear power has been an energy source since the late 1950s, but no nuclear power plant has been built in the United States since 1973. There are currently 111 nuclear power plants in operation, licensed for forty years (with the year 2000 being the expiration year for the oldest licenses). It is possible to extend the licenses for a decade or two to relieve the burden of losing this power source. Nuclear energy is no longer the inexpensive energy solution that its proponents once touted. In 1997 the U.S. nuclear power industry generated one-fifth of the nation's electricity.

Fossil fuels thus remain the major energy resource for the United States. Alternative energy sources such as solar power, wind power, and geothermal development have not received a significant amount of investigation or government support. Since these are renewable energy resources, the incentive for private or industry development has been absent.

The impact of the energy crisis was the reduction of fuel supplies, which resulted in long lines at gas stations and dramatic price increases for home fuel oil. America's continuing dependency on oil and the international oil supply might be a losing proposition, even though international oil prices were stable through the late 1990s with a robust supply. As long as the supply of oil continues to exceed demand and the pricing structure for oil remains stable, U.S. policymakers will not pursue an energy policy agenda that searches for alternatives to our reliance on fossil fuels.

See also: Energy: Corporate Average Fuel Economy Standards; Energy Policy and Conservation Act of 1975

References: Clarke E. Cochran et al., *American Public Policy: An Introduction* (1996); David H. Davis, *Energy Politics* (1993); Donald T. Wells, *Environmental Policy* (1996).

Energy Policy and Conservation Act of 1975

The Energy Policy and Conservation Act of 1975 was designed to add to previous conservation policies developed to counter the reduced supply of foreign oil. The bill set mileage standards for automobiles and efficiency standards for home appliances; it also established a Strategic Petroleum Reserve for the nation. The law also dealt with pricing structures (the establishment of price controls) for newly discovered crude oil and gave the president authority to relax controls as well. Section 546 of the legislation established building standards of 65 degrees Fahrenheit in the winter and 78 degrees Fahrenheit in the summer. Many homeowners also purchased wood-burning stoves during this time to aid in conservation efforts and to avoid the increasingly high prices of home fuel oil. This legislation did have a lasting effect on energy conservation and made conservation a priority for Americans during the late 1970s.

See also: Energy: Energy Policy

References: Frederick R. Anderson, Daniel Mandelker, and A. Dan Tarlock, *Environmental Protection: Law and Policy* (1984); David H. Davis, *Energy Politics* (1993); Dennis J. Palumbo, *Public Policy in America: Government in Action* (1988).

Federal Energy Regulatory Commission

In 1920 Congress passed the Water Power Act, creating the Federal Power Commission (FPC) to license and regulate power plants. Over the years, FPC was granted the authority to regulate interstate transmission of electricity, and in 1977, when it passed the Department of Energy Reorganization Act, Congress replaced FPC with the Federal Energy Regulatory Commission (FERC). This new agency was responsible for regulating American water resources, but its authority grew to include oversight of transmission and sale of electric power, natural gas, oil by pipeline and interstate commerce, and private, municipal, and state hydroelectric projects. Today, FERC is a part of the Department of Energy, its legal authority being derived from several laws: the original Federal Power Act of 1935, the Natural Gas Act of 1938, and the Natural Gas Policy Act of 1978. The five members of FERC, appointed by the president with the advice and consent of the Senate, serve staggered five-year terms.

See also: Energy: Department of Energy; Energy Policy

References: David H. Davis, *Energy Politics* (1993); Earl R. Kruschke and Byron M. Jackson, *Nuclear Energy Policy: A Reference Handbook* (1990); Jacqueline V. Switzer, *Environmental Politics: Domestic and Global Dimensions* (1994).

Federal Power Commission

See Energy: Energy Policy

Groves, Leslie (1896–1970)

Brig. Gen. Leslie Groves, an engineer by training, headed the Manhattan Project, the secret U.S. effort to develop an atomic bomb during World War II. Groves was appointed in 1942 to establish the scientific and technical team that created the bomb, directing activities at two primary facilities, in Oak Ridge, Tennessee, and Los Alamos, New Mexico. Groves's role in atomic energy continued after World War II; he served on a committee that provided recommendations to Pres. Harry Truman on international uses of atomic energy. Groves became associated with the Atomic Energy Commission when he was appointed by President Truman to lead the Military Liaison Committee. Groves played the role of military and security liaison between the Atomic Energy Commission, Congress, and the president.

See also: Energy: Atomic Energy Commission; Nuclear Energy Policy

References: Steven M. Neuse, *David E. Lilienthal: The Journey of an American Liberal* (1996); Allan M. Winkler, *Life under a Cloud: American Anxiety about the Atom* (1993).

Jackson, Henry (1912–1983)

Sen. Henry Jackson served in the U.S. Congress for 42 years as a representative (first elected in 1940) and senator from Washington State (1953). Senator Jackson was an avid supporter of the development of nuclear power and was one of the original members on the Joint Committee on Atomic Energy during the late 1940s and early 1950s. Jackson was chiefly responsible for the development of the government's nuclear reactor facility and reservation at Hanford, Washington. During Senate subcommittee discussions on nuclear waste disposal, Senator Jackson once suggested that spent nuclear fuel rods be encased in stainless steel and taken to Antarctica for safe storage. "Scoop" Jackson was known for his unflagging support of nuclear power and was a major influence on U.S. nuclear energy policy.

See also: Energy: Nuclear Energy Policy

References: Earl R. Kruschke and Byron M. Jackson, *Nuclear Energy Policy: A Reference Handbook* (1990).

Lilienthal, David (1899–1981)

David Lilienthal was an important part of two major technological projects during the mid-20th century. He was founding director of the Tennessee Valley Authority (TVA), a controversial, monumental effort to transform the Tennessee Valley watershed into an agriculturally productive and economically prosperous area. Prior to serving with TVA, Lilienthal was director of the Wisconsin Public Service Commission. He worked with TVA from 1933 until 1946, using his impressive political skills to win over Congress, powerful Tennesseeans, and critics.

In 1947 Lilienthal was selected to be the first chair of the U.S. Atomic Energy Commission (AEC). He served a four-year term as chair, leading the United States into the atomic age. While serving with AEC, Lilienthal maintained an ideal for peaceful use of the atom and nuclear energy, fighting the U.S. military, which wanted to the preserve secrets of nuclear power. Eventually, cold warriors wore him down; he left the AEC in 1950, returning to private enterprise and public service. He was a dedicated public servant who understood the use of technology for social good.

See also: Energy: Atomic Energy Commission

References: David E. Lilienthal, *The Journals of David Lilienthal* (1964–1983); Steven M. Neuse, *David E. Lilienthal: The Journey of an American Liberal* (1996).

Low-Level Nuclear Waste Policy Act of 1980

One of the major problems of the nuclear power industry, including any businesses using radiation and uranium for medical and technological purposes, is the disposal and storage of waste. The U.S. Department of Energy oversees the disposal of nuclear waste. Prior to 1970 all low-level radioactive waste was dumped in sites in Nevada, South Carolina, and Washington. In 1979 U.S. Rep. Butler Derrick, a Democrat from South Carolina, proposed that each state manage storage of low-level radioactive waste. Under Butler's proposal, each state would build its own low-level radioactive waste dump or join neighboring states to create a regional dump. In December 1980 Congress passed the measure, yet the bill did not receive full hearings in the House and Senate; also it did not detail how the states were to choose waste dump sites or how to work in regional compacts to develop sites. The target date for each state to conform to the bill's requirements was January 1, 1986. The bill did not account for variations in state radioactive waste production.

In 1985 Congress amended the act to set more realistic compliance dates; by late 1998 ten regional compacts for low-level radioactive waste disposal had been entered; Texas's waste site is still awaiting congressional approval.

See also: Energy: Department of Energy; Nuclear Energy Policy; Environment: Environmental Policy

References: Donald L. Bartlett and James B. Steele, *Forevermore: Nuclear Waste in America* (1985); David H. Davis, *Energy Politics* (1993).

Natural Gas

See Energy: Energy Policy

Nuclear Energy Policy

In 1945 the United States became the first nation to develop and explode atomic weapons. In August of that year the United States, seeking a Japanese surrender in World War II, dropped the bomb on Hiroshima and Nagasaki, both on the Japanese mainland; this brought about the end of the war (Germany had already surrendered). America thus entered the atomic age, eventually becoming the world's foremost nuclear power. In 1948 the Soviet Union exploded its first atomic weapon.

In 1946 Congress passed the Atomic Energy Act, which established the Atomic Energy Commission, responsible for controlling the development of nuclear energy and exploring the peaceful uses of the atom. In 1954 Congress passed the Atomic Energy Act, which revised the 1946 legislation and provided for commercial development of nuclear energy. In 1957 Congress passed the Price-Anderson Act, which encouraged private utility companies to invest in nuclear power facilities and provided financial protection to the public and to Atomic Energy Commission licensees and contractors in the event of a major accident involving a nuclear power plant. This legislation was designed to free potential owners and builders of nuclear power facilities from the liability issues that could inhibit development of the industry. On March 28, 1979, an accident happened in the reactor facility of the Three Mile Island Nuclear Power Plant near Harrisburg, Pennsylvania. This was the most serious accident to occur at a commercial nuclear power facility in the United States.

Regulation of the nuclear power industry changed in 1977 when Pres. Jimmy Carter signed the Energy Reorganization Act, which created the Department of Energy. The Atomic Energy Commission was replaced by the Nuclear Regulatory Commission, which was given authority to regulate and inspect the nation's nuclear power facilities. In 1983 Pres. Ronald Reagan signed the Nuclear Waste Policy Act, designed to develop a disposal program for high-level radioactive waste and spent nuclear fuel rods. During the 1990s nuclear power plants continued to store spent nuclear fuel rods on site. Two long-term depositories have been selected but have yet to go into full operation: Yucca Mountain, 100 miles northwest of Las Vegas, Nevada, and the WIPP site in New Mexico. Long-term storage is problematic because of the life span of spent nuclear fuel rods, which remain "hot" (radioactive) for thousands of years and can contaminate air, water, and soil. Long-term storage sites must be free from earthquake activity, free from precipitation and soil percolation from rain seepage, and free from soil conditions that promote penetrable conditions.

The future of nuclear power as an energy source in the United States is uncertain. At the turn of the century some 100 nuclear power plants were operational, generating one-fifth of the nation's electricity. During the next thirty years the number of plants may shrink somewhat due to early closings and expirations of the oldest existing licenses (which might be extended under certain circumstances). No nuclear plant has been built since 1973 in light of the high costs and recurring safety issues. One-third of the existing licenses for nuclear reactors will expire by 2015, and nuclear power still remains among the cleanest energy-producing industries, avoiding the need to burn hundreds of millions of tons of coal, tens of millions of barrels of oil, and some 1 trillion cubic feet of natural gas; it reduces annual carbon dioxide emissions by some 150 million tons. And though the industry continues to promote the environmental cleanliness of nuclear energy, it struggles to solve the problem of long-term storage of spent fuel rods.

See also: Energy: Atomic Energy Act of 1946; Energy Policy; Three Mile Island; Environment: Environmental Policy

References: Lynton V. Caldwell, *Environment as a Focus for Public Policy* (1995); David H. Davis, *Energy Politics* (1993); Earl R. Kruschke and Byron M. Jackson, *Nuclear Energy Policy: A Reference Handbook* (1990); Walter Rosenbaum, *Environmental Politics and Policy* (1998).

Nuclear Regulatory Commission

See Energy: Nuclear Energy Policy

Nuclear Waste

See Energy: Nuclear Energy Policy

Tennessee Valley Authority

See Energy: Lilienthal, David

Three Mile Island

The most serious nuclear accident in the United States occurred at the Three Mile Island Nuclear Power Plant on the Susquehanna River south of Harrisburg, Pennsylvania, in 1978. As a result, the Nuclear Regulatory Commission increased requirements for emergency planning at commercial nuclear power plants. Following this accident, demand for more nuclear power plants diminished, and communities questioned the location of nearby nuclear power plants. Although no deaths resulted from the accident at Three Mile Island, the negative publicity surrounding this accident, as well as that at Chernobyl, Ukraine, in 1986, made it extremely difficult for the nuclear power industry to change American opinion about the overall safety of commercial plants.

See also: Energy: Nuclear Energy Policy

References: Donald L. Bartlett and James B. Steele, *Forevermore: Nuclear Waste in America* (1985); Earl R. Kruschke and Byron M. Jackson, *Nuclear Energy Policy: A Reference Handbook* (1990).

Entitlement Programs

Chronology

1930 Herbert Hoover appointed Col. Arthur Woods to head the president's Emergency Committee for Employment.

1931 The President's Organization on Unemployment Relief was created to replace Emergency Committee for Employment.

1932 Emergency Relief Act was passed to help states fund assistance and unemployment programs.

1933 Rise of the Townshend movement to give people over 60 years old a monthly stipend.

1935 Social Security Act passed, establishing income maintenance program for elderly, poor, blind, and disabled and an early form of Aid to Families with Dependent Children.

1964 Food Stamp Act passed as a means-tested food and nutrition program for the poor, disadvantaged, and children.

1972 Establishment of Supplemental Security Income, which offered guaranteed income to eligible aged, blind, and disabled.

1979 Food Stamp Act was targeted at reducing fraud, waste, and abuse in the Food Stamp Program.

1996 Welfare Reform Bill directed at putting welfare recipients to work and training programs to reduce the welfare rolls.

Aid to Families with Dependent Children

This government assistance program was one of the first of what we call welfare programs. It was replaced in 1996 by Temporary Assistance to Needy Families (TANF), which eliminated the open-ended entitlement and instituted time-limited cash assistance. Aid to Families with Dependent Children (AFDC) and TANF are means-tested assistance programs. Recipients of aid must demonstrate the need for cash payments to supplement or provide income for needy children. AFDC was established in 1935 as a part of the Social Security Act, which enabled states to provide cash payments for needy children who had been deprived of parental support because the father or mother was continuously absent from home. AFDC became synonymous with welfare, and AFDC recipients have been typically single mothers, unwed mothers, and other caregivers to children who do not have traditional parental support. AFDC has been the object of complaints and criticism about alleged waste, fraud, and abuse. The Food Stamp Program is the principal nutrition assistance program, in the form of coupons or electronic benefits that may be exchanged for food in authorized stores. Some food stamp recipients also receive AFDC or Supplemental Security Income (SSI), although a large portion of recipients do not receive AFDC or SSI. A companion program to AFDC is the Aid to Families with Dependent Children and Unemployed Parent (AFDC-UP). The average number of families participating in the AFDC programs between the years 1970–1973 increased by 64 percent, from 1.9 million to 3.1 million. The number of AFDC recipients increased again in 1989, with a high of 5.1 million families, but has declined since, with 4.4 million families participating in August 1996.

In August 1996 Congress passed the Personal Responsibility and Work Opportunity Reconciliation Act, which changed reporting and eligibility requirements for families to receive aid. There are no individual guarantees of benefits under this reform law, which is intended to reduce family dependence on assistance by promoting job skills, work, and marriage.

See also: Entitlement Programs: Social Security Act of 1935; Welfare Policy

References: Dennis J. Palumbo, *Public Policy in America: Government in Action* (1988); Frances Fox Piven and Richard A. Cloward, *Regulating the Poor: The Functions of Public Welfare* (1971).

Cash Benefit Programs

Cash benefit programs are federal and state social programs that provide assistance in the form of money to supplement personal income. These programs are designed for the deserving poor and are tied to minimum-income criteria or to a recipient's previous self-contributions. Examples of cash benefit or assistance programs are welfare and Social Security. These are means-tested assistance programs, available to eligible low-income families. There are three cash benefit or assistance programs in the United States: (1) Aid to Families with Dependent Children was established in 1935 and provided cash payments for needy children who had been deprived of parental support or care because of an absent father or mother; (2) the Food Stamp Program is the principal nutrition assistance program in the United States and provides nutrition assistance through coupons or electronic benefits; and (3) the Supplemental Security Income program provides assistance to three categories of recipients—low-income elderly, low-income and disabled nonelderly adults, and disabled children living in low-income families.

Cash benefit programs are under constant scrutiny in American politics, and therefore public assistance is sometimes difficult to obtain, even for those who qualify. Other kinds of income subsidies, such as those for agriculture, transportation companies, small businesses, and large corporations, receive less attention.

See also: Entitlement Programs: Aid to Families with Dependent Children; Food Stamp Act of 1964; Supplemental Security Income; Welfare Policy

References: Charles Bonser, Eugene B. McGregor Jr., and Clinton V. Oster Jr., *Policy Choices and Public Action* (1996); Clarke E. Cochran et al., *American Public Policy: An Introduction* (1996); Frances Fox Piven and Richard A. Cloward, *Regulating the Poor: The Functions of Public Welfare* (1971).

Entitlement Programs

Entitlement programs are frequently discussed in the context of the federal budget and uncontrolled spending. Entitlement programs are government programs that guarantee benefits to anyone who is eligible. These automatic spending programs cost the federal government $762 billion in 1992–1993, more than half of all government spending. Eligibility requirements for entitlement programs are usually class-based, which means that age, income, disability, unemployment, and veteran status determine recipients' eligibility. Social Security, welfare and food stamps (Aid to Families with Dependent Children), Medicare and Medicaid, federal employees' retirement, veterans' benefits, and unemployment compensation are entitlement programs. These entitlement programs are not altogether uncontrollable, as critics in Congress claim. Congress can alter the original spending formulas but risks political battles when attempts are made to reduce spending in these programs. The 1996 federal budget committed 54.1 percent of spending to entitlement programs, and one-third of Americans receive some form of government benefits.

See also: Entitlement Programs: Aid to Families with Dependent Children; Medicaid; Medicare; Social Security Act of 1935; Welfare Policy

References: Thomas R. Dye and L. Harmon Ziegler, *The Irony of Democracy: An Uncommon Introduction to American Politics* (1996); Paul C. Light, *A Delicate Balance: An Essential Introduction to American Government* (1997).

Family Support Act of 1988

The issue of welfare and welfare dependency has been a hot debate in Congress since the early 1980s. The Family Support Act of 1988, championed by Sen. Daniel P. Moynihan, has four major provisions: a job-training program for most adults receiving Aid to Families with Dependent Children (AFDC) payments; child care for job-training program participants; child care and Medicaid for 12 months after a participant leaves AFDC to take a job; and strengthened child-support enforcement programs. State implementation of these programs has been slow, and the job-training programs have not been fully funded. The Job Opportunities and Basic Skills (JOBS) program is required for public assistance recipients. The Family Support Act as policy demonstrated the shift of welfare policy from cash benefit programs, upon which recipients became dependent, to work incentive programs, such as the Personal Responsibility and Work Opportunity Reconciliation Act of 1996.

See also: Entitlement Programs: Aid to Families with Dependent Children; Welfare Policy

References: Clarke E. Cochran et al., *American Public Policy: An Introduction* (1996); Thomas R. Dye, *Understanding Public Policy* (1995); B. Guy Peters, *American Public Policy: Promise and Performance* (1993).

Food Stamp Act of 1964

The federal Food Stamp Program was initiated as a pilot program in 1961 and was formally established as a federal program by the Food Stamp Act of 1964. The original program had 22 states participating; by 1970 all but five states participated in the program. By 1975 all the states were participants in the federally funded Food Stamp Program. In the original program, food stamp coupons were purchased by participating families. They received allotments of food stamps that were large enough to purchase a nutritionally adequate diet; free food stamps were provided to the poorest recipients. In 1977 the purchase requirement for food stamps was eliminated, and families received what was called the bonus value of stamps (the difference between the face value of the coupons and the amount the participant paid). The rules were liberalized in 1985 with the passage of the Food Security Act, which required states to implement employment and training programs for food stamp recipients; provided automatic food stamp eligibility for AFDC and Social Security Insurance recipients; and prohibited the collection of sales taxes on food stamps purchases.

Food stamp benefits are available to all households that meet federal eligibility requirements for limited monthly income. The Food Stamp Program operates in all 50 states, the District of Columbia, Guam, and the Virgin Islands. The major purpose of food stamps is to increase the food purchasing power of low-income households to maintain a nutritionally adequate, low-cost diet. The program requires that a household devote 30 percent of monthly cash income to food purchases. If a household has no cash income, its members receive the maximum monthly allotment of food stamps per the household size.

See also: Entitlement Programs: Aid to Families with Dependent Children; Welfare Policy

References: Frances Fox Piven and Richard A. Cloward, *Regulating the Poor: The Functions of Public Welfare* (1971); U.S. Department of Health and Human Services, *Indicators of Welfare Dependence and Well-Being* (1996).

Food Stamps

See Entitlement Programs: Food Stamp Act of 1964

Goldberg v. Kelly

See Entitlement Programs: Welfare Policy

Harrington, Michael (1917–1989)

In 1962 Michael Harrington wrote *The Other America,* a detailed and troubling account of poverty. Harrington portrayed an economic underworld that had no hope of getting out of poverty. He discussed the problems of the rural poor and the vast extent of poverty in Appalachia and the South. He detailed the poverty and living conditions of African Americans in northern cities, the problems of the elderly poor, as well as the poverty of those who no longer sought help from government, namely, alcoholics and the homeless.

Harrington estimated that 40 percent of Americans were in poverty, regardless of the national statistics. Harrington's book received a major amount of attention and prompted Pres. John F. Kennedy to introduce antipoverty programs, which were carried on by Pres. Lyndon B. Johnson after Kennedy's assassination in 1963. Until the publication of *The Other America,* poverty in America was not an important matter on the public agenda. Like Rachel Carson's important work on the abusive use of pesticides in *Silent Spring* and its concomitant impact on restricting the use of DDT, Harrington's *Other America* grabbed the nation's attention, leading the country toward solutions for poverty.

See also: Entitlement Programs: Poverty Policy

References: Michael Harrington, *The Other America* (1963); Dennis J. Palumbo, *Public Policy in America: Government in Action* (1988).

Medicaid

In 1965 Congress amended the Social Security Act of 1935 and created the Medicaid program, a federal program operated through the states to provide poor people access to health care. Medicaid met its goal of improving health care access for the poor. By 1993 enrollment had increased to 28.9 million people. Medicaid recipients are required to demonstrate eligibility primarily through welfare programs, but not all categories of poor people are eligible for welfare. Medicaid pays for one in three of all births, pays for the care of one in four American children, and offers a health insurance mechanism for 60 percent of the poor.

Medicaid accounts for half of all nursing home care and is heavily involved in providing health care for people with HIV-AIDS. Medicaid is implemented as a joint federal-state program and is administered by the Health Care Finance Administration. During the late 1990s cost-cutting in health care has been the norm, affecting access to health care through Medicaid as well. With increasing costs of health care, the problems of access, service, enrollment, and reimbursements to physicians and institutions have become more acute.

See also: Health: Health Maintenance Organization Act of 1973; Health Policy

References: Theodore Litman and Leonard S. Robins, *Health Politics and Policy* (1997); Theodore K. Marmor, *Understanding Health Care Reform* (1994); Kant Patel and Mark E. Rushefsky, *Health Care Politics and Policy in America* (1995).

Medicare

A health care program for the elderly had been a goal of the American political system since Harry Truman's administration in 1950. The means to finance such a health care program was the major stumbling block for Congress. In 1965 Congress amended the Social Security Act of 1935 and created Medicare for the elderly. Before 1965, conservative forces in Congress obstructed passage of comprehensive health care or health insurance programs, including programs for the elderly. During the Johnson administration of the mid-1960s the necessary majorities were in place to pass health care legislation for the poor and elderly.

Medicare is the single largest health insurance program in the United States. The program serves 38 million elderly and disabled people; in 1996 the cost of the program was $178 billion. The Health Care Finance Administration has administrative responsibility to operate the program. Medicare has been a successful program because it is efficient, it does not have a large force of administrators, and the elderly—its clients—appear to be satisfied. Medicare works with insurance companies to process claims; the program allows the elderly and disabled to choose their health care providers. Costs for the program have been kept at a relatively low level, but state attempts to cut budgets and costs across many social programs raise the question whether Medicare might suffer from inadequate state funding. States are the major implementers of the Medicare programs, and thus the financial health of states will have an effect on the quality of health care service available to Medicare clients.

See also: Health: Health Maintenance Organization Act of 1973; Health Policy

References: Theodore Litman and Leonard S. Robins, *Health Politics and Policy* (1997); Theodore K. Marmor, *Understanding Health Care Reform* (1994); Kant Patel and Mark E. Rushefsky, *Health Care Politics and Policy in America* (1995).

Moynihan, Daniel Patrick (b. 1927)

Sen. Daniel Patrick Moynihan was first elected to Congress in 1976. Moynihan, a Democrat, had previously served in the Kennedy, Johnson, Nixon, and Ford presidential administrations. He served as U.S. ambassador to India in 1973 during the Nixon administration; in 1975 Moynihan was appointed by Gerald Ford as ambassador to the United Nations, where he served only eight months before returning to a faculty position at Harvard University.

Moynihan came to public attention in 1965 when he wrote a report, "The Negro Family," warning that the growth of single-parent families contributed to the problems of inner cities. During this time Moynihan stated that "benign neglect" was preferable to continuing massive welfare spending for the urban poor. As a U.S. senator, Moynihan has played an important role in shaping the debate over Social Security. During the early 1990s Moynihan proposed separating Social Security from the Department of Health and Human Services. He has actively sought to reform Social Security and has been the leading Democrat on the Senate Finance Committee, which oversees taxes, Social Security, Medicare, Medicaid, and welfare. Moynihan chaired the Senate Finance Committee in 1993 and 1994 and has been a major force in developing Social Security policy in the Senate.

See also: Entitlement Programs: Social Security Act of 1935

References: Michael Barone and Grant Ujifusa, eds., *Almanac of American Politics* (1995).

Poverty Policy

The U.S. government has never established a comprehensive policy to correct problems caused by poverty. During the late 19th and early 20th centuries, the prevailing belief was Social Darwinism, essentially that individuals needed to fend for themselves and account for their own problems and poverty. The belief in individualism and the free enterprise system did not promote policies directed at relieving the effects of poverty.

In 1935 the Social Security Act was passed, the first federal law to attack the problems of indigence, but only as poverty and indigence applied to the elderly and the disabled. Over the years, children and unemployed mothers of needy children were included in Social Security provisions. With the New Deal legislation, the federal government had come to the aid of people in need.

The private sector dealt with poverty through the development of jobs and through charity, the latter not a role for the government. Charity had always come from volunteer efforts, like the Red Cross. During the 1960s Michael Harrington wrote *The Other America,* which raised the visibility of poverty. For the first time, the federal government acknowledged a role in eliminating poverty nationwide. Pres. Lyndon B. Johnson's Great Society programs targeted poverty as a major national problem. Many of these so-called poverty programs were designed to help the urban poor help themselves. The programs did not relieve much and were criticized for wasting federal money.

Since the poverty programs of the 1960s, joint participation between the federal government and private employers to encourage and stimulate job training and skills development is the norm. During the 1990s the nation's economy grew, and the unemployment rate was extremely low. Income was up and poverty was down in all age, racial, and regional groups. Yet there was no change in the income gap between rich and poor; children remain the most likely to be poor. Legislators will continue to pursue policies that promote economic growth as the chief means to employment opportunities for the nation's poor and disadvantaged.

See also: Labor: Employment Policy

References: Michael Harrington, *The Other America* (1963); David B. Robertson and Dennis R. Judd, *The Development of American Public Policy: The Structure of Policy Restraint* (1989); U.S. Bureau of the Census, *Statistical Abstract of the United States* (1998).

Poverty Programs

The concept of poverty programs was derived from Lyndon Johnson's Great Society programs and his War on Poverty, between 1963 and 1968. Although poverty has always existed, government-sponsored programs to attack poverty are primarily a 20th-century phenomenon. The New Deal programs of the 1930s were efforts to create conditions for employing American workers who had lost jobs because of the Great Depression. The first public housing and financial support programs to protect homeowners from foreclosure also came during this era. The Social Security Act of 1935 was a massive effort to provide for older Americans as well as poor families and their children.

The poverty programs of the Great Society era were employment and vocational training programs, the expansion of welfare programs (food stamps and cash assistance programs), Medicare and Medicaid, public housing programs and urban housing programs that provided mortgage support and financing, mental health programs, and education support programs for the poor (college-level, educational, equal-opportunity programs). Since 1990 the focus has shifted to the plight of homeless people throughout the United States. Welfare reform has shifted public assistance efforts from cash assistance to work and education programs.

See also: Entitlement Programs: Aid to Families with Dependent Children; Harrington, Michael; Poverty Policy

References: Frances Fox Piven and Richard Cloward, *The New Class War* (1982); Laura Waxman and Remy Trupin, *A Status Report on Hunger and Homelessness in America's Cities* (1997).

Public Assistance

See Entitlement Programs: Aid to Families with Dependent Children

Social Security Act of 1935

The Social Security Act was a monumental piece of New Deal legislation. Congress had long resisted old-age and health insurance programs; it finally gave in to an old-age pension program that was more acceptable to the conservative forces in Congress. Pres. Franklin D. Roosevelt had shown enthusiasm for old-age security programs when he was governor of New York. One of the elements of the Social Security Act was the development of old-age pensions and disability insurance programs (Old Age Survivors Disability Insurance). The act created the Social Security Administration to administer Social Security policy. The program offers benefits for survivors of workers who die before retirement. It also provides benefits for children of deceased workers until they reach the age of 18, if they are not employed.

Social Security taxes support the financing of Social Security programs. The Social Security tax is not really viewed as a tax per se; it supports the pay-as-you-go system, where current contributions (from workers) are paid out to current recipients (retirees). It is assessed through a payroll deduction and is viewed by many as a contribution to a retirement insurance fund. Medicare was not an element of the original act but is linked with Social Security as a means of financing Medicare. The act also includes unemployment insurance and workers compensation. A popular element of the Social Security Act is the retirement provision. In 1935 life expectancy for males was less than 65 years, but during the 1990s male life expectancy was more than 70.

The Aid to Families with Dependent Children program was part of the 1935 legislation. It provided cash payments for needy children who had been deprived of parental support because the father or mother was absent from the home on a continuous basis or was incapacitated, deceased, or unemployed. The 1935 Social Security Act has served as the foundation for the public welfare system in the United States; during the late 1960s it became the platform upon which the current welfare program was built.

See also: Entitlement Programs: Aid to Families with Dependent Children; Welfare Policy

References: Jeffrey E. Cohen, *Politics and Economic Policy in the United States* (1997); Frances Fox Piven and Richard A. Cloward, *Regulating the Poor: The Functions of Public Welfare* (1971); T. H. Watkins, *The Great Depression: America in the 1930s* (1993).

Social Security Administration

See Entitlement Programs: Social Security Act of 1935

Social Security Taxes

See Entitlement Programs: Social Security Act of 1935

Supplemental Security Income

Supplemental Security Income (SSI) is a welfare program created in 1974, part of the Social Security Act providing public assistance to eligible recipients who are aged, blind, disabled, and otherwise have no means of income and support. SSI has grown from 4 million recipients in 1974 to more than 6.6 million people in 1996, with increases in disabled and child recipients. In 1974 the government paid $5.3 billion to SSI; in 1995, the federal expenditure was more than $27 billion. SSI benefits are tied to the national poverty level. When poverty indicators are high, the number of SSI program recipients increases. The number of elderly people receiving SSI benefits has declined since 1974.

See also: Entitlement Programs: Aid to Families with Dependent Children; Food Stamp Act of 1964; Welfare Policy

References: Frances Fox Piven and Richard Cloward, *The New Class War* (1982); U.S. Department of Health and Human Services, *Indicators of Welfare Dependence and Well-Being* (1996).

Temporary Assistance to Needy Families

See Entitlement Programs: Aid to Families with Dependent Children

Townshend Movement

In 1933 Dr. Francis E. Townshend developed a following among groups who favored his idea of creating a government pension plan for everyone over sixty. Townshend's idea was that the pension would involve a monthly stipend ($150–200), which had to be spent within a month. The immediate spending would put the money back into the economy, which would create a continuing need for goods and services and also create employment opportunities. Townshend proposed that the plan be financed by a national sales tax on all goods and commodities.

Life was difficult for everyone during the Great Depression, but the elderly suffered most. Townshend's plan did not receive approval from government officials, but most people in Congress agreed that something had to be done to help the nation's aged and poor. Congress did not pass the Townshend plan when it was introduced, despite widespread public support. Congress would soon create the Social Security Act of 1935.

See also: Economics: New Deal

References: Robert Goldston, *The Great Depression: The United States in the Thirties* (1968); T. H. Watkins, *The Great Depression: America in the 1930s* (1993).

Welfare Policy

Welfare policy comprises a series of public policies directed at specific groups categorized as needy. During the early 20th century, the federal government was reluctant to enter the business of helping poor people. Poverty was relieved through private efforts, not government. This changed during the Great Depression, marked by the Roosevelt administration and his New Deal policies. Unemployment legislation, work programs, and the Social Security Act all passed in 1935, changing the federal government's approach to helping the indigent.

During the mid-1960s, after the economic boom of the 1950s and early 1960s, Pres. Lyndon B. Johnson introduced his Great Society programs to attack poverty and unemployment.

Aid to Families with Dependent Children (1935), the Food Stamp Program (1970), and Supplemental Security Income (1974) are components of U.S. welfare policy. Since the development of these programs, and the earlier Social Security programs for the aged and infirm, the numbers of recipients has risen. The government spends billions of dollars for welfare programs. The 1970 U.S. Supreme Court case *Goldberg v. Kelly* had a lasting effect on welfare policy and the rights of welfare recipients. It affirmed the right to a hearing for welfare recipients who faced the prospect of termination of benefits. It extended due process requirements for evidentiary hearings in state administrative matters, particularly in welfare hearings.

The major issues associated with welfare policy and programs are the large numbers of recipients, abuses of the welfare system, the movement to get people off of welfare instead of making welfare a way of life, and replacing welfare with work incentives. The newest dimensions in welfare policy are the Personal Responsibility and Work Opportunity Reconciliation Act of 1996 and the Workforce Investment Act of 1998. Both programs are directed at work training and removing welfare recipients from the relief rolls. The Personal Responsibility and Work Opportunity Reconciliation Act eliminated the federal entitlement program, Aid to Families with Dependent Children, and created a block grant for states to provide time-limited cash assistance for needy families (Temporary Assistance to Needy Families). This new bill promotes opportunities for welfare-dependent people to seek work opportunities. It targets reducing dependency on welfare by promoting job preparation, work, and marriage; preventing out-of-wedlock pregnancies; and encouraging the formation and maintenance of two-parent families. The bill also offers states complete flexibility in determining eligibility, means of assistance, and benefit levels for eligible recipients. Adults in families receiving federal-funded assistance under the block grant are required to participate in work activities after receiving assistance for 24 months.

Cash assistance under the previous AFDC format is replaced with state administered and controlled programs that will determine forms and amounts of assistance.

In August 1998 Pres. Bill Clinton signed the Workforce Investment Act, which consolidates and coordinates employment training, literacy, and vocational education programs. This is a major adult education bill directed at solving welfare problems by attacking some of the symptoms that contribute to welfare dependency, such as low levels of education, which prevent people from qualifying for employment.

Welfare during the 1990s has been a policy under attack. Reform has been the leading goal of members of Congress, and the 1996 legislation has a goal of getting people off of welfare and into gainful employment, never an easy task given the circumstances of welfare recipients. Conquering poverty and welfare dependence is not simple, but perhaps the work-oriented philosophy of the reform efforts will provide the opportunities that are needed.

References: Leif H. Carter and Christine B. Harrington, *Administrative Law and Politics: Cases and Comments* (1991); Thomas R. Dye, *Understanding Public Policy* (1995); U.S. Department of Health and Human Services, *Indicators of Welfare Dependence and Well-Being* (1996).

Welfare Reform

See Entitlement Programs: Welfare Policy

Environment

Chronology

1899 Refuse Act passed, making it illegal to dump refuse into navigable waterways without a permit.

1948 Federal Water Pollution Control Act set standards for treatment of municipal water waste before discharge.

1955 Air Pollution Control Act passed, authorizing federal research programs for air-pollution control.

1962 Rachel Carson published *Silent Spring.*

1963 Clean Air Act passed, providing assistance to state and local governments to establish air pollution control programs and coordinate research.

1965 Clean Air Act amendments established automobile emission standards beginning with 1968 models.

1965 Solid Waste Disposal Act passed to provide assistance to local and state governments for control programs.

1965 Water Quality Act passed, setting standards for discharges into waters.

1967 Air Quality Act established air quality regions with acceptable pollution levels.

1969 National Environmental Policy Act passed, establishing the Council for Environmental Quality to coordinate federal pollution control programs. Also authorized the establishment of the Environmental Protection Agency.

1972 Federal Water Pollution Control Act amendments set water quality goal of restoring polluted waters to swimmable, fishable levels by 1973.

1972 Federal Environmental Pesticide Control Act required all pesticides used in interstate commerce to be approved and certified as effective for their stated purpose. They also needed to be certified that they would not be harmful to humans, animal life, animal feed, and crops.

1973 The Endangered Species Act passed, protecting plants and animals designated as endangered or threatened.

1974 Safe Water Drinking Act set federal standards for water suppliers serving more than 25 people.

1976 Resource Conservation and Recovery Act passed, encouraging conservation and recovery measures for hazardous waste.

1980 Comprehensive Environmental Response, Compensation, and Liability Act established the Superfund to clean up waste dumps.

1990 Oil Pollution Act established the liability for the cleanup of navigable waters after oil spill disasters.

Acid Rain

The problem of acid rain, or precipitation that contains high concentrations of acid, has become more than just a U.S. environmental problem. Acid rain is an atmospheric pollution that comes from burning fossil fuels (primarily coal), predominantly by factories in the Midwest and north-central states along the Canadian border. Acid rain in sufficient amounts makes once-prime habitat uninhabitable to fowl, fish, and other lifeforms. Acidification caused primarily by sulfur dioxides and nitrogen oxides from industrial plants and motor vehicles gathers in clouds and rains down an acidic mixture that sterilizes remote lakes and defoliates forests.

The problem of acid rain and its effects became acute during the early 1970s, when scientists in New England, Upstate New York, and Quebec noticed numerous lakes in which fish had died. The lakes had become acidic as a result of the burning of high-sulfur coal in factories and electric plants thousands of miles away. The sulfur oxides form high in the atmosphere and are deposited miles away. The greater the accumulation of acidic particles, the more devastating the effects are in the water and on the land. The greatest impacts have been felt in the Midwest and in the eastern United States and Canada.

Acid rain has become an international environmental policy problem as a source of transboundary pollution. U.S. public policy initially focused on regulating factories burning fossil fuels. Many were required to comply with Environmental Protection Agency emission standards that offered the option of installing "stack gas scrubbers" to remove pollutants from the burned particles before they were emitted into the air, converting to oil, or using low-sulfur coal. The Canadian government and U.S. policymakers have been engaging in talks to identify the sources of acid rain; the U.S. government took its first steps to control air pollution through the Clean Air Act of 1963. Amendments to the Clean Air Act were designed to strengthen the original provisions, but the issue and problem of acid rain and transboundary pollution continue to have serious effects on lakes and wildlife in the United States and Canada.

See also: Environment: Clean Air Acts; Environmental Protection Agency; Transboundary Pollution

References: John Allen, ed., *Annual Editions: Environment 95/96* (1995); Lynton K. Caldwell, *Environment as a Focus for Public Policy* (1995); David H. Davis, *Energy Politics* (1993); Jacqueline V. Switzer, *Environmental Politics: Domestic and Global Dimensions* (1994).

Air Pollution Policy

The problem of air pollution during the 20th century is the result of smoke and soot, sulfur dioxide, and automobile emissions. During the early 1900s industrial smoke in urban areas brought the first public ordinances to control air pollution. The major sources of air pollution are automobiles and other motor vehicles, lead smelters, electric utility boilers, combustion from industry, forest fires, windblown dust, and oil and chemical refineries. The U.S. Environmental Protection Agency (EPA) was created by executive order in 1970. EPA shares jurisdiction over the implementation of most of the nation's environmental policies with the Department of Interior. EPA is an independent agency in the executive branch, headed by an administrator, deputy, and nine assistant administrators. EPA is a regulatory agency that issues permits, sets and monitors standards, and enforces federal laws. EPA identified six conventional pollutants: carbon monoxide, lead, nitrogen oxides, ozone, particulate matter, and sulfur oxides. These pollutants are found in the atmosphere; most are manmade. Some of the pollutants are the result of fine particles of dust and vegetation. Conventional pollutants fall into three general categories: stationary or point sources, such as factories and power plants; mobile sources, including cars, trucks, and aircraft; and domestic sources, such as home heating or consumer products. Ozone is the most serious air pollution problem in North America.

Since air pollution was largely a problem of industrial smoke in urban areas during the early 20th century, air pollution was not seen as a federal or national issue. In 1912 the Bureau of Mines did a study of smoke control, which was considered at that time to be the only source of air pollution. The U.S. Public Health Service investigated the effect of carbon monoxide in automotive gas in 1925. The Clean Air Act of 1963 was the federal government's first attempt to tackle air pollution as a national problem. Four members of Congress were instrumental in crafting the first air pollution legislation in the United States: Edmund Muskie, senator from Maine; Abraham Ribicoff, senator from New York; Kenneth Roberts, U.S. representative from Alabama; and Paul Schenk, U.S. representative from Ohio. The 1963 Clean Air Act established the foundations of national air pollution policy. The act expanded research and technical assistance programs in air pollution; gave the federal government investigative and abatement authority, which allowed the government to seek out, analyze, and correct (or have corrected) air pollution problems; and encouraged the automobile and petroleum industries to develop exhaust-control devices. There have been several amendments to the original 1963 legislation that have shifted responsibility to state and local governments, relaxed standards for automobile emissions, and provided for flexible application of business and industry requirements for reducing pollution from plants. In 1990 Pres. George Bush signed the 1990 Clean Air Act to take the nation into the next century. A major feature of the bill was that it set new deadlines on five categories of American cities meeting federal standards for compliance with air pollution laws. The problem of acid rain in the form of transboundary pollution continues to present problems between Canada and the United States regarding identification of sources of discharge of industrial air pollutants and reduction and elimination of air pollution.

See also: Environment: Clean Air Acts; Environmental Protection Agency

References: John Allen, ed., *Annual Editions: Environment 95/96* (1995); Lynton K. Caldwell, *Environment as a Focus for Public Policy* (1995); Jacqueline V. Switzer, *Environmental Politics: Domestic and Global Dimensions* (1994).

Air Quality Act of 1967

The Air Quality Act was passed by Congress in 1967 as a response to the growing need to place pollution control restrictions on coal- and oil-fired plants in urban areas. This legislation also provided a stimulus to the nuclear power industry at a time when nuclear power was seen as the most likely future energy source.

See also: Environment: Air Pollution Policy; Environmental Policy

References: John Allen, ed., *Annual Editions: Environment 95/96* (1995); Jacqueline V. Switzer, *Environmental Politics: Domestic and Global Dimensions* (1994).

Carson, Rachel (1907–1964)

In 1962 Rachel Carson published *Silent Spring,* which called attention to the devastating effects of the extensive application of chemical pesticides on wildlife and human beings. This very influential book helped launch the environmental movement. Carson described the horror of a spring without the usual sounds of birds and animal life, and her book helped to make citizens and policymakers understand the possible effects of the pollutants—especially insecticides like DDT—being poured into the air and water of the United States.

During the early 1960s Americans were unaware of the danger posed by the millions of gallons of toxic chemicals that were routinely being applied, poured, and dumped into waterways and wildlife habitats. Carson fought to have her work published in *Silent Spring,* and she had to continue to fight to have her arguments for control of pollutants in the environment accepted by the scientific community, the general public, and by commercial pesticide producers. Chemical companies that produced herbicides and pesticides engaged in a campaign to discredit her work. Carson testified before Congress to make the government and public aware of the severity of the damage to the natural environment caused by uncontrolled usage of chemical agents in agriculture and for public health purposes. Her work to expose the dangers of rampant use of chemical pesticides alerted the government to the dangers of toxic contamination and the potential for health problems in humans.

See also: Environment: Environmental Policy

References: Rachel Carson, *Silent Spring* (1962); B. Guy Peters, *American Public Policy: Promise and Performance* (1993); Jacqueline V. Switzer, *Environmental Politics: Domestic and Global Dimensions* (1994).

Chlorofluorocarbons

A major issue in environmental policy debate is the depletion of the ozone layer, the atmospheric layer that insulates the Earth from the Sun. There is widespread agreement that something is happening to the ozone layer, but the extent and causes of the depletion are subjects of intense debate. The depletion of the ozone layer is attributed to the presence of chemicals such as chlorine and chlorofluorocarbons (CFCs), which are used as refrigerants, aerosols, and solvents. CFCs are any gaseous compounds that contain carbon, chlorine, fluorine, and sometimes hydrogen. In combination, these compounds act against the ozone layer and result in increased levels of skin cancer and cataracts; they damage human and animal immune systems and destroy plant life. The Montreal Protocol on Substances That Deplete the Ozone Layer is an international treaty (signed by Pres. George Bush in 1989) designed to encourage governments to place restrictions on the free use of CFCs in the upper atmosphere. In 1990 Congress passed, and Pres. George Bush signed, the amendments to the Clean Air Act, with a target of phasing out CFCs in the United States by January 1996. Action to ban CFCs is a more difficult problem in developing countries due to limited technology and lack of political will.

See also: Environment: Clean Air Acts; Environmental Policy

References: John Allen, ed., *Annual Editions: Environment 95/96* (1995); David H. Davis, *Energy Politics* (1993).

Clean Air Acts

With industrial development and economic growth come environmental pollution and waste. Industrial pollution became a problem in nations that were developing their industrial capacities during the mid-19th-century industrial revolution. During the early 20th century the primary components of pollution were smoke and soot and sulfur dioxide, which were waste products from home heating, industrial facilities, and utility power plants. As industrialization increased and the production of the automobile became a mass enterprise, the list of pollutants and emissions was expanded. There are six conventional pollutants today that are identified by the Environmental Protection Agency (EPA): carbon monoxide, lead, nitrogen oxides, ozone, particulate matter, and sulfur oxides. Other air toxins include regional and global pollutants, such as acid rain, carbon dioxide, and chlorofluorocarbons. The sources for environmental pollutants are classified in three primary categories: stationary or point sources, such as factories and power plants; mobile sources, such as automobiles, trucks, and airplanes; and domestic sources, such as home heating units or consumer products that require aerosol containers.

The federal government was not aggressively interested in air pollution legislation and only saw smoke as the major pollution problem. During the early 1960s four members of Congress used their influence to begin the air pollution policy debate in the federal legislature. Edmund Muskie, senator from Maine; Abraham Ribicoff, former secretary of the Department of Health, Education, and Welfare; Kenneth Roberts, U.S. representative from Alabama; and Paul Schenk, U.S. representative from Ohio, led the initial discussion of air quality and air pollution policy. Their advocacy for air quality policy led to the passage of the 1963 Clean Air Act. The act provided for expanded research and technical assistance programs in air pollution and air quality measurement; it provided the federal government with investigative and abatement authority; and it encouraged the automobile and petroleum industries to develop exhaust-control devices. This initial air quality bill was followed in 1967 with another Clean Air Act, signed by Pres. Lyndon B. Johnson. This bill gave the major responsibility for air pollution control to state and local governments. It also suggested that the federal government look into the establishment of national automobile emissions standards.

The 1970 Clean Air Act required the newly created EPA to develop national air quality standards, establish emission standards for motor vehicles (effective in fiscal year 1975), and develop emission standards and hazardous emission levels for new stationary sources (factories, power plants, etc.) and mobile sources. The 1970 act was important because it authorized EPA to regulate fuels and fuel additives and required states to prepare emission reduction plans. The act called for a partial preemption strategy that allowed EPA to set air quality standards, which would be implemented by the states. The act also established the first National Ambient Air Quality Standards. These standards came in two forms: primary standards directed at the health of the vulnerable, especially the elderly and children, and secondary standards that protected such things as visibility, buildings, crops, and water. The act introduced a new element in environmental regulations by requiring EPA to consider the costs, energy requirements, and environmental effects of each standard. This was the first consideration of cost-benefit issues in the development of environmental regulations. EPA was also given flexibility with timetables for controlling automobile and truck emissions.

The first amendments came in 1977 as a result of industry pressure to relax emission standards on automobiles. The 1977 amendments suspended the deadlines for automakers and also extended the deadlines by which states were to have met federal standards in implementation plans to 1982. The Sierra Club influenced a provision of the 1977 amendments requiring industries to install the best available control technology (BACT) to certify that any potential pollution was minimized.

The next series of amendments to the Clean Air Act came in 1990. Pres. George Bush signed legislation that established five categories of cities termed nonattainment areas (marginal, moderate, serious, severe, or extreme) and set new deadlines by which they were required to meet federal standards. The Los Angeles/South Coast Air Basin was the only region classified as extreme by EPA. The regional air quality authority was given 20 years to meet federal standards. President Bush believed strongly in the 1990 amendments and called them "the cornerstone of our environmental agenda."

The creation of air quality legislation is a complex and difficult business. Each of the Clean Air Acts and amendments was pursued aggressively in Congress by proponents of environmental policy and air quality and by those opposed because of the impact of regulations on business and industry. Implementation of this legislation remains difficult, cumbersome, and clouded in ambiguity as local regions try to understand how to meet national standards. The cost-benefit requirement in air quality regulations also raises interesting questions, because industries cannot be expected to implement pollution control measures if they threaten profits. Therefore, the cost of reducing industrial emissions or waste cannot exceed the air quality benefits sought by EPA. Industry costs for meeting ambient air quality standards must be feasible and not so exorbitant that the costs of regulation outweigh the benefits to health and safety.

See also: Environment: Air Pollution Policy; Environmental Protection Agency; Sierra Club; Key Concepts: Cost-benefit Analysis

References: David Edwards and Alessandra Lippucci, *Practicing American Politics: An Introduction to American Government* (1998); Jacqueline V. Switzer, *Environmental Politics: Domestic and Global Dimensions* (1994); Donald T. Wells, *Environmental Policy* (1996).

Clean Water Act of 1972

The Clean Water Act of 1972 is the primary legislation that addresses surface water pollution. The 1972 law is an amendment that strengthens 1948 legislation that dealt with surface water regulation. Therefore, the Clean Water Act of 1972 is a series of amendments to the original 1948 legislation; the 1972 legislation is called the Federal Water Pollution Control Act Amendments. The 1972 amendments provided for the improvement of the nation's municipal sewage treatment plants and the reduction of industrial effluents (industrial waste products) to zero discharge by 1985. Timetables were designated for reducing industrial effluents (1985) and for making surface waters fishable and swimmable (1983). As is the case with most environmental regulations and policy, the timetables and deadlines for improvement or correction of environmental problems has been difficult and, in some cases, impossible to attain. The 1972 amendments provided federal funding for the widespread construction of municipal sewage treatment plants. Given the population growth and expansion of suburbs, the construction of municipal sewage treatment plants and the managing of wastewater have become major public enterprises.

The Clean Water Act was amended in 1987 with two major provisions: industries had until 1989 to use the best available technology to reduce effluent discharge to zero, with the threat of enforcement action if the industries failed to meet the standard and deadlines; and a transition from federal to state and local funding responsibility for meeting standards after 1994. The amendments also required states to identify "hot spots" in surface waters that remained polluted after the application of the best available technology.

The primary enforcement mechanism of the Clean Water Act is the National Pollutant Discharge

Emanation System (NPDES) permit. A five-year, renewable NPDES permit is required for all new and existing industrial and municipal dischargers. The Environmental Protection Agency and state-certified programs issue the permits. The Safe Drinking Water Act of 1974 is also legislation that is designed to ensure a safe water supply specifically through the control and monitoring of contaminants.

As with most environmental regulations and policy, success has not been easy. Water quality issues have political, social, economic, and moral implications. In the United States, recent attention has been directed at groundwater quality and pollution, the next major area of public policy debate, development, regulation, and enforcement.

See also: Environment: Environmental Policy; Safe Drinking Water Act of 1974; Key Concepts: Interest Groups; Public Interest Research Groups

References: Lynton K. Caldwell, *Environment as a Focus for Public Policy* (1995); David Edwards and Alessandra Lippucci, *Practicing American Politics: An Introduction to American Government* (1998); Jacqueline V. Switzer, *Environmental Politics: Domestic and Global Dimensions* (1994); Donald T. Wells, *Environmental Policy* (1996).

Comprehensive Environmental Response Act of 1980

The march toward economic development, national expansion, and industrial progress during the 20th century exacted a mighty, sometimes devastating toll on the natural environment. The creation of mines to extract minerals for fuel and metals for industry and consumer products, the clearing of forests for building homes and offices, and the construction of factories to produce industrial and consumer goods for the national and international economies caused problems throughout the United States. On many occasions, waste byproducts of industry were improperly contained, stored, housed, and managed, creating health and safety hazards for local populations.

In 1980 Congress passed the Comprehensive Environmental Response Act (also known as the Comprehensive Environmental Response, Compensation, and Liability Act), which established the Superfund for cleaning up toxic and hazardous waste sites. The Environmental Protection Agency identified more than 20,000 potential sites, and 1,245 of these sites were at the top of the EPA's National Priority List. The purpose of the Superfund legislation was to make federal money available to assist in the cleaning, removal, and disposal of the wastes. It authorizes EPA to clean up a toxic or hazardous waste site when a release or a threatened release of waste occurs; EPA recovers the costs of the cleanup from whoever generated the wastes at the site; from whoever transported the wastes to the site; whoever operated the site at the time of the disposal; or the current owner or operator. In many cases, owners of the industries that created the waste sites were required to clean up the sites themselves, but the cost of solving the problems of toxic and hazardous waste dumps was prohibitive for the owners, and EPA and the federal government assumed the burden of responsibility and funding for the cleanup.

The Superfund program has not received sufficient funding from presidents and Congress since 1982 to seriously affect the problem of hazardous and toxic wastes. By the early 1990s, 84 of the 1,245 designated sites on the National Priority List had been cleaned up at a cost of $11.1 billion. The Superfund problem and hazardous waste removal is under continuous review because the cost-benefit ratio in cleaning up hazardous waste sites may not be worth the investment. This is one area of environmental policy in which there is legislation but no simple or direct solutions for solving the problems of hazardous waste.

See also: Environment: Environmental Policy; Environmental Protection Agency

References: Lynton K. Caldwell, *Environment as a Focus for Public Policy* (1995); Thomas R. Dye, *Understanding Public Policy* (1995); Steffen W. Schmidt, Mack C. Shelley II, and Barbara A. Bardes, *American Government and Politics Today* (1997).

Conservation

During the first two decades of the 20th century the conservation movement, the predecessor of the later environmental movement, was at its peak. *Conservation* refers to planned, efficient progress and rational use of the U.S. public lands. The leading belief of conservationists was that sustainable exploitation of natural resources was possible. The original ideals of the conservation movement came from forest management practices that were popular in Europe. Early American conservationists included Frederick H. Newell, George Maxwell, Francis G. Newlands, and

Gifford Pinchot. Pres. Theodore Roosevelt presided over the approval of several conservation-oriented policies. He believed that conservation required that the nation not squander its natural resources and undertook to educate the American electorate about conservation to secure legislative action. In 1902 the Newlands Act was passed during Roosevelt's administration; it appropriated money received from the sale of public lands in the West and Southwest for the construction of irrigation projects. Roosevelt also led the campaign to preserve special lands as national parks. As president, he set aside 148 million acres in timber reserves and withdrew from sale all public lands that contained minerals until Congress could safeguard the mineral resources with proper lease arrangements.

The use of national waterways also illustrates the conservationist idea of efficient use of natural resources. The Internal Waterways Commission was created and appointed by Roosevelt to promote a system of internal waterways, facilitate transportation, promote irrigation projects, and develop waterpower sites. In 1908 Roosevelt called a National White House Conference, where he appointed the National Conservation Commission, directed by Gifford Pinchot. Thirty-six state conservation commissions were also created to work with the national commission.

The conservation movement would split into two camps: the conservationists and the environmentalists. John Muir led the environmentalist group, which sought to preserve wilderness areas for strictly recreational and educational use. Muir is recognized for encouraging and championing the protection of the Yosemite Valley in California's Sierra Nevada Mountains. The environmentalist movement did not have the national character of the conservationists, who had the blessing of the president. The conservation movement was an outgrowth of the earlier Progressive movement of the late 19th century; it spawned the growth of national conservation organizations such as the National Audubon Society (1905), the National Parks Association (1919), and the Izaak Walton League (1922). Environmentalism began to rise during the 1930s, when Aldo Leopold founded the Wilderness Society to lobby for the protection of public lands and the National Wildlife Federation (1936) was created to educate the public about conservation programs.

See also: Environment: Environmental Policy

References: Francis Sandbach, *Environment, Ideology, and Policy* (1980); Jacqueline V. Switzer, *Environmental Politics: Domestic and Global Dimensions* (1994).

Department of Interior

The executive-branch Department of Interior was created in 1849 to take responsibility for the nation's internal affairs, which originally included the construction of the District of Columbia's water system; the colonization of freed slaves in Haiti; exploration of the continental western wilderness; oversight of the jail in the nation's capital; regulation of territorial governments; management of hospitals and universities; management of public parks; and oversight of Native American issues, public lands, patents, and pensions. Important agencies within the Department of Interior include the U.S. Geological Survey (1879); the National Park Service (1916); and the U.S. Fish and Wildlife Service (1940). The secretary of the interior leads the agency, appointed by the president with the advice and consent of the Senate.

In 1977 Congress passed the Surface Mining Control and Reclamation Act, which created the Office of Surface Mining in the Department of Interior. The Office of Surface Mining had the responsibility for regulating mining with the assistance of the Bureau of Mines and focused much of its attention on the 27 states that engaged in coal mining. The area of mine regulation and enforcement has been a controversial issue for the Department of Interior, as environmentalists want aggressive enforcement of surface mining regulations. The Department's public lands leasing for coal, oil, and natural gas development and exploration has also been challenged by environmentalists.

During the 1990s the Department of the Interior employed some 80,000; its principal duties include the supervision of federally owned lands and parks; the operation and management of federal hydroelectric power facilities; and the supervision of Native American affairs. Key subagencies are the U.S. Fish and Wildlife Service, the National Park Service, the Bureau of Indian Affairs, and the Bureau of Land Management. The Clinton administration focused on the following missions: restoring and maintaining the health of federally managed lands, waters, and renewable resources; preserving the nation's natural and cultural heritage for future generations;

providing recreational opportunities for the public to enjoy natural and cultural resources; providing for the appropriate commercial use and development of federally managed natural resources in an environmentally sound manner; encouraging the preservation of diverse plant and animal species and protection of the habitat critical to their survival; working to transfer federal program operations to tribal governments through Indian self-determination and self-governance agreements; protection and conservation of American Indian and Alaska Native tribes and working with these tribes to enhance education, economic opportunities, and quality of life for their members; conducting scientific research and monitoring to improve understanding of the interactions of natural and human systems to reduce the impact and hazards caused by human systems on the natural environment; providing scientific information for sound resource decisionmaking; and applying laws and regulations fairly and effectively.

See also: Environment: Environmental Policy

References: David H. Davis, *Energy Politics* (1993); Steffen W. Schmidt, Mack C. Shelley II, and Barbara A. Bardes, *American Government and Politics Today* (1997); Donald T. Wells, *Environmental Policy* (1996).

Endangered Species Act of 1973

The Endangered Species Act of 1973 (ESA) protects plants and animals that have been designated as endangered or threatened. There are four categories of protection: migratory and game birds, wild horses and burros, marine mammals, and endangered species. ESA was an attempt to incorporate previous endangered species legislation (Endangered Species Preservation Act of 1966 and the Endangered Species Conservation Act of 1969) in a broader, more specific law. ESA requires all federal agencies to seek to conserve endangered species; expands conservation measures by including methods and procedures for protection of species, rather than just focusing on habitat protection; expands the definition of wildlife to include any member of the animal kingdom; and creates two classes of species, those endangered (in danger of extinction) and those threatened (species likely to become endangered). An important element of this act is that it offers protection of habitat as well as the animal species. The law also requires the development of a recovery plan for species designated as endangered. Plants also fall within the protections of ESA.

ESA has been criticized by conservative antienvironment groups who feel it limits the rights of private property owners, especially the logging industry. Other critics have asserted that the act causes economic problems for communities that rely heavily on extractive industries (logging, mining, and fisheries). Initially, the act called for the protection of 109 species; since then, the list has expanded to 1,135 species.

See also: Environment: Conservation; Environmental Policy

References: Frederick R. Anderson, Daniel Mandelker, and A. Dan Tarlock, *Environmental Protection: Law and Policy* (1984); Lynton K. Caldwell, *Environment as a Focus for Public Policy* (1995); Jacqueline V. Switzer, *Environmental Politics: Domestic and Global Dimensions* (1994).

Environmental Externalities

See Environment: Environmental Policy

Environmental Impact Statement

In 1969 Congress passed the National Environmental Policy Act (NEPA). NEPA created the Council for Environmental Quality and mandates that an environmental impact statement (EIS) be developed for any recommendation or report on legislation or federal actions that significantly affect the quality of the environment. EISs are also required at the state and local levels, where major developments (housing construction, business or manufacturing construction, roads and bridges) are planned with federal money. The EIS analyzes the nature of the disruption to natural environments, the impact of the development on the land and animal and wildlife habitats, and the costs and benefits of development. The EIS procedure requires that developers and government agencies agree on large-scale development coordination and design. EISs at one time were controversial, but during the 1990s the EIS has become an accepted part of any federally supported project that impacts the environment.

See also: Environment: Environmental Policy; National Environmental Policy Act of 1969

References: Steffen W. Schmidt, Mack C. Shelley II, and Barbara A. Bardes, *American Government and Politics Today* (1997); Frank S. So and Judith Getzels, eds., *The Practice of Local Government Planning* (1988).

Environmental Policy

The growth of industrialism between 1870 and 1900 caused many, especially Progressives, to call for policies that addressed industrial pollution and waste. Around 1900 conservationists, led by Pres. Theodore Roosevelt and his forester-colleague Gifford Pinchot, pioneered the conservation movement, advocating the setting aside of public lands for national parks and forests. The beginning of the modern environmental movement was April 22, 1970, the very first Earth Day.

During the late-19th-century Progressive era, environmental issues were being coordinated for the first time, starting at the local level where pollution was worst. The conservation movement that followed on its heels spawned the first environmental organizations, such as the National Audubon Society and the National Conservation League, and states developed legislation to control pollution and industrial waste. Beginning in 1948, however, a series of federal laws were passed, marking the federal government's full-blown involvement in environmental issues. During the early 1960s Rachel Carson published *Silent Spring*, a compelling argument against the widespread use of the pesticide DDT. Her book prompted a national discussion on the use of chemicals and their impact on wildlife. *Silent Spring* thus helped place the environment squarely on the public agenda, and legislation followed, dealing with issues like preservation of land; management of surface and underground water sources; oceans; air quality; acid rain and industrial emissions; and endangered species and habitats.

The 1948 Federal Water Pollution Control Act set federal standards for the treatment of municipal wastewater before discharge. It established a limited federal role in regulating interstate water pollution. Although the act expected cooperation between states and the federal government to meet standards, it did not have enforcement authority, and government support for sewage treatment facilities was lacking. The 1955 Air Pollution Control Act was the first federal legislation directed at air pollution, authorizing research into problems related to air pollution. The 1963 Clean Air Act focused on state and local governments and offered incentives to automobile manufacturers and petroleum industries to develop exhaust-control devices. It also provided federal technical assistance and funds for research into problems of air pollution. The first federal standards for automobile exhaust emissions (for 1968 models) were set in the 1965 Clean Air Act amendments. The series of Clean Air Acts breaks down as follows: the 1967 Air Quality Act, which established air quality regions; the 1970 Clean Air Act amendments, which authorized the Environmental Protection Agency to set national air pollution standards and restricted the discharge of six major pollutants into the lower atmosphere, also setting a deadline for meeting the emissions reduction standard in the auto industry; the 1977 Clean Air Act amendments, which postponed that deadline; and the 1990 Clean Air Act amendments, which created formulas for new gasoline mixtures to be burned in areas with high smog and pollution levels (it also placed restrictions on toxic pollutants).

In 1969 Congress passed the National Environmental Policy Act, which established the Council for Environmental Quality (CEQ), the coordinating body for all federal pollution control programs, and the Environmental Protection Agency. In 1972, the Clean Water Act established a legal framework for restoring the nation's waters, setting standards for the protection of wildlife, recreation, and drinking water sources. The primary target of the Clean Water Act was industry, which has caused significant pollution to the nation's waterways. The 1972 Water Pollution Control Act amendments set water-quality goals for restoring polluted waters to swimmable and fishable conditions by 1983. The 1972 Federal Environmental Pesticide Control Act dealt with pesticide controls and required approval of all pesticides used in interstate commerce. These pesticides had to be certified as harmless to humans, animal life, animal feed, and crops. The 1976 Resource Conservation and Recovery Act encouraged conservation and recovery of resources and provided guidelines for solid waste management. The 1980 Comprehensive Environmental Response, Compensation, and Liability Act created the Superfund to clean up toxic waste dumps. The 1990 Oil Pollution Act established liability for the cleanup of navigable waters after oil-spill disasters.

Environmental policy is very much the work of interest groups that shepherd environmental issues onto the public agenda to protect the environment. These groups include the Environmental Defense Fund, Environmental Policy Institute, Friends of the

Earth, Greenpeace USA, the Isaak Walton League of America, League of Conservation Voters, the National Audubon Society, the National Wildlife Federation, the Natural Resources Defense Council, the Sierra Club, and the Wilderness Society.

Clean air, clean water, wildlife habitats free of pesticides and pollutants, clean oceans, and a safe natural environment are the goals of environmental groups and of public policy. These goals are expected to be balanced with the competing goals inherent to a free-market economy. These issue will continue to drive local, state, and federal policymakers.

See also: Environment: Air Quality Act of 1967; Carson, Rachel; Clean Air Acts; Clean Water Act of 1972; Comprehensive Environmental Response Act of 1980; Environmental Protection Agency; Federal Water Pollution Control Act and Amendments; National Environmental Policy Act of 1969; Key Concepts: Interest Groups

References: John Allen, ed., *Annual Editions: Environment 95–96* (1995); Frederick R. Anderson, Daniel Mandelker, and A. Dan Tarlock, *Environmental Protection: Law and Policy* (1984); Lynton K. Caldwell, *Environment as a Focus for Public Policy* (1995); David H. Davis, *Energy Politics* (1993); Francis Sandbach, *Environment, Ideology, and Policy* (1980); Jacqueline V. Switzer, *Environmental Politics: Domestic and Global Dimensions* (1994); Donald T. Wells, *Environmental Policy* (1996).

Environmental Protection Agency

The 1969 National Environmental Policy Act authorized the creation of the Environmental Protection Agency (EPA) to implement the policies of the Council for Environmental Quality. EPA was formed as an independent agency in the federal executive branch in 1970, with an administrator, a deputy, and nine assistant administrators. The president nominates each of the administrators, who are confirmed by the Senate. EPA has a mixture of regulatory and administrative functions. Pres. Bill Clinton replaced the original Council for Environmental Quality with the White House Office of Environmental Policy.

EPA is a so-called second-generation regulatory agency (established after the first phase of regulation and the New Deal). EPA combines legislative, judicial, and executive functions: it makes rules and sets standards in environmental policy; it has enforcement power over the application of its rules and regulations; and it acts as an independent executive agency for making policy to affect the environment. The agency was initially assigned responsibility for enforcing the Clean Air Act amendments, and in 1972 it was given responsibility for improving the quality of American waterways. The 1972 Noise Control Act gave EPA the authority to regulate noise pollution.

The EPA's mission during the 1990s has been to protect human health and to safeguard the natural environment—air, water, and land. EPA acts to reduce environmental risk by collecting, disseminating, and acting upon scientific data and information that it has acquired. EPA has improved air quality in American cities, but the agency still struggles to meet air-quality standards for various pollutants. Global air quality and transboundary pollution remain problems. Approximately 60 percent of American rivers, lakes, and estuaries are clean enough to meet basic uses such as fishing and swimming. Oil spills have declined in volume and frequency since the 1970s, and ocean dumping of sewage sludge, industrial waste, plastic debris, and medical waste have been banned. Wastewater standards have prevented millions of pounds of toxic pollutants from being dumped, and industrial plants are now required to operate under pollution-control permits and pretreatment requirements. Groundwater conditions have improved as a result of groundwater standards and programs; pesticide runoff is the leading cause of water pollution in the United States.

See also: Environment: Clean Air Acts; Environmental Policy; National Environmental Policy Act of 1969

References: Leif H. Carter and Christine B. Harrington, *Administrative Law and Politics: Cases and Comments* (1991); Steffen W. Schmidt, Mack C. Shelley II, and Barbara A. Bardes, *American Government and Politics Today* (1997); Jacqueline V. Switzer, *Environmental Politics: Domestic and Global Dimensions* (1994).

Federal Pesticides Control

See Environment: Environmental Policy

Federal Insecticide, Fungicide, and Rodenticide Act

The original 1947 legislation was designed to control toxic wastes, especially the use of pesticides in agricultural applications by requiring the registration of labels (e.g., pesticides were required to be "registered" before they could be marketed). Any pesticide that was highly toxic, that persisted in the environment, or that posed risks to nontarget organisms (those organisms that were not the subject of eradication) were denied registration. In 1972 the act was revised to update standards and to improve implementation procedures.

The original act was amended in 1972, 1975, 1978, and 1988. Each amendment strengthened the requirement for premarket review of potential health and environmental effects. As a result, the Environmental Protection Agency is required to evaluate more than 50,000 individual pesticide products containing more than 600 active ingredients and 900 inert ingredients. This evaluation process is complex and costly.

See also: Environment: Environmental Policy; Environmental Protection Agency

References: Walter Rosenbaum, *Environmental Politics and Policy* (1998); Jacqueline V. Switzer, *Environmental Politics: Domestic and Global Dimensions* (1994); Donald T. Wells, *Environmental Policy* (1996).

Federal Water Pollution Control Act and Amendments

Congress passed the first water pollution control regulations in 1948 through the Water Pollution Control Act, which established the federal government's first attempts in regulating interstate water pollution. The 1972 Federal Water Pollution Control amendments established the regulatory structure for surface-water quality and amended the earlier 1948 act and 1956 amendments. More amendments to the 1972 act were passed in the Water Quality Act of 1987. The 1972 legislation gave the Environmental Protection Agency (EPA) six specific deadlines to grant permits to water pollution sources, issue effluent (wastewater) guidelines, require sources to install water pollution technology, and eliminate discharges into the nation's waterways to make them fishable and swimmable. The legislation also established the National Pollution Discharge Elimination System, which requires a federal permit to release discharges.

The 1987 Water Quality Act had six key provisions: (1) goals for technological innovations to control pollutants; (2) standards for discharges into navigable waterways with effluent limits that were acceptable; (3) pretreatment standards to prevent the discharge of pollutants; (4) federal and state power to enforce standards; (5) $18 billion to assist local communities to build wastewater treatment facilities; and (6) a requirement for each state to establish an EPA-approved plan to control pollution from nonpoint sources.

This important legislation provided standards for water quality and introduced technological means to aid in improving water quality and controlling the discharge of effluents by polluters in local communities.

See also: Environment: Environmental Policy

References: Alfred A. Marcus, *Promise and Performance: Choosing and Implementing an Environmental Policy* (1980); Walter Rosenbaum, *Environmental Politics and Policy* (1998); Jacqueline V. Switzer, *Environmental Politics: Domestic and Global Dimensions* (1994).

Forest Service

The U.S. Forest Service (USFS) is an agency within the Department of Agriculture. USFS is responsible for promoting the best uses and practices on American forests (some 170 million acres). Forest rangers, administrators, and other specialists staff regional and district offices throughout the United States. With the growth of "multiple use" over the years, the role of USFS has changed. Public use on national forests has increased substantially, and USFS has expanded it role to serve the public, manage range and forest lands, regulate grazing on government land, oversee sales and management of timber, and preserve the natural environment. USFS also plays a role in research and preservation of forest products and timber. During the late 20th century, USFS has been at the center of the controversy over the proper use of federal lands, especially regarding policies on clear-cutting as well as access to old growth forests for timber.

See also: Environment: Environmental Policy

References: Walter Rosenbaum, *Environmental Politics and Policy* (1998); Steffen W. Schmidt, Mack C. Shelley II, and Barbara A. Bardes, *American Government and Politics Today* (1997).

Friends of the Earth

An offshoot of the Sierra Club, Friends of the Earth is an activist public interest group that focuses on environmental issues. Created by David Brower, a renowned and dedicated environmentalist, Friends of the Earth combines lobbying and public pressure to move environmental issues onto the public agenda.

Friends of the Earth was incorporated in 1969, but the idea for the organization started with Brower in 1957, when he pushed the Sierra Club toward a more active role in pursuing environmental causes. The original Friends of the Earth combined with the League of Conservation Voters to push its agenda on an international basis. Stewart Ogilvie assisted Brower, and he eventually became honorary president. Friends of the Earth aggressively advocates and lobbies for preservation of old growth forests, preservation of the Alaska Wildlife Refuge and other wildlife refuges from development, reduction of worldwide pollution, and reduction and elimination of aerosol production to eradicate ozone-destroying chlorofluorocarbons, among other important environmental causes.

See also: Environment: Environmental Policy; Sierra Club

References: David Brower, *For Earth's Sake: The Life and Times of David Brower* (1990); Walter Rosenbaum, *Environmental Politics and Policy* (1998).

Global Warming

One of the most important environmental problems of the 20th century is global warming, the result of air pollution and other activities. Scientists and environmentalists have recorded evidence that Earth is warming and climatic zones shifting. Glaciers are melting; greenhouse gases, like carbon dioxide, methane, and chlorofluorocarbons, are increasing in the atmosphere; and plants, wildlife, and the oceans are showing the effects of global air pollution.

The extent of damage to the planet caused by global warming is unclear, but serious effects occur. Some scientists believe that Earth's biological capacity to adapt and correct the problems of pollution is such that global warming is not the acute problem that many environmentalists claim. Yet there is clear evidence of global temperature changes and effects to plants, wildlife, and the oceans. And some environmentalists claim that Earth's ability to adjust to these problems is limited. Public policy solutions to global warming are not easy and require intense study and research. Unfortunately, finding solutions is subject to partisan politics, with conservatives believing that environmental issues are the province of liberals. Finding solutions to the planet's environmental problems will require bipartisan efforts to understand, control, and reverse environmental degradation.

See also: Environment: Acid Rain; Chlorofluorocarbons; Environmental Policy

References: John Allen, ed., *Annual Editions: Environment 95/96* (1995); Charles Bonser, Eugene B. McGregor Jr., and Clinton V. Oster Jr., *Policy Choices and Public Action* (1996); Lynton K. Caldwell, *Environment as a Focus of Public Policy* (1995); Albert Gore, *Earth in the Balance: Ecology and the Human Spirit* (1993); Jacqueline V. Switzer, *Environmental Politics: Domestic and Global Dimensions* (1994).

Green Index

The green index is a combination of elements that classifies how a company (or even a nation) scores in its relationship to environmental issues and its approach to environmental and species preservation and protection in product development. The Green Revolution that was begun by environmentalists during the late 1960s and early 1970s focused on the national production of food grains (rice and wheat), reduction in the use of pesticides, and better land and agricultural management techniques. An outgrowth of the Green Revolution was green consumerism, which emphasized lifestyle changes in communities and nations that were based on the principle of simplicity and maximizing experiences in nature. Simplicity of consumption is affected by the quality and quantity of products bought, sold, and consumed.

Environmental consciousness during the 1970s promoted consumer products that were safe to humans and the environment, biodegradable, and free of harmful chemicals. The environmental and consumer movements combined their interests and goals during the 1980s to educate people and influence public policy. In 1990 the Green Cross Certification Company and Green Seal Company began issuing their stamp of ecological approval to American companies that made environmental marketing claims. Environmental groups challenged these labels and sought Federal Trade Commission (FTC) review of the approval seal. FTC issued guidelines in 1992 that were not legally enforceable but that required reliable and competent scientific investigation of environmentally safe claims. The major area of concern was the use of terms such as "recyclable," "biodegradable," and "environmentally safe" in marketing and packaging. The green index concept has had broad exposure, and many companies, large corporations, and even nations have adapted practices and policies toward environmental safety.

See also: Environment: Environmental Policy

References: Jacqueline V. Switzer, *Environmental Politics: Domestic and Global Dimensions* (1994); Donald T. Wells, *Environmental Policy* (1996).

Marine Protection, Research, and Sanctuaries Act of 1972

One of the important issues during the early 1970s was the condition of the world's oceans. In 1972 the Environmental Protection Agency (EPA) sent Congress the proposed Marine Protection, Research, and Sanctuaries Act. The bill created strict standards for dumping trash in the oceans and established a research program to find ways to minimize or end dumping of waste materials. As a result of passage of the act, ocean dumping was subject to a permit system jointly regulated by EPA and the U.S. Army Corps of Engineers. EPA's intent was to eventually bring an end to all ocean dumping.

In 1981 the City of New York applied for a permit to continue dumping sewage sludge in the ocean, but EPA sought to end all dumping after 1981. The city filed a federal lawsuit, which it won; this caused EPA to withdraw from its firm position against all ocean dumping, and EPA became more flexible in its policy. The Marine Protection, Research, and Sanctuaries Act brought attention to the effects of dumping sewage and waste in the oceans.

See also: Environment: Environmental Policy

References: James P. Lester and Joseph Stewart Jr., *Public Policy: An Evolutionary Approach* (1996); Walter Rosenbaum, *Environmental Politics and Policy* (1998).

Montreal Protocols

In the international battle against global warming and the reduction of chlorofluorocarbons (CFCs) in the atmosphere, 140 nations signed an agreement in 1987 that committed them to reduce CFC production 50 percent by 1998. The United States met its target for reducing CFC production by eliminating the domestic production of new freon and by applying a tax on CFC production and other related chemicals. This commitment to reducing freon production has had a major impact, as CFC-12 freon is used in 80 million U.S. automobiles built before 1992; freon replacement will have to come from existing or recycled stocks of CFC-12. By acting quickly at considerable expense in the short term, the United States and other nations positively affected a serious problem in a way that would have important long-term benefits.

See also: Environment: Environmental Policy

References: Lynton K. Caldwell, *Environment as a Focus for Public Policy* (1995); Walter Rosenbaum, *Environmental Politics and Policy* (1998).

Motor Vehicle Air Pollution Control Act of 1965

The Motor Vehicle Air Pollution Control Act of 1965 was a relatively minor attempt to improve air-quality regulation. It introduced weak hydrocarbon standards and carbon monoxide standards for automobile emissions. It was an early attempt to set air quality standards and reduce automobile emissions. The legislation was bolstered through 1970 amendments that mandated a 90 percent reduction in the level of hydrocarbons and carbon monoxide emissions by 1975. Even though tougher standards were implemented, emission reductions did not necessarily occur. The existing technology for reducing emissions to the tougher levels was not sufficient, and more work on "technology forcing" standards in the automobile industry commenced. The quality of air did improve as a consequence of the new emission control regulations, leading to other clean air policy initiatives during the 1980s and 1990s.

See also: Environment: Clean Air Acts; Environmental Policy

References: Frederick R. Anderson, Daniel Mandelker, and A. Dan Tarlock, *Environmental Protection: Law and Policy* (1984); B. Guy Peters, *American Public Policy: Promise and Performance* (1993); Walter Rosenbaum, *Environmental Politics and Policy* (1998).

National Environmental Policy Act of 1969

In 1969 Pres. Richard M. Nixon declared the next ten years as the environment decade. Congress passed the National Environmental Policy Act (NEPA) of 1969, the foundation for future environmental legislation. The act created the Council on Environmental Quality (CEQ) to make policy recommendations to the president and evaluate environmental protection programs in the executive branch. CEQ was replaced during the first Clinton administration by the White House Office of Environmental Policy. NEPA requires federal agencies to prepare environmental impact statements; calls for citizen participation in environmental decisionmaking; and authorizes citizens to file lawsuits against agencies for failure to implement environmental laws. The legislation also grants federal judges the authority to apply the "hard look" doctrine to critically review regulatory decisions made by environmental agencies. This review authority created an important check on the implementation of environmental policy.

See also: Environment: Environmental Impact Statement; Environmental Policy

References: Lynton K. Caldwell, *Environment as a Focus for Public Policy* (1995); David H. Davis, *Energy Politics* (1993); Walter Rosenbaum, *Environmental Politics and Policy* (1998); Jacqueline V. Switzer, *Environmental Politics: Domestic and Global Dimensions* (1994).

National Wildlife Federation

See Environment: Environmental Policy

Natural Resources Defense Council

The Natural Resources Defense Council (NRDC) is an environmental interest group that has used litigation as a means to protect public lands and preserve the environment, thereby challenging the government to make policy that supports protection and preservation.

See also: Environment: Environmental Policy; Key Concepts: Interest Groups

References: Jacqueline V. Switzer, *Environmental Politics: Domestic and Global Dimensions* (1994).

NIMBY

NIMBY is the acronym for "not in my backyard," referring to the common response of people who oppose government projects in or near their communities. In the context of environmental politics, the NIMBY syndrome is the typical knee-jerk reaction to any project that has a potential for hazards, blight, or unsightliness. People organize, picket, demonstrate, or do whatever it takes to thwart the project and its perceived problems. Public policy is influenced at times by overly vocal NIMBYism, thus the implications of any public policy need to be considered prior to the implementation.

See also: Key Concepts: Interest Groups

References: Jacqueline V. Switzer, *Environmental Politics: Domestic and Global Dimensions* (1994).

Noise Control

See Environment: Environmental Protection Agency

Resource Conservation and Recovery Act of 1976

Toxic waste in the environment is a consequence of industrialization. In 1976 Congress passed the first of two pieces of legislation regulating toxic waste: The Resource Conservation and Recovery Act (RCRA) of 1976 (the second law was Superfund). RCRA requires the Environmental Protection Agency (EPA) to determine what chemicals are hazardous; it also specified methods for disposal of hazardous chemicals. EPA was required to develop a permit system to ensure that hazardous chemicals were disposed of safely and effectively. Other provisions of the act include the development of environmentally safe disposal sites; the regulation of all hazardous waste; promotion of commercialization of waste recovery; state implementation requirements; and deadlines and waste-by-waste review. These requirements were not implemented until 1980. During the early years of the Reagan administration EPA was attacked for regulatory excesses, and the agency's funding was cut, adding to the failure to fulfill RCRA's requirements. During George Bush's presidency, RCRA came under renewed attack, and many waste disposal regulations were removed. Although RCRA ultimately was seen as going too far during a time of deregulation, it is still in effect.

See also: Environment: Comprehensive Environmental Response Act of 1980; Environmental Policy

References: B. Guy Peters, *American Public Policy: Promise and Performance* (1993); Walter Rosenbaum, *Environmental Politics and Policy* (1998); Jacqueline V. Switzer, *Environmental Politics: Domestic and Global Dimensions* (1994).

Safe Drinking Water Act of 1974

In 1974 Congress passed the first Safe Drinking Water Act to protect groundwater from contamination by organic and inorganic chemicals, radionuclides, and microorganisms. Designed to control contaminants in the nation's drinking water, the act placed regulations on contaminant levels and protection of underground water by placing minimum standards for injecting waste in wells. In 1986 the act was amended to put into place enforceable standards and maximum contaminant level goals. The Clean Water Act of 1948 (amended in 1972 and 1987) had been the primary surface water legislation.

Clean water legislation is developed and implemented primarily by the Environmental Protection Agency (EPA). EPA was given rulemaking authority to set standards and conduct research on contaminants in the nation's water. Safe drinking water directly affects every American and is highly dependent on the use of science and technology to test, treat, and distribute water. This is one of the most important public and environmental policy areas.

See also: Environment: Clean Water Act of 1972; Environmental Policy

References: Edward J. Calabrese, Charles E. Gilbert, and Harris Pastides, eds., *Safe Drinking Water Act: Amendments, Regulations, and Standards* (1989); Donald T. Wells, *Environmental Policy* (1996).

Sierra Club

The Sierra Club is an environmental advocacy and interest group that was created in 1892 by John Muir. Muir's purpose in establishing the Sierra Club was to preserve the natural beauty of the Sierra Nevada Mountains in California and to protect wilderness areas in the Mountain West. Since Muir's time, the Sierra Club has grown into one of the most active, well-financed, and largest environmental advocacy groups in the world. The group emphasizes political action through government, using traditional techniques like organizing, educating the public, coalition-building, and creating national environmental agendas. The Sierra Club's major purpose has been to influence the public policy process toward environmental and resource preservation.

See also: Environment: Environmental Policy

References: Walter Rosenbaum, *Environmental Politics and Policy* (1998); Donald T. Wells, *Environmental Policy* (1996).

Soil Conservation and Domestic Allotment Act of 1936

This legislation supported farmers during the Great Depression by offering payments for soil conservation practices (rather than by controlling the crops that were planted). This was one of the first soil conservation initiatives, coming at a time when soil conservation and erosion were serious problems. The Dust Bowl, created in the drought-stricken southwestern United States during the early years of the Great Depression, alerted the federal government to the need for soil conservation.

See also: Agriculture: Agricultural Adjustment Act of 1933; Agricultural Adjustment Act of 1938; Economics: New Deal

References: Don E. Albrecht and Steve H. Murdock, *The Sociology of U.S. Agriculture* (1990); Judith I. de Neufville, ed., *The Land Use Policy Debate in the United States;* T. H. Watkins, *The Great Depression: America in the 1930s* (1993).

Solid Waste Disposal Act of 1965

Municipal waste (trash) is a serious problem for communities, which sometimes resort to dumping in unsightly local dumps, regional landfills, or even the oceans. Dumping solid waste in this way is a problem for the environment and for human health and safety. The first federal action to regulate solid waste was the Rivers and Harbors Act of 1899, which regulated the dumping of refuse into surface waters and prohibited the discharge of solid waste into navigable waters. The goal was not to improve or protect water quality but rather to prevent interference with shipping lanes.

The Solid Waste Disposal Act of 1965 was developed as a result of growing concerns in Congress over burning waste in city dumps, backyards, and incinerators, which was causing air pollution. The act called for research of solid waste disposal and introduced a new line of thinking that eventually led to many of the recycling policies that are common today. As a result of this legislation, scientists and environmentalists learned about soil and water contamination problems caused by dumping. Communities reconsidered the use of landfills and set policies governing landfill development. Since the 1965 legislation, solid-waste pollution has become a major issue for all levels of government. Agricultural wastes, residential and commercial wastes, industrial wastes, and mineral wastes account for billions of tons of solids. This early effort led to the development of other laws to control, restrict, and monitor the dumping of toxic materials.

See also: Environment: Environmental Policy; Resource Conservation and Recovery Act of 1976

References: Frederick R. Anderson, Daniel Mandelker, and A. Dan Tarlock, *Environmental Protection: Law and Policy* (1984); Charles Bonser, Eugene B. McGregor Jr., and Clinton V. Oster Jr., *Policy Choices and Public Action* (1996); Clarke E. Cochran et al., *American Public Policy: An Introduction* (1996); Jacqueline V. Switzer, *Environmental Politics: Domestic and Global Dimensions* (1994).

Superfund

See Environment: Comprehensive Environmental Response Act of 1980

Surface Mining Control and Reclamation Act of 1977

Strip mining is one of the most environmentally damaging practices in the mining industry, as it requires huge amounts of topsoil to be removed in order to get at the minerals beneath. Strip mines take the minerals (primarily coal) from the exposed surface without digging shafts. It is seen as an efficient and safer form of mining, but it leaves the land destroyed and useless. Taxpayers paid for reclamation of lands defaced by strip mines until the 1977 Surface Mining Control and Reclamation Act, which created the Office of Surface Mining in the Department of Interior to enforce legislation regarding reclamation of lands that were strip mined. The reclamation requirements have proven to be difficult to enforce, and mining companies are able to avoid many of the regulations requiring restoration and reclamation. The Office of Surface Mining issues fines to companies that have not complied with the reclamation rules, but many companies have been slow to pay such fines.

See also: Environment: Environmental Policy

References: Dennis J. Palumbo, *Public Policy in America: Government in Action* (1988); Jacqueline V. Switzer, *Environmental Politics: Domestic and Global Dimensions* (1994).

Toxic Substances Control Act of 1976

The first legislation to focus on the regulation, creation, manufacture, and distribution of chemical substances was the Toxic Substances Control Act of 1976, designed to begin the process of understanding the effect of toxic substances on humans and the environment and to prevent these substances from becoming a part of the ecosystem. The act authorizes the Environmental Protection Agency to gather information and scientific data on chemicals; screen the development of new chemicals; test the chemicals for their harmful qualities; control the distribution, use, and disposal of the chemicals; control the spread of asbestos in schools and public buildings; and develop plans to remove or manage asbestos-containing materials in buildings. Rachel Carson's book *Silent Spring*, which questioned the use and harmful effects of chemicals in the environment, spurred the nation into action. It also helped set in motion environmental legislation that addressed toxic substances, solid waste, safe water, and hazardous waste disposal.

See also: Environment: Carson, Rachel; Solid Waste Disposal Act of 1965

References: Walter Rosenbaum, *Environmental Politics and Policy* (1998).

Tradable Emissions Allowances

The tradable emission allowance is a mechanism by which industries can reduce emissions of pollutants; its purpose is to encourage innovation in emission-reduction technology. Emission allowances were established by the Environmental Protection Agency in 1992 for utilities, refineries, and other industries that routinely emitted pollutants into the atmosphere, and the target goals were measured in tons of harmful chemical pollutants. The allowances were "tradable" in that some industries were more or less able to reduce emissions and keep within target limits. If a company's emission levels came under the set target, then it sold the unused balance to other factories or industries for a profit. This is a highly technical policy dimension that had questionable value in limiting emission of pollutants. It was intended to erect economic incentives for limiting pollution, that is, it would be in the financial interest of utilities and industries to reduce emissions and meet targets. Such market incentives are one alternative in the battle for clean air and clean water.

See also: Environment: Environmental Policy

References: Thomas R. Dye, *Understanding Public Policy* (1995); Michael D. Reagan, *Regulation: The Politics of Policy* (1987).

Transboundary Pollution

Acid rain (water that is acidified by chemicals, minerals, or other carcinogens) is the result of burning industrial fuels and wastes, as heavy emissions enter the atmosphere. Released gases and toxic agents travel long distances and eventually settle on the ground or in water hundreds or thousands of miles away. The Canadian government has claimed for decades that the decline of forests in Canada's eastern provinces is the result of toxic particles released into the air by American industries in the Midwest. This is an example of transboundary pollution.

Transboundary pollution can affect water, air, and soil quality. Acid rain affects forests, lakes, plant and animal life, and humans. The United States and Canada have agreed to talk about reducing industrial transboundary pollution. The United States still has problems with polluters in Mexico along the Rio Grande and the Colorado Rivers. Transboundary pollution requires international conferences and agreements to establish policy to control and restrict polluters and pollution.

See also: Environment: Acid Rain; Environmental Policy; Montreal Protocols

References: Lynton K. Caldwell, *Environment as a Focus for Public Policy* (1995); Walter Rosenbaum, *Environmental Politics and Policy* (1998); Jacqueline V. Switzer, *Environmental Politics: Domestic and Global Dimensions* (1994).

Uranium Mill Tailings Reclamation Act of 1980

Mining uranium presents special problems not found in mining of other minerals. Uranium creates radon gas, which is harmful to miners, and uranium tailings are radioactive, which presents another set of hazards. Uranium tailings were ground into a fine sand and sold to construction companies as a building material in Colorado, which introduced radioactivity to some homes in that state. Congress passed the Uranium Mill Tailings Reclamation Act in 1980 to finance the identification and removal of uranium tailings near residences in the Rocky Mountains. This legislation came in direct response to the problem of uranium, its tailings, and the presence of radon gases caused by uranium in the mining and building construction processes. The legislation also resulted in the scrutiny of building products and restrictions on the use of uranium ore and byproducts in buildings.

See also: Environment: Environmental Policy

References: David H. Davis, *Energy Politics* (1993); Jacqueline V. Switzer, *Environmental Politics: Domestic and Global Dimensions* (1994).

Water Pollution

See Environment: Environmental Policy

Health

Chronology

1798 Disabled Seamen and Marine Hospital Service Act passed to help sick and disabled seamen and establish the first Marine Hospital.

1847 American Medical Association was established.

1872 American Public Health Association was founded.

1899 National Hospital Superintendent's Association was created; it later became the American Hospital Association.

1912 U.S. Public Health Service was formed from the Marine Hospital Service.

1921 Sheppard-Towner Act created the first federal grant program for women's and children's health clinics.

1928 Sheppard-Towner Act was terminated.

1929 Blue Cross was established.

1930 National Institutes of Health established to discover the causes, prevention, and cure of disease.

1935 Social Security Act passed, providing unemployment compensation, old-age benefits, and aid to the blind and infirm.

1937 National Cancer Act was passed, creating the National Cancer Institute.

1939 Murray-Wagner-Dingell bill is proposed, offering national health insurance.

1946 National Hospital Survey and Construction Act mandated federal funding to subsidize construction of hospitals.

1965 Medicare and Medicaid bills are passed as amendments to the Social Security Act of 1935.

1966 Comprehensive Health Planning Act passed to implement health care facilities planning throughout the states.

1973 Health Maintenance Organization Act is passed to encourage development of HMOs to induce competition in the health care marketplace.

1981 Omnibus Budget Reconciliation Act passed, affecting growth rates in Medicaid, reducing the number of those eligible for welfare, and changing Medicare policy.

1983 The Prospective Payment System (PPS)

began. It classified illnesses into categories for reimbursement.

1988 The Pepper Commission Report is released, calling for coverage for long-term care and for universal coverage for those under the age of sixty-five.

1993 Family and Medical Leave Act passed, guaranteeing emergency leave for family illness.

Acquired Immunodeficiency Syndrome

Acquired immunodeficiency syndrome (AIDS), became a serious public health problem during the early 1980s. What started as a series of illnesses common to gay men became a worldwide problem for heterosexuals as well. AIDS is caused by the human immunodeficiency virus (HIV), which is primarily transmitted through sexual intercourse, sharing contaminated needles between intravenous (IV) drug users, introducing contaminated blood through blood transfusions or spattering, and infected pregnant mothers to their infants. In 1995 more than 75 percent of new AIDS cases in the United States occurred in two population groups: gays and IV-drug users. The number of women with HIV is rapidly growing. In underdeveloped countries (e.g., Uganda and Kenya), AIDS is primarily a heterosexual disease spread between men and women.

The response of public policy to AIDS has taken on different forms as a public health issue. The majority of government spending to fight AIDS has come from the federal government. There have been efforts directed at education and prevention. Biomedical research, support, and funding have come from the federal Department of Health and Human Services, the Food and Drug Administration, the National Institutes of Health, the Centers for Disease Control, the Health Resources and Services Administration, and the Health Care Financing Administration.

Development of a comprehensive and aggressive AIDS policy has been a major challenge for the U.S. government. Policy needs related to HIV infection include medication and costs of purchasing medication, the cost of continuous treatment and hospitalization of AIDS patients, and home health care and housing needs of AIDS patients. The AIDS activist group ACTUP has focused on publicizing the severity of the AIDS problem. ACTUP and AIDS activists feel that public policy has been unresponsive to AIDS sufferers. During the late 1990s AIDS infections shifted from predominantly white gays to African American and Hispanic IV-drug users. Health policy directed at AIDS will continue to focus on the health effects of the disease, the increasing number of AIDS cases, priorities in biomedical research, the effectiveness of AIDS/HIV awareness and education, and the management of the costs of care.

See also: Health: ACTUP; Department of Health and Human Services; Health Policy

References: Theodore J. Litman and Leonard S. Robins, *Health Politics and Policy* (1997); Stella Z. Theodoulou, *AIDS: The Politics and Policy of Disease* (1996).

ACTUP

When it was determined that illnesses among the U.S. gay population were attributed to acquired immunodeficiency syndrome (AIDS) during the early 1980s, the federal government began taking its first steps toward AIDS awareness, prevention, and cure. AIDS is caused by the human immunodeficiency virus (HIV) and has become a problem for heterosexuals as well. Since then, the government has been accused of giving insufficient attention and resources to problems associated with AIDS. One of the groups that has engaged in the most direct forms of AIDS activism is the AIDS Coalition to Unleash Power (ACTUP).

ACTUP was founded in 1987 in response to the perception that the government and medical community were not putting forth enough effort to find a cure for AIDS. ACTUP is an interest group that brings attention to the magnitude of the worldwide AIDS problem and pressures the medical establishment to engage in testing and approval of effective drugs to help HIV-infected people. The activist members of ACTUP have deliberately chosen to pursue controversial and visible tactics and strategies to influence American health policy.

See also: Key Concepts: Interest Groups

References: Theodore J. Litman and Leonard S. Robins, *Health Politics and Policy* (1997); Kant Patel and Mark E. Rushefsky, *Health Care Politics and Policy in America* (1995); Stella Z. Theodoulou, *AIDS: The Politics and Policy of Disease* (1996).

Advisory Committee on Smoking and Health

This committee met for the first time in November 1962. It was composed of scientists selected by the U.S. surgeon general from lists of names submitted by the tobacco industry, health policy groups, professional associations, and federal agencies. This was to be an expert advisory committee, the first to tackle the controversial issue of health warnings and tobacco usage. It issued the first clear health warning regarding tobacco use in a January 1964 report. The members concluded unanimously that "cigarette smoking is a health hazard of sufficient importance in the United States to warrant appropriate remedial action." This report was the formal beginning of federal government attempts to issue rules requiring packaging and advertisement warnings as to health hazards associated with cigarette smoking.

See also: Health: Health Policy; Key Concepts: Advisory Committees

References: A. Lee Fritschler and James M. Hoefler, *Smoking and Politics: Policy Making and the Federal Bureaucracy* (1996).

AIDS

See Health: Acquired Immunodeficiency Syndrome

Alcohol, Drug Abuse, and Mental Health Administration

Within the U.S. Public Health Service, several separate agencies serve a public health function. The Alcohol, Drug Abuse, and Mental Health Administration is an agency that supports research, treatment, and demonstration programs that focus on these three policy areas. Under the Clinton administration the agency name changed to the Substance Abuse and Mental Health Services Administration (SAMHSA). SAMHSA comprises three centers that carry out the agency's mission of providing substance abuse and mental health services: The Center for Mental Health Services, the Center for Substance Abuse Prevention, and the Center for Substance Abuse Treatment. Six other offices lend support: the Office of Applied Studies, the Office of Managed Care, the Office on AIDS, the Office for Women's Services, the Associate Administrator for Alcohol Prevention and Treatment Policy, and the Associate Administrator for Minority Concerns. SAMHSA works directly to support public health policy issues and services and uses grants and contracts with state and local agencies to conduct various programs.

See also: Health: Acquired Immunodeficiency Syndrome; Health Policy

References: Theodore Litman and Leonard S. Robins, *Health Politics and Policy* (1997); Stella Z. Theodoulou, *AIDS: The Politics and Policy of Disease* (1996).

American Cancer Society

One of the most deadly diseases in modern industrial societies is cancer. The American Cancer Society, founded in 1913, performs cancer research, provides information on prevention of cancer, and advocates at all policy levels for cancer survivors and for issues related to cancer. During the late 20th century the American Cancer Society has focused its efforts on laws and regulations dealing with the use, sale, distribution, and marketing of tobacco products to young people; improved access for Americans to health care services toward prevention, diagnosis, and treatment of cancer; increased federal funding and incentives for private sponsorship of cancer research; support for the dissemination of cancer information; and advocacy for the rights of cancer survivors. The American Cancer Society acts as an interest and advocacy group and works through volunteer participation. The organization reaches 10–12 million American people through its community-based programs. It has been a leading advocate in the national crusade against tobacco and smoking.

See also: Health: Health Policy

References: A. Lee Fritschler and James M. Hoefler, *Smoking and Politics: Policy Making and the Federal Bureaucracy* (1996); Robert L. Rabin and Stephen D. Sugarman, *Smoking Policy: Law, Politics, and Culture* (1993).

American Health Security Act

During Pres. Bill Clinton's first term, the right to health care was at the heart of health care reform debates. Clinton proposed a new health care initiative in 1993, the American Health Security Act, to guarantee health care insurance and health care access to all citizens. Much of the work to restructure America's health care system came out of a committee headed by First Lady Hillary Rodham Clinton. The health security proposal promoted managed competition among health care providers through the formation of alliances of providers; guaranteed access to health care for all citizens and legal residents; provided a choice of variable cost health plans; provided that most of the costs of health plans would be paid by employers; and established a new national health board to set a national health care budget and allocate money to health care alliances throughout the United States. Known as a "single-payer" bill, it intended to include long-term care services (institutional, community-based, and home) into an overall package of national health insurance. It also made provision for phasing out Medicaid and would provide for copayments for long-term care services and subsidization for low-income people.

There was support for this ambitious health reform plan, but it failed in Congress in 1994. The reform bill was another in a series of attempts in the executive branch and Congress to change the health care system. Critics and opponents of the Health Security Act complained that the reform would present extraordinary administrative problems and would not cut the costs of health care. Others expressed fears of not having true competition in the health care marketplace, where there would be extensive government involvement. Health policy is incremental, and this bill was a means of attacking the problem of access to health care, underinsured and uninsured Americans, and cost containment in the health insurance and health care industries.

See also: Health: Health Policy; Key Concepts: Incrementalism

References: Clarke E. Cochran et al., *American Public Policy: An Introduction* (1996); Thomas R. Dye, *Understanding Public Policy* (1995); Theodore Litman and Leonard S. Robins, *Health Politics and Policy* (1997).

American Hospital Association

The American Hospital Association (AHA) is an interest group founded in 1893 by an eight-person organization of hospital superintendents. Today AHA, with its headquarters in Chicago, Illinois, has some 54,500 members including individuals; hospitals; nursing executives/administrators; health care corporations and health maintenance organizations (HMOs); substance abuse centers; hospices; and other types of hospitals. AHA represents the interests of health and hospital professionals. It works to influence health care policy and hospitalization issues and to assist political campaigns through its political action committee, PAC of AHA, which was founded in 1976.

See also: Health: Health Maintenance Organization Act of 1973; Key Concepts: Interest Groups

References: Clarke E. Cochran et al., *American Public Policy: An Introduction* (1996); Theodore Litman and Leonard S. Robins, *Health Politics and Policy* (1997).

American Medical Association

The American Medical Association (AMA) was founded in 1847 as a result of a meeting of 222 delegates from 23 states. One of the first acts was to adopt a code of ethics that addressed the obligations of physicians to patients and to each other and the duties of the medical profession to the public at large. The early years were devoted to establishing national standards for medical education and for medical care in hospitals. Today, AMA has more than 290,000 physician members and 54 state groups. It represents more than 40 percent of all U.S. physicians. Many young doctors are apathetic about joining AMA, and most members are more than 45 years old. AMA is a very powerful interest group for physicians and has a well-funded and aggressive political action committee (PAC), AMPAC, which was founded in 1961. AMPAC is among the top five contributors to national political campaigns. During the 1993–1994 national election cycle, AMPAC gave $2,562,368 to political candidates and campaigns, the largest among all health care and health insurance PACs.

During the 20th century AMA has opposed almost all government intervention in the health care field. The AMA has been very effective in generating support in Congress and state legislatures in furthering the interests of physicians and the medical profession. Its most visible activity has come in its opposition to national health insurance proposals from the states and those introduced before Congress.

See also: Health: American Health Security Act; Health Maintenance Organization Act of 1973; Health Policy; Key Concepts: Interest Groups

References: Theodore Litman and Leonard S. Robins, *Health Politics and Policy* (1997); Kant Patel and Mark E. Rushefsky, *Health Care Politics and Policy in America* (1995).

Anti-tobacco Policy

The emergence of public interest lobbying during the 1960s altered the balance of influential players in the realm of tobacco and public policy during the 1990s. Until the 1960s, the tobacco industry and its subsidiaries were in a dominant position regarding federal support for tobacco and the industry—tobacco growers, marketing organizations, and cigarette manufacturers. Other important players in tobacco policy are members of Congress who represent tobacco constituencies; the four subcommittees in Congress that handle tobacco legislation and appropriations; and officials in the Department of Agriculture who are connected to tobacco programs.

Since 1964 health-related organizations have played a major role in tobacco politics. The American Cancer Society and the American Medical Association now advocate a total ban on cigarette advertising. State and local governments have also been active in passing antismoking ordinances in public places. The U.S. tobacco industry generates $48 billion per year in revenues. It represents a potent economic force, with some 47,000 workers and providing $2.8 billion in crop income for more than 100,000 farmers in 16 states. North Carolina and Kentucky grow two-thirds of the total U.S. tobacco crop.

The research findings regarding the health effects of smoking and tobacco use gave the U.S. government reason to begin warning consumers about the related health dangers. The first scientific study that linked smoking and lung cancer was published in 1939. In 1954 cigarette manufacturers established the Council for Tobacco Research, a public relations organization that spent more than $200 million during the next 40 years to fund research that cast doubt on links between smoking and health problems. In January 1964 the U.S. surgeon general issued a report written by the Advisory Committee on Smoking and Health that summarized research on smoking and health hazards. In 1965 Congress passed the Cigarette Labeling and Advertising Act, which required that a health warning appear on all cigarette packages. In 1970 the Public Health Cigarette Smoking Act of 1969 was passed. The act banned ads from radio and television and addressed rulemaking restrictions on the Federal Trade Commission. Anti-tobacco legislation during the 1990s has been directed at the tobacco industry's culpability for knowledge of health risks and addictive qualities of tobacco. The issue of secondhand smoke and its related health effects have also been the subject of recent lawsuits against the tobacco industry. The claim is based on cigarette producers' manufacturing a faulty product that threatens the health of persons near smokers. The continuing question is the proper role of government, specifically, whether the government should pursue health and safety or protect the economic interests of a major agricultural industry threatened by health-related interest groups.

See also: Economics: Federal Trade Commission; Health: Advisory Committee on Smoking and Health; Health Policy

References: A. Lee Fritschler and James M. Hoefler, *Smoking and Politics: Policymaking and the Federal Bureaucracy* (1996); A. Stanton Glantz et al., *The Cigarette Papers* (1996); Robert L. Rabin and Stephen D. Sugarman, *Smoking Policy: Law, Politics, and Culture* (1993).

Catastrophic Health Insurance

The United States is a nation that does not offer universal health insurance, and many citizens do not have health insurance or are underinsured. For them, the specter of a catastrophic health problem is a daunting image. The occurrence of a serious accident or illness, for any person regardless of financial status, can lead to personal bankruptcy. A means to offset and prevent financial disaster is catastrophic health insurance. Such a plan would be based on individual income and supplement costs of medical care beyond the patient's ability to pay. Some catastrophic health insurance plans require individuals to invest in medical savings plans to encourage or force them to save or borrow to cover large deductibles. These plans require users to plan ahead for serious health problems and only are available to individuals who have the financial ability to set aside money in medical savings accounts.

Medical savings plans would not be necessary under a national health insurance system in which health care is a right and not something based on ability to pay. Under a national health insurance plan, individuals and businesses would pay into a risk pool of funds that is based on a universal coverage principle and designed to cover all reasonable health expenditures. This is one form of universal health insurance in effect in Canada, and it has been proposed by proponents of U.S. national health insurance. In the ongoing debate on health care policy in the United States, the issue of catastrophic coverage receives considerable attention due to the potential financial consequences for the U.S. population.

See also: Health: Health Policy

References: Charles Bonser, Eugene B. McGregor Jr., and Clinton V. Oster Jr., *Policy Choices and Public Action* (1996); Theodore Litman and Leonard S. Robins, *Health Politics and Policy* (1997).

Centers for Disease Control and Prevention

Located in Atlanta, Georgia, the U.S. Centers for Disease Control and Prevention (CDC) is a federal public health agency that conducts medical research, traces disease and health problems, and engages in testing of possible cures and vaccines for many types of illnesses. CDC plays a major role in research, education, and prevention of HIV/AIDS, emphasizing a public health approach.

See also: Health: Acquired Immunodeficiency Syndrome; Health Policy

References: Theodore Litman and Leonard S. Robins, *Health Politics and Policy* (1997); Stella Z. Theodoulou, *AIDS: The Politics and Policy of Disease* (1996).

Cipallone v. Liggett Group

The U.S. tobacco industry has been under attack since the 1950s, when studies became more definitive in linking smoking to health problems. By 1988 there were approximately 135 liability cases that challenged the tobacco companies to prove that cigarette smoking was not the cause of illness and death in smokers or their families. In *Cipallone v. Liggett Group,* a U.S. circuit court of appeals ruled that tobacco companies have limited immunity from liability because of the presence of warning labels on tobacco products. In this case, the heirs of Rose Cipallone were awarded $400,000 from Liggett Group, Inc., a tobacco company, at the trial phase. In January 1990 the appeals court threw out the damage award against the Liggett Group on the grounds that the plaintiffs had not proven that Rose Cipallone either saw or believed Liggett's claims about the health benefits of smoking. Since the *Cipallone* ruling, plaintiffs and anti-tobacco activists have been successful in getting tobacco companies to admit awareness of the addictive properties of nicotine; the companies have also been held liable for deaths related to the use of tobacco products.

See also: Health: Anti-tobacco Policy; Health Policy

References: A. Lee Fritschler and James M. Hoefler, *Smoking and Politics: Policymaking and the Federal Bureaucracy* (1996).

Common Sense Legal Reform Act

In 1995 congressional Republicans, as part of the "Contract with America," introduced the Common Sense Legal Reform Act. The bill was designed to establish legal standards and procedures for product liability litigation. Its proponents sought to achieve a balance between rights of claimants and defendants in civil lawsuits and to curb abuses in tort laws. The bill would enact "loser pays" laws and establish limits on punitive damages in civil lawsuits. The thrust of the bill was to limit excessive litigation. The bill passed the House and Senate but was vetoed by Pres. Bill Clinton and did not receive the required two-thirds vote to override the veto.

See also: Key Concepts: Congress, United States

References: Charles Bonser, Eugene B. McGregor Jr., and Clinton V. Oster Jr., *Policy Choice and Public Action* (1996); David Edwards and Alessandra Lippucci, *Practicing American Politics: An Introduction to American Government* (1998).

Comprehensive Health Manpower Training Act of 1971

A major issue in national health care planning is controlling health care–related costs. Cost-control measures focus on the growth of hospitals in comparison to the need for hospitals throughout the country. In 1946 Congress passed the Hospital Survey and Construction Act at a time when there was a clear need for the development and construction of new hospitals. Since the 1970s a major goal in the health care industry has been to reduce increases in hospital costs; one way to do that is to reduce the number of hospitals and improve medical treatment while reducing time spent in hospitals. States are involved in mandating rate-setting in hospital costs. A form of mandated rates is capitation, which provides cash payments by states for each eligible patient to the health care service provider (hospital). To help increase the number of physicians in the United States, Congress passed the 1971 Comprehensive Health Manpower Training Act, providing capitation grants to medical schools based on the number of students enrolled. The gist of this legislation was to increase the supply of physicians in key geographical areas, but, like subsequent legislation, it met with limited success.

See also: Health: Emergency Health Personnel Act of 1973; Health Policy

References: Theodore J. Litman and Leonard S. Robins, *Health Politics and Policy* (1997); Theodore Marmor, *Understanding Health Care Reform* (1994); Dennis J. Palumbo, *Public Policy in America: Government in Action* (1988).

Comprehensive Smoking Education Act of 1984

Much of the early antismoking activity of the Federal Trade Commission (FTC) came in the form of educating the public about the scientific and health effects of smoking. During the early 1980s FTC sought to further educate the American public about the dangers of cigarette smoking, calling for more effective health warnings on cigarette packaging and advertising. Congress eventually passed the Comprehensive Smoking Education Act in 1984, which replaced 1970 language with stronger, more specific warnings about the dangers of smoking. FTC sought this stronger language and larger type on packaging because it appeared that many cigarette smokers were not fully aware of the dangers of smoking, even with the inclusion of warnings on packaging up to that time.

See also: Health: Anti-tobacco Policy; *Cipallone v. Liggett Group*

References: A. Lee Fritschler and James M. Hoefler, *Smoking and Politics: Policymaking and the Federal Bureaucracy* (1996).

Consumer Product Safety Act of 1972

Consumer product safety regulation emerged during the late 1960s and early 1970s, mainly in preventive policy areas such as health care, the environment, and health and hazards in the workplace. This policy area was heavily influenced by consumer protection advocates, notably Ralph Nader, who argued on behalf of automobile safety. A Nader book, *Unsafe at Any Speed,* exposed the safety defects in Corvair automobiles. His group of staff assistants, "Nader's Raiders," became the core of a large group of consumer activists who pressured Congress to adopt consumer product safety legislation.

The consumer movement was an extension of the Great Society programs under Pres. Lyndon Johnson. The Consumer Product Safety Act was passed in 1972. It created the Consumer Product Safety Commission, an independent regulatory commission with jurisdiction over all consumer products except food and drugs. The act also developed regulations and safety standards for common consumer products like paints, children's clothing, toys, and bedding articles. The policy role of the Consumer Product Safety Commission is to administer protective regulation. Consumer advocates have been less successful in their attempts to exert pressure for regulations in product safety since the active regulatory years of the 1960s and 1970s. Nevertheless, their early efforts laid the foundation for product safety, standards, regulations, and laws that have had lasting impact as protective regulatory policy.

See also: Health: Food and Drug Administration; Nader, Ralph; Key Concepts: Regulation

References: Jeffrey E. Cohen, *Politics and Economic Policy in the United States* (1997); Richard Harris and Sidney Miklis, *The Politics of Regulatory Change* (1996); Dennis J. Palumbo, *Public Policy in America: Government in Action* (1988); Susan Welch et al., *Understanding American Government* (1997).

Council for Tobacco Research

A function of a lobby is to provide information and advocate policies or programs that serve the interests of client groups represented by the lobby. The tobacco industry saw the need in the 1950s to counter health groups' growing activism regarding the health effects of using cigarettes and other tobacco products. One tactic was to found the Tobacco Industry Research Committee. Now called the Council for Tobacco Research, it provides funding for scientific research into the health effects of tobacco. A. Lee Fritschler and James Hoefler, in *Smoking and Politics: Policymaking and the Federal Bureaucracy,* state that during the first 25 years of operation the Council for Tobacco Research awarded 744 grants totaling $64 million to 413 scientists at 258 hospitals, laboratories, research organizations, and medical schools with 1,882 published reports that acknowledged council support.

The Council for Tobacco Research saw its task as

countering criticism of smoking by funding research reports and an active public relations campaign. The Council for Tobacco Research was one of the earliest lobbying groups created by the tobacco industry to respond to the growing interest in the deleterious health effects of smoking and tobacco use.

See also: Health: Anti-tobacco Policy

References: A. Lee Fritschler and James M. Hoefler, *Smoking and Politics: Policymaking and the Federal Bureaucracy* (1996); A. Stanton Glantz et al., *The Cigarette Papers* (1996); Robert L. Rabin and Stephen D. Sugarman, *Smoking Policy: Law, Politics, and Culture* (1993).

Department of Health and Human Services

An executive department, the Department of Health and Human Services (HHS) is responsible for promoting the public health, enforcing pure food and drug laws, and engaging in health-related research. Headed by the secretary of health and human services, it was formed in 1979 (it was previously housed within the Department of Health, Education, and Welfare). The department employs some 125,000 in the following subagencies: the Food and Drug Administration (FDA); the Administration for Children and Families; the Health Care Finance Administration; and the Public Health Service. The department advises the president and Congress on legislative measures and carries out congressional mandates in the health care and social services areas.

HHS has a broad mandate and set of responsibilities to address health and safety matters in the nation. Much of the current work on drug testing and efficacy trials for drugs comes through FDA; much of the work and policy on HIV/AIDS is carried out by individuals in this federal agency. The functions of this agency are divided into the general categories of public health, human development services, and Social Security. The Public Health Service is responsible for conducting medical and biomedical research; developing and administering programs for the prevention of disease and alcohol and drug abuse; the delivery of health services; and coordinating the activities of its subagencies. The Office of Human Development Services administers programs for the elderly, children, families, Native Americans, disabled people, and rural residents. The Health Care Financing Administration administers the Medicare and Medicaid programs.

See also: Entitlement Programs: Medicaid; Medicare; Health: Acquired Immunodeficiency Syndrome; Health Policy

References: Theodore Litman and Leonard S. Robins, *Health Politics and Policy* (1997); Theodore K. Marmor, *Understanding Health Care Reform* (1994); Kant Patel and Mark E. Rushefsky, *Health Care Politics and Policy in America* (1995).

Diagnosis-related Groups

In *Understanding Health Care Reform,* Theodore Marmor defines diagnosis-related groups (DRGs) as a classification system adopted by Medicare in 1983 to set standard payments for hospitalization.

During the early 1980s the federal government sought to reduce the costs of health care and to reduce such costs within federally supported programs like Medicare. In 1981 the Omnibus Budget Reconciliation Act was passed to control federal spending. The act had a provision for reducing Medicare spending and reimbursements. The Tax Equity and Fiscal Responsibility Act of 1982 was also designed to control public spending. This bill included a Medicare element that established a limit on the rate of increase over time in Medicare hospital payment rates; it also set a new payment index (or category) that was based on diagnosis-related groups. The bill set an efficiency goal for hospitals that offered incentives for attention paid to the reimbursement based on DRGs.

Payments to hospitals are based on the patient's diagnosis, which is adjusted for the average cost of health care in the geographical area. A physician's diagnosis is used as a basis for reimbursement to the hospital regardless of the specific costs of a Medicare beneficiary's hospitalization. There are 468 categories of DRGs that are recognized and will be reimbursed by Medicare. The use of DRGs as a reimbursement plan was an important health care reform initiative that supported the prospective payment system model to provide hospitals with a built-in incentive for considering treatments and costs that would be more economically efficient.

See also: Entitlement Programs: Medicare; Health: Health Policy

References: Theodore Litman and Leonard S. Robins, *Health Politics and Policy* (1997); Theodore K. Marmor, *Understanding Health Care Reform* (1994); Kant Patel and Mark E. Rushefsky, *Health Care Politics and Policy in America* (1995).

Emergency Health Personnel Act of 1973

A major health care issue is the unavailability of adequate care in rural areas and of general practitioners in so-called critical shortage areas. The Emergency Health Personnel Act of 1973 was passed to relieve the shortage of general practitioners in rural and nonmetropolitan areas. The legislation approved project grants to improve medical school programs to train and encourage doctors for general practice in rural and critical shortage areas. The legislation did little to correct the doctor shortage and geographical imbalances. Employment trends for physicians indicate that urban areas have a stronger appeal to doctors, that general practice does not fulfill the lifestyle and financial needs of newly licensed physicians. The Health Professions Educational Assistance Act of 1976 replaced the programs in the Emergency Health Personnel Act with a greater emphasis on correcting the geographical imbalance, but that legislation also fell short in achieving objectives.

See also: Health: Comprehensive Health Manpower Training Act of 1971; Health Policy

References: Theodore Litman and Leonard S. Robins, *Health Politics and Policy* (1997); Theodore K. Marmor, *Understanding Health Care Reform* (1994); Dennis J. Palumbo, *Public Policy in America: Government in Action* (1988).

Family and Medical Leave Act of 1993

The Family and Medical Leave Act requires all employers with 50 or more workers to guarantee unpaid leave to employees who have illness or family responsibilities that will legitimately keep the employees from working. Any worker who has been employed for one year and for at least 25 hours a week can take up to 12 weeks of unpaid leave during any 12-month period for the following reasons: birth or adoption of a child; serious illness of a child, spouse, or parent; or a serious illness that prevents the worker from doing the job. Upon returning to work, the employee has a right to his or her old job or an equivalent position. In 1998, 40 percent of employees were covered by the Family and Medical Leave Act.

The Family and Medical Leave Act attempts to relieve families of the burden of missing work during family medical emergencies. This legislation was championed by women activists and the Women's Defense Fund. Hearings were held before the House Select Committee on Children, Youth, and Families, where expert witnesses spoke about the need for working people to have paid time off to care for newborns. The act covers all public-sector employees, including federal employees.

See also: Health: Health Policy

References: James E. Anderson, *Public Policymaking* (1997); Charles Bonser, Eugene B. McGregor Jr., and Clinton V. Oster Jr., *Policy Choices and Public Action* (1996).

Fauci, Anthony S. (b. 1941)

Dr. Anthony S. Fauci is the director of the National Institute of Allergy and Infectious Diseases at the National Institutes of Health. Dr. Fauci has been in the forefront in the battle against HIV-AIDS. Dr. Fauci has a medical degree from Cornell University and has been at the National Institutes of Health since 1971. Dr. Fauci became director of the National Institute of Allergy and Infectious Diseases in 1984. His work has contributed to the understanding of how HIV destroys the body's defenses, leading to susceptibility and the onset of AIDS. Dr. Fauci has been a leader in the scientific investigation of HIV-AIDS and in the development of immunotherapy programs that have been instrumental in prolonging the lives of many HIV-AIDS sufferers.

See also: Health: Acquired Immunodeficiency Syndrome

References: Emily J. McMurray, ed., *Notable Twentieth-Century Scientists* (1995).

Federal Emergency Management Agency

During times of natural or accidental disasters, victims readily call on the federal government for aid and relief. The U.S. government has been prepared to aid citizens who have suffered injury from floods, wildfires, earthquakes, tornadoes, and hurricanes. The Federal Emergency Management Agency (FEMA) was founded in 1979 and is responsible for emergency preparedness and for rapid response to all types of emergencies that seriously threaten or affect American lives and property.

During the 1990s Americans in the Midwest and the West suffered flooding caused by excessive rainfall, snow, and runoff. State governors often called on the president to declare affected regions federal disaster areas. Once the declaration is made FEMA coordinates federal relief, providing financial and other assistance to communities and residents, including low-cost loans and emergency housing. Ultimately, the mission of FEMA is to reduce the loss of life and property and to protect the nation's critical infrastructure from all types of disasters and hazards. This national emergency program works to mitigate injury, promote preparedness, and respond immediately to loss of life and property.

References: Edward S. Greenberg and Benjamin I. Page, *The Struggle for Democracy* (1993).

Federal Motor Vehicle Safety Standards Act of 1968

Automobile safety emerged as a matter of public interest and policy during the 1960s, when the consumer product safety movement became highly visible. Led by consumer advocates such as Ralph Nader, the issue of automobile safety was placed on the public agenda, and in 1968 the Federal Motor Vehicle Safety Standards Act was passed. The act required all automobiles to be equipped with lap or shoulder (or a combination of both) belts. The Ford Motor Company acted alone in 1955 to improve automobile safety when it made lap safety belts optional in its automobiles. The matter of automobile safety was an important issue, and by 1964 14 states required that cars sold have lap belts. Though seatbelts are commonplace today, airbags are also standard in most new automobiles. The 1968 legislation is an example of the development of public policy in response to the mobilization of people by a public interest group, namely, the consumer protection movement that took hold during the 1960s.

See also: Health: Nader, Ralph; Key Concepts: Interest Groups; Public Interest Research Groups

References: Dennis J. Palumbo, *Public Policy in America: Government in Action* (1988).

Food and Drug Administration

The U.S. Food and Drug Administration (FDA) is an agency in the Department of Health and Human Services that administers the 1938 Food, Drug, and Cosmetic Act as well as the laws regarding dangerous drugs, food, medical devices, and cosmetics. FDA, within the Public Health Service, is responsible for regulating and assuring that food, cosmetics, medicines, and medical devices are safe and effective. The agency also inspects and ensures the safety of feed and drugs for pets and farm animals. FDA regulates labeling of consumer products for truth and accuracy. The Food, Drug, and Cosmetic Act required manufacturers to list the ingredients of products on the labels, prohibited the misbranding of food products, and forbade false advertising.

FDA has some 1,100 investigators and inspectors and regulates 95,000 businesses through 157 local offices. In its review of product safety, the agency finds 3,000 products a year as unfit for consumers; these products are withdrawn from the market by voluntary recall or court-ordered seizure. The agency has some 2,100 scientists, including chemists and microbiologists working in 40 laboratories in Washington, D.C., and around the United States.

FDA has been active during the last ten years in biomedical research policy in its development and testing of drugs for treating AIDS. All drugs to counter the spread of AIDS are required to undergo review and efficacy tests by FDA, a process that has been criticized by AIDS activists because of the perceived slowness and overcaution. FDA has had to satisfy calls for efficient drug review while balancing the need for sound science.

See also: Health: Acquired Immunodeficiency Syndrome; Health Policy; Key Concepts: Regulation

References: Theodore Litman and Leonard S. Robins, *Health Politics and Policy* (1997); Dennis J. Palumbo, *Public Policy in America: Government in Action* (1988).

Galbraith v. R. J. Reynolds Industries

In the battle against smoking, the tactics of antitobacco crusaders have taken on a variety of dimensions. One was to demonstrate that cigarette smoking caused cancer and other health problems and that manufacturers of cigarettes should be held legally liable for the inherent dangers of their products. Even after tobacco companies were required to place health warnings on packaging, some opponents declared it was useless and that tobacco companies were still liable. The case of *Galbraith v. R. J. Reynolds Industries* was one such case. In this case, argued by renowned attorney Melvin Belli, Mr. Galbraith claimed he was addicted to tobacco and that health warnings were useless and did not deter him from smoking cigarettes. The jury found against Mr. Galbraith.

This and other cases that favored tobacco companies, including *Green v. American Tobacco Company,* were not to last. During the 1990s tobacco companies were held liable for distributing products that led to serious health problems.

See also: Health: Anti-tobacco Policy

References: A. Lee Fritschler and James M. Hoefler, *Smoking and Politics: Policymaking and the Federal Bureaucracy* (1996); A. Stanton Glantz et al., *The Cigarette Papers* (1996).

Hammond, E. Cuyler (b. 1912)

The battle against cigarette smoking had its origins in the scientific work of Drs. E. Cuyler Hammond and Daniel Horn, who conducted scientific studies on the harmful effects of smoking. Led by Hammond, scientists made the link between cigarette smoking and lung cancer. Hammond found that the death rate for male smokers between the ages of 45 and 64 was twice as high as that for nonsmokers. The results of the 1954 studies conducted by Hammond and Horn were instrumental in demonstrating a health hazard from smoking tobacco products, which provided an important impetus for the development of labeling and anti-tobacco policy.

See also: Health: Anti-tobacco Policy

References: A. Lee Fritschler and James M. Hoefler, *Smoking and Politics: Policymaking and the Federal Bureaucracy* (1996).

Hazardous Substances Labeling Act of 1960

One of the major elements in the opposition to use of tobacco products and cigarette smoking was the labeling of cigarette packages with warnings about the hazards of smoking. In 1960 Congress passed the Hazardous Substances Labeling Act, which empowered the Food and Drug Administration to control the sale of substances that had the capacity to produce illness or health problems through inhalation. Cigarettes were not specifically targeted as being among this group of hazardous substances at the time. It was not until 1964 that actual labeling of cigarettes as being potentially hazardous became policy.

See also: Health: Anti-tobacco Policy

References: A. Lee Fritschler and James M. Hoefler, *Smoking and Politics: Policymaking and the Federal Bureaucracy* (1996).

Health Care Industry

The health care industry comprises medical doctors, nurses, hospitals, hospital support staff, laboratories, drug companies, health maintenance organizations, insurance companies, attorneys whose clients are predominantly affiliated with the medical community and insurers, manufacturers of medical instruments and equipment, emergency medical transport companies (ambulance operators), the American Medical Association, and the American Hospital Association. There are numerous other actors in the health care industry that have an interest and stake in issues related to health care.

The U.S. health care industry is one of the largest and most influential private industries. The predominant issues that affect the health care industry are access to health care, the cost and financing of health care, the availability of health insurance, the quality of health care, the rise of managed care systems and the power of health maintenance organizations, and reform of the national health care system. Health care reform is a political issue that will continue to affect the health care industry during the 21st century. The focus of reform efforts has been to make the health care delivery system more efficient and less costly. One approach has been to encourage competition in health care markets, but this approach has not proven to be more efficient or less costly. The American Medical Association has been the major opponent of improving access, reducing costs, and producing workable reform efforts.

See also: Health: Health Maintenance Organization Act of 1973; Health Policy

References: Theodore Litman and Leonard S. Robins, *Health Politics and Policy* (1997); Theodore K. Marmor, *Understanding Health Care Reform* (1994).

Health Maintenance Organizations (HMOs)

See Health: Health Maintenance Organization Act of 1973

Health Maintenance Organization Act of 1973

A health maintenance organization (HMO) is a group practice plan in which members are treated by any of the physicians employed by the organization. Congress passed the Health Maintenance Organization Act of 1973 and required employers to offer HMOs as an alternative to regular health insurance. This act created a national market for a competitive, cost-effective managed health care system. One of the characteristics of health care during the 1990s was the proliferation and predominance of HMOs in the health care industry. The 1973 legislation overturned state laws that prevented the establishment of prepaid group practices. It required all employers with more than 25 employees to offer the choice of an HMO if one was available in the employees' area of residence. The goal was to open up competition and control costs. Preferred provider organizations have been established to enter agreements with employers to serve employees with discounted fees in return for employers' offering employment incentives to use the preferred provider HMO. If an employee uses a health provider not approved by the preferred provider plan, the employee must then pay the full costs of treatment instead of a discounted rate.

See also: Health: Health Policy

References: Theodore Litman and Leonard S. Robins, *Health Politics and Policy* (1997); Dennis J. Palumbo, *Public Policy in America: Government in Action* (1988).

Health Planning and Resources Development Act of 1974

Throughout the 1930s and 1940s the lack of hospitals in rural and poor areas was evident. To correct the problem, Congress passed the Hospital Survey and Construction Act of 1946 (also known as the Hill-Burton Act). The provisions of the act were popular because politicians and the public agreed that new hospitals were needed. Numerous hospitals were built and millions of dollars were appropriated to construct hospitals.

By 1974 hospital usage had doubled. Congress passed the Health Planning and Resources Development Act of 1974 with the purpose of establishing 200 health systems agencies (HSAs) to construct and analyze data, review the adequacy of health resources in the regions served by HSAs, prepare five-year health plans, and set priorities for spending and program development. HSAs would become clearinghouses for requests for the construction of new hospitals. Another goal of the law was to control costs of hospital care and health care in general. This did not happen, and HSAs did not function according to plan. Hospital and health care costs continued to escalate; the provisions of this legislation did little to assist planning of health care facilities.

See also: Health: Health Policy; Health Systems Agencies

References: Theodore K. Marmor, *Understanding Health Care Reform* (1994); Dennis J. Palumbo, *Public Policy in America: Government in Action* (1988).

Health Policy

Over the decades, there has been no concerted national effort to create a comprehensive health care policy process with a set of common goals that offer direction to health planning. Health policy and program development have been found at the local, state, and federal levels of government, yet there has also been substantial development of health policy in the private sector. One of the first health policies was Pres. John Adams's signing of an act that provided relief for sick and disabled seamen and created the first Marine Hospital. The American Medical Association was formed by physicians in 1847; the American Public Health Association was founded in 1872. The Public Health Service provides social and economic assistance in health problems. The National Institutes of Health (NIH) was established in 1930 to discover the causes, preventions, and cures of disease. In 1934 the Federal Emergency Relief Administration (FERA) provided the first federal grants to local governments for public assistance to the poor, which included financial support for health care. The Social Security Act was signed into law in 1935 and provided unemployment compensation, old-age benefits, and other benefits. In 1937 Congress passed the National Cancer Act, which created the National Cancer Institute. In 1946 the National Hospital Survey and Construction Act was passed, providing federal funding for hospital construction, particularly in rural areas.

Although there has not been a comprehensive and planned approach to health care policy in the United States, the government has been significantly involved in providing health care during the 20th century. In 1990 the federal government provided $7.7 billion to medical research. The role of government in health care is larger than most citizens would expect. During the 1990s health care costs were extremely high, almost unmanageable. Approximately 40 million Americans have no medical insurance, and with numbers like these there have been continuing calls for a national health insurance program. Attempts have been made in Congress to provide Americans with better health care coverage. In 1971 Sen. Ted Kennedy called for a version of national health insurance for Americans. Kennedy backed away from his ambitious plan to align with Sen. Wilbur Mills to propose a Health Security Act that did not get majority support in Congress. Kennedy's original plan was a comprehensive program of free medical care and would have replaced all public and private health plans in a federally operated health insurance system. Budget restraints would have been a provision of the plan. Opponents called it socialized medicine, a claim that has the force of certain defeat. In 1993 Pres. Bill Clinton proposed the Health Security Act, which called for comprehensive health care reform. The plan attempted to create report cards to bring about informed consumer choice of health plan options (reports on costs, access, and quality). Opponents claimed that the plan was fraught with problems in implementation, and the plan never gained the required support in Congress.

During the 1960s the Medicare and Medicaid programs were created by Congress. Medicare is a medical assistance program for the elderly; Medicaid is directed at health care for the poor. Both programs were passed as amendments to the Social Security Act of 1935. Medicare was designed to be a compulsory health insurance program for the elderly, financed through payroll taxes; it would be a voluntary insurance program for physicians' services subsidized through general revenues. Medicaid is a means-tested program administered by states. Both programs have been successful and have increased access to health care. The major problem has been the rising costs of health care. Reimbursement to physicians was generous during the early years of these programs, but rising costs have caused the government to focus more on controlling the costs of health care in general.

During the Reagan administration, attempts were made to cut and control health care costs through the Deficit Reduction Act of 1984. The act called for the mandating of a prospective payment system (PPS), which would be a form of reimbursement to hospitals under Medicare. The purpose of the PPS system was to reduce the costs of Medicare and make hospitals more efficient. Another element of this legislation was the creation of diagnosis-related groups (DRGs), in which illnesses would be classified into one of 468 DRGs, with each category assigned a treatment rate; hospitals would be reimbursed according to these rates. The use of DRGs went into effect in 1987. Another cost-cutting measure during the Reagan administration was the Medicare Catastrophic Coverage Act of 1988. It was repealed by Congress in 1989 because it met with major protests from primarily affluent elderly citizens for the act's requirement that Medicare recipients contribute more to long-term nursing home care.

Health care policies often focus on reducing costs while attempting to ensure access to the elderly and poor. The American Medical Association (AMA) has aggressively opposed most legislation that reduces the costs of health care. AMA is a powerful lobbying force in the U.S. health care industry. Health care in the United States remains primarily a private system. Any attempts by federal or state governments or by public interest groups to bring about comprehensive, government-funded health care are resisted heavily by AMA and other industry lobbies. The issues of access, costs, and quality of health care are policy problems that will continue into the 21st century. The United States remains the only large industrial democracy without a universal health care system for its citizens.

See also: Health: American Medical Association; Diagnosis-related Groups; Health Maintenance Organization Act of 1973; Health Planning and Resources Development Act of 1974

References: Charles Bonser, Eugene B. McGregor Jr., and Clinton V. Oster Jr., *Policy Choices and Public Action* (1996); Theodore Litman and Leonard S. Robins, *Health Politics and Policy* (1997); Theodore K. Marmor, *Understanding Health Care Reform* (1994); Kant Patel and Mark E. Rushefsky,

Health Care Politics and Policy in America (1995); B. Guy Peters, *American Public Policy: Promise and Performance* (1993).

Health Professionals Educational Assistance Acts of 1963 and 1976

To offset the high cost of studying medicine and biomedical research, Congress passed the Health Professionals Educational Assistance Act of 1963. The act was intended to provide assistance to finance graduate education in the health professions, especially to students who wanted to work in research programs. This was the first federal program that offered direct financing for students to attend medical schools. The 1976 act required medical schools to provide training to American medical students who were studying abroad. American medical schools opposed this new provision, and Congress withdrew the requirement for continued financing from the legislation.

See also: Health: Health Policy

References: Theodore J. Litman and Leonard S. Robins, *Health Politics and Policy* (1997).

Health Systems Agencies

Health systems agencies (HSAs) are health planning agencies created under the auspices of the Health Planning and Resources Development Act of 1974. The act created a framework for implementing and planning health care policy. The act created more than 200 HSAs to administer certificate-of-need laws for local areas. Certificate-of-need requirements establish the priorities and needs of local communities regarding their health care requirements. Community needs specify hospital availability and the costs of building or improving hospitals and of health care for communities. The purpose of HSAs was to cut the costs of health care and engage in more realistic community health planning. The HSA concept never worked as designed, and the Health Planning and Resources Development Act of 1974 was abandoned by the Reagan administration in 1983. The HSAs established under the 1974 legislation were eliminated in favor of health maintenance organizations. HSAs were seen by opponents as regulatory agencies that did not provide for the competition necessary to reduce costs and produce efficiency.

See also: Health: Health Planning and Resources Development Act of 1974; Health Policy

References: Theodore Litman and Leonard S. Robins, *Health Politics and Policy* (1997); Dennis J. Palumbo, *Public Policy in America: Government in Action* (1988); Kant Patel and Mark E. Rushefsky, *Health Care Politics and Policy in America* (1995).

Hill-Burton Act

See Health: Health Planning and Resources Development Act of 1974

HIV/AIDS

See Health: Acquired Immunodeficiency Syndrome

Kennedy, Sen. Edward

See Health: Kennedy-Corman Bill

Kennedy-Corman Bill of 1974

U.S. Sen. Edward Kennedy, youngest brother of the assassinated Pres. John F. Kennedy, has been a staunch liberal in the U.S. Senate. Along with his belief in social and poverty programs, Senator Kennedy has been a champion of universal health care legislation. In 1974 he attempted to get passage of a comprehensive health care bill that closely resembled the universal health care system in Canada. The bill proposed that the federal government play a major role in providing universal health insurance to all Americans by replacing all public and private health insurance plans. The underlying philosophy of any universal health care program is that it would be accessible to all, not just to those who are eligible under a certain set of rules or conditions. Kennedy's program was to be financed by payroll taxes and general revenues to the federal government, with no copayments or cost-sharing obligations expected of program recipients. This sweeping approach did not receive the necessary support and was not approved.

A compromise 1974 bill, the Kennedy-Mills bill, never received the required support in Congress. The Kennedy-Mills bill relied on a 4 percent payroll tax to fund the health care plan. The Kennedy-Mills bill had an estimated annual cost of $103 billion a year. In most of the comprehensive health care policy initiatives proposed since 1970, the major issues have been the extraordinary cost for government implementation, the exclusion of the private health care industry from free competition in the health care marketplace, and the opposition of the American Medical Association for any government-controlled or -dominated health insurance proposals.

See also: Health: Health Policy

References: Theodore Litman and Leonard S. Robins, *Health Politics and Policy* (1997); Theodore K. Marmor, *Understanding Health Care Reform* (1994); Dennis J. Palumbo, *Public Policy in America: Government in Action* (1988); Kant Patel and Mark E. Rushefsky, *Health Care Politics and Policy in America* (1995).

Kennedy-Mills Bill of 1974

See Health: Kennedy-Corman Bill of 1974

Kerr-Mills Act of 1960

The Kerr-Mills Act (also known as the Medical Assistance Act) was designed to provide medical assistance to the elderly and medically needy. Recipients included the blind, elderly, low-income, and disabled people. It was a part of a government strategy during the early 1960s to avoid comprehensive health care legislation—and all of the political problems that would invite in targeting key groups designated as "needy." The bill made state participation in the program optional and allowed states to set eligibility requirements. The bill was ineffective and did not reach the target population. In 1963 a Senate subcommittee on the health of the elderly found that only 1 percent of the nation's elderly received benefits and assistance from the program. The failure of this program set the tone for further discussions in Congress about how to fund and provide workable health care programs for the elderly and medically indigent. Congress eventually passed the Medicare program in 1965, which addressed the need for effective and manageable health care programs for the elderly. The Medicaid program, also passed in 1965, targeted the indigent. Both Medicaid and Medicare were amendments to the Social Security Act of 1935.

See also: Health: Health Policy

References: Theodore Litman and Leonard S. Robins, *Health Politics and Policy* (1997); Kant Patel and Mark E. Rushefsky, *Health Care Politics and Policy* (1995); David B. Robertson and Dennis R. Judd, *The Development of American Public Policy: The Structure of Policy Restraint* (1989).

Managed Care

See Health: Health Maintenance Organization Act of 1973

Marine Hospital Service Act of 1798

See Health: Health Policy

Marsee v. U.S. Tobacco

In the battle against cigarette smoking and the use of tobacco products, numerous lawsuits have been filed on behalf of individuals who have suffered serious health problems as a result of tobacco use. In 1985, in *Marsee v. U.S. Tobacco,* a woman filed a lawsuit against a U.S. tobacco company, seeking damages because her son died of oral cancer as a consequence of his prolonged use of oral snuff, a tobacco product. The jury decided on behalf of the tobacco company. This was one of a series of liability suits filed against tobacco companies to make them responsible for the health problems suffered by tobacco users. Since this lawsuit, a public advertising campaign has aggressively tried to educate and inform individuals—especially young people—about the health dangers related to the use of oral snuff and other tobacco products.

See also: Health: Anti-tobacco Policy

References: A. Lee Fritschler and James M. Hoefler, *Smoking and Politics: Policymaking and the Federal Bureaucracy* (1996).

Mississippi v. American Tobacco Company et al.

In the campaign against tobacco use, one tactic has been to sue tobacco companies for health problems caused by their products. In another tactic, states sue tobacco companies to recover tobacco-related health costs. In *Mississippi v. American Tobacco Company et al.,* Mississippi sued to recover smoking-related health care costs. This was part of a pattern by several states to sue or to make legislation allowing states to sue tobacco companies to recover Medicaid payments. Florida passed such a law in 1994 that also prohibited tobacco companies from claiming immunity from liability. Since 1994, 36 states and Puerto Rico have filed Medicaid suits against the tobacco industry. In 1997, the State of Mississippi settled its Medicaid case with the tobacco industry for

$3.4 billion. Florida settled its 1994 Medicaid suit against the tobacco industry for $11.3 billion. In 1998, Texas settled its Medicaid suit against the tobacco industry for a record $14.5 billion.

See also: Health: Anti-tobacco Policy

References: A. Lee Fritschler and James M. Hoefler, *Smoking and Politics: Policymaking and the Federal Bureaucracy* (1996).

Nader, Ralph (b. 1934)

Ralph Nader is a political activist who set the tone during the 1960s for citizen involvement in the political process. Nader wrote *Unsafe at Any Speed,* which exposed the safety problems with the Chevrolet Corvair; he waged a consumer advocacy campaign against the automobile industry and General Motors Corporation to force the industry and the corporation to produce safer, more reliable products. Nader created the public interest group Public Citizen in 1971 as a vehicle for engaging American citizens in activist causes that would enable them to successfully challenge American corporations in the political process. Nader feels that corporations have too much influence over the political process; one way to blunt corporate power is for American citizens to organize against it. Nader's advocacy inspired the development of public interest research groups (PIRGs) throughout the United States. PIRGs engage in research and activism to illustrate and publicize environmental, consumer, labor, health, and business issues that are important to quality of life. In 1996 Nader wrote *No Contest: Corporate Lawyers and the Perversion of Justice in America,* which attacks the role of corporate lawyers and the power of corporations in American politics. Nader was also a candidate for president during the 1992 and 1996 elections. Most recently, Nader has supported the Green Party as a means for citizen activism and political change in American politics.

See also: Health: Consumer Product Safety Act of 1972; Key Concepts: Interest Groups; Public Interest Research Groups

References: J. David Gillespie, *Politics at the Periphery: Third Parties in Two-Party America* (1993); William McGuire and Leslie Wheeler, eds., *American Social Leaders* (1993).

National Cancer Act of 1937

See Health: National Institutes of Health

National Health Insurance

Most Western democracies have national health insurance systems that are low- or no-cost, have universal access, and offer excellent care for citizens at all economic levels. There have been several attempts in Congress to introduce national health insurance; the closest to reach that goal is the Medicare program created in 1965, which serves the elderly and disabled. During Woodrow Wilson's administration, national health insurance was considered, but the onset of World War I, the adoption of national health insurance by the Germans, and the opposition of the American Medical Association prevented any action on national health insurance until the New Deal of the 1930s. In 1939 the Murray-Dingell bill was introduced, but it did not receive the support needed to pass. This has been the case throughout the 20th century regarding national health insurance legislation. Republicans and the American Medical Association (AMA) have managed to mount enough opposition to ensure that national health insurance bills always fail in Congress.

During Pres. Bill Clinton's first term, he introduced the Health Security Act, which would provide comprehensive health insurance based on a system of managed competition. Clinton's plan was not well received and did not receive serious consideration. National health insurance is a difficult proposition in the United States because of the decentralized health care system and the incremental health care policy environment that prevails. AMA has never favored government involvement in the health care industry; AMA has the political resources to influence members of state legislatures and members of Congress to vote against universal health care plans. National health insurance would be a complex, costly enterprise. Because of the structure of American politics, economics, and the current decentralized private health care system, an American national health insurance policy that is universal, low- or no-cost, and easily accessible would require a major structural change in the way we conduct our politics, health care, and business.

See also: Entitlement Programs: Medicaid; Medicare; Health: Health Policy

References: Theodore Litman and Leonard S. Robins, *Health Politics and Policy* (1997); Theodore K. Marmor, *Understanding Health Care Reform* (1994); Kant Patel and Mark E. Rushefsky, *Health Care Politics and Policy in America* (1995).

National Hospital Survey and Construction Act of 1946

See Health: Health Policy

National Institutes of Health

The federal government funds agencies, institutions, and research groups that contribute and lend support to aspects of health care policy. One of those is the National Institutes of Health (NIH), founded in 1930 to research the cause, prevention, and cure of diseases. Much of the work is biomedical research. Recently, NIH activity has focused on research in HIV and AIDS.

See also: Health: Acquired Immunodeficiency Syndrome; Health Policy

References: Charles Bonser, Eugene B. McGregor Jr., and Clinton V. Oster Jr., *Policy Choices and Public Action* (1996); Kant Patel and Mark E. Rushefsky, *Health Care Politics and Policy in America* (1995).

Occupational Safety and Health Act of 1970

The Occupational Safety and Health Act of 1970 created the Occupational Safety and Health Administration (OSHA), which is responsible for ensuring health and safety in the workplace through the setting of standards. In setting health and safety standards, OSHA was required to make certain they would not have disruptive effects on the whole industry. Industries that opposed OSHA sought to apply cost-benefit analysis to its standards; Pres. Ronald Reagan supported the cost-benefit requirements. OSHA was eventually required to weigh the costs to industries adopting new workplace health and safety standards against the health benefits that would be derived from the standards.

The agency revoked and reduced thousands of its original safety regulations, and its regulations are frequently challenged. A so-called second-generation regulator, OSHA does not have the regulatory authority it once did; businesses and industries continue to be wary of OSHA regulations, and the unsupportive regulatory environment continues to challenge the OSHA mission.

See also: Economics: Deregulation; Health: Occupational Safety and Health Policy

References: Leif H. Carter and Christine B. Harrington, *Administrative Law and Politics: Cases and Comments* (1991); Dennis J. Palumbo, *Public Policy in America: Government in Action* (1988).

Occupational Safety and Health Administration

See Health: Occupational Safety and Health Act of 1970

Occupational Safety and Health Policy

Occupational safety and health policy did not begin with the passage of the Occupational Safety and Health Act in 1970. Although that act established federal regulations and remedies for widespread problems related to industrial accidents, the issue of workplace safety and health dates to the mid-19th century. Factory conditions for workers were a serious problem during the 19th century and the issue worsened with the growth of the population of workers and industrialization.

The railroad and mining industries have always served as examples of dangerous and risky work situations. During the early 20th century, the railroads and mining industries were major sources of industrial accidents, and working conditions in both industries were extremely hazardous. The growth of unionization during the 1920s drew increasing public and government attention to working conditions, and the issue of industrial accidents was thrust onto the public agenda as an issue for labor negotiations. When the National Labor Relations Act in 1934 was passed, conditions and worker health and safety became part of most collective bargaining discussions. During this period states became more involved in establishing workers' compensation policies that focused on assisting injured workers.

The Occupational Safety and Health Act of 1970 created the Occupational Safety and Health Administration (OSHA), which generated policy directed at improving health and safety in the workplace. OSHA met with substantial resistance and made many errors in its first ten years of existence. OSHA policies drew so many complaints that some members of Congress introduced bills to amend OSHA's authority. OSHA aggressively pursued its charge to improve worker health and safety during the early 1970s and issued many infractions against industries for violations of health and safety policies. During its first ten years of operation, OSHA was forced to retract many of its claims of health and safety violations.

OSHA has continued its regulatory course but has drawn back from its initial aggressiveness. The agency's charge has not changed, but its methods for enforcing health and safety codes have been modified to preserve the agency's credibility. OSHA continues to issue violations of health and safety codes, but the regulatory environment has changed since the 1970s, and the trend during Congress in the 1990s was to move toward deregulation and away from government intervention in the workplace.

See also: Health: Occupational Safety and Health Act of 1970; Labor: Industrial Accident Commission of California; National Labor Relations Act of 1935

References: Philippe Nonet, *Administrative Justice* (1969); Dennis J. Palumbo, *Public Policy in America: Government in Action* (1988).

Pepper, Claude (1900–1989)

Claude Pepper was a member of the U.S. Senate and the House of Representatives. Most of his time in Congress was spent as a member of the House of Representatives representing Florida. Claude Pepper is significant in the context of public policy because of his strong and unwavering support for older Americans and the poor. Pepper was a staunch advocate for issues related to health insurance and health care for older Americans. He was one of few senators to serve in the House of Representatives after failing to win reelection to the U.S. Senate.

Pepper's upbringing had something to do with his advocacy for the poor and disadvantaged. He was born into poverty and worked his way through the University of Alabama. He professed to be a New Dealer in his approach to politics before the onset of the New Deal programs of the Roosevelt administration during the 1930s. Pepper was a different kind of southern politician, supporting liberalism and racial moderation as a young man. Early during his political career, Pepper favored a minimum-wage law, universal health insurance, and labor unions. This support alerted opponents in Congress, and Pepper became one of the early targets of McCarthyism in 1950. Claude Pepper served 26 years in the House of Representatives and 14 years in the Senate. He was a defender of social security and Medicare and led the fight to eliminate the required retirement age (65 years). Pepper's activism in support of Social Security and health care for older Americans established him as a champion for the elderly; he was able to mobilize support from various interest groups who supported health care and Social Security. The U.S. Bipartisan Commission on Comprehensive Health Care was known as the Pepper Commission in honor of Pepper's advocacy for health care.

See also: Entitlement Programs: Social Security Act of 1935; Health: Health Policy

References: Claude Pepper with Hays Gorey, *Pepper: Eyewitness to a Century* (1987).

Preferred Provider Organizations (PPOs)

See Health: Health Maintenance Organization Act of 1973

Sheppard-Towner Act of 1921

The Sheppard-Towner Act added to an evolving package of legislation that focused on children's health and creating and funding community health centers for women and children. It was not a major piece of legislation, but it did support health care for women and children who were disadvantaged and thus not ensured of adequate health care. This legislation came at a time when health care was still considered a private matter and not an area of public responsibility. The federal government provided grants-in-aid to state health agencies for maternal and child health care. The American Medical Association opposed this legislation; the act passed into oblivion and lost its funding by 1929.

See also: Health: Health Policy

References: Theodore Litman and Leonard S. Robins, *Health Politics and Policy* (1997); Dennis J. Palumbo, *Public Policy in America: Government in Action* (1988).

Shilts, Randy (1951–1994)

Randy Shilts was a journalist and the leading chronicler of gay life and the AIDS epidemic. He wrote one of the major works on the spread of the AIDS epidemic, *And the Band Played On: Politics, People, and the AIDS Epidemic*, which was published in 1987. Shilts resided in San Francisco, California, and wrote for the *San Francisco Chronicle*. One of his assignments was to write about gay life and the subsequent

AIDS epidemic. Shilts also wrote a book about discrimination of gays and lesbians in the U.S. military, *Conduct Unbecoming,* which was published in 1993. Shilts's first book was *The Mayor of Castro Street: The Life and Times of Harvey Milk,* which told the story of Harvey Milk, a gay San Francisco supervisor who was shot and killed along with the mayor of San Francisco, George Moscone, in 1979 by a disgruntled former supervisor, Dan White. Shilts wrote newspaper articles during the 1980s about the gay bathhouse culture in San Francisco, and he criticized the gay establishment in San Francisco for not acting sooner against the spread of AIDS through unrestricted bathhouse sexual escapades. Shilts died from AIDS in 1994.

See also: Health: Acquired Immunodeficiency Syndrome

References: J.V. Smith, "Writer Randy Shilts Dies: Chronicled Rise of AIDS" (1994).

Soldiers and Sailors Civil Relief Act of 1918

See Health: Health Policy

Housing

Chronology

1913 Federal Reserve Act helped liberalize prohibitions against real estate lending by nationally chartered banks, allowing commercial banks to provide real estate loans in urban areas.

1918 Soldiers and Sailors Civil Relief Act forbade eviction of military dependents from nonluxury rental housing.

1933 Homeowners Refinancing Act created the Homeowners Loan Corporation to provide emergency loans to homeowners in danger of foreclosure.

1934 National Housing Act created the Federal Housing Administration and introduced federal regulation and support of housing credit systems through Federal Housing Administration insurance.

1954 Housing Act focused housing efforts from urban redevelopment to urban renewal. The act also encouraged comprehensive planning and required that cities develop plans to attack urban decay.

1968 The Housing Act encouraged mortgage insurance for home purchases in blighted areas. It also required that housing be insured for disadvantaged people and created the Government National Mortgage Association (Ginnie Mae).

1974 The Housing and Community Development Act passed, creating a block-grant program directed at new construction. It also emphasized direct subsidy of tenants' rent as the basis for assistance and federal subsidy of mortgages for people of moderate income.

1987 McKinney Act expanded emergency food and shelter grants administered by the Federal Emergency Management Agency. The act also funded Emergency Shelter grants and other programs creating shelter space.

1990 The National Affordable Housing Act created a tenant-based assistance program through vouchers and certificates using existing standard housing. Gave control of the housing program to local governments to create a central strategy of home ownership to assist low-income households and integrate social services with housing programs.

Department of Housing and Urban Development

In 1965 Congress passed the Department of Housing and Urban Development Act, which created the Department of Housing and Urban Development

(HUD). Robert Weaver was the first secretary of HUD. This federal executive agency was created to develop and administer policy to affect the nation's housing needs, develop and rehabilitate urban communities, and promote improvement in city streets and parks. The agency grew out of the previous Housing and Home Finance Agency. The agency has some 13,000 employees who work in the following subagencies: the Assistant Secretary for Community Planning and Development; the Government National Mortgage Association; the Assistant Secretary for Housing; and the Assistant Secretary for Fair Housing and Equal Opportunity.

The federal government's initial involvement in housing policy came in 1934 when the Congress passed the National Housing Act, designed to aid the housing needs of families during the Great Depression. The act came as a response to the widespread loss of jobs and income during the Depression; foreclosures and evictions had become commonplace as borrowers and creditors responded to the national economic crisis. The National Housing Act of 1934 created the Federal Housing Administration (FHA) to help broaden the segment of the American population that could afford a home. FHA provided mortgage insurance but did not offer a significant amount of assistance to the poor who could not afford to purchase homes. The Housing Act of 1949 set the long-range goal of "a decent home and living environment for every American family." This was a challenging rhetorical statement for national housing policy to live up to. Major funding and a national commitment to housing, especially for low-income families, came during the Johnson administration when the Housing Act of 1968 was passed. The act established the Government National Mortgage Association (Ginnie Mae) to expand availability of mortgage funds for moderate-income families using government guaranteed, mortgage-backed securities. Pres. Richard M. Nixon halted this bold thrust to stimulate housing construction and financing for the poor when, in 1973, he called a moratorium on housing and community development assistance. The moratorium reversed most of the goals of the 1968 act.

The current state of affairs in HUD is one of "reinventing" the agency and its purpose. The agency's budget suffered severely during the 1980s as part of the budget cuts aimed at social programs. Congress has not shown a willingness to reinvigorate HUD programs. During the Reagan and Bush administrations, HUD was rocked with scandal when its secretary, Samuel Pierce (appointed in 1981 by Reagan), used HUD programs and leadership positions as sources of political favors for Republican Party supporters. Congress has been reluctant to appropriate resources to HUD programs because of the agency's dismal record in accomplishing established goals and living up to commitments. HUD's goals during the Clinton administration have been to demonstrate commitments to community, to families, to providing an economic lift in society, to reciprocity and balancing individual rights and responsibilities, and to reducing racial separation and variations in income in American life.

See also: Housing: Federal Housing Administration; Housing Policy

References: R. Allen Hays, *The Federal Government and Urban Housing: Ideology and Change in Public Policy* (1995); Gail Radford, *Modern Housing for America* (1996).

Federal Housing Administration

Housing for Americans was a serious problem during the 1930s, and the federal government acted during the New Deal era to positively affect the situation. The National Housing Act of 1934 was developed to aid families in need of adequate housing. Loss of jobs and income with little hope for improvement brought about large-scale evictions and foreclosures. This resulted in a drop in housing construction, which led to unemployment in the building trades. The Federal Housing Administration (FHA) created a mortgage insurance program to aid American families of modest means. This program benefited middle- and working-class families but segregated African Americans and refused to underwrite mortgages in central urban neighborhoods. FHA helped many Americans, but African Americans were not served effectively by FHA programs.

FHA changed its treatment of African Americans with the passage of the Housing Act of 1968, which relaxed restrictions on FHA loans for homes in blighted urban areas. The act also created the Government National Mortgage Association (Ginnie Mae), which is a government-sponsored, low-income mortgage buyer. The act also created programs that subsidized mortgage payments to people of modest income who wanted to buy a home. The Federal National Mortgage Association (Fannie Mae) is another program under FHA that supports mortgages for moderate-income purchasers of homes. FHA also administers public housing programs for low-income populations.

FHA during the 1990s has focused on minority and first-time homebuyers. FHA's major role is to help individuals become homeowners and to improve neighborhoods.

See also: Housing: Housing Policy

References: R. Allen Hays, *The Federal Government and Urban Housing: Ideology and Change in Public Policy* (1995).

Fuller, Millard

See Housing: Habitat For Humanity

Habitat for Humanity

During the early 1980s the problem of housing for the poor and disadvantaged became especially acute. Throughout the 20th century, in fact, the issues of housing for the poor and public housing have been a concern for the federal government as well as local governments. During the early 1980s, however, the homeless, the thousands of Americans who had no shelter of their own and who in large numbers resided on urban streets or under the cover of bushes and trees, came to the forefront of the debate. In cities throughout the United States, homeless people reside in public plazas or near city streets.

In 1976 Millard Fuller founded Habitat for Humanity. Fuller was a millionaire who felt a moral obligation to help solve a public problem. Habitat for Humanity is a worldwide, nonprofit Christian housing ministry that is run by volunteers who have built homes together with 65,000 families in more than 1,300 U.S. cities and other countries. Habitat for Humanity is among the top twenty homebuilders in the United States.

Jimmy Carter, former president of the United States, and his wife, Rosalyn, have been regular participants and volunteers with Habitat for Humanity projects in the United States and overseas. Habitat for Humanity is an example of a nonprofit, independent project that was developed to solve an immense public policy problem—inadequate housing. Under the Habitat for Humanity philosophy, families help build the houses alongside volunteers. This has been a very successful program throughout the world.

See also: Housing: Housing Policy

References: Millard Fuller, *A Simple, Decent Place to Live* (1995); R. Allen Hays, *The Federal Government and Urban Housing: Ideology and Change in Public Policy* (1995).

Home Owners Refinancing Act of 1933

In 1933 the Home Owners Refinancing Act became one of the New Deal programs to help and protect homeowners. The act created the Home Owners Loan Corporation to issue bonds to refinance nonfarm mortgages. The Home Owners Loan Corporation eventually refinanced 20 percent of all mortgaged urban private homes. The immediate thrust of the act was to provide emergency loans to homeowners in imminent danger of foreclosure. The long-term effect of the act was to restructure the way people borrowed money for home purchases. This was a successful program that came under the authority of the Federal Housing Administration. This legislation helped middle- and working-class homeowners and would-be homeowners but did little for those who were too poor to own or purchase a home.

See also: Economics: New Deal; Housing: Housing Policy

References: R. Allen Hays, *The Federal Government and Urban Housing: Ideology and Change in Public Policy* (1995); Gail Radford, *Modern Housing for America* (1996).

Homeless Policy

See Housing: Homelessness

Homelessness

Between 1970 and 1988 the number of poor people increased by almost 26 percent, from 25.4 million to 31.9 million. The U.S. Bureau of the Census reported that by 1996 36.5 million Americans lived in poverty. Poverty and joblessness among low-skilled and undereducated workers and the decline in public assistance have contributed to the rise of homelessness. Declining wages means much of the poverty-stricken population cannot afford housing. The inability to find affordable housing and the inadequacy of housing assistance programs have contributed to homelessness during the 1990s. Other factors include lack of affordable health care, eviction resulting from an illness, domestic violence, mental illness, and chemical dependency and drug abuse.

Many cities across the nation have been forced to create shelters to accommodate shifting homeless populations; rural areas have few or no shelters for the homeless. Homelessness is a temporary circumstance, not a permanent condition, which makes it difficult to accurately count the number of homeless people. There is widespread disagreement among all levels of government as to the proper role of government in this very difficult policy area.

See also: Entitlement Programs: Welfare Policy; Housing: Housing Policy

References: R. Allen Hays, *The Federal Government and Urban Housing: Ideology and Change in Public Policy* (1995); Paul Koegel et al., "The Causes of Homelessness," in *Homelessness in America* (1996); Laura Waxman and Remy Trupin, *A Status Report on Hunger and Homelessness in America's Cities* (1997).

Homestead Act of 1862

The Homestead Act was one of a series of laws passed during the Civil War to stimulate the national economy. The act offered any citizen (or any alien who intended to become a citizen) who was the head of a family 160 acres after five years of continuous residence and payment of a registration fee of $10. The Morrill Land Grant Act of 1862 granted each Union state 30,000 acres for each senator and representative in Congress to endow an agricultural college. The Pacific Railway Act of 1862 authorized a central transcontinental railroad, loaned it money, and granted it a right-of-way and five alternate sections of land on each side of the railroad for every mile built. Two other acts of Congress—the Immigration Act of 1864 and the Department of Agriculture Act of 1862—completed the Civil War economic development proposals. Each of these acts was successful in that they stimulated the economy and made land available for private and commercial development.

See also: Economics: Economic Development Administration

References: Joseph R. Conlin, *The American Past: A Survey of American History* (1993).

Housing and Community Development Act of 1974

This legislation was a departure from previous housing assistance policy in that it focused on providing a direct subsidy of a tenant's rent as the basis for assistance. The act had broad eligibility requirements; the specific provisions for supplementing rent and housing payments are referred to as "Section 8" provisions. The act tried to limit very-low-income people from using the program, and it attempted to avoid concentrating poor people in housing project developments.

The act also required the development of a Housing Assistance Plan to make local communities responsible for planning their community's housing needs. The Community Development Block Grant Program, part of the Housing and Community Development Act, completed the shift of responsibility for local housing needs and planning from the federal level to communities. This was a successful program that engaged local communities in making important decisions on local housing needs. The Reagan administration attempted to impose dramatic cuts in the program during the early 1980s, which exacerbated the homeless problem. The Clinton administration has attempted to revive many of the features of the original legislation and block grants. Much of the emphasis of the Clinton plan has been on reforming the Department of Housing and Urban Development by making the agency financially stable and to reestablish local public housing authorities to promote their flexibility in planning and decisionmaking.

See also: Housing: Housing Policy

References: R. Allen Hays, *The Federal Government and Urban Housing: Ideology and Change in Public Policy* (1995).

Housing Policy

Interest in housing policy began during the late 19th century, when advocates called for housing improvements to relieve the pressures of tenement life in the nation's cities. Rapid urbanization during the 19th century, as many Americans and immigrants left the farms for factory jobs in urban areas, caused massive population shifts to cities; local governments were unable to accommodate the migration.

The federal government's role in providing housing did not begin in earnest until the Depression. Until the Great Depression, the general attitude was that the federal government had no formal responsibility. States and local governments were seen as the ones to aid the poor and those without adequate housing. Two major New Deal programs changed the federal government's role. The National Housing Act of 1934 was designed to aid families in need of housing. The Home Owners Loan Corporation provided emergency loans to homeowners in danger of foreclosure. This program introduced long-term, low-down payment mortgage. As a result, more Americans were able to purchase and keep homes.

The passage of the National Industrial Recovery Act also changed the government's posture toward housing. The act established a federal housing program through the auspices of the Public Works Administration. The Housing Division assisted in the construction of housing for the poor; its focus was on the development of urban residential environments. The Housing Division constructed 51 projects in 36 American cities. Many of the sites were in former slum areas, which made it easier to acquire land inexpensively for development. An important element of the Housing Division's projects was the promise to set aside one-third of the construction projects for African American tenants. This was unique among New Deal programs because many federal and state legislators deliberately excluded African Americans from the benefits of most New Deal programs. The Housing Division also demonstrated concern for architectural suitability in its housing projects, and the Public Works Administration received critical acclaim for its attention to aesthetic appeal. The Federal Housing Administration (FHA) was also created in 1934 by the National Housing Act to provide home loans and to finance construction of new homes.

After World War II, Veterans Administration home loan programs stimulated the housing market and made it possible for more Americans than ever to own homes. The Housing Act of 1949 established the long-term goal of a decent home for every American family. FHA lasted beyond the Depression years, unlike the Housing Division of the Public Works Administration, and during the 1960s the Federal Housing Administration turned its attention to urban housing problems to solve the problems of the urban poor who were in need of better housing. The Housing Act of 1961 devoted $6.1 billion for housing programs. The Housing Act of 1968 authorized programs for creating opportunities for mortgage insurance in blighted urban areas and targeted the disadvantaged in central cities for housing programs. The act also created the Federal National Mortgage Association (Fannie Mae) to buy mortgages on higher-risk, low-income housing projects. The act also offered a subsidy of mortgage payments to people with low incomes who wanted to purchase homes.

During the 1960s a unique alliance took place between the National Association of Home Builders and the federal Housing and Home Finance Agency. This combined set of groups became in 1966 the Department of Housing and Urban Development. The federal strategy for improving low-cost housing was made up of three elements: FHA single-family mortgage insurance; public housing; and programs that offered direct subsidies to private builders. During the Nixon administration, much of the progress was stopped, and the federal role in housing changed. The Reagan years were a time of massive federal budget cuts; with them, housing programs were also cut. After 1980 homelessness became a major public and social policy issue. The Clinton administration has emphasized urban economic development. Urban empowerment zones stimulated housing and urban development during the late 1990s. A renewed federal commitment to housing is not likely during the early 21st century.

See also: Housing: Department of Housing and Urban Development; Federal Housing Administration; Homelessness

References: R. Allen Hays, *The Federal Government and Urban Housing: Ideology and Change in Public Policy* (1995); Nathaniel Keith, *Politics and the Housing Crisis* (1973); Gail Radford, *Modern Housing for America* (1996).

National Affordable Housing Act of 1990

Affordable housing for Americans has been a policy goal since the New Deal era of the Roosevelt administration. The 1990 National Affordable Housing Act came after years of congressional distrust of housing programs following major problems in the administration of housing programs by top officials in the Department Housing and Urban Development.

The 1990 program has four major provisions: (1) a voucher-assisted housing program was made available to support tenancy in existing housing units; (2) housing programs would be locally controlled and operated through nonprofit community development corporations; (3) the strategy focused on home ownership as a goal for helping low-income households; and (4) other relevant social services would be integrated into housing programs to ensure comprehensive family support efforts in housing. Communities that participate in this program are also required to submit a Comprehensive Housing Affordability Strategy that considers a market strategy for developing housing needs, a consideration of housing quality and conditions, and the development of action plans to implement housing programs. This would be a broad-based program that invited participation from various government, nonprofit, and private housing officials to encourage public participation in the setting of community housing needs.

See also: Housing: Housing Policy

References: R. Allen Hays, *The Federal Government and Urban Housing: Ideology and Change in Public Policy* (1995); Gail Radford, *Modern Housing for America* (1996).

National Housing Act of 1934

See Housing: Housing Policy

Labor

Chronology

1883 Pendleton Act created civil service and merit systems in promotion and hiring in federal government.

1890 Sherman Antitrust Act prohibited labor actions as restraint of trade and subject to tort action.

1913 Lloyd-LaFollette Act moved toward due process in the handling of government employees. The act gave employees threatened with dismissal the right to respond to charges.

1932 Norris-LaGuardia Act restricted use of injunctions in labor disputes and made "yellow dog" contracts unenforceable in federal courts.

1933 Federal Emergency Relief Act passed, creating the Federal Emergency Relief Administration to help states care for the unemployed.

1933 National Industrial Recovery Act instituted collective bargaining in labor and management relations.

1934 Civil Works Relief Act passed, creating the Civil Works Administration.

1935 Wagner Act (National Labor Relations Act) created National Labor Relations Board and guaranteed right to workers to collectively bargain and organize.

1943 Smith-Connally Act gave power to president to take over industries during time of national emergency.

1946 Full Employment Act was passed to guarantee full employment during the post–World War II years.

1964 Economic Opportunity Act protected workers from discrimination because of race and sex.

American Federation of Labor–Congress of Industrial Organizations

During the 1880s the American Federation of Labor (AFL) was a loose collection of craft unions whose members were predominantly skilled workers. Between 1863 and 1873 many national trade (craft) unions developed. Early attempts at consolidating the various unions failed when the National Labor Union collapsed in 1872. This was a period of intense labor activity as industrialization took hold in urban centers. In 1886 the AFL was created as a federation of craft unions. Led by its first president,

Samuel Gompers, the organization sought higher wages, an eight-hour workday, and the right to collective bargaining. By 1904 the AFL had 1,676,200 out of 2,067,000 total union members.

During the early Depression years in the 1930s, labor activity was directed at improved work conditions and pay for nonskilled workers. The AFL had been slow in organizing industrial workers; when it did organize industrial workers, the AFL favored the interests of craft workers over the interests and demands of industrial workers. In November 1935, John L. Lewis, president of the United Mine Workers of America, and Sidney Hillman, of the garment unions, and other industrial union leaders formed the Committee for Industrial Organization (CIO) within the AFL to organize industrial workers. In November 1938 the CIO left the AFL and became the Congress of Industrial Organizations, with Lewis serving as president. The CIO was known as more radical, aggressive, and politically and socially conscious of the large labor organizations in the United States. By 1955 the AFL and CIO had put aside their differences over ideology and the direction of the labor organization and merged into a powerful, 15 million member organization. During the late 1990s the organization was a voluntary federation of more than 100 national and international unions operating with more than 13 million members. The AFL-CIO of the 1990s was a powerful, organized, well-funded organization that lobbied on behalf of working people.

The AFL-CIO does much of its interest-group activity and advocacy on behalf of American workers through its political action committee (PAC). The organization is able to appeal to, access, and influence candidates because of its substantial resource base. The AFL-CIO provides political campaign support through money contributions to candidates and causes that will benefit workers. During national congressional or presidential elections, candidates deliberately address issues related to working people with the hope that the AFL-CIO will provide campaign contributions to candidates. The AFL-CIO has traditionally supported candidates that favor legislation promoting the needs of workers.

See also: Labor: Labor Policy

References: Susan Welch et al., *Understanding American Government* (1997).

Child Labor Laws

As the industrial revolution took hold during the mid-19th century, waves of immigrants came to America in search of dreams, fortunes, and opportunities for better lives. Lewis Hine, a photographer commissioned by the U.S. Immigration and Naturalization Service during the 1880s to keep a photographic record of immigrants passing through Ellis Island, New York, noticed scores of child immigrants. After his commission expired, Hine followed immigrant families to factory towns in the Northeast and Atlantic Seaboard to photograph conditions of work and life for child immigrants. What Hine saw and discovered astounded and disturbed him. He went on to develop a photographic record. As a result, Hine and others joined forces to notify state and local governments about the deplorable conditions of child labor. Most of the early efforts resulted in local and state ordinances, but child labor advocates frequently encountered resistance because of the interest of communities to protect the rights of entrepreneurs in factory towns. In 1851 New Jersey enacted a child labor law that restricted employment of minors to ten-hour workdays in cotton, wool, silk, paper, glass, and flax factories. The law also set the age floor at ten years. Utah created the Utah Smelter Acts in 1896, which limited the floor at 14 years in any mine or smelter in Utah.

Hine and others had some success in alerting local and state governments to the issues of child labor, but at the outset of World War I in 1914 many of their claims fell on deaf ears in favor of the interests of production of war materiel. No national legislation was developed in the area of child labor until 1938.

Congress then passed the Fair Labor Standards Act of 1938, restricting work done by children under 16 and establishing a minimum wage and maximum hours for all workers—adults and children. Congress placed legal liability on businesses by banning the shipment of goods illegally produced by children. In 1939 a new series of federal regulations were developed to allow 14- and 15-year-olds to do specific, nonhazardous jobs. In 1949 Congress prohibited oppressive child labor in addition to the shipment of goods they produced. Parents were no longer allowed to employ their own children under 16 in occupations considered hazardous. Much of the subsequent federal child labor regulations focused on children working on farms. In 1990 the U.S. Department of Labor began an investigative program called Child Watch to monitor illegally employed minors. In 1997 some 100,000 children between the ages of 16 and 17 were employed illegally. That same year, some 60,000 children under 14 years of age were employed illegally.

See also: Labor: Hine, Lewis W.; Labor Policy

References: Sigmund Nosow and William Form, *Man, Work, and Society* (1962); Dennis J. Palumbo, *Public Policy in America: Government in Action* (1988).

Civil Service

A civil service system is one in which government employment is based on merit and the premise that similar employees performing like functions should be treated and paid the same. The British civil service system served as the model for the American civil service system that was adopted in the Pendleton Act of 1883. The impetus for the United States to reform its system of hiring and staffing in the federal government came when Pres. James Garfield was assassinated by Charles Guiteau, who was upset because he was not appointed to the patronage position of American consul to France. Congress was in the middle of discussions about reforming the spoils system that dominated government when Garfield was assassinated. The Pendleton Act created the U.S. civil service system, replacing patronage with a nonpartisan, career employment system based on merit. The act also created the U.S. Civil Service Commission to recruit employees and fill vacancies through open, competitive examinations.

The purpose of a civil service system is to ensure that merit guides hiring, staffing, and promotions in government. All states have varying types of civil service systems. Local and city governments have also adopted civil service models in hiring, staffing, and promotions. In 1978 Pres. Jimmy Carter encouraged Congress to reform the U.S. civil service system, resulting in the Civil Service Reform Act of 1978. The act abolished the old Civil Service Commission and replaced it with two new agencies: the Office of Personnel Administration and the Merit Systems Protection Board. The act also tried to improve the productivity of managers and supervisors in the federal government. It also established the Senior Executive Service, which would make use of a corps of 8,000 federal executives in mobile troubleshooting and consulting positions throughout the federal government. This program has not met with the success that was hoped for upon its creation. The American civil service system has as its ideal the strength of merit-based hiring, staffing, and promotions.

See also: Labor: Civil Service Reform Act of 1978

References: Fred A. Kramer, *Dynamics of Public Bureaucracy: An Introduction to Public Management* (1981); Ronald E. Pynn, *American Politics: Changing Expectations* (1993).

Civil Service Reform Act of 1978

One of Pres. Jimmy Carter's priorities during the four years of his administration was to reform the U.S. civil service system. In 1978 Congress passed the Civil Service Reform Act to eliminate the old U.S. Civil Service Commission, create the Office of Personnel Management, establish the Merit Systems Protection Board, and institute the new Senior Executive Service. A major element of the act was to establish productivity improvement among senior executives, managers, and supervisors as a measure for advancement and merit-pay increases. This new emphasis on performance appraisal measures was consistent with the reform initiatives in the act and was designed to decentralize personnel decisionmaking authority, separate the personnel executive and the merit protection functions, and establish links between compensation and performance. It was hoped that the law would strengthen public personnel management at all levels of government and reassert the importance of the merit principle in staffing, compensation, advancement, and retention based on the employee's ability, education, skills, experience, and job performance. Many of the goals of merit-based hiring set in the Civil Service Reform Act of 1978 were subverted during the Reagan administration during attempts to place politically reliable personnel in positions of leadership in federal agencies that were obligated to apply merit principles in hiring and promotions. The Senior Executive Service ideals were never realized because of the complexity of moving federal executives around from agency to agency without proper notice, the absence of agency or executive interest and commitment, and the general reluctance of senior agency executives to take on new and ambiguous assignments.

See also: Labor: Civil Service; Office of Personnel Management

References: Fred A. Kramer, *Dynamics of Public Bureaucracy: An Introduction to Public Management* (1981).

Civil Works Emergency Relief Act of 1934

In February 1934 Congress passed the Civil Works Emergency Relief Act to provide funds for civil works projects and relief under the Federal Emergency Relief Administration. This program became the Works Progress Administration in 1935 and was responsible for placing 2,500,000 unemployed people to work by January 1935. This program was a part of Pres. Franklin D. Roosevelt's New Deal. An outgrowth of this act was the Civil Works Administration (CWA), also established by President Roosevelt. Harry Hopkins was the administrator for CWA, and he was assigned the task of creating jobs for millions of unemployed Americans from a budget of almost $1 billion. When CWA was inaugurated, its managers proclaimed a goal of giving employment to 4 million people within 30 days; that goal was reached in 60. This was the largest public employment project in history and was created with astounding rapidity. CWA jobs included repair and maintenance of roads and highways, building and repairing of schools and public buildings, the developing of public playgrounds, and the hiring of more than 50,000 teachers to staff adult education courses in towns and communities across the United States.

CWA was criticized by private business owners and local business councils as wasteful and unnecessary. CWA was highly popular with the ranks of the unemployed. It lasted until March 1934, when it was subsumed under the Federal Emergency Relief Administration. President Roosevelt was sensitive to claims that CWA was a drain on the federal budget, and he allowed it to be merged, transferring other projects to state and local administrations. It did not function as successfully under state and local control because of the competing interests and criticisms of local and state business organizations. CWA programs that emerged out of the Civil Works Emergency Relief Act were just one example of the federal government's response to desperate economic conditions caused by the Great Depression.

See also: Economics: New Deal; Labor: Federal Emergency Relief Act of 1993

References: Robert Goldston, *The Great Depression: The United States in the Thirties* (1968).

Coal Mine Health and Safety Act of 1969

The Coal Mine Health and Safety Act was passed by Congress in 1969. It required that better working conditions be present in the mines, specifically regarding roof and wall collapses, dust and methane control, electrical equipment and mechanical safety, increased monitoring of safety requirements, sampling of air quality, and stricter enforcement of safety regulations. The coal mining industry had been one of the most difficult and dangerous industries ever. During the early part of the 20th century safety was frequently left to chance, unregulated by national or state governments. The average number of coal mining fatalities ranged between 2,000 and 3,000 per year until 1931, when these fatalities declined following unionization in the mines. The number of fatalities was down to 500 per year by 1953. Safety in the mines had little to do with the decline in fatalities by 1953, however; the actual reason for the reduction was that fewer people were working the mines.

The 1969 act is an example of congressional action to remedy problems of health and safety in the workplace. Mine safety regulations historically have been flaunted by companies; inspection and enforcement were lax, corruption in inspection practices was common, and miners were willing to risk health and safety for the sake of steady employment. Congress has also been sensitive to claims by the coal industry that safety regulations lead to loss of jobs. With the pressure from environmental groups to improve national air quality by reducing the burning of fossil fuels, which leads to reduction on the reliance on coal as a fuel source, coal industry lobbyists today claim that the industry is under attack. The Coal Mine Health and Safety Act has had mixed success. The numbers of coal mining–related injuries and fatalities have been reduced significantly since 1969, but black lung disease and maintenance of health standards for workers remain problems for the coal industry.

See also: Environment: Environmental Policy

References: Dennis J. Palumbo, *Public Policy in America: Government in Action* (1988).

Comparable Worth

The term *comparable worth* means equal pay for equal work. The term generally applies to the matter of gender equality in the workplace. Comparable worth is based on a person receiving equal pay for different jobs that require equal levels of skill, training, respectability, and responsibility. The discussion of equal pay began during the 20th century, with the growth of labor unions and the diversification of the American workforce. The initial challenges for equal pay were based on discriminatory policies and activities directed toward African American workers. These challenges finally were met in 1964 with the passage of the Civil Rights Act, which laid the groundwork for correcting discrimination in the workplace.

In 1963 Congress passed the Equal Pay Act, which provided wage protection to some female workers; it was not a comprehensive bill that would aid all female workers. Congress amended the Equal Pay Act in 1972 to include certain professions, but equal pay has yet to become reality for all women. A wage gap between men and women still exists, with males earning 20–30 percent more than women (based on different wage levels). This devaluation of women in the labor marketplace places them at an economic disadvantage, which for single mothers is especially difficult to overcome. Equal pay and comparable worth will continue to be a major labor issue during the 21st century.

See also: Civil Rights: Civil Rights Acts; Labor: Equal Pay Act of 1963

References: Clarke E. Cochran et al., *American Public Policy: An Introduction* (1996); David Edwards and Alessandra Lippucci, *Practicing American Politics: An Introduction to American Government* (1998).

Comprehensive Employment and Training Act of 1973

In 1969 Pres. Richard M. Nixon introduced "new federalism," a plan to decentralize federal responsibilities to the states. One of the programs was the Comprehensive Employment and Training Act of 1973 (CETA), designed to streamline and decentralize federally sponsored, grant-based employment programs. CETA became a publicly subsidized employment program that permitted state and local governments to use federal CETA funds to create public jobs. CETA programs at the state and local levels grew rapidly; in 1975 CETA spent $4.5 billion on public employment and funded 725,000 jobs.

CETA programs were implemented during the mid-1970s, when local governments were strapped; many city governments converted their staff workers to CETA employment with CETA funding. In some city governments, CETA funds were used to fill patronage positions. This was not the intent of the original CETA bill, and the program came under heavy criticism. When Ronald Reagan was elected president in 1980, he quickly dismantled the public-jobs program, shifting responsibility for funding to state jurisdictions and engaging the private sector in job creation and training. In 1982 the Job Training Partnership Act (JTPA) was passed, incorporating many of the private job-training aspects of the previous CETA legislation.

See also: Labor: Employment Policy

References: James E. Anderson, *Public Policymaking* (1997); B. Guy Peters, *American Public Policy: Promise and Performance* (1993); David B. Robertson and Dennis R. Judd, *The Development of American Public Policy: The Structure of Policy Restraint* (1989).

Department of Labor

Congress created the Department of Labor in 1913 to foster, promote, and develop the welfare of working people. Congress also felt that the department should aid in improving working conditions and opportunities for profitable employment for Americans. In 1903 the Department of Labor was a branch of the Department of Commerce and Labor. The original agencies in the Department of Labor were the Bureau of Labor Statistics, Bureau of Immigration, Bureau of Naturalization, and the Children's Bureau. With the changing needs of workers in a growing industrial society, the Department of Labor's functions and responsibilities grew as well. The department grew during and after World War I as new demands of industrial production and labor became leading issues that faced the national economy. To meet the requirements for production of materials in support of the war, the secretary of labor created the War Labor Administration within the Department of Labor. Its function was to mobilize workers for agriculture, shipbuilding, and defense plants and deal with wages, hours and working conditions, recruitment of women and minorities, race relations in the workplace, and worker safety and health issues.

During the Great Depression, the Department of Labor faced its biggest challenges. Pres. Franklin D.

Roosevelt appointed the first female cabinet member, Secretary of Labor Frances Perkins. She served from 1933 to 1945, the longest tenure for any secretary at that time. During Perkins's tenure, the department instituted many New Deal programs that exist today: minimum wage, overtime and child labor standards, unemployment insurance, and public employment service. Perkins was also instrumental in developing the original Social Security program.

Following World War II, the Department of Labor focused on veterans' employment rights. Since the early 1950s much of the department's activity has centered on worker health and safety, culminating in the development of the Occupational Safety and Health Act in 1970 (the first major industrial safety law passed by Congress) and, in 1978, safety and health in mines. The department's efforts to eliminate discrimination in employment resulted in the passage of the Manpower Development and Training Act of 1962, the Comprehensive Employment and Training Act of 1973 (CETA), the Job Training Partnership Act of 1982, and equal employment opportunity bills, such as the Equal Pay Act of 1963 and the Age Discrimination in Employment Act of 1974.

During the 1990s the Department of Labor administered labor laws, promoted the interests of workers, set standards in worker safety, and enforced and set penalties for violations. The Department of Labor is seen as a clientele department, which means that its functions are designed to serve a selected clientele—working people, injured workers, and those involved with management and labor issues. The current important subagencies in the Department of Labor are the Occupational Safety and Health Administration; the Bureau of Labor Statistics; the Employment Standards Administration; and the Office of Labor-Management Standards.

See also: Labor: Comprehensive Employment and Training Act of 1973; Equal Pay Act of 1963; Labor Policy; Manpower Development and Training Act of 1962; National Labor Relations Act of 1935

References: James E. Anderson, *Public Policymaking* (1997); Leif H. Carter and Christine B. Harrington, *Administrative Law and Politics: Cases and Comments* (1991); Douglas L. Leslie, *Labor Law in a Nutshell* (1979); Robert Reich, *Locked in the Cabinet* (1997); David B. Robertson and Dennis R. Judd, *The Development of American Public Policy: The Structure of Policy Restraint* (1989).

Earnings Gap

The earnings gap is the gap in income and earnings that exists between men and women, speaking to the issue of gender inequality in the U.S. economy. Women earned approximately 72 percent of men's earnings, due to the manner in which work is divided and compensated. Traditionally, perceived "female" occupations are in the lower pay scales. To correct the problem, female activists have sought to ensure equal access for women in traditional male occupations, which should have the effect of narrowing the earnings gap between men and women.

The Civil Rights Act of 1964 contained an antidiscrimination provision to protect against discrepancies in wages between the sexes. The best way to close the earnings gap will be for more women to hold positions in male-dominated occupations. The call for "equal pay for equal work" is central. Although the Equal Pay Act of 1963 banned wage discrimination on the basis of sex in jobs requiring equal skill, effort, and responsibility, the matters of differences in pay and the earnings gap still affect women.

See also: Civil Rights: Civil Rights Acts; Women's Movement; Labor: Comparable Worth; Equal Pay Act of 1963

References: Thomas R. Dye, *Understanding Public Policy* (1995).

Economic Opportunity Act of 1964

The Great Society programs initiated by Pres. Lyndon B. Johnson were designed to solve domestic problems during the early 1960s. One of the Great Society programs was the Economic Opportunity Act of 1964, part of the War on Poverty. This act created work-study programs for college students, a Job Corps program, and the new Urban and Rural Community Action Programs, which included Head Start. The Head Start program provided preschool training for children from poor educational and economic backgrounds. Among urban populations, Head Start was popular and necessary. As an antipoverty program, Head Start did not so much relieve the effects of poverty as provide education incentives for children from poor families. Pres. Bill Clinton has supported expanding Head Start because of the success it has had in helping preschool children in poor urban areas.

Local participation in Community Action Programs and other poverty programs provided residents with jobs, which resulted in valuable work experience and other opportunities; but it also resulted in misdirection, mismanagement, and lack of focus for many urban poverty programs. Head Start, Community Legal Services, and Community Action Agency programs have been the most successful, although each has come under criticism for too much government spending. The Economic Opportunity Act expired on September 30, 1981. Some of the Community Action Programs were continued under the Community Service Block Grant, and Head Start is still intact, albeit at a reduced level. As a policy approach that targeted urban poverty, this legislation had mixed reviews, but it did improve the lives of many participants.

See also: Education: Head Start; Entitlement Programs: Poverty Programs

References: Sheldon H. Danziger, Gary D. Sandefur, and Daniel H. Weinberg, *Confronting Poverty: Prescriptions for Change* (1994); Charles Murray, *Losing Ground: American Social Policy, 1950–1980* (1984); Dennis J. Palumbo, *Public Policy in America: Government in Action* (1988); James T. Patterson, *America's Struggle Against Poverty, 1900–1980* (1981).

Emergency Relief Appropriations Act of 1935

Work relief programs were one of the solutions to mass unemployment during the Great Depression. The Emergency Relief Appropriations Act of 1935 offered work programs instead of direct relief or cash benefits. This legislation authorized the expenditure of $5 billion for a works program for the unemployed. The program was administered under the Works Progress Administration (WPA), led by Harry Hopkins. WPA programs included the Federal Theater Project, the Federal Writers' Project, and the Federal Art Project. These work relief programs provided skills and made use of the talents of millions of unemployed workers. Although work relief programs and WPA came under criticism for waste and inefficiency, these programs stimulated the economy by adding to the national purchasing power and lifted the dignity of previously unemployed and unemployable workers.

See also: Economics: National Industrial Recovery Act of 1933

References: Joseph R. Conlin, *The American Past: A Survey of American History* (1993); Robert Goldston, *The Great Depression: The United States in the Thirties* (1968).

Employment Act of 1946

The mass unemployment of the Depression years made it clear to American legislators that continued, large-scale unemployment after World War II created a potential for labor and social unrest, which had contributed to the onset of war in Europe in the first place. Full employment was the broad goal of postwar legislators, but it was an unreasonable goal. In 1946 "full employment" was defined as 4 percent unemployment. The definition changed shortly thereafter to 4.5 percent, then to 5 percent. Such manipulation made it easier for the federal government to claim progress toward solving unemployment. In 1946 Congress passed the Employment Act to maintain maximum employment. Under this bill, the Council of Economic Advisers and the Congressional Joint Economic Committee were created to study economic problems and to plan policy responses to economic and employment issues. The original intent was to promote employment, production, and purchasing power. The act did not provide money for jobs or create work. The Korean War in 1950 took away the focus on employment legislation, and the low jobless rate during the early 1950s did little to renew attempts by the federal government to engage in employment programs.

See also: Economics: Council of Economic Advisers; Labor: Employment Policy

References: B. Guy Peters, *American Public Policy: Promise and Performance* (1993); David B. Robertson and Dennis R. Judd, *The Development of American Public Policy: The Structure of Policy Restraint* (1989).

Employment Policy

The rise of industrialization during the second half of the 19th century gave rise to a massive influx of immigrants seeking work and new opportunities. Between 1865 and 1900 the U.S. population more than doubled, from fewer than 36 million to 76 million. The extent of wealth grew rapidly as well, and by the end of the Civil War the annual production of goods was valued at $2 billion, reaching $13 billion by 1900. In 1860 the United States was the fourth largest industrial nation in the world and was still largely an agricultural nation; more than a million people (including many women and children) worked in industrial labor. By 1900 more than 5 million Americans worked in industrial jobs; by 1890 the United States had overtaken Great Britain as the world's foremost industrial nation. Yet the industrial worker was powerless to change or improve work conditions and remained relatively weak.

As people moved to cities in search of work at the turn of the century, the available workforce expanded. Mass industry became more organized during the early 20th century, and skilled laborers were in demand. Unskilled workers were an excess commodity, the most likely to suffer exploitation. Large-scale enterprises became more productive, and fewer workers were needed to sustain output. The stock market crash in October 1929 brought about major changes in employment and created the conditions for federal government involvement in employment policy.

During the first year after the crash, 4 million American workers lost their jobs. By 1931 100,000 workers were fired each week. By 1935 25 percent of the American workforce was unemployed (35 percent among African Americans). These conditions led to massive federal involvement, including the Federal Emergency Relief Act of 1933 (the federal government's attempt to create public employment opportunities through public works and relief programs), the Social Security Act of 1935, the U.S. Employment Service, and, later, the Employment Act of 1946 (designed to make the federal government responsible for full employment).

Another series of federal programs to aid the unemployed followed. In 1961 the Kennedy administration passed the Area Redevelopment Act, which gave grant assistance to counties to help develop employment opportunities in depressed communities. The Manpower Development and Training Act, an employment retraining bill, was passed in 1962, administered in state vocational education departments. The War on Poverty programs of the Johnson administration also created retraining and vocational education programs that grew out of the Economic Opportunity Act of 1964. In 1973 Congress passed the Comprehensive Employment and Training Act (CETA), which created public jobs for unemployed workers. CETA was another series of grant-based programs that eventually were used to relieve cities' budget problems but did little to help unemployed workers. Pres. Ronald Reagan eliminated the CETA public jobs program in 1981. In 1982 the Job Training Partnership Act was passed to channel job training through private enterprises.

The history of employment policy is one of shifting emphases from federal government leadership to administration of job creation and job training programs through the states. The prevailing government philosophy into the 21st century is one in which government encourages and promotes a strong national economy through private economic growth.

See also: Economics: New Deal; Labor: Comprehensive Employment and Training Act of 1973; Economic Opportunity Act of 1964; Employment Act of 1946; Federal Emergency Relief Act of 1933

References: Jeffrey E. Cohen, *Politics and Economic Policy in the United States* (1997); Joseph R. Conlin, *The American Past: A Survey of American History* (1993); Thomas R. Dye, *Understanding Public Policy* (1995); Robert Goldston, *The Great Depression: The United States in the Thirties* (1968); Rhonda F. Levine, *Class Struggle and the New Deal: Industrial Labor, Industrial Capital, and the State* (1988); David B. Robertson and Dennis R. Judd, *The Development of American Public Policy: The Structure of Policy Restraint* (1989).

Equal Pay Act of 1963

In 1938 the federal government made bold moves for working people. Congress passed the Fair Labor Standards Act, which established a minimum wage and a maximum workweek and forbade child labor. The Equal Pay Act of 1963 amended the Fair Labor Standards Act of 1938, correcting wage differentials based on gender.

The Equal Pay Act of 1963 requires equal pay for both genders for jobs requiring substantially equal skill, effort, and responsibility and for jobs that have similar working conditions. Remedies include civil and criminal penalties. The provisions of the Equal Pay Act of 1963 remain in force today. During the 1980s activists in the women's movement challenged the narrow scope of the Equal Pay Act.

See also: Civil Rights: Equal Rights Amendment

References: Irving Bernstein, *Turbulent Years: A History of the American Worker, 1933–1941* (1970); Leif H. Carter and Christine B. Harrington, *Administrative Law and Politics: Cases and Comments* (1991); Kermit L. Hall, William M. Wiecek, and Paul Finkelman, *American Legal History* (1991).

Fair Labor Standards Act of 1938

See Labor: Equal Pay Act of 1963

Federal Emergency Relief Act of 1933

Under pressure from Pres. Franklin D. Roosevelt, Congress passed the Federal Emergency Relief Act of 1933, which created the Federal Emergency Relief Administration (FERA) to provide direct grants to states and cities in support of relief efforts. FERA was authorized to distribute $500 million to state relief agencies. President Roosevelt appointed Harry Hopkins, former director of New York's relief programs, to head FERA. Most programs were public works programs, designed to immediately put millions of unemployed workers back to work. FERA laid the groundwork for future employment and social programs that helped Americans during the postwar years. By 1938 FERA had run its course. World War II was on the horizon, and before long millions of Americans went to war or worked in war-related industries.

See also: Economics: New Deal; Labor: Employment Policy

References: Irving Bernstein, *Turbulent Years: A History of the American Worker, 1933–1941* (1970); Robert Goldston, *The Great Depression: The United States in the Thirties* (1968).

Griggs v. Duke Power Company

Griggs v. Duke Power Company (1971) established the standard that employment tests must be job-related. Certain employment tests or screening devices may have a disparate impact on a particular racial, sexual, or ethnic group. In *Griggs,* the Duke Power Company in North Carolina required all employees to have a high school diploma to be eligible for certain promotions. In North Carolina, it was established that 34 percent of white males had completed high school, whereas only 12 percent of black males did. The U.S. Supreme Court found that high school graduation did not affect the ability of a person to perform at Duke. The Court decided that the policy had a negative racial effect without a valid relation to specific job requirements. This case established the principle that employment tests should not have a disparate impact on racial, sexual, or ethnic groups and that employment tests or prequalifications could not be valid unless such tests are clearly related to job requirements.

See also: Civil Rights: Affirmative Action

References: Steven J. Cann, *Administrative Law* (1998); Leif H. Carter and Christine B. Harrington, *Administrative Law and Politics: Cases and Comments* (1991).

Hawthorne Effect

Between 1927 and 1932 a series of studies was conducted by Elton Mayo, Fritz Roethlisberger, and others at the Hawthorne Works Western Electric Company in Chicago, Illinois. The studies looked at how the physical conditions of work (lighting and seating arrangements) affected productivity. The researchers expected that increasing lighting would positively affect output. But the studies found that workers to a large extent were responding to the experiments themselves rather than to changes in work conditions (like illumination). The workers appreciated the attention being paid to them, and they responded by increasing productivity.

Since the conclusion of the Hawthorne studies, research at the Western Electric wiring room showed that workers tend to respond to changes in work environment or formal organization as groups rather than as individuals. These experiments also demonstrated that people behave differently when they know they are being watched. This behavioral change in people who are being watched or studied is called the Hawthorne effect. It is important to understand that programs might appear to be successful because the participants know that they are being studied or monitored. The newness of a program might also lead to initial indicators of program success, but only because new programs receive a significant amount of attention.

See also: Key Concepts: Evaluation

References: Thomas R. Dye, *Understanding Public Policy* (1995); David H. Rosenbloom, *Public Administration: Understanding Management, Politics, and Law in the Public Sector* (1998).

Help Through Industrial Training Act of 1982

One aspect of employment policy has been the partnering between government and the private sector to build employment programs for the unemployed. One attempt at partnering the federal government with private employers was the Help Through Industrial Training program in 1982. This program sought to involve large corporations, targeting unemployed Vietnam War veterans, economically disadvantaged young people, and the long-term unemployed. The program had an ambitious goal of hiring 100,000 people, a goal it never met. The Job Training Partnership Act of 1982 was another government and industry cooperation program that had more success in accomplishing program goals.

See also: Labor: Comprehensive Employment and Training Act of 1973; Employment Policy

References: George J. Gordon and Michael E. Milakovich, *Public Administration in America* (1998); Dennis J. Palumbo, *Public Policy in America: Government in Action* (1988).

Hine, Lewis W. (1874–1940)

Lewis Hine was a photographer who was moved by the plight of immigrants to the United States as they landed at Ellis Island, New York. Hine was an early photojournalist; his photography was distinctive, as his subjects were usually children in terrible working conditions or people who were poor and downtrodden. Hine is best known for his work with the National Child Labor Committee, which he started in 1906. After Hine made an extensive photographic record of immigrants at Ellis Island, he decided to follow immigrant families to the cities and heartland to see how these new Americans built lives and fortunes. What he discovered was the extraordinary sacrifices made by children as they were put to work in the nation's mines, factories, sweatshops, and fields in support of families. Hine was an early leader in the child labor movement, and his photographs of children at work helped the development of public policy.

See also: Labor: Child Labor Laws

References: Daile Kaplan, *Lewis Hine in Europe: The Lost Photographs* (1988).

Immigration and Naturalization Service

The U.S. Immigration and Naturalization Service (INS) is an agency within the Department of Justice. Its function is to protect U.S. borders and to implement and enforce the nation's immigration policy and laws. The INS was established in 1891, originally within the Department of Labor when it was still just a government agency; INS was transferred to the Department of Justice in 1940. INS handles all applications for citizenship, residency, and work permits for nonresidents. The U.S. Border Patrol is a part of the INS and has the chief responsibility over illegal aliens and illegal goods entering the United States. INS has a reputation of being understaffed and slow to act.

See also: Labor: Immigration Policy

References: Frank J. Coppa and T. J. Curran, eds., *The Immigrant Experience in America* (1976).

Immigration Policy

The United States is a nation that was constructed by immigrants. Although indigenous people were present in the territory that would become the United States along with people of Spanish, African, and Chinese descent, the structure of government and the emerging society were founded by people of Western European origin. The first attempts to restrict the influx of immigrants into the United States took place during the 1880s, when the bulk of immigrants were from Eastern Europe and regions along the Mediterranean Sea. These restrictions took on antiforeign, racist overtones. Jews and Catholics were targeted as undesirable in the mix of immigrants to the northeastern United States. In the West, Asians from China and Japan came under immigration restrictions. One early restriction came in the form of literacy tests for immigrants, which was supported by the American Federation of Labor in 1897. By 1917 Congress passed a literacy test requirement for all immigrants, which resulted in a decline of immigration.

Following World War I the first quota law set a total of approximately 360,000 immigrants from European nations. Northern and Western European nations were allowed a higher quota than other regions, because of a preference in Congress for white immigrants that were not Italian or Eastern European in origin. During the 1930s only 528,000 immigrants were permitted into the United States. Prior to World War I, 1 million immigrants might arrive every year. By the start of World War II, however, immigration controls had stemmed the flow. The federal government had the major responsibility for creating restrictive legislation and for carrying out the laws. The U.S. Border Patrol was created in the 1930s and focused much of its activity along the southwestern borders to restrict Mexican immigrants from seeking work opportunities in the Southwest and California.

In 1952 Congress passed the McCarran-Walter Immigration Act, which imposed small-nation-origin quotas for many countries. The quotas were set for various nations. One of the problems caused by World War II was the huge number of displaced people in Europe. Congress passed the Displaced Persons Acts of 1948 and 1950 and the Refugee Relief Act of 1953 to allow for the admission of 600,000 European refugees into the United States. In 1965 congress passed the Immigration Act of 1965 (also known as the Hart-Celler Act), which replaced national origin quotas with a system of preferences for people with special skills. The next immigrant wave to affect the United States occurred when Fidel Castro successfully overthrew the regime of Fulgencio Batista in Cuba. Following Castro's takeover, Cuban immigration to the United States came in swells, and by 1980 thousands of Cubans who were allowed to leave Cuba fled to Florida in the Mariel boatlift. Another immigrant wave came with the fall of Vietnam and the movement of Indochinese refugees from Southeast Asia. The population of Indochinese refugees in the United Sates by 1980 had risen to 1 million, and in reaction to the refugee influx Congress passed the Refugee Act of 1980.

Congress passed the Immigration Reform Act of 1986 (the Simpson-Rodino Act), which was designed to place limits on immigration of all types. It was the most comprehensive immigration legislation in 35 years. The bill had two major provisions: It attempted to stem the flow of immigrants by applying employer sanctions and by legalization. The sanctions provided for penalties to employers of undocumented immigrants; legalization was meant to allow certain illegal immigrants to become lawful residents and to lead toward citizenship. The Immigration and Naturalization Service (INS) was responsible for implementing the provisions of the act. The requirements of the 1986 bill placed a tremendous burden on INS, an agency not previously known for efficiency of operations.

The Immigration Act of 1990 is the most recent major change in immigration policy; it increased immigration by 35 percent. The largest numbers of immigrants to the United States during the 1990s have come from Asia, Mexico, and Latin America. State policy toward immigrants drew significant attention during the 1994 California elections; voters passed Proposition 187 to bar illegal immigrants from receiving welfare and education benefits. The upshot was that illegal immigrants were denied access to public education systems, nonemergency medical care, and cash benefits from welfare programs. California went even farther in restricting education benefits for Spanish-speaking immigrants by passing Proposition 209 to end bilingual education in California schools.

Immigration policy during the early 20th century ebbed and flowed along with economic prosperity. The second half of the century saw much immigration result from refugee crises and movements. The people of the United States have shown a confusing intolerance toward nonwhite immigrants during the 20th century, which goes against the very principles upon which the nation was founded. However, the willingness of American policymakers to welcome refugees to the United States continues to confound the race- and ethnic-origin limitations that dominated immigration policy prior to World War II.

See also: Labor: Immigration and Naturalization Service

References: Jason Juffras, *Impact of the Immigration Reform and Control Act on the Immigration and Naturalization Service* (1991); David Reimers, *Unwelcome Strangers: American Identity and the Turn Against Immigration* (1998).

Industrial Accident Commission of California

Industrial accidents during the early 20th century caused the loss of countless man-hours of work. Industrial accidents were linked to poor working conditions, poor work habits, lack of worker safety rules, and disregard for the general welfare of factory workers. Moreover, companies saw injured workers as a burden and treated them either as welfare clients (which was the more benevolent approach) or as replaceable parts of the industrial enterprise, which meant that the injured worker lost the job because of the injury and was replaced by a healthy worker. There was no workers' compensation during the late 19th and early 20th centuries, until California created the Industrial Accident Commission in 1911.

The California State Assembly passed the Roseberry Act, creating the seven-member Industrial Accident Commission, which took appeals from injured workers and granted welfarelike compensation to injured workers until they were healthy enough to return to work. The commission was one of the first workers' compensation boards, guided by a philosophy that viewed the injured worker as someone who needed "relief" while recovering from injury. The Industrial Accident Commission decided the extent of injury and the extent of relief.

By 1950 the commission was replaced by the State Workmen's Compensation Appeals Board, which operated differently. During the early 1950s workers had the aid of workers' compensation attorneys and unions who advocated on behalf of injured workers; the status of the injured worker thus changed from one who sought relief to one who had a workers' compensation claim that under law had to be heard and settled. Every state now has very clearly developed workers' compensation policies, and the relationship among the injured worker, the employer, and the insurance company is now one in which workers' rights are protected by law. Many critics point out abuses by injured workers who attempt to take advantage of the system by claiming monetary compensation that goes beyond the true nature of the injury.

See also: Labor: Labor Policy

References: Philippe Nonet, *Administrative Justice* (1969).

Job Creation and Wage Enhancement Act

This bill was proposed as a part of the Republicans' "Contract with America," led by U.S. Rep. Newt Gingrich in 1994. The "Contract with America" comprised a series of symbolic legislative proposals, most of which lacked majority support in Congress and thus did not pass. The purpose of the Job Creation and Wage Enhancement Act was to create small business incentives for job creation and to restrict government regulation of businesses by requiring a cost-benefit analysis of all new business regulations. The intent was to further deregulate the business environment, which Republicans in Congress felt would stimulate savings and reinvestment in small businesses, which in turn would lead to job creation.

See also: Key Concepts: Congress, United States; Labor: Employment Policy

References: Charles Bonser, Eugene B. McGregor Jr., and Clinton V. Oster Jr., *Policy Choices and Public Action* (1996).

Job Training Partnership Act of 1982

See Labor: Employment Policy

Job Training Programs

Job training programs have been an important element of employment policy. During the 1920s the first vocational training and rehabilitation programs were created by the federal government. The New Deal introduced many job training programs, but the focus was on "make work" programs to immediately put people to work. Job training became federal employment policy with the Great Society programs of the Lyndon B. Johnson administration. Johnson's War on Poverty specified the development of the Economic Opportunity Act, which set up the Job Corps for vocational training; an Office of Economic Opportunity to organize education and training programs; and the Volunteers in Service to America (VISTA) program.

Job training programs in various forms are popular policy programs that legislators assume lead to employment. Rather than making jobs or giving jobs to individuals, the prevailing philosophy is that those most in need of jobs to improve their economic status in the long run would benefit most directly from vocational programs that teach skills. Job training and vocational programs are important components of employment policy.

See also: Labor: Employment Policy

References: Clarke E. Cochran et al., *American Public Policy: An Introduction* (1996).

Labor Policy

Current labor policy is the result of a series of changes in attitude toward organized labor since the 1800s. Labor policy shifted with the growth of industrialization. As the nation became more industrial and economic prosperity increased, more people left farms and sought out opportunities in cities, where the factories were located; labor clashes between workers and employers followed. Working conditions during the 19th century were generally poor, and workers had no means to challenge the powers that be to improve worker safety and health.

The only recourse was to stop or delay the production process; in most cases, the workers were fired if they went on strike in this way. One of the earliest cases of workers refusing to work was *Com-*

monwealth of Pennsylvania v. Pullis (1806). Workers refused to work because they were dissatisfied with their wage rate. As was the case during much of the 19th century, workers were convicted of criminal conspiracy for refusing to work at a specified wage rate and for attempting to prevent others from working at a lower rate. Worker attempts to unionize to improve wages and working conditions were considered violations of criminal law. One of the first instances reflecting the shift from criminal conduct to civil liability of workers' unions was *Commonwealth of Massachusetts v. Hunt* (1842). Workers in this case refused to work for employers who paid less than union scale.

After the Civil War the large factory system developed in the U.S. economy, introducing machinery, the use of immigrants as a ready labor supply, long hours, low wages, and poor working conditions. Between 1863 and 1873 many national trade unions developed. Most were skilled craft unions that included railway engineers and firemen, machine molders, and wood craftsmen. In 1868 Congress passed an eight-hour workday for certain federal workers. The Knights of Labor, founded in 1869, grew rapidly and encouraged membership of all ethnic and racial groups. In 1886 the American Federation of Labor was created in Columbus, Ohio, predominantly from craft unions; its president was Samuel Gompers, a famed labor leader.

In 1890 the Sherman Antitrust Act was passed; union tactics to stop work or to organize and use economic pressure against employers were viewed as a violation of the restraint-of-trade provisions in the act. The penalty for such violations fell under civil liability, which meant that unions were required to pay damages suffered by the business owners caused by economic pressure applied by the unions. Congress shifted its posture in 1914, when the Clayton Act was passed with provisions that protected labor activity. Employers found that requiring unions to pay damages for using economic pressure was insufficient; they turned to the more immediate means of controlling union activity by seeking injunctive relief to stop, with government assistance, union pressure.

The passage of the National Industrial Recovery Act of 1933 established collective bargaining for American workers. Section 7 guaranteed labor the right to organize and collectively bargain and established the National Labor Board to negotiate disputes. This bill set the stage for much of the labor action that was protected by the Norris-LaGuardia Act of 1932, which changed government responses to labor activity. The act withdrew the power of federal courts to issue injunctions in nonviolent labor disputes; protected picketing and refusals to work from injunctions; asserted the neutral posture of the federal government by removing the power of federal courts to make rules governing labor policy; and resulted in the federal government's direct permission for labor unions to organize and grow.

The National Industrial Recovery Act had set the stage for the development of collective bargaining for labor organizations during the 1930s. The National Labor Relations Act of 1935 (also known as the Wagner Act) replaced section 7a of the National Industrial Recovery Act after the U.S. Supreme Court declared the National Industrial Recovery Act illegal. The Wagner Act represented another shift in the government's attitude toward labor, creating rules and conditions for employee rights and setting the groundwork for collective bargaining between unions and employers. The act established the National Labor Relations Board (NLRB) to administer and interpret unfair labor practices and the union representation provisions of the legislation. The act also provided for judicial review of challenges to the provisions of the act. The 1930s were tumultuous years in terms of labor and union activity. Many strikes occurred, and employees and employers' security forces often battled in streets and factories. Many unskilled workers who were excluded by the American Federation of Labor (AFL) were being courted to become members of another labor collective, the Congress of Industrial Organizations (CIO). Some of the most violent strikes and labor actions took place among longshoremen, autoworkers, steelworkers, textile workers in the South, and miners. Walter Reuther was a leader of the autoworkers in Michigan, and during the late 1940s he became president of the United Auto Workers (UAW).

After World War II public opinion began to sour on labor's "immunity." Some members of Congress were intolerant of socialists in the labor movement and viewed socialist influence as an extension of international communism. Congress passed the Labor-Management Relations Act (Taft-Hartley Act) in 1947 to restrict "union bad practices." The legislation specifically prohibited secondary boycotts and provided remedies for parties injured by secondary boycotts. The Labor-Management Reporting and Disclosure Act (the Landrum-Griffin Act) was passed in 1959, requiring a union membership bill of rights, financial disclosure measures for unions, union election procedures, and civil and criminal penalties for abuses by union officers. The era of full government neutrality toward union activity had ended, but the rights of unions and collective bargaining were firmly in place.

Since 1960 the pace of union activity has slowed. During the 1980s and 1990s, union activity grew in public employee unions and associations. Union membership in the private economic sector has declined since 1970, and the 1980s and 1990s saw widespread decertification (a vote by union members to disband the union) in some industries. Unions remain a powerful political force and use political action committees (PACs) to lobby political candidates. Collective bargaining is a part of the economic landscape, and both public and private unions and employee associations rely on collective bargaining mechanisms to bring about favorable employment contracts and work agreements.

See also: Labor: American Federation of Labor–Congress of Industrial Organizations; Employment Policy; National Labor Relations Act of 1935

References: Leif H. Carter and Christine B. Harrington, *Administrative Law and Politics: Cases and Comments* (1991); Douglas L. Leslie, *Labor Law in a Nutshell* (1979); David B. Robertson and Dennis R. Judd, *The Development of American Public Policy: The Structure of Policy Restraint* (1989).

Landrum-Griffin Act of 1959

See Labor: Labor Policy

Manpower Development and Training Act of 1962

This legislation was one of the Great Society programs under the administration of Pres. Lyndon B. Johnson. The Manpower Development and Training Act of 1962 authorized the Department of Labor to distribute grants to retrain workers. It attempted to provide job skills, training, and help to the poor to find employment. It tried to bypass state vocational education programs. The Department of Labor had little confidence in the state bureaucrats who ran vocational education programs, as funds were often diverted for selfish gain. Often the poor received little benefit from the state-run programs, which were often plagued by racial discrimination and financial waste.

See also: Labor: Employment Policy

References: Dennis J. Palumbo, *Public Policy in America: Government in Action* (1988); David B. Robertson and Dennis R. Judd, *The Development of American Public Policy: The Structure of Policy Restraint* (1989).

Mills, C. Wright (1916–1962)

C. Wright Mills was an eminent sociologist who wrote on philosophical pragmatism, social stratification, and the intricacies of sociological practice. He understood and wrote about the importance of the historical tradition of social science. Mills recognized the importance of individual and societal change and how that change affected groups of people. Mills wrote a classic work in sociology, *The Sociological Imagination,* delineating the aspects of occupationalism and professionalism in the discipline of sociology.

Mills is best known for his work in stratification in *White Collar* and *The Power Elite.* His theory of the power elite laid new ground in the area of who gets political power and how that power is used. Mills proposed that certain types of individuals attain political power as a result of birth, connections, occupations in leading corporations and industries, wealth, and political positions; they will always be able to dominate the interests of the majority of citizens because of their access to political and social power. Mills's work has been important in studies of political power and political participation.

See also: Key Concepts: Political Behavior

References: Irving L. Horowitz, *C. Wright Mills: An American Utopian* (1983).

Mine Safety and Health Administration

The Mine Safety and Health Administration (MSHA) is a federal agency in the Department of Labor that is responsible for inspecting mines and enforcing health and safety requirements in the mining industry. This agency holds a difficult and controversial role, particularly in its relationship with the coal industry. Many of the nation's coal mines are in regions of the country (such as Appalachia) in which coal mining is the sole industry, occupation, and way of life. Although many miners know of the unsafe and unhealthy conditions of coal mines, they work in the mines despite the conditions, as they have little choice. When a complaint is made to the Mine Safety and Health Administration about unsafe conditions, there is the possibility that MSHA will shut down the mine until conditions are improved. Such action seriously affects the livelihoods of the miners as well as the profits of the mine owners. There have been numerous occasions when MSHA has shut down a coal mine due to unsafe conditions. MSHA also manages issues related to black lung disease in coal miners. As the enforcers and implementers of public policy dealing with the health and safety issues in the mining industry, MSHA has a huge responsibility in serving the interests of clients and government policy.

See also: Key Concepts: Regulation

References: Dennis J. Palumbo, *Public Policy in America: Government in Action* (1988).

Model Cities Program

The Model Cities Program was part of Pres. Lyndon B. Johnson's War on Poverty. It was designed to rehabilitate poor neighborhoods, engage the poor in local community programs to improve urban areas, and create self-help programs for youth and the jobless by offering employment opportunities to develop urban improvement projects in inner-city areas. The Model Cities Program was an ambitious idea that provided the urban poor with opportunities to make decisions about urban needs and projects themselves. Housing agencies, social service agencies, and other public agencies coordinated efforts to find solutions to urban poverty, which was common in American cities during the 1960s and early 1970s. Critics claimed that this was an example of merely throwing federal money at a problem. It was difficult to prove positive results, yet many inner-city residents became employed in positions that had previously eluded them because of their poor education opportunities and lack of job skills.

See also: Labor: Employment Policy

References: Dennis J. Palumbo, *Public Policy in America: Government in Action* (1988); B. Guy Peters, *American Public Policy: Promise and Performance* (1993).

National Labor Relations Act of 1935

The National Industrial Recovery Act set the stage for the development of collective bargaining for labor organizations during the 1930s. The National Labor Relations Act of 1935 (also known as the Wagner Act) replaced section 7a of the National Industrial Recovery Act after the Supreme Court declared the National Industrial Recovery Act illegal. U.S. Sen. Robert Wagner of New York sponsored the bill, which was a major step in promoting the rights of labor and workers. The act required management to collectively bargain with labor unions. This meant that workers were permitted by law to organize and to have unions represent their interests in negotiating work contracts and agreements with management. The act also forbade management from preventing or interfering with union organizing activities. The act created the National Labor Relations Board to hear, arbitrate, and decide disputes between labor and management. The act itself was designed to promote equal status between labor and management, a 180-degree turnabout in the traditional philosophy of management toward labor. This philosophy capitalized on a "master-servant" relationship, with management as the master and labor as the servant.

The passage of the National Labor Relations Act made it possible for thousands of union elections to occur, and the newly created National Labor Relations Board heard thousands of cases of alleged unfair labor practices. The board corrected injustices created by companies that were antagonistic to unions. The NLRB intervened in disputes, disbanded 2,000 "unions" imposed by companies as opposed to formed by workers, and reinstated thousands of workers who were fired from companies for engaging in union organizing. This was an intense period for labor and workers; the National Labor Relations Act permanently changed the character of labor in America.

See also: Economics: National Industrial Recovery Act of 1933; Labor: Labor Policy

References: Irving Bernstein, *Turbulent Years: A History of the American Worker, 1933–1941* (1970); Rhonda F. Levine, *Class Struggle and the New Deal: Industrial Labor, Industrial Capital, and the State* (1988).

National Labor Relations Board

See Labor: National Labor Relations Act of 1935

National Labor Relations Board v. Jones and Laughlin Steel Corp.

After the passage of the National Labor Relations Act of 1935, the relationship between labor and management did not dramatically improve. In *National Labor Relations Board v. Jones and Laughlin Steel Corp.* (1937), the U.S. Supreme Court upheld the National Labor Relations Act, which created the National Labor Relations Board (NLRB). The major issue had to do with whether the federal government, acting through the NLRB, had the authority to regulate the private property interests of a corporation in the corporation's decisions to dismiss, intimidate, and discriminate against employees because of their participation in union organizing activities. The steel corporation challenged the jurisdictional authority of the NLRB, stating that the National Labor Relations Act had no authority to regulate the activities of private businesses in their dealings with employees. The Court decided that the National Labor Relations Act worked in favor of preserving and protecting public and private rights in the area of general health and welfare for society.

See also: Labor: Labor Policy; National Labor Relations Act of 1935

Norris-LaGuardia Act

See Labor: Labor Policy

Oakland Project

The Oakland Project was an economic development project to which the U.S. Economic Development Administration (EDA) committed $23 million to create jobs for unemployed minority workers in Oakland, California. In 1968 the U.S. Department of Commerce had authorized EDA to spend the money to create jobs to employ people in Oakland, California. The project never lived up to its promises; in fact it represented a massive failure, an example of federal funds being thrown at a "make work" program that had not considered issues critical to success.

The failure of EDA's mission was the subject of a study by Jeffrey Pressman and Aaron Wildavsky, two political scientists from the University of California–Berkeley who turned a critical eye toward programs that spent millions of dollars to create jobs. Pressman and Wildavsky point out that lack of implementation of public policy is not related to failure so much as it is to the inability to follow through with plans. The lesson learned was that capital subsidy plans are paid out on promises, which rarely come true. The implementation of any program of this type should be simple, not complex. Public policy is always improved if implementation is given due consideration during the development of policy.

See also: Key Concepts: Implementation

References: Jeffrey L. Pressman and Aaron B. Wildavsky, *Implementation* (1973).

Office of Personnel Management

The central federal personnel office is the Office of Personnel Management (OPM). OPM was created as a part of the reorganization of the federal government in 1979. The personnel function for the federal government was previously performed by the Civil Service Commission, which was abolished. OPM would now be responsible for recruiting, hiring, and testing for executive branch agencies. In 1993 Vice Pres. Al Gore introduced the National Performance Review, which called for the federal government and its agencies to engage in better customer service to citizens and clients of the agencies. To that end, many of the personnel functions previously handled by OPM shifted to the separate agencies, which have since developed their own personnel rules, testing procedures, and merit examinations. OPM still has the responsibility of administering federal retirement and health programs, and it conducts training sessions through the Federal Executive Institute.

See also: Key Concepts: Administrative Agencies

References: President Bill Clinton and Vice President Al Gore, *Putting Customers First, 1995: Standards for Serving the American People,* National Performance Review (October 1995); David H. Rosenbloom, *Public Administration: Understanding Management, Politics, and Law in the Public Sector* (1998); James Q. Wilson and John J. DiIulio Jr., *American Government: The Essentials* (1998);

Pendleton Act

See Labor: Civil Service

Sherman Antitrust Act of 1890

See Labor: Labor Policy

Smith-Connally War Labor Disputes Act of 1943

Although the National Labor Relations Act gave workers the right to organize and established a neutral posture for the federal government, numerous labor strikes during World War II prompted the federal government to act against organized labor. The late 1930s saw thousands of strikes by organized labor, and these strikes continued into the war years. Pres. Franklin D. Roosevelt took over the eastern coal mines in 1943 and forced the president of the United Mine Workers, John L. Lewis, to call off the miners' strike the day after he took over the mines. On June 25, 1943, Congress passed the Smith-Connally War Labor Disputes Act, which strengthened the president's power to address strikes that interfered with the war effort. Roosevelt also seized the railroads for approximately one month between December 1943 and January 1944 to avoid a railroad strike. Following the war, Congress moved to blunt the influence and actions of labor unions.

See also: Labor: Labor Policy

References: Irving Bernstein, *Turbulent Years: A History of the American Worker, 1933–1941* (1970); Rhonda F. Levine, *Class Struggle and the New Deal: Industrial Labor, Industrial Capital, and the State* (1988).

Smith-Hughes Act of 1917

The Smith-Hughes Act of 1917 provided vocational education opportunities through a program in which funding would be shared by states. It represented one of the first vocational training programs adopted by the federal government; in partnering with states, however, the program met with limited success. One of the problems was that some members of Congress from southern states were reluctant to allow African Americans to benefit from the program, and they felt that the program was really intended to aid northern cities. The program was important in that it marked meaningful federal involvement in vocational and employment training.

See also: Labor: Employment Policy

References: Irving Bernstein, *Turbulent Years: A History of the American Worker, 1933–1941* (1970).

Wagner Act

See Labor: National Labor Relations Act of 1935

Workers' Compensation

See Labor: Industrial Accident Commission of California

Bibliography

Abraham, Henry J. 1988. *Freedom and the Court: Civil Rights and Liberties in the United States*. New York: Oxford University Press.

Albrecht, Don E., and Steve H. Murdock. 1990. *The Sociology of U.S. Agriculture*. Ames: Iowa State University Press.

Alexander, C. C. 1975. *Holding the Line: The Eisenhower Era, 1952–1961*. New York: Little, Brown.

Alger, Dean E. 1989. *The Media and Politics*. Englewood Cliffs, NJ: Prentice Hall.

Allard, C. Kenneth. 1991. *Command Control and the Common Defense*. New Haven: Yale University Press.

Allen, John, ed. 1995. *Annual Editions: Environment 95/96*. Belmont, CA: Dushkin Publishing.

Allison, Graham, and Gregory F. Treverton, eds. 1992. *Rethinking America's Security: Beyond the Cold War to New World Order*. New York: Norton.

Anderson, Frederick R., Daniel R. Mandeker, and A. Dan Tarlock. 1984. *Environmental Protection: Law and Policy*. Boston: Little, Brown.

Anderson, James E. 1997. *Public Policymaking*. Boston: Houghton Mifflin.

Bacon, Donald C., Roger H. Davidson, and Morton Keller, eds. 1995. *The Encyclopedia of the United States Congress*. New York: Simon and Schuster.

Baker, James, with Thomas M. DeFrank. 1995. *The Politics of Diplomacy*. New York: Putnam's Sons.

Baker, Ross K. 1995. *House and Senate*. New York: W. W. Norton.

Barker, Lucius J., and Mack H. Jones. 1994. *African Americans and the American Political System*. Englewood Cliffs, NJ: Prentice Hall.

Barone, Michael, and Grant Ujifusa, eds. 1995. *Almanac of American Politics*. New York: E. P. Dutton.

Bartlett, Donald L., and James B. Steele. 1985. *Forevermore: Nuclear Waste in America*. New York: W. W. Norton.

Bell, Charles, and Charles Price. 1988. *California Government Today: Politics and Reform?* Chicago: Dorsey.

Berkman, Ronald, and Laura W. Kitch. 1986. *Politics in the Media Age*. New York: McGraw-Hill.

Bernstein, Irving. 1970. *Turbulent Years: A History of the American Worker, 1933–1941*. Boston: Houghton Mifflin.

Berry, Jeffrey M. 1977. *Lobbying for the People: The Political Behavior of Public Interest Groups*. Princeton: Princeton University Press.

———. 1997. *Interest Group Society*. New York: Longman.

Bittner, Egon. 1980. *The Functions of Police in Modern Society*. Cambridge: Oelgeschlager, Gunn, and Hain.

Blackstock, Nelson. 1976. *COINTELPRO: The FBI's Secret War on Political Freedom*. New York: Vintage Books.

Blasius, Mark. 1994. *Gay and Lesbian Politics: Sexuality and the Emergence of a New Ethic*. Philadelphia: Temple University Press.

Bonser, Charles, Eugene B. McGregor Jr., and Clinton V. Oster Jr. 1996. *Policy Choices and Public Action*. Englewood Cliffs, NJ: Prentice Hall.

Bornet, Vaughn D. 1983. *The Presidency of Lyndon B. Johnson*. Lawrence: University of Kansas Press.

Bowker, Lee H. 1982. *Corrections: The Science and Art*. New York: Macmillan.

Brower, David. 1990. *For Earth's Sake: The Life and Times of David Brower*. Salt Lake City, UT: Peregrine Smith Books.

Browning, Robert X. 1986. *Politics and Social Welfare Policy in the United States*. Knoxville: University of Tennessee Press.

Brownlee, W. Elliot. 1996. *Federal Taxation in America: A Short History*. New York: Cambridge University Press.

Burns, James MacGregor. 1978. *Leadership*. New York: Harper and Row.

Burns, James MacGregor, J. W. Peltason, Thomas E. Cronin, and David B. Magleby. 1996. *Government by the People*. Upper Saddle River, NJ: Prentice Hall.

Cain, Bruce, and Roger G. Noll, eds. 1995. *Constitutional Reform in California*. Berkeley: Institute of Governmental Studies.

Calabrese, Edward J., Charles E. Gilbert, and Harris Pastides, eds. 1989. *Safe Drinking Water Act: Amendments, Regulations, and Standards*. Chelsea, MI: Lewis Publishers.

Caldwell, Lynton K. 1995. *Environment as a Focus for Public Policy*. College Station: Texas A&M Press.

Cann, Steven J. *Administrative Law*. 1998. Thousand Oaks, CA: Sage Publications.

Carmichael, Stokeley, and Charles V. Hamilton. 1967. *Black Power: The Politics of Liberation in America*. New York: Random House.

Carson, Rachel. 1962. *Silent Spring*. Boston: Houghton Mifflin.

Carter, Leif, and Christine Harrington. 1991. *Administrative Law and Politics*. New York: HarperCollins.

Case, Karl E., and Ray C. Fair. 1989. *Principles of Economics*. Englewood Cliffs, NJ: Prentice Hall.

Central Intelligence Agency. 1996. *The World Fact Book, 1996–1997*. Washington, DC: Brassey's.

Chubb, John E., and Terry M. Moe. 1990. *Politics, Markets, and American Schools*. Washington, DC: Brookings Institution.

Cigler, Allen, and Burdett Loomis. 1990. *Interest Group Politics*. Washington, DC: Congressional Quarterly Press.

Clarke, Jonathan, and James Clad. 1995. *After the Crusade: American Foreign Policy for the Post-Superpower Age*. Englewood Cliffs, NJ: Prentice Hall.

Clinton, Bill, and Al Gore. 1995. *Putting Customers First, 1995: Standards for Serving the American People*. Washington, DC: U.S. Government.

Cochran, Clarke E., Lawrence C. Mayer, T. R. Carr, and N. Joseph Cayer. 1996. *American Public Policy: An Introduction*. New York: St. Martin's.

Cochrane, Willard W., and Mary E. Ryan. 1976. *American Farm Policy, 1948–1973*. Minneapolis: University of Minnesota Press.

Cohen, Jeffrey E. 1997. *Politics and Economic Policy in the United States*. New York: Oxford University Press.

Cohen, Richard E. 1992. *Washington at Work: Back Rooms and Clean Air*. New York: Macmillan.

Cole, George F., and Marc G. Gertz. 1998. *The Criminal Justice System: Politics and Policies*. Belmont, CA: West/Wadsworth Publishing.

Conlin, Joseph R. 1993. *The American Past: A Survey of American History*. Fort Worth: Harcourt Brace.

Cook, Fred J. 1964. *The FBI Nobody Knows*. New York: Macmillan.

Coppa, Frank J., and T. J. Curran, eds. 1976. *The Immigrant Experience in America*. Boston: Twayne Publishers.

Coulter, Edwin M. 1994. *Principles of Politics and Government*. Madison: Brown and Benchmark.

Cramer, Gail J., and Clarence W. Jensen. 1991. *Agricultural Economics and Agri-business*. New York: John Wiley & Sons.

Dahl, Robert. 1968. *A Preface to Democratic Theory*. Chicago: University of Chicago Press.

Danziger, Sheldon H., Gary D. Sandefur, and Daniel H. Weinberg. 1994. *Confronting Poverty: Prescriptions for Change*. Cambridge, MA: Harvard University Press.

Davidson, Roger H., and Walter Oleszek. 1994. *Congress and Its Members*. Washington, DC: Congressional Quarterly Press.

Davies, David. 1986. *U.S. Taxes and Tax Policy*. New York: Cambridge University Press.

Davis, Charles E. 1993. *The Politics of Hazardous Waste*. Englewood Cliffs, NJ: Prentice Hall.

Davis, David H. 1993. *Energy Politics*. New York: St. Martin's.

DeBow, Ken, and John C. Syer. 1994. *Power and Politics in California*. Boston: Allyn and Bacon.

Deckard, Barbara Sinclair. 1979. *The Women's Movement*. New York: Harper and Row.

Downs, Anthony. 1972. "Up and Down with Ecology—The Issue Attention Cycle," *Public Interest* 28:28–50.

DuBois, W.E.B. 1961. *The Souls of Black Folk: Essays and Sketches*. New York: Dodd, Mead.

———. 1971. *The Autobiography of W.E.B. DuBois: A Soliloquy on Viewing My life from the Last Decade of Its First Century*. New York: International Publishers.

Dugger, Ronnie. 1982. *The Politician: The Life and Times of Lyndon B. Johnson*. New York: Norton.

Dunn, William N. 1993. *Public Policy Analysis: An Introduction*. Englewood Cliffs, NJ: Prentice Hall.

Dye, Thomas R. 1995. *Understanding Public Policy*. Englewood Cliffs, NJ: Prentice Hall.

Dye, Thomas R., and Harmon Ziegler. 1996. *The Irony of Democracy*. Orlando: Harcourt Brace.

Edmondson, Harold, ed. 1972. *Journey to Amtrak: The Year History Rode the Passenger Train*. Milwaukee: Kalmbach Books.

Edwards, David, and Alessandra Lippucci. 1998. *Practicing American Politics: An Introduction to American Government*. New York: Worth Publishers.

Etzioni, Amitai. 1995. *Rights and the Common Good: The Communitarian Perspective*. New York: St. Martin's.

Finn, Chester E., Jr. 1991. *We Must Take Charge: Our Schools and Our Future*. New York: Free Press.

Fischer, Frank. 1995. *Evaluating Public Policy*. Chicago: Nelson Hall Publishers.

Flexner, Eleanor. 1975. *Century of Struggle: The Women's Rights Movement in the U.S.* Cambridge: Harvard University Press.

Fowler, Robert Booth. 1991. *The Dance with Community*. Lawrence: University of Kansas Press.

Franklin, John Hope, and Isidore Starr, eds. 1967. *The Negro in the 20th Century in America*. New York: Harcourt Brace.

Freedman, James O. 1978. *Crisis and Legitimacy: The Administrative Process and American Government*. Cambridge: Cambridge University Press.

Fritschler, A. Lee, and James M. Hoefler. 1996. *Smoking and Politics: Policymaking and the Federal Bureaucracy*. Englewood Cliffs, NJ: Prentice Hall.

Froman, Lewis. 1968. "The Categorization of Policy Contents." In Austin Ranney, ed., *Political Science and Public Policy*. Chicago: Markham.

Fuller, Millard. 1995. *A Simple, Decent Place to Live*. Dallas, TX: Word Publishing.

Galbraith, John K. 1958. *The Affluent Society*. Boston: Houghton Mifflin.

———. 1967. *The New Industrial State*. Boston: Houghton Mifflin.

———. 1981. *A Life in Our Times: A Memoir*. Boston: Houghton Mifflin.

Garrettson, Charles L., III. 1993. *Hubert H. Humphrey and the Politics of Joy*. New Brunswick, NJ: Transaction Publishers.

Garrow, David. J. 1994. *Liberty and Sexuality: The Right to Privacy and the Making of* Roe v. Wade. New York: Macmillan.

Geisler, Charles C., and Frank J. Poppen. 1984. *Land Reform, American Style*. Montclair, NJ: Rowman and Allanheld.

Gillespie, J. David. 1993. *Politics at the Periphery: Third Parties in Two-Party America*. Columbia: University of South Carolina Press.

Glantz, A. Stanton, et al. 1996. *The Cigarette Papers*. Berkeley: University of California Press.

Goggin, Malcolm, Ann O'm. Bowman, James P. Lester, and Lawrence O'Toole. 1990. *Implementation Theory and Practice*. Glenview, IL: Scott, Foresman.

Goldston, Robert. 1968. *The Great Depression: The United States in the Thirties*. New York: Bobbs-Merrill.

Gordon, George J., and Michael E. Milakovich. 1998. *Public Administration in America*. New York: St. Martin's.

Gore, Albert. 1993. *Earth in the Balance: Ecology and the Human Spirit*. Boston: Houghton Mifflin.

Greenberg, Edward S., and Benjamin I. Page. 1993. *The Struggle for Democracy*. New York: HarperCollins.

Hafner, Katie, and Matthew Lynon. 1996. *Where Wizards Stay Up Late: The Origins of the Internet*. New York: Simon and Schuster.

Hall, Kermit L., William M. Wiecek, and Paul Finkelman. 1991. *American Legal History*. New York: Oxford University Press.

Harrigan, John J. 1984. *Politics and Policy in States and Communities*. Boston: Little, Brown.

Harrington, Michael. 1963. *The Other America*. Baltimore: Penguin Books.

Harris, Richard, and Sidney Milkis. 1996. *The Politics of Regulatory Change*. New York: Oxford University Press.

Hays, R. Allen. 1995. *The Federal Government and Urban Housing: Ideology and Change in Public Policy*. Albany: State University of New York Press.

Heffron, Florence, and Neil McFeeley. 1983. *The Administrative Regulatory Process*. New York: Longman.

Hoogenboom, Ari, and Olive Hoogenboom. 1976. *A History of the ICC: From Panacea to Palliative*. New York: W. W. Norton.

Horowitz, Irving L. 1983. *C. Wright Mills: An American Utopian*. New York: Free Press.

Inciardi, James A. 1984. *Criminal Justice*. New York: Academic Press, Inc.

Jacob, Herbert. 1986. *Law and Politics in the United States*. Monterey, CA: Brooks/Cole.

Jones, Charles O. 1984. *An Introduction to the Study of Public Policy*. Monterey, CA: Brooks/Cole.

Juffras, Jason. 1991. *Impact of the Immigration Reform and Control Act on the Immigration and Naturalization Service*. Santa Monica, CA: Rand Corporation.

Kaplan, Daile. 1988. *Lewis Hine in Europe: The Lost Photographs*. New York: Abbeville Press.

Keith, Nathaniel. 1973. *Politics and the Housing Crisis*. New York: Universe Books.

Kelly, Alfred H., Winfred A. Harbison, and Herman Belz. 1983. *The American Constitution: Its Origins and Development*. New York: W. W. Norton.

Kerwin, Cornelius M. 1994. *Rulemaking: How Government Agencies Write Law and Make Policy*. Washington, DC: Congressional Quarterly Press.

King, Coretta Scott. 1969. *My Life With Martin Luther King*. New York: Holt, Rinehart, and Winston.

Koegel, Paul, et al. 1996. "The Causes of Homelessness," in Jim Baumohl, ed., *Homelessness in America*. Phoenix, AZ: Oryx Press.

Kramer, Fred A. 1981. *Dynamics of Public Bureaucracy: An Introduction to Public Management*. Cambridge, MA: Winthrop.

Kruschke, Earl, and Byron M. Jackson. 1990. *Nuclear Energy Policy: A Reference Handbook*. Santa Barbara: ABC-CLIO.

Lerner, Allan W., and John Wanat. 1992. *Public Administration*. Englewood Cliffs, NJ: Prentice Hall.

Leslie, Douglas L. 1979. *Labor Law in a Nutshell*. Minneapolis: West Publishing.

Lester, James P., and Joseph Stewart Jr. 1996. *Public Policy: An Evolutionary Approach*. Minneapolis: West Publishing.

Levine, Rhonda F. 1988. *Class Struggle and the New Deal: Industrial Labor, Industrial Capital, and the State*. Lawrence: University of Kansas Press.

Levitan, Sar A. 1980. *Programs in Aid of the Poor for the 1980s*. Baltimore: Johns Hopkins University Press.

Lewis, Anthony. *Gideon's Trumpet*. 1966. New York: Vintage.

Light, Paul C. 1992. *Forging Legislation*. New York. W. W. Norton.

———. 1997. *A Delicate Balance: An Essential Introduction to American Government*. New York: St. Martin's.

Lilienthal, David. 1984. *The Journals of David Lilienthal*. Seven volumes, 1964–1983. New York: Harper and Row.

Lincoln, C. Eric, ed. 1970. *Martin Luther King Jr.: A Profile*. New York: Hill and Wang.

Lindblom, Charles F. 1980. *The Policy Making Process*. Englewood Cliffs, NJ: Prentice Hall.

Lippmann, Walter. 1955. *The Public Philosophy*. New York: Mentor Books.

Litman, Theodore J., and Leonard S. Robins. 1997. *Health Politics and Policy*. Albany, NY: Delmar.

Lowi, Theodore. 1974. *The End of Liberalism: The Second Republic of the U.S.* New York: Norton.

———. 1984. *The Personal President: Power Invested, Promise Unfulfilled*. Ithaca: Cornell University Press.

Lowi, Theodore J., and Benjamin Ginsberg. 1998. *American Government: Freedom and Power*. New York: W. W. Norton.

Lynn, Naomi, and Aaron Wildavsky. 1990. *Public Administration: The State of the Discipline*. Chatham, NJ: Chatham House Publishers.

Marcus, Alfred A. 1980. *Promise and Performance: Choosing and Implementing Public Policy*. Westport, CT: Greenwood Press.

Marmor, Theodore. 1994. *Understanding Health Care Reform*. New Haven: Yale University Press.

McCartney, John T. 1992. *Black Power Ideology*. Englewood Cliffs, NJ: Prentice Hall.

McCool, Daniel C. 1995. *Public Policy: Theories, Models, and Concepts*. Englewood Cliffs, NJ: Prentice Hall.

McGuire, William, and Leslie Wheeler, eds. 1993. *American Social Leaders*. Santa Barbara, CA: ABC-CLIO.

McMurray, Emily J., ed. 1995. *Notable Twentieth-Century Scientists*, vol. 2. New York: Gale.

Meyer, John R., and Clinton V. Oster Jr. 1987. *Deregulation and the Future of Intercity Passenger Travel*. Cambridge: MIT Press.

Milkis, Sidney. 1993. *The President and the Parties: Transformation of the American Party System*. New York: Oxford University Press.

Murray, Charles A. 1984. *Losing Ground: American Social Policy, 1950–1980*. New York: Basic Books.

Nakamura, Robert, and Frank Smallwood. 1980. *The Politics of Implementation*. New York: St. Martin's.

Neufville, Judith I. De, ed. 1981. *The Land Use Policy Debate in the United States*. New York: Plenum Press.

Neuse, Steven M. 1996. *David E. Lilienthal: The Journey of an American Liberal*. Knoxville: University of Tennessee Press.

Neustadt, Richard. 1960. *Presidential Power: The Politics of Leadership*. New York: Wiley.

Nonet, Philippe. 1969. *Administrative Justice*. New York: Russell Sage Foundation.

Nosow, Sigmund, and William Form. 1962. *Man, Work, and Society*. New York: Basic Books.
Paarlberg, Don. 1980. *Farm and Food Policy: Issues of the 1980s*. Lincoln: University of Nebraska Press.
Packer, Herbert. 1968. *Limits of the Criminal Sanction*. Palo Alto: Stanford University Press.
Palumbo, Dennis J. 1988. *Public Policy in America: Government in Action*. San Diego: Harcourt Brace Jovanovich.
Paris, David C., and James F. Reynolds. 1983. *The Logic of Policy Inquiry*. New York: Longman.
Patel, Kant, and Mark E. Rushefsky. 1995. *Health Care Politics and Policy in America*. Armonk, NY: M. E. Sharpe.
Patterson, James T. 1981. *America's Struggle Against Poverty, 1900–1980*. Cambridge: Harvard University Press.
Pepper, Claude, and Hays Gorey. 1987. *Pepper: Eyewitness to a Century*. San Diego: Harcourt Brace Jovanovich.
Perlmutter, Felice D. 1997. *From Welfare to Work: Corporate Initiatives and Welfare Reform*. New York: Oxford University Press.
Peters, B. Guy. 1993. *American Public Policy: Promise and Performance*. Chatham, NJ: Chatham House Publishers.
Peters, B. Guy, and Brian W. Hogwood. 1985. "In Search of the Issue Attention Cycle," *Journal of Politics* 47:238–253.
Piven, Frances Fox, and Richard Cloward. 1971. *Regulating the Poor: The Functions of Public Welfare*. New York: Vintage Books.
———. 1982. *The New Class War*. New York: Pantheon Books.
Prados, John. 1991. *Keepers of the Keys: A History of the National Security Council from Truman to Bush*. New York: William Morrow.
Pressman, Jeffrey L., and Aaron B. Wildavsky. 1973. *Implementation*. Berkeley: University of California Press.
Price, David E. 1992. *The Congressional Experience*. Boulder: Westview Press.
Pye, Lucian W. 1965. *Political Culture and Political Development*. Princeton: Princeton University Press.
Pynn, Ronald E. 1993. *American Politics: Changing Expectations*. Madison: Brown and Benchmark.
Quinney, Richard. 1977. *Class, State, and Crime*. New York. St. Martin's.
Rabin, Robert L., and Stephen D. Sugarman. 1993. *Smoking Policy: Law, Politics, and Culture*. New York: Oxford University Press.
Radford, Gail. 1996. *Modern Housing for America*. Chicago: University of Chicago Press.
Rainey, Hal G. 1997. *Understanding and Managing Public Organizations*. San Francisco: Jossey-Bass.
Randall, J. G., and David Donald. 1961. *The Civil War and Reconstruction*. Boston: D.C. Heath.
Reagan, Michael D. 1987. *Regulation: The Politics of Policy*. Boston: Little, Brown.
Reagan, Michael D., and John G. Sanzone. 1981. *The New Federalism*. New York: Oxford University Press.
Redman, Eric. 1973. *The Dance of Legislation*. New York: Simon and Schuster.
Reich, Robert. 1997. *Locked in the Cabinet*. New York: Knopf.
Reimers, David. 1998. *Unwelcome Strangers: American Identity and the Turn Against Immigration*. New York: Columbia University Press.
Ripley, Randall, and Grace Franklin. 1982. *Implementation Theory and Practice*. Homewood, IL: Dorsey Press.
Robertson, David B., and Dennis R. Judd. 1989. *The Development of American Public Policy: The Structure of Policy Restraint*. Glenview, IL: Scott, Foresman.
Robinson, Glenn O., Ernest Gellhorn, and Harold H. Bruff. 1979. *The Administrative Process*. Minneapolis: West Publishing.
Rosenbaum, Walter. 1998. *Environmental Politics and Policy*. Washington, DC: Congressional Quarterly Press.
Rosenbloom, David H. 1998. *Public Administration: Understanding Management, Politics, and Law in the Public Sector*. New York: McGraw Hill.
Rowan, Carl T. 1993. *Dreammakers, Dream Breakers: The World of Thurgood Marshall*. Boston: Little, Brown.
Sampson, Roy J., Martin T. Farris, and David L. Shrock. 1985. *Domestic Transportation: Practice, Theory, and Policy*. Boston: Houghton Mifflin.
Sandbach, Francis. 1980. *Environment, Ideology, and Policy*. Montclair, NJ: Allanheld, Osmun.
Schick, Allen. 1980. *Congress and Money: Budgeting, Spending, and Taxing*. Washington, DC: Urban Institute.
Schlesinger, Arthur M., Jr. 1965. *A Thousand Days: John F. Kennedy in the White House*. Boston: Houghton Mifflin.
Schmidt, Steffen W., Mack C. Shelley II, and Barbara A.

Bardes. 1997. *American Government and Politics Today*. Minneapolis: West Publishing.
Senna, Joseph, and Larry Siegel. 1993. *Introduction to Criminal Justice*. Minneapolis: West Publishing.
Shafritz, Jay M., and E. W. Russell. 1997. *Public Administration*. New York: Longman.
Sidlow, Edward, and Beth Henschen. 1998. *America at Odds*. Belmont, CA: Wadsworth Publishing.
Skerry, Peter. 1993. *Mexican Americans: The Ambivalent Minority*. New York: Free Press.
Skolnick, Jerome, and David Bayley. 1988. *Community Policing: Issues and Practices around the World*. Washington, DC: National Institute of Justice.
Skowronek, Stephen. 1993. *The Politics Presidents Make: Leadership from John Adams to George Bush*. Cambridge: Harvard University Press.
Smith, J.V. "Writer Randy Shilts Dies: Chronicled Rise of AIDS," *Washington Post*, February 18, 1994: B7.
So, Frank S., and Judith Getzels, eds. 1988. *The Practice of Local Government Planning*. Washington, DC: International City Management Association.
Sorenson, Theodore. 1965. *Kennedy*. New York: HarperCollins.
Spaeth, Harold J. 1979. *Supreme Court Policy Making: Explanation and Prediction*. San Francisco: W. H. Freeman.
Stanko-Glantz, A. 1996. *The Cigarette Papers*. Berkeley: University of California Press.
Starling, Grover. 1998. *Managing the Public Sector*. Fort Worth: Harcourt Brace.
Steinmo, Sven. 1993. *Taxation and Democracy*. New Haven: Yale University Press.
Switzer, Jacqueline V. 1994. *Environmental Politics: Domestic and Global Dimensions*. New York: St. Martin's.
Talbot, Ross, and Don F. Hadwiger. 1968. *The Policy Process in American Agriculture*. San Francisco: Chandler Publishing.
Thelen, David P. 1996. *Robert LaFollette and the Insurgent Spirit*. Madison: University of Wisconsin Press.
Theodoulou, Stella Z. 1996. *AIDS: The Politics and Policy of Disease*. Englewood Cliffs, NJ: Prentice Hall.
Thiele, Leslie P. 1997. *Thinking Politics: Perspectives in Ancient, Modern, and Postmodern Political Theory*. Chatham, NJ: Chatham House.
Tobias, Sheila. 1997. *Faces of Feminism: An Activist's Reflections on the Women's Movement*. Boulder: Westview Press.
U.S. Bureau of the Census. 1997. *Statistical Astract of the United States* (117th edition). Washington, DC: U.S. Government.
———. 1998. *Statistical Abstract of the United States* (118 th edition). Washington, DC: U.S. Government.
U.S. Department of Health and Human Services. October 1996. *Indicators of Welfare Dependence and Well-Being*. Interim Report to Congress. Washington, DC: U.S. Government.
Waldman, Steven. 1995. *The Bill: How Legislation Really Becomes Law—A Case Study of the National Service Bill*. New York: Penguin Books.
Warren, Kenneth F. 1982. *Administrative Law in the Political System*. St. Paul, MN: West Publishing.
Wasby, Stephen L. 1988. *The Supreme Court in the Federal Judicial System*. Chicago: Nelson-Hall Publishing.
Watkins, T. H. 1993. *The Great Depression: America in the 1930s*. Boston: Little, Brown.
Waxman, Laura, and Remy Trupin. 1997. *A Status Report on Hunger and Homelessness in America's Cities*. Washington, DC: U.S. Conference of Mayors.
Webber, Carolyn, and Aaron Wildavsky. 1986. *A History of Taxation and Expenditure in the Western World*. New York: Simon and Schuster.
Welch, Susan, John Gruhl, Michael Steinman, John Lomer, and Jan P. Vermeer. 1997. *Understanding American Government*. Minneapolis: West Publishing.
Wells, Donald T. 1996. *Environmental Policy*. Upper Saddle River, NJ: Prentice Hall.
Wildavsky, Aaron. 1988. *The New Politics of the Budgetary Process*. Glenview, IL: Scott, Foresman.
Wilson, James Q. 1968. *Varieties of Police Behavior: Management and Law and Order in Eight Communities*. Cambridge: Harvard University Press.
———. 1975. *Thinking About Crime*. New York: Basic Books.
Wilson, James Q., and John J. DiIulio Jr. 1998. *American Government: The Essentials*. Boston: Houghton Mifflin.
Winfree, L. Thomas, Jr., and Howard Abadinsky. 1996. *Understanding Crime: Theory and Practice*. Chicago: Nelson-Hall Publishers.
Winkler, Allan M. 1993. *Life under a Cloud: American Anxiety about the Atom*. New York: Oxford University Press.
Woodward, C. Vann. 1957. *The Strange Career of Jim Crow*. New York: Oxford University Press.
Zuboff, Shoshana. 1988. *In the Age of the Smart Machine: The Future of Work and Power*. New York: Basic Books.

Index